PEOPLE IN SPITE OF HISTORY

TIBOR VÁRADY

PEOPLE IN SPITE OF HISTORY

Stories Found in an Attorney Archive in the Banat Region

CEU PRESS

Central European University Press
Budapest–New York

Published in 2021 by Central European University Press

Nádor utca 9, H-1051 Budapest, Hungary
Tel: +36-1-327-3138 or 327-3000 | Fax: +36-1-327-3183
E-mail: ceupress@press.ceu.edu | Website: www.ceupress.com

Translated by János Boris (chapter vii–viiii), Owen Good
(chapter i–iii, except II/2, and v),
and Péter Balikó Lengyel (chapter ii/2 and iv)

isbn 978-963-386-407-4 (hardback)
isbn 978-963-386-408-1 (ebook)

Library of Congress Cataloging-in-Publication Data

Names: Varady, Tibor, 1939- author. | Boris, János, translator. | Good,
Owen, translator. | Lengyel Balikó, Péter, translator.
Title: People in spite of history : stories found in an attorney archive in
the Banat region / Tibor Várady ; [translated by] János Boris, Owen
Good, Péter Lengyel Balikó.
Description: Budapest, Hungary ; New York : Central European University
Press, 2021.
Identifiers: LCCN 2020048005 (print) | LCCN 2020048006 (ebook) | ISBN
9789633864074 (hardback) | ISBN 9789633864081 (pdf)
Subjects: LCSH: Practice of law--Serbia--Zrenjanin--History. |
Lawyers--Serbia--Zrenjanin--History. | Law
offices--Serbia--Zrenjanin--History. |
Lawyers--Serbia--Zrenjanin--History.
Classification: LCC KKS1162.9 .V37 2021 (print) | LCC KKS1162.9 (ebook) |
DDC 340.092/24971--dc23
LC record available at https://lccn.loc.gov/2020048005
LC ebook record available at https://lccn.loc.gov/2020048006

CONTENTS

FOREWORD

FOR MORE THAN A CENTURY, three generations of a family of lawyers run a firm founded in 1893 in a small city, first a part of the Austro-Hungarian Habsburg monarchy, then of Hungary, then of Germany, then of Yugoslavia and finally of Serbia. All files, folders and documents of the law office remain in existence. In them we find the raw material for this remarkable book.

In Becskerek, a market town of 20,000 souls before the Second World War and within two decades thereafter a provincial administrative capital of some 60,000, the multiplicity of languages and religions was a matter of course. The daily relationships of folks who at home spoke German, Hungarian, Serbian or Yiddish was simply normal life—until it once, then again and then a third time was not. Some of this variety is still found even today, but no longer in its earlier breadth and no longer in the unremarkable and self-evident manner in which it had manifested itself over the many earlier centuries.

The records concern marriages, divorces, births and testaments; they record expulsions, emigrations, incarcerations and releases of these rural and small-town populations. But what is found in the letters, affidavits, complaints and decisions involving these apparently mundane situations are only the individual building blocks. Transforming their reflection of the march of those times through war, peace, revolution and counter-revolution, serfdom and freedom, comfort and poverty into affecting and vivid vignettes requires an impressive narrative talent—and Tibor Várady possesses and demonstrates this gift in full measure.

The context always, and essentially, is intimate; one of house and home, of family and neighbors. But the tragedies and abominations of the larger history that mark this century and marked these people give the small stories that were brought to this law office their deeper meaning. A divorce may spare one of the parties the expulsion from the homeland, only then to drive the other party away. A marriage may rescue the fortune of the in-laws, a testament prevent a confiscation of their property—but then again may not.

Várady selects and comments on the selected files with a light hand. But his uncommon ability to braid together the two levels they reflect, the history and the stories, without sentimentality but with human empathy, casts a light on this era that lends these records a novelistic depth.

Research into court dossiers that aim to illuminate the effects of decisions of even the courts of an authoritarian state on the lived world of their subjects are no longer a complete novelty. Inga Markowits' book, *Justice in Lueritz*, describing the garden variety of cases dealt with by a local court of the German Democratic Republic, can serve as an exemplar of this genre. But even such empirical studies concern already structured judicial acts, embed the parties in the stylized protocol dictated by the court. What is unique in the vivid narratives Várady presents is that they arise directly from the lives of those involved, from their own accounts spoken in their own words. The petitions and letters crossing between client and attorney, accompanied by the raw material of witnesses' and officials' statements—those provide the raw materials of later decisions and the reader's fascination.

But they are not only stories from "below" or only to be thus understood by their readers. The book at the same time is affecting evidence that the attorney is not only, or is required to be, a civil servant of the state. On the contrary, this law office—these three generations of the Várady family—in heartening fashion demonstrates that the profession permits and in difficult times even requires its members to defend the "ordinary" man and woman against the higher and often stronger powers of state and society. It deserves the praise implicit in its recognition as a liberal profession. And for those of us fortunate enough not to be subject to government or party commands dictating our professional conduct, the human and forensic arguments mounted against those constraints by those who, as here, are subject to them only deepen our respect for their work.

Várady does not analyze these aspects of the material for us; they speak for themselves. He sets the scene in which these actors speak, and places them within the scenarios of each particular era. He deepens our understanding of the larger context within which these people find themselves by revealing the constraints and limits they and their attorney faced as they acted. But he also reveals their autonomy, their agency, even as these historical epochs engulfed their lives.

Two vividly rendered vignettes may serve to exemplify the dilemmas this push against inescapable constraints produces. The first concerns the pseudonymous István Tóth, who, as Várady puts it, "sold goose-feather down [that he smuggled into Hungary] while ignoring national borders—whatever those borders were between 1942 and 1944." With the profits from those transactions, he returned the favor by smuggling other items from Hungary into the Banat, then under German occupation—items such as shoe polish, two meters of tailor's cloth, 100 cigarette papers, a comb and so forth. Unfortunately, on the last of these forays he was caught by the German occupation authorities, confessed, but in mitigation pleaded the household's poverty and his wife's ill health. Sentenced to a fine he could not pay, he faced the alternative of jail at a conversion rate that netted him 5,000 days of potential imprisonment.

István Tóth received a "choice": imprisonment in a notorious concentration camp or mandatory service as a guard there. He chose the second option. And that, after the liberation, brought him the imprisonment he had earlier avoided. Because of testimony from former prisoners that he had not been among the worst guards, he was sentenced to serve only three years, or approximately one-fourth of the earlier sentence. Of course, with liberation arriving in late 1944, the actual time would have been about the same, but István Tóth could not foresee the future.

The second vignette arcs over almost the entire twentieth century. It concerns the fate of the Eckstein Leather Factory, which existed for 75 years and experienced every fate that could befall a Jewish property owners during those times: forced sale, confiscation, restitution, nationalization, refusal of later restitution because of the family's emigration, and finally the hypothetical possibility of compensation.

Várady concludes this family saga with a comment that also might serve to place the files of this remarkable law office themselves ad acta:

> The matter of compensation for the nationalized property was never resolved. In 2011 the Serbian Parliament passed the Asset Recovery Act. I believe that in accordance with this, it would now be possible to make a claim in connection to the Becskerek leather factory. But I don't know whether there is anyone left to do so.

RICHARD BUXBAUM, PROFESSOR EMERITUS,
University of California, Berkeley

WHAT IS THIS BOOK ABOUT?

THIS BOOK IS A BASED ON A COINCIDENCE that later turned out to be good luck. My father and my grandfather were well-known attorneys. My younger brother too. But there were other well-known attorneys too, even close by. What's unprecedented—at least in our part of the world—is that all the files of a family legal archive remained in storage after more than one hundred years (the files piled up from 1893 through 2014). While in the meantime, countries changed, as well as beliefs, ideologies, and languages, many of which were nearly lost. Yet languages proved to be somewhat more enduring than the beliefs and ideologies. The prevailing new worlds and new powers proved to be ruthless with archives. And with memories too.

I can no longer ask my father or my grandfather why all the documents remained, but I know that both held the conviction that "nothing was to be thrown out." Not long ago, in a drawer I found the electricity bills from 1949 to 1967. There was also the fact that the attorney's profession continued in the family. And we lived in a small town, where it was no great financial sacrifice to keep up a stable, which later became a file room. About eight years ago, after putting things off time and again, I started to read the files in the archives of my father and my grandfather when I began to see the family file room differently than before. For decades I had said to myself and to others that "the files are there." And then, after my mother also departed and the house was empty, I started to say: "the files were left there." Once I noticed this, I realized that something ought to be done.

The office operated in Becskerek (pronounced "betchkerek"). This was the original town name that became layered in history. Under the Austro-Hungarian Monarchy the official name was Nagybecskerek, but the local Serbians knew it as Veliki Bečkerek, and the local Germans as Gross-betschkerek. For a few years it was Petrovgrad, and then in the years after World War Two it took the name of a partisan hero, Zrenjanin, although the Hungarian Nagybecskerek remained in official use. The residents—Serbs, Hungarians, and others—preferred to use the original name. They spelled it differently, but pronounced it roughly the same: "betchkerek." Given that most of the documents refer to "Becskerek," I'll use the same spelling. I deliberated a lot over the names of other towns and villages. There are towns and cities which have developed names in English: "Beograd" in Serbian, and "Belgrád" in Hungarian, is "Belgrade" in English, therefore I'll use "Belgrade." But most settlements don't have names in English, moreover, with time the official names have changed, too, including in lawsuits. And then there's the matter that most of the towns and villages are in the Banat region in Serbia, and even today localities in this region have several names in official use. The names are mostly Hungarian and Serbian, but occasionally Romanian, Slovak and Ruthenian. This is how the region of Banat is. Thus, in this English text I shall try to tiptoe between different names of the same locations, and to explain what I can. In the Hungarian version of my texts I relied mostly on Hungarian names. Here I shall indicate Serbian names as well.

When the office opened, Becskerek belonged to the Austro-Hungarian Monarchy. After World War One it became part of the State of Slovenes, Croats and Serbs, then of the Kingdom of Yugoslavia, then of the Territory of the German Military Commander in Serbia, then of the Federal People's Republic of Yugoslavia, then of the Socialist Federal Republic of Yugoslavia, then of Serbia and Montenegro, then of Serbia. The Becskerek families (if they didn't leave) remained Becskerek families. In the family office the "main desk" remained for more than one hundred years.

My father can be seen in this picture. My grandfather also used the same desk. I too would have become the heir to this desk, but I chose instead to follow an academic career. My father was followed by my younger brother. I didn't find a photo of my grandfather in the office, but this is a photo from around the time I knew him:

There are all sorts of things in the documents which have been lost elsewhere. There is the everyday life. One can still find in history books, and to some degree in living memory, how the world wars, fascism and communism ended. But the neighbors, and the little people, who stumbled into history and staggered through it (or hid from it), trying to survive, have been forgotten. At the end of the nineteenth century some dueled, even with friends, so as not to be squeezed out of the world of nobility. I can see that behind certain names which have now become mere legends, there stood real people, like Karolin Messinger. And in these files one can see how attorneys, most often unsuccessfully, tried to defend Jews and Jewish assets. There were marriages between local Jews and Germans which may have been shaken by human frailty, but survived Nazism. In many cases, however, survival remained a mere hope. In the background, concentration camps took form. There were sham divorces which, even if the court archives had remained, wouldn't be detectible. In the family attorney's office, however, there have remained letters in which a Christian wife writes in 1942 that she doesn't want to divorce her Jewish husband, but if there's no other means to improve their child's fate, and to save a part of their property, then she asks my father to file the divorce claim, hoping that the marriage will be reinstated "if this ever comes to an end." After World War Two, German husbands became the defendants in sham divorces.

I read that on February 5, 1946 Péter Balgó (who lived near us) was sentenced to one year in prison and forced labor. The crime for which he was convicted was the following: "the slaughtering of a calf without the people's approval." The appeal doesn't say that this is ridiculous, but that he decided to slaughter the calf "in a time of extreme necessity," and that a few months later his wife would give birth, and so he couldn't leave her for prison. It is worth noting that the calf was his own, but at the time it wasn't only property which could be expropriated, but rationality too. (This possibility continued in later times too, in differing forms.) There are trials that show how fascism and antifascism came into household use in neighborly disputes, for example in the case of the 82-year-old Aunt Jemrics. Or the case during the first years of communism when three drunk peasants took a barrel of rum from an even drunker drayman (albeit, while pocketing a thousand dinars). According to the prosecutor and the judge, those who had taken the barrel of rum had "expropriated a part of the total people's property."

The documents have remained, but the purposes of the papers have changed. It is no longer the outcomes of the proceedings that are interesting, but the world in which they came to be. By looking from a new perspective, and with a new curiosity, it turns out this world too has been recorded in these files. Reading the documents brings one closer to the emotions that formed on the brink of wars, during wars and in their wake, and those environments of excitation, which were once the everyday reality, become visible. The people, too, come to life. If I was a prosecutor, in many cases I would change the classification of the act committed. I would say that the actors had in fact committed novels.

Not long ago, in Belgrade, I passed a cinema which I had frequented as a student. The wall had been sprayed with large red letters:

NO MORE CINEMA SHOWS. COME BACK YESTERDAY.

This is what I'm trying to do.

I.

ON THE RELEVANCE OF HISTORY

MÁRIA ORMOS V. MATHIAS ALBRECHT

File No. 12254

It is September 1944. These are the last days of German occupation in Becskerek. I am five years old, and besides me there are roughly another 50,000 people living in the town. The majority were Serbians, but a good number of Hungarians and Germans, too. In the street people alternated between three languages. The Jews started turning to remembrance, but their deportation was still too recent, that daily life in which they'd had a part was too close, and they hadn't yet broken away from the Becskerek reality. Moreover, those few who were in hiding or who were concealing their identities were still among us. In Becskerek there were Romanians and Slovaks, too, a few Russians and one old French woman. The town had two official names in September 1944: Grossbetschkerek in German and Petrovgrad in Serbian. ("Petrovgrad" was a name adopted recently. The traditional Serbian name was Veliki Bečkerek.) The Hungarian name, Nagybecskerek, was also in use, though not officially. The people preferred to say "Becskerek" (pronounced as "betchkerek"). I will use the same in English.

Uncertainty was rife. Beacons lighting the way ahead faded out one after the other. People must have felt as though they were teetering along a path between uncertainty and the abyss. Life went on, but every frame of reference had become utterly pliable. In my grandfather's diary on September 11, 1944 is the following entry (indicating the month with Roman numerals):

> *11.IX. tax negotiations, rates of taxation have been increased. I've ceased all payments of taxes. It is impossible to know who is authorized to collect them. The Germans have carried everything off; the question is whether or not the following power will recognize these payments. We're waiting.*

While everyone was waiting, on the very same day, an indignant woman came into my father's office. Her name was Mária Ormos, a day-laborer. The story begins with her own handwritten record. I suppose my father requested she register her complaint in writing (probably with a clerk's assistance) while she was waiting. Mária Ormos's record is on the back of a document dated 1914, due to the paper shortage. The text is written in black ink, in Serbian—difficult to make out, but legible. The format of the paper is no longer in use. It is as wide as an A4, but five or six centimeters longer. The card file, holding the documents, is also made to fit this format. From the text it becomes clear, Mária Ormos was the victim of slander. Her problem was very much a peacetime problem.

It is difficult to aptly translate her text, which struggles not only with the incident itself, but also with the Serbian language. Expressing herself in a solicitor's office and in her second language (rather than in Hungarian, her mother tongue), it isn't easy to accurately reflect in yet a third language the authentic frailties of the day-laborer without making her a caricature, which would be unfair—but then there's no need to polish her words either. Perhaps then, it might be translated as follows:

> My landlord without reason stood himself in my doorway where I had just been scolding my stepson István Csikós, and he started hurling insults, that I was a bloody whore and an old whore, that I wasn't my husband's wife, but his whore and that I didn't have sexual intercourse with my husband, Livius Ursulescu, with whom I've been living in cohabitation for 11 years, but only with his dog. Moreover, he said he'll kill me and my stepson if we didn't leave the house at once. Then he grabbed me from behind and pushed me out of the kitchen across the courtyard towards the street.
> Moreover, he said myself and my stepson were thieves without saying what we stole.

> I've been living in his house with my cohabiting husband since May 15, 1943. The landlord doesn't live in the same building, he only has a still here for making pálinka.
> Evidence: 1. Mária Lázár, Szentmihály 2. István Csikós
> When I told him I would take him to court, he said, fuck my horse-dick solicitor, my solicitor can't touch him, he has money.
> Please make a criminal report.

Both the beginning and the end of the report are dated. The beginning reads September 11, the end, September 12. Either it was written over two days, or she made a mistake at the beginning or the end. Or maybe she wrote it on the twelfth, and she meant to indicate that it had happened on the eleventh. This will now never be known. From the documents it becomes clear that Mária Ormos and her partner Livius Ursulescu lived as tenants in the house of the Becskerek farmer Mathias Albrecht. The proprietor only ever visited the house to make *pálinka* (spirit). It isn't revealed what initiated the argument. To that end, we would need to hear Mr. Albrecht's stance, but such a statement isn't included in the documents. There were some Albrechts in Becskerek. I went to school with an Albrecht, but I don't know if he was of any relation to Mathias—and of course at the time I knew nothing of the case. In the daily paper *Magyar Szó* there was at one point a journalist called János Albrecht. Today there aren't any Albrechts left in Becskerek, or any Germans really. I don't know whether in September 1944 the hail of insults really did begin without reason, nor do I know whether Mária Ormos offered any rhetorical ripostes, but Mária's description of Mathias's actions and words is utterly vivid. It would seem to be an incident which pushed everything else into the background, and (most likely for the first time in her life) urged Mária Ormos to turn to a solicitor.

Furthermore, as key words in the Serbian text are included in Hungarian, it's apparent the exchange must have taken place in Hungarian. At crucial points of the accusation the recorded Serbian text strives to conform to an almost bureaucratese: the Hungarian original *lófasz* (horse-dick) is refined to "the horse's genital organ." Those concerned include the Hungarian day laborer/tenant, who has a Romanian husband, and the German farmer/landlord. The case takes place in a street named after a legendary Serbian ruler who fell in the 1389 Battle of Kosovo (Cara Lazara street

43/a). The town is under German occupation. At the time in Becskerek, affairs were also handled in German (in addition to Serbian), but Hungarian wasn't restored to official use. My father writes the criminal charge on September 13. It is addressed: *Sreskom krivičnom sudu—Bečkerek* (Criminal Court of the District of Becskerek).

Allow me to quote my grandfather's diary entry from the following days (September 18– October 1):

> *18. IX. and the following days, German preparations for their escape. The arrival of Swabians from Romania, they scatter themselves among the ethnically German villages. –Shocking news from Transylvania and the Székely Land. Evictions. The loss of Arad and Belényes. Grave news broadcasts on the radio.*
>
> *26. IX. cold all day, autumn rain. The migration of the unfortunate evicted emigrants, bitterly cold, soaked to the bone.*
>
> *27. IX. the radio makes no secret of it: due to the joint Romanian and Russian attacks Hungary is in a rather grave situation. Today already the fighting has reached the southern streets of Nagyvárad. The Hungarians have evacuated Battonya, Belényes, Makó. The enemy is approaching Szeged, Szőreg.*
>
> *29. IX. … Fierce fighting is taking place along the entire defensive line. – From Budapest 80,000 children have been evacuated to the countryside. For the refugees, in particular for those unfortunates evicted from Transylvania, the Budapest red cross have organized an inquiry office especially, so that inquirers may more easily learn where their relatives have taken shelter. It has been raining constantly for two days. Those poor fleeing evictees. What a horrific fate. As for us in the Banat region, we are still able to hold on to our homes. From Romania a great deal of fleeing Germans have been dispersed among the Swabian villages of Banat. Their fate is no more enviable. Whatever portable possessions they could fit onto one or two carts they brought with them; the rest was left behind…*
>
> *30. IX. Fleeing Germans drove roughly 700 carts down the main street, headed for Aradácz. They're coming from the areas of Leibling and*

Zsombolya, and are headed for Bácska. Beaten by the rain for the length of the journey. There are covered carts among them, but the majority are open, with children and women. Here and there a cow tied to the forage rack; sometimes two. Well-nourished horses, cows in good strength.

1st October 1944. Sunday. The line of fleeing carts is unbroken. The rain beats down on these unfortunate people. We are told these people are fleeing Romanian territories, as Romania, according to the terms of peace, is required to donate a workforce of 1,400,000 men and women to the Soviets. Romania will fulfil this accepted requirement by transporting Hungarians and Germans from its territories to Russia. The more well-to-do Germans are fleeing this fate. Hence the great migration.

There is an entry in the file, too, dated October 1. This is another sheet of paper of the same format, no longer in use. Printed in Hungarian are "client," "opponent," "subject," and "file number." Also, on the form are the receipts and expenses. Mária Ormos paid 500 dinars on September 12. This is noted in the receipts column. In the expenses column are the costs of sending a criminal charge and of a deed stamp: 40 plus 33 dinar, and the date of September 15. After the amounts on the form there is only one note, in Hungarian:

"The accused German has fled. The case has been discontinued. 01.10.1944."

Thus, in the days following the exchange, the Germans, too, are the victims of fate. In Becskerek, the German occupation and authority still stand, but it slowly becomes clear that a change is approaching, which even the most wishful of thinkers is forced to acknowledge. The future is no longer a guessing game, it is presented quite plainly by those fleeing the Romanian territories of Banat in droves. Nor does one know to whom the taxes should go. The undercurrent of fear becomes prevalent. The Germans in Banat have the most reason, but fear spreads among the Hungarians too. Many Serbians are also afraid; they are afraid of the remaining Germans, but many are also afraid of communism, of the unknown. Perhaps it is only among those few Jews who are still in hiding in Becskerek (and those hiding their identities) that there were people who no longer feared the change. As they saw it, circumstances for them couldn't possibly get any worse, and they were right. So, then the Germans in Becskerek began to flee. I've heard many stories about this, most of which say that those with connections to fascism left, and those who had no guilty conscience stayed. There's certainly some truth in this, but local oral tradition tells of many cases in which it wasn't down to guilt that people left, but rather fear. And then, those who stayed were hit by reprisals.

I remember a story that I heard in my grammar school days. Now, as I write this text, I'm trying to recall the names and to look into it, for validity's sake, but I have had no luck. Those in my parents' generation may remember this, but none remain. I ought to have asked in time. According to the story, a well-to-do German (his given name initial was K.), who had many Hungarian and Serbian friends, couldn't decide (like many others) to stay or go. He asked one of his Serbian friends (an engineer in Becskerek who had joined the partisans and could only come into town in secret) whether or not he ought to flee if the partisans come. K.'s Serbian friend reassured him that the partisans he was with weren't like the fascists. They know K. is a decent man that has helped many of his Serbian friends, and he can rest assured. And so, K. stayed. According to the story, the partisan may have been honest, but he was wrong. After the change there were indeed atrocities, and K. was killed. When the Serbian arrived home and learned what had happened, he committed suicide. I read similar stories in Greek tragedies in grammar school in Becskerek.

Returning to File Number 12254; during the two weeks of dread before the new forces arrived, Mathias Albrecht is making *pálinka*, calling his tenant a whore, furthermore, a whore having sexual relations not with her partner, he explains, but with dogs. The woman isn't troubled by either fascism or antifascism, she isn't crippled with conjecture over what the arrival of the Russians might bring, but instead is wrapped up in being called a whore, and turns to a solicitor. And the solicitor, my father, proceeds as usual. Albrecht boasts of his wealth, he has properties, he has a *pálinka* still—and two weeks later none of this matters.

On October 1, 1944 the *Torontál* daily newspaper appears. There in the header, we can read that it is in its seventy-third year, "published every morning," "Price: 3 dinars." Inside the cover is a call for subscriptions. From the very next day there is no longer a Hungarian daily in Becskerek.

On October 2, the Russian troops and their allies arrive in Becskerek. My grandfather writes about this in his diary:

> *02. X. Monday. We've been told that the invading army via the occupation of Módos, has reached Szécsány. In the afternoon hours the villages of Szárcsa, Lázárföld, Klekk all fell. The artillery fire could be heard throughout the night, all day today it has been creeping closer. Some shrapnel has already come into Becskerek. One fragment killed Cvejanov, the trade association president in Piroska's [my aunt's] street. Zorka [my mother] and the children are taking cover in the cellar. Some form of air pressure, it would appear, has caused one of the windows in the hall and the skylight over the girl's room to shatter; at which the family ordered me into the cellar, too.*
>
> *I remember taking cover in the cellar. I was five. My sister Piroska was one. I remember the damp, the petroleum lamp, that we were there a long time (though I don't know how long). My parents were playing cards. My grandfather just sat in a chair. Then he went up into the apartment, ignoring the appeals of my parents. The diary continues:*
>
> *I couldn't stand it for long of course. News of the enemy's advances were spreading. Artillery fire and now machine gun fire could both be heard close by. –In the course of the day the German civic leaders left the town one after the other; reportedly they were fleeing in the direction of Aradác, Zsablya and some for Titel. –The German soldiers withdrew from the town without resistance. This saved Becskerek from shelling and devastation.*

Mathias Albrecht didn't belong among the "German civic leaders." Perhaps he fled because he was affiliated with the occupiers, perhaps he had done something, but perhaps the crimes he took away with him didn't surpass his calling Mária Ormos a whore.

And then, what the Germans of Becskerek most feared became a reality. In the first days, the arriving Russians and partisans display no violence, they speak of freedom, and they initiate discourse with a number of the ethnic groups living here. But then, the news of an incident (later revealed to be false) opened up free ground for the heated tensions of war. Another entry from grandfather's diary:

> *10th October. On this day the immaculate conception of the announced freedom came to an end. News spread that last night a Serbian was murdered in the street somewhere behind the Lutheran church. In response the partisans blocked off certain parts of the town and in the German street in particular rounded up 68 people according to some, 150 according to others, whom were taken to where the alleged murder took place, there the unfortunate people had to remove their upper garments and shoes, and were shot in the head, one-by-one. Among the victims were Dr József Weiterschan, solicitor and vice-chair of the Roman Catholic religious community; Dr Alajos Heinermann, the doctor; two butchers by the name of Porcseller etc. Cindrényi-Gimpel and Benkovich would have been among those arrested; but the former was released because one of the partisans recognized him, stating he is the only pediatrician in Becskerek, the other meanwhile assured them he was Hungarian; and so these two were released. The rest perished on the spot.*

Was K. also among them? Would Mathias Albrecht have ended up among them if he had stayed? Did fleeing save his life? I have no answer to these questions. I don't even know what happened to Mária Ormos. I know that certain people ran into difficulties purely because they lived with Germans. Would this have concern Mária Ormos and her partner Ursulescu? Or perhaps the criminal report was of help to them? Did this influence their safe classification in the new system of prejudices? Under the Germans, Jewish descent resulted in discrimination. A special law required the confiscation of all Jewish and Gypsy property. After liberation, the Germans were in the firing line. According to one law, the property of all Germans was to be confiscated, if the respective German hadn't "fought in the ranks of the people's liberating army," (that is, was not a partisan). There are one or two case documents in the archives in which my grandfather and father try to protect a Jewish landowner from confiscation (to no avail), and then the owner, who has survived the horrors, is confronted by the uninformed officials of the new power, again targeting the very same house as a German property, because the owner's name is German.

Two weeks before fleeing, Mr. Albrecht is safe in his world of disrespectful tantrums, into which he drags Mária, too. In this world, being a German, Hungarian, or Romanian does not make one a target. Fascism and communism are not even issues. What is important and divisive is property and its everyday consequences, the countless tensions of sorts between men and women, perhaps jealousy and certainly arrogance. And this is the same world that survived ethnic discrimination, ethnic prejudice and persecution, fascism and communism.

There are two ways I can end this story: Firstly, I went to Cara Lazara 43/a. There was nobody there by the name of Ormos, or Ursulescu, or Albrecht, or even the memory of any of them. Case 12254 is beyond closed. And here we could stop. But we could search for a conclusion elsewhere, too. In April 1993, in a very interesting piece of writing (it appeared in the Belgrade magazine *Republika*) Mirko Tepavac discusses the communities and divisions shaped by the fevers of the Milošević regime. He explains the "*Samo sloga Srbina spašava*" (Only unity saves the Serbs) slogan in the context of the war, and writes:

> Unity alone will no longer save the Serbs. If the war finally becomes untenable, the hopelessly destitute and those drunk on money, the power-hungry leaders and the forsaken followers will no longer be bound by any unity. Those promoting the war know very well why "war is better," hence why it lasted so long, hence why it was so bitter. The time has come for the false divisions to make way for the true divisions, and maybe this is the one good outcome of this whole tragedy.

Mária's and Mathias's remain among the true divisions. It is difficult to say whether these divisions (which continued in spite of history) or history better represent human reality.

II.

THREE BECSKEREK STORIES

Featuring Local Jews and Germans in the Leading Roles

AN ANACRUSIS

AMONG THE FILES I DISCOVERED coffeehouse songs, too. From the years around the war in particular. These are criminal cases, and the charge in each case is "incitement and propaganda." In 1912, when Becskerek still belonged to the Austro-Hungarian Empire, my grandfather was defending a Serbian group who had been singing suspicious Serbian songs. And there were others. In 1945, for example, it was suspicious Hungarian songs to which the prosecutor had pricked up their ears, and this time my father defended the accused. At that time, tapping technologies hadn't yet been perfected, so the clamor of the coffeehouse may have been valuable towards learning how those who thought differently thought. Today there are different methods. The NSA has options that go beyond the pub.

During our teenage years, my friends and I didn't know about these issues, but we knew there were sensitive cases and sensitive songs. Most of my friends got a glimpse of the world of coffeehouse music. So did I, but the memories have faded. For such a show, the first stage that I came to know was the most notorious restaurant in Becskerek. It had changed names plenty of times. By the time I was a guest there in the late '50s it was *Vojvodina*, but we preferred an older name, the *Rózsa* (rose, in Hungarian). My Serbian peers also preferred to call it the *Rózsa*, perhaps *Ruža* (rose, in Serbian), which isn't far off. I usually went there with my classmates; we must have been 16–17 years old. The garden that leads down to the Bega

River was beautiful. Now there is no garden and no River Bega in town either. I also remember there being some awareness of danger linked to these sing-alongs, an awareness of the reality. Over the years, this or that zeal or form of nationalism embroidered even the simpler lines here and there with symbols and tensions. We even felt the tension when we didn't truly understand it, but this only served to pique our interest. In my secondary school years, Becskerek was a multicultural town (earlier even more so, and afterward unfortunately less so). Sat at my table were usually Hungarians, sometimes Hungarian and Serbians. Many of us had learned German even before school, in addition to Hungarian and Serbian. At this time, everyone was aware that two ethnic groups (the Jewish and the Germans) had practically vanished during our childhoods. There were personal memories; the friendly ties of our parents were still fresh. After, there remained a feeling of absence. I think this too has disappeared by now.

In the Rózsa—when there happened to be a mixed company—certain patrons would request Hungarian and Serbian songs bordering on unsafe. On one occasion a Romanian fellow at the table, after great hesitation, requested a Romanian song. Nobody understood it and I still don't know what it was about. The gypsies knew every song and granted every request. They knew a Jewish one, too, which my classmate E. requested more than once. Translated line for line, the song goes:

Comes the Jew and buys two geese
buys two geese
Black and spotty, so are these
so are these
Hello Jew, go fuck your geese
fuck your geese
Buy equal ones c'mon please
c'mon please

For a while I hesitated as to whether or not I should include this song in the text. My classmate requested it proudly. I am not entirely sure whether his pride was boosted because the song affirmed his identity or because he knew such a cracking tune. As I remember, E. was of Jewish descent, though never once was it mentioned between us. The question arose then, was it an ironic Jewish song, or some sort of anti-Semitic inspired verse? E. evidently saw it as a Jewish song. When we requested a Hungarian tune, then a Serbian one, this was the one he would request to feel included. But did he know what he was playing? I didn't have many Jewish peers. These people, like myself, were born during or just before the war, but in their case, their identity was never disclosed to them as it could be life-threatening. I remember what a drama it had been at home when, at three years old, I climbed up to the loft and found someone there. We had a conversation, too. At that age, my father would show me pictures and explain to me things from the *Brehm's Life of Animals* book. On the shelf at home there stood at least ten volumes of Brehm's thick blue books. I had also seen Brehm's books on my classmates' shelves. At that time, I was most interested in lions, and so in the loft I brought up lions. The gentleman told me he was in fact a lion-hunter, and regaled me with exciting anecdotes from his hunting expeditions around Becskerek. When I came back down, I asked why there was a stranger in the loft. An aunt, who wasn't particularly circumspect, explained to me that this man was a Jew, the Germans didn't like the Jews, and that was why he was hiding in the loft. My father went completely white when I repeated this to him. I wasn't let out onto the street for months so that I wouldn't tell anyone (though my father's friend only hid in our loft for a few days). Since I had enjoyed his stories so much, I often asked if the Jewish man was still in the loft. My father corrected me every time: "the lion-hunter." It was less dangerous this way.

The parents of my Jewish classmates didn't let them know they were Jewish; their parents and relatives hid their own identities from them. For many, these methods went on after the danger had passed. How much could E. have known about the community he was from? Arguably little. There may have remained the memories of customs; there may have remained objects or stories told differently by each different acquaintance. But now and again the bulge of some buried identity may have become apparent. And it was then he might have discovered this song. Was this the sort of thing which his parents (or their acquaintances) hummed playfully with a sense of community, or had something been buried which his parents and relatives considered no worse than the (harmless) banter of others?

I didn't know the answer to this in my secondary school days or later either, until during a conversation in Budapest I asked János Kenedi (a writer and historian, who was much better informed in these matters), whether he happened to know something about this song. He wasn't sure, and asked me to hum it, in case the melody jogged his memory. I sang it (for the first time in half a century), and Jancsi said that this was an ironic, Hasidic song.

It was interesting to compare the Becskerek in which I grew up with the one painted by the stories of my grandfather and parents. Whenever any pre-war public events or gatherings came up in conversation, one felt the tangible presence of a Jewish community and their associated celebrations and events, to which they invited members of the other communities, too. I know (I have heard) that in 1945, those Jews who had successfully gone into hiding in Becskerek (or had successfully hidden their identities), and those Jews returning from Hungary and elsewhere, founded the Becskerek Jewish Council, but then they vanished. Many did leave for Israel or other countries, perhaps other towns. Of course, some did stay, I knew for example that Uncle Jancsi (one of my father's colleagues) and his sister, Aunt Iduska (my English tutor), were Jews. Memories remained, too. Many times in my family I heard the story of the Borsodi family (the writer, Lajos Borsodi and his son, Ferenc Borsodi). During my father's university years in Zagreb, Ferenc Borsodi had been his roommate. When they were first hauled to the camps, it was indeed according to fascist law, but within the law there was still a tiny amount of room for maneuver where one could at least try to appeal. The following case, number 11964, shows such an attempt. My father had somehow managed to legally secure the release of the Borsodis. But sometime later they were hauled off to the camps once again, and then there was no coming back. In my childhood, the anecdotes harking back to the university years with Feri Borsodi were a part of some form of Becskerek reality. Now this (virtual) reality is gone, too.

Then we became witnesses to the vanishing of another community. Everyone in my age group, myself included, knew German, although some better than others. It was the norm. German identity in the last years of the war and the first years following the war became burdened. As it had been with the Jews, the weighing up of the Germans' affiliations and the judgement of their various ties became of upmost importance. There's pedantry, too, in madness.

On May 22, 1941 the German Military Command issued a series of decrees that concerned culture across all of the Serbian territories. In paragraph 7 of the decree concerning cinemas, for example, it was stated that there was to be no employment (as ticket sellers, ticket collectors, or even ushers) of Jews, Roma, or anyone married to a Jew or a Roma. Not only did it give rise to the condemnation of ethnic and racial affiliation, but also of maintaining a relationship with the discriminated ethnicity or race. And then, in everyday life, there arose questions of borderline cases to this absurd law. What about those who were divorced? Who were widowed? After the withdrawal/expulsion of the German forces, it was the local Germans who ended up as the targets of laws and condemnation. Once again there arose questions of borderline cases.

There was one woman—a cook of Czech descent. She was born in Daruvár, where there had once been a Czech community. In Becskerek, a few months before the war, she had married a German worker. Being German, her husband had quickly been recruited to the German army and ended up on the Russian front where he died. Their marriage had only lasted a few months. Yet this was enough for her to be pigeonholed. In my grandfather's diary is the following:

> *20. IV. 1945. Friday. At one hour after midnight I awoke to a loud conversation coming from the hallway. I recognized Józsi's and then Zorka's voices. Then I hear that an unfamiliar voice is speaking into the telephone. I open the door to the hallway. Józsi is debating with two partisans, and to my question answers that the partisans are carrying off the cook, Maska (Marija); her husband, Annau served as a soldier for the Germans. Maska, being of Czech descent, received personal legitimacy, but with a note: "udata za Nemca" [wife to a German]. The partisans compiled a list of the cook's chattels which were here in our house. Two partisans slept here. The first slept on the divan in the office, the second on the bench in the hallway, doubtless to ensure that none of the listed chattels go missing during the night. – All next morning we hear from the complainants swarming to our door, that in the night, some manner of a raid had swept through the town and carried off anyone with a German name. We get news that people are also being taken from the nearby German villages and escorted to the town, and from here, they'll either be deported towards Austria, or carried off to Russia. Mere scaremongering? It's still impossible to say. – At one o'clock in the afternoon a long dray pulls up in our yard. They loaded the unfortunate cook's possessions;*

> *a couple of worn pieces of furniture (a wardrobe, a bed), her clothes, a pair of shoes, stockings, handkerchief; and took them away. I stared at the poverty heaped onto the cart. I felt a deep pity for those unfortunate people, and a deep disgust for the degeneration of humanity. Just as from our own yard they had carted off what little the cook had gathered over a lifetime, later I saw, while walking the streets throughout the day, one cart after another, piled high with furniture.*

The means of escaping this fate were also marked by frenzy. Once again, I'd like to quote from my grandfather's diary:

> *09. XII. 1944. For the last three days I have lent my room to Piros and Józsi, who alongside the clerk Ivkovics are receiving and hearing out complaints. Here they record the details in writing and prepare the petition. Over the last 3 days the stream of complaints has been endless. Somehow news spread that the fate is less grim for those women who file for divorce against their—German—husbands. These unfortunate women are lining up at the door. They are crammed into the corridor, and into my own room from 7 in the morning until the evening. The complaints are being written; the divorce suits are being prepared. Everything of course is done on favor, pro bono. Today we accept money from nobody; one person, a woman who escaped from the camps, brought 10 liters of wine into the kitchen out of gratitude.*

And let me add that during such turbulent times, even mercy found its place in the zealous coordinate system and zealous rhetoric. Another diary entry:

> *25. V. 1945. … –At noon, Maska the cook, overjoyed, arrived back from the lager, and was soon called upon by Mrs. Dr Pupa Kleits and Mrs. Dragan. So the news turned out to be true, those in mixed marriages have been released. In Becskerek several hundred have been released. Today is the birthday of Marshal Tito, we have been told that the release is an act of mercy for the occasion.*

In the local transit camps many Germans (or those pigeonholed as Germans) lost their lives. The majority however—in contrast to the Jews carried off to transit camps a few years ago—survived the torments and returned. Not much of their personal property, however, could be saved. All Jewish and Roma property was seized according to the law of the German occupiers. Similar laws were then created by the newer powers driving out the Germans. All German personal property was seized, with exception for the property of those Germans who joined the partisans. Of which there were some, but very few. There were many more German Becskerek citizens whose names couldn't be associated to any heroism, or wrongdoing. The property of these, too, was seized. In many cases, before the authorities, the pivotal question came down to who was a German? In Becskerek there weren't many families which didn't contain a mixed marriage. And so, the affiliation was a question of choice. Now, however, the authorities could decide who was affiliated to whom. And then in the '50s, a compromise was made between Tito and the German chancellor. Germany agreed that the value of the German property seized in Serbia would be compensated to those who emigrated to Germany. At the same time, Yugoslavia would presumably lower its demands for reparations. This opened up an opportunity for those whose property had been seized because they were Germans (or because they hadn't successfully proven they were not). I remember how the German names dwindled from class during my secondary school years. Like the Jewish community before it, the German community disappeared from Becskerek.

I found three documents in the archives of my grandfather's and father's lawyer's office in which, I believe, I can trace this occurrence. In the first part I will write about the Eckstein file.

1. THE ECKSTEIN CASE

File No. 11964

In February 1937, in the Becskerek weekly paper, *Tükör*, the following news item was published:

The Jews are celebrating. This may sound strange when these people are being exposed to the harshest and most inhumane persecution. Yet this celebration is more relevant than ever, because it lends hope to this people that the new Hamans, too, will perish, as in the time of Ahasuerus. And today this isn't the will of Jews alone, but the better part of the population would happily welcome the day when the bloody sword of the new Hamans is lost to oblivion.

Lili Eckstein, the daughter of the leather manufacturer, János Eckstein, on 21 February stood at the altar in Budapest with the nobleman Károly Molnár. Crowds of well-wishers celebrated the young couple.

A zsidók örömünnepet ülnek. Talán furcsán hangzik ez ma, amikor ez a nép a legdurvább és legembertelenebb üldözéseknek van kitéve. De ez az örömünnep mégis aktuálisabb mint valaha, mert reményt ad ennek a népnek, hogy az uj Hamanok is ugyanugy elpusztulnak mint Ahasverus idején. És ez ma nemcsak a zsidó nép kivánsága, hanem az emberiség legnagyobb része is örömmel várja azt a napot, amikor az uj Hamanok véres kardja a feledésbe merül.

✩

Eckstein Lilit, Eckstein János bőrgyáros leányát, február 21-én vezette oltár elé Budapesten nemes Molnár Károly. A fiatal párt tömegesen keresték fel szerencsekivánatokkal.

Réh Pál a petrovgradi fiatal iparosgárda közkedvelt tagja vasárnap, március 7-én délelőtt fél 8 órakor esküszik örök hüséget László Manci urleánynak, néhai László Márton petrovgradi kereskedő leányának. A polgári esküvőt csütörtökön, március 4-én tartják. A tanui tisztet a menyasszony részéről Eckstein Hermann, a vőlegény részéről pedig Hajduska Lajos töltik be. A Tükör szerkesztősége őszinte szerencsekivánatait küldi a fiatal párnak.

Gábor Antal petrovgradi állatorvost, a „Jugoslavija" biztositótárság helyi fiókjának tisztviselőjét Beogradba, a „Jugoslavija" biztositó központjába helyezték át.

Ma este rendezi a helybeli cionista szervezet hagyományos purimbálját a Parisien összes helyiségeiben. A bál iránt nagy érdeklődés nyilvánul meg a petrovgradi bálozók körében és igy jogosult az a remény, hogy az idei purimbál méltó lesz az eddigi purimbálakhoz hangulatban és kedélyben.

The owner and responsible editor of *Tükör* was Jenő László B. He also wrote poems, short lampoons, under the penname of Vékony Náci.[1] One well-known (nowadays we'd say cult-classic) was "The Scribbles and Scrawls of Vékony Náci." I came across this by chance decades ago in the family library. I read it several times.

But Vékony Náci wrote other things, too. In an argument with Iván Nagy (who is remembered in history as a radical Hungarian politician of Bácska), Jenő László B. writes:

> Good Sir, I was honored to read your recent article in *A Nép*, in which, by taking aim at my religion, you suggest I cannot understand the struggles of Hungarians. I can assure the worthy, cock-eyed, butcher editor of *A Nép* (who aims one way and shoots the other), that in all probability, I understand better and can empathize better than they! [...] It's not in my nature to pull up a pair of frayed knickers and act the magyar, but that's what I am, in all weathers, and this fact cannot be altered by any law. As opposed to those who only ever choose better weather.

This article appeared on April 6, 1940. A year later, *Tükör* no longer existed. Lili Eckstein was in Budapest with her husband (in the file it is later revealed that they lived in the 4th district, at 7 Petőfi Street). Becskerek was under German occupation. The occupiers established a new law and order. A decree was issued according to which all Jewish and Roma property was to be seized. I was already a lawyer, when, in amongst a pile of papers, the May 22, 1941 issue (the 5th issue) of *Verordnungs-Blatt* (Journal of Decrees) came into my hands. In the 1941 Journal of Decrees there featured a decree about the press, another about the theatre, a third about the cinema, and a fourth about the cabaret and variety shows.

1 "Náci," short for the given name Ignác (Ignatius). But this short name is pronounced "Natsy," just as "Nazi." While "Vékony" is a surname meaning "thin." A translation in English might be "Natsy Thin," though the Hungarian is at an advantage, as in the language surnames come before given names, i.e., "THIN Natsy."

VERORDNUNGSBLATT
DES MILITÄRBEFEHLSHABERS IN SERBIEN
Bestellungen nehmen alle Kommandanturen der Militärverwaltung an.
Einzelnummern nur bei diesen. Einzelpreis 0.20 RM.

ЛИСТ УРЕДАБА
ВОЈНОГ ЗАПОВЕДНИКА У СРБИЈИ
Поруџбине примају све командатуре војних управа. Поједини бројеви само код њих. Примерак 0·20 рајхсмарака.

№ 5	Belgrad, 22 Mai - Београд, 22 маја	1941

INHALT — САДРЖАЈ — Seite — Страница

1. Verordnung betreffend die Presse im serbischen Gebiet (Presseverordnung) 47
Уредба о штампи на српској територији . . . .
2. Verordnung über den Betrieb von Theatern 51
Уредба о позориштима . . . .
3. Verordnung über den Betrieb von Lichtspieltheatern und den Verleih von Filmen 53
Уредба о раду биоскопа и изнајмљивању филмова . . . .
4. Verordnung über das Kabarett- und Varietéwesen 56
Уредба о кабаретима и вариетеима . . . .

Verordnung — Уредба

In every decree it was repeated precisely what forms of work Jews and Roma, or those married to Jews and Roma, cannot perform. There were also nuances. In the decree concerning cabarets and variety shows it is stated in the first and third paragraphs that anyone who wishes to run a cabaret or variety show must gain permission from the Military Headquarters, for which one would need proof of their working capital, and whether it contained any Jewish capital. There was no mention of Roma capital, and, according to the letter of the law, the presence of Jewish capital merely obligates it be declared. Jewish and Roma women, or any women with a Jewish or Roma husband, couldn't become dancers (paragraph 5). In section 4 it was detailed that the works of Jewish authors or composers could not be published or produced (at this point, Roma or those married to Jews were not excluded). Paragraph 4 also specifies that there were to be no *compères* (announcers) in cabarets or variety shows.

In May of 1941, how could they have found time for such delicately tenacious embroidery of prejudice?! Who wrote such laws? Victor Klemperer writes of the step-by-step progress of this lunacy, that for a while in

Germany Jews were permitted to walk in parks, but they weren't permitted to sit on the benches. In the memoirs of Rudolf Schlesinger, who started out as a lawyer in Munich, then fled fascism to America, where he became one of the most renowned teachers of comparative law, he describes in detail the process of the deconstruction of normality in everyday life, how madness spread inch by inch.[2] He writes that in 1933, a German "reform" stated that Jews may not take doctorates. In a manner characteristic of the normal times and circumstances, for a while the new lunatic-laws came with introductory periods. Their enactment was fixed to a deadline. In May 1933 Schlesinger was called up by his teacher, Mueller-Erzbach. He was told the new law was being written, but Jewish doctorates are still permitted until the end of the summer semester. He had the support of a non-Jewish teacher, Kisch. Schlesinger writes highly of both. He had originally planned to take his doctorate at the end of the year, but then he sped up the work. He didn't finish everything as he would have originally liked, but he managed the dissertation and the oral exams by the end of the summer. He graduated summa cum laude. Afterwards, a large garden dinner party was held for family and friends. He describes how much he enjoyed being called *Herr Doktor.* And then, according to one law, Jews could not become members of the Bar; only those Jews can remain members who were accepted twenty-five years prior, and those who had seen combat duty in World War One. And so, Schlesinger's father could remain a lawyer, but he himself couldn't gain acceptance into the Bar. However, he could work as a house counsel in a private bank and take part in court trials, but he couldn't make oral pleadings.

It isn't easy to put this into perspective. Were these steps essential from a fascist point of view? After a certain stage of civilization, can inhumanity only be reached in gradients? Do the emerging, tragically pedantic laws denote these steps? In order to deconstruct normality, is there a necessity first for the bizarre? And how should we regard those who wrote these laws? Nowadays, those who drafted these laws merge with those who followed up the "walking yes, sitting-on-a-bench no" norm with the gas chambers. Among those who drafted the offensive, discriminative (for a while, more grotesque than bloodstained) laws, were there people who stopped (or would have stopped) at the point when Jews could stroll but

2 Rudolf B. Schlesinger, *Memories* (Universita degli studi di Trento, 2000).

couldn't sit on a bench, or could be legal counsels but couldn't be members of the Bar, or when Jews, Roma and those married to Jews or Roma couldn't be ticket collectors in a cinema?

But let me get back to Lili Eckstein, whose wedding was mentioned in *Tükör* as a joyful celebration of the Becskerek Jews in 1937. Lili Eckstein's father was a leather manufacturer and, according to the Eckstein file, he had a good few lawsuits to his name and earned a pretty penny. Lili, according to my parents' stories, was pretty, kind and sympathetic. She married at twenty-seven years old. Among the documents, there is a handwritten letter dated August 14, 1940, which Lili Eckstein sent from Budapest to my grandfather, addressed Dear Uncle Imre (Lili Eckstein was my parents' contemporary). In the letter, among other things she writes:

> Please may I ask that you go to the German authorities to request they pay arrears of the rent of my property, 2 Kraljica Marija, as far back as the occupation. From the rent, please, Uncle Imre, settle all of my outstanding debts, and put the rest towards supporting Hungarian students.

Besides this matter, I can see there was at least one more matter to be taken care of, her letter of request isn't there, but the petition is. Lili had a share of 600,000 dinars in the Eckstein company, and from February 11, 1937 it bore 8% interest. In the petition my grandfather requested the payment of this from the authorities. According to the papers, these 600,000 dinars were Lili's loan to the Eckstein family company. It was much more likely that at the time this was classified as a loan for tax purposes. Presumably the case could not have been that the girl had given a loan to her factory-owning father, but that the father had allowed his daughter 600,000 dinars and any extras.

In August 1941, when the letter was written, the Kraljica Marija Street house and the company had both been seized as Jewish property. My grandfather turned to the authorities with Lili Eckstein's request. I can see that the petition is rather thorough. It was written in German, addressed to *Deutsche Volksgruppe im Banat, Kreisamt für Volkswirtschaft—Juden Abteilung* (the Banat German People's Group, District Economic Bureau—Jewish Department). The reply was written on November 15 and is rather curt. My grandfather is informed that his client "according to our information is a pure Jew [Volljüdin]," and therefore, as according to the decree on Jewish and Roma property, can no longer own the property. The letter ends "Heil Hitler."

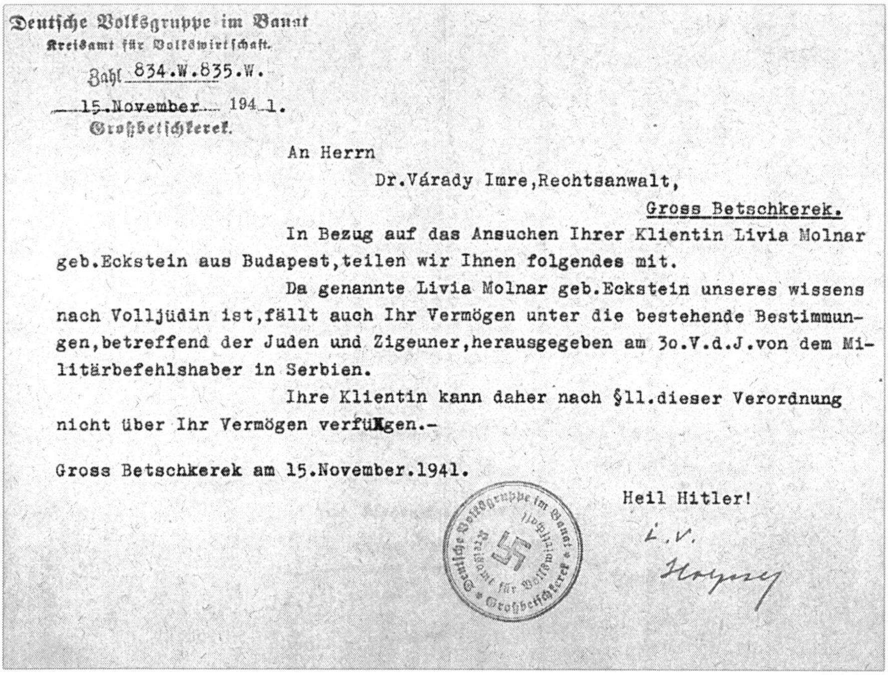

Deutsche Volksgruppe im Banat
Kreisamt für Volkswirtschaft.
Zahl 834.W.835.W.
15.November 194 1.
Großbetschkerek.

An Herrn
Dr.Várady Imre,Rechtsanwalt,
Gross Betschkerek.

In Bezug auf das Ansuchen Ihrer Klientin Livia Molnar geb.Eckstein aus Budapest,teilen wir Ihnen folgendes mit.

Da genannte Livia Molnar geb.Eckstein unseres wissens nach Volljüdin ist,fällt auch Ihr Vermögen unter die bestehende Bestimmungen,betreffend der Juden und Zigeuner,herausgegeben am 30.V.d.J.von dem Militärbefehlshaber in Serbien.

Ihre Klientin kann daher nach §11.dieser Verordnung nicht über Ihr Vermögen verfügen.-

Gross Betschkerek am 15.November.1941.

Heil Hitler!
i.V.

This is followed by a second attempt. I can see here my grandfather drifted towards the territory of private international law. I taught private international law for decades in Novi Sad. The file came into my possession not long ago, and until then I hadn't known my grandfather had experience in this domain. One of the supporting arguments is the certificate from the Hungarian city of Székesfehérvár which verifies that Károly Molnár, Lili Eckstein's husband, is Lutheran. Another paper shows that Károlyné Molnár née Lívia Eckstein is a Hungarian citizen. My grandfather's petition of February 9, 1942 in German explained that Lívia Molnár is a Hungarian citizen, and according to which, decrees of the Serbian (German) Military Command did not apply to her. While in Hungary, there were no decrees on the seizure of Jewish and Roma property. Therefore, the Hungarian law was applicable, and Károlyné Molnár was still the rightful owner. According to the petition, the citizenship, rather than the situation of the property was decisive in the question of which law was applicable. Then the rhetoric intensified: "The living individual rather than the dead property is the deciding momentum."

Reluctantly, I must note that this is not what I taught. When it concerns real estate, the dominant position in private international law is that the property's situation is more important than the owner's citizenship. But then, other lawyers also used arguments which similarly didn't reflect the dominant positions of the law.

The decision most probably didn't depend upon private international law. There is no refusal order among the documents, but from the correspondence it is revealed that the attempt was unsuccessful. Among the documents is a letter dated February 28, 1942 in which my grandfather is summoned to appear in front of an Obersturmführer named Pamer at the request of the Security Service concerning the Lívia Molnár case. This letter also signs off with a "Heil Hitler."

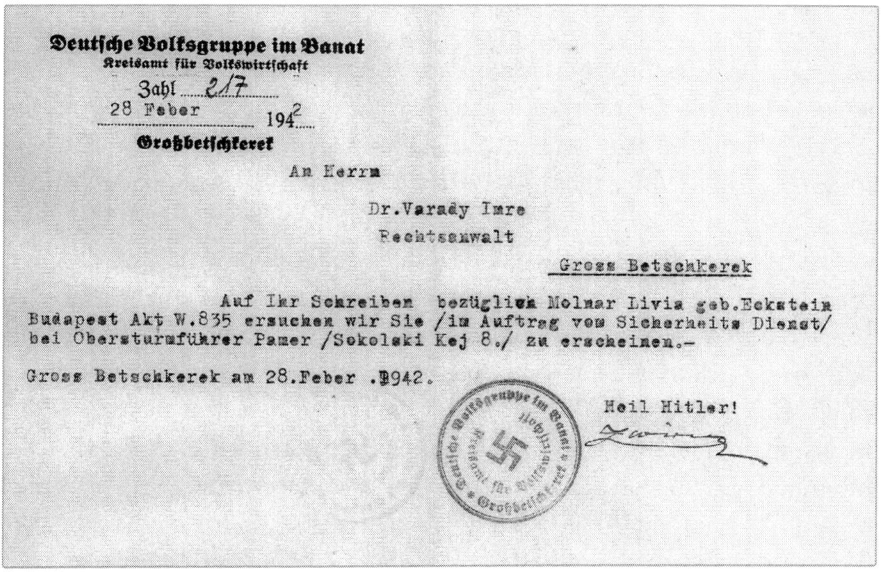
Deutsche Volksgruppe im Banat
Kreisamt für Volkswirtschaft
Zahl 217
28 Feber 1942
Großbetschkerek

An Herrn

Dr.Varady Imre
Rechtsanwalt
Gross Betschkerek

Auf Ihr Schreiben bezüglich Molnar Livia geb.Eckstein Budapest Akt W.835 ersuchen wir Sie /im Auftrag vom Sicherheits Dienst/ bei Obersturmführer Pamer /Sokolski Kej 8./ zu erscheinen.-

Gross Betschkerek am 28.Feber .1942.

Heil Hitler!

I don't know what happened in this questioning. The closed case was opened up again by the change of power. Lili Eckstein survived the horrors of war, but her marriage didn't. In 1945 she returned to Becskerek. My father took over her affairs. In Lili Eckstein's letters, *Dear Uncle Imre* becomes *Dear Jóska*. On the authorization is the signature "Livija Ekštajn," and again in Cyrillic, so as not to take any chances. The matter at hand remained the same, Lili Eckstein's property, but the language changed to Serbian, and new zeals have to be avoided. The addressees also changed. The former, simple "mayor's office," in Hungarian or Serbian, was first replaced by the "Banat German People's Group." And then followed a long, sermonizing period of renaming things. The addressee became the *Gradski narodno-oslobodilački odbor*, namely, the People's Liberation Commission. The fervent closing words initiated four years prior, remained, however *Heil Hitler!* was been replaced by *Smrt fašizmu, sloboda narodu!* (Death to fascism, freedom to the people!). And in an interesting development, not only did the bureau sign off thus, but the civilian writing to the bureau as well. Albeit somewhat more reservedly, perhaps with an abbreviation: S.F.–S.N. Lili Eckstein closed her petition to the People's Liberation Commission "S.F.–S.N.," which may after all have been easier than Heil Hitler.

From the remaining documents and letters, it is not completely clear on what grounds the new powers withheld Eckstein's property from her. I have heard stories that a German name brought with it a new grotesque pigeonholing which also entailed the seizure of property. Those Jews who had German surnames, and who hadn't been murdered by the German occupiers, had to prove that they weren't Germans. This was made difficult by the fact that while concealing their identities, the people had done their best to free themselves of any papers which referred to their (Jewish) identities. My father had one such case in which, before the People's Liberation Commission, he offered as evidence the order of the Banat German People's Group, District Economic Bureau–Jewish Department, according to which someone's property had been seized as Jewish property. By which means, of course, my father and his client had intended to prove that the individual was not German, and therefore the new orders on the seizure of property did not apply. The proud, laconic response was "we cannot take into consideration fascist documents."

Among the documents I see no clear evidence, though it is probable, that the new power tried to take possession of the Eckstein property as German property. Therefore, it had to be proven the Ecksteins were Jews, not Germans. One of the pieces of evidence may have been the Zionist identity card of Lili's father, János Eckstein, which is also included among the papers.

I can't see a date, but it states that Jovan/János Eckstein was seventy-one. Considering he was born in 1866, the card must have been issued in 1937. The New Zionist Organization issued the card in which their fundamental aims were stated in Serbian, Hebrew, English and French. This seems sufficiently convincing proof that the Eckstein Jews were not Germans.

As an aside, the Eckstein leather factory was founded in 1863. Its telephone number was 104. It was still the same in 1912, when János Eckstein wrote to my grandfather, addressing him "Dear Imre." The telegraphic address was also simple; there was no need for a street or a house number, merely "János Eckstein."

From the documents there emerges one more reason as to why they had wanted to seize the Eckstein property, and this was "collaboration with the occupiers," which resulted in confiscation. In Becskerek, and elsewhere too, collaboration was understood in rather broad terms. The well-known Bencze furniture factory was also seized because the factory had "collaborated with the fascist occupiers." The judgement provided their definition of collaboration: the furniture factory had manufactured and sold furniture not only to the civilians of Becskerek, but also to the fascist occupiers. That was it.

János Eckstein, the owner of the leather factory (a secondary school classmate of my grandfather) had been hauled off in 1942 to Belgrade, where he was killed. I heard several times that the deported Jews from Becskerek, and likely other towns, were loaded into lorries in Belgrade, gas was released among the passengers, and this was how they lost their lives. I am not sure, but according to my knowledge, the operation of the leather factory wasn't directly taken over by the German occupiers. Whatever the case may have been, in all likelihood, the factory sold leather to whomever wanted to buy it and had the money (or just took it, money or no), and so the fascist occupiers could get leather too. It is possible that this is how the Eckstein leather factory was assessed, and this led to the confiscation.

This stigma fell away regardless, as can be seen in the letter of the factory's director, dated June 4, 1951. The subject of the letter is the claim of Livia Lepedat; Lili Eckstein had married anew, and her new husband's name was Dušan Lepedat. The letter concerns the Eckstein leather factory, but the factory's name was now *Fabrika Kože Svetozar Marković-Toza*, named after a Yugoslav war hero, and was under the ownership of Zrenjanin (Becskerek) city and the state. The letter declared that the assessment has changed. Originally, on March 1, 1950, the factory had been seized, but then was transferred to state hands by right of nationalization. In other words, the factory had been taken as a Jewish property, then the new power which ousted the German occupiers made efforts to claim the factory as a German property—because "Eckstein" is a German name—and because during occupation the factory had collaborated with occupiers, in that leather was sold to the Germans, too. Then, once it had been successfully refuted that Eckstein was German or that he had collaborated with the occupiers, the fact still remained, it was a property. All properties above a certain size were nationalized. The only option was for Lili Eckstein to try to claim compensation from the Svetozar Marković-Toza leather factory.

There were other problems, too, for which Lili Eckstein had asked for legal help. The new authorization was written in May 1945, and my father is mentioned as a lawyer of Petrovgrad (therefore, the town was no longer Grossbetschkerek or Nagybecskerek, and it hadn't yet become Zrenjanin). The first petition (May 10, 1945) requested permission for Lívia Eckstein to take residence in Becskerek. For this, however, she needed a certificate of political and moral conduct (*Uverenje o političkom i moralnom vladanju*), and when issued, her relations with the occupiers were closely scrutinized. (I don't know whether the linguistic shift happened merely by chance, but in Hungarian and Serbian, the word order of the phrase "political and moral" altered, and was replaced by "moral-political," *moralno-političko* in Serbian.) In her request for the certificate, Lili Eckstein wrote:

> ...I'm of Jewish nationality, and as such I escaped the German authorities. I was born in Petrovgrad on 12.III.1910, my father is Jovan [János], my mother is Gizella Polák, who were executed by the fascist occupiers.
> ...As a Jew, I simply could not have compromised myself on the side of the occupiers, my politics therefore are respectable.

In the last sentence between the lines I sense an amount of exasperation. On the back of the petition, the comment of an office clerk is noted in pencil: "The certificate will be issued within a few days." And it was.

A day after writing the petition requiring the certificate of moral-political conduct (May 11, 1945) another application was written. This one was intended for the Supply Department of the City People's Liberation Commission. Stated at the top of the page is the subject of the application: "The request of LÍVIA ECKSTEIN, Petrovgrad housewife (Kr. Marije St. 2), that allowance be granted for the purchase of one women's summer dress." In which Lili Eckstein writes the following (in Serbian):

> ... I fled Petrovgrad to escape the German occupation. I returned on 8 May 1945.
> Besides one winter dress, I have nothing.
> I kindly ask that it be permitted I buy enough material for one summer dress, namely of a material which is washable.
> Petrovgrad, 11.V.1945
> S.F.–S.N.

There is no reply among the documents, but as she was granted certification of suitable political-moral conduct, I suppose that the procurement of a summer dress also became possible. Moreover, I don't remember who told me, but I heard that Lili Eckstein also wanted to include in the request that the reason she needed the dress was because she wanted to walk on the *korzó* again, the promenade. My father dissuaded her from writing this. In Becskerek the korzó was as important as the Hungarian writer Sándor Márai holds it to be in *The Confessions of a Haut-Bourgeois (Egy polgár vallomásai).* The korzó in Becskerek was Main Street (we used this name, and still do, even after many name changes). I heard that the korzó hadn't disappeared entirely under fascism, and that there had been a difference between its two sides. According to Márai, one side was upper-class, and along the other strolled "the maids, the infantrymen and the more modest members of society." I don't know whether this was entirely true in Becskerek, but there did exist a distinction. I began going to the korzó in the mid-'50s, at that time it was still an unavoidable factor of the town's social life, and some sort of distinction did exist between the left and right sides of the korzó. I couldn't say that it was a class-based distinction, but we all knew that the left side (when walking away from the town hall and the catholic temple) was the main stage. On the right side were the students from the countryside, who still hadn't connected with town life, and the couples who wanted to be alone and to avoid the constant greeting and stopping for exchanges with acquaintances. And there were some who walked along both sides.

In May 1951 a more serious result was achieved in the Ecsktein affair. I'm reading the protocol signed on May 31, 1951 by Nikola Preradović, the chief of the Department of State Buildings, Milorad Popović, the director of the Municipal Property Company and my father, as lawyer to Lívia Lepedat, née Eckstein. According to the protocol, the house and land under 13 Makedonska Street was to be given over to Lívia Lepedat in its entirety, in addition to the house under 12 Balkanska Street and half the land. The estate would be given in its present condition and taken over by the parties without objection. It isn't revealed in the papers whether this is the return of two earlier confiscated estates, or whether new estates were given instead of the seized one. In any case, they had succeeded in getting something back from the nationalized estates.

After this, I would like to cite two letters sent from Maribor (now a city in Slovenia). Duško Lepedat was from the town of Kikinda in Banat, and for a while the married couple lived in Kikinda. It is possible the letters sent from Maribor were written during the summer vacation, but it is also possible the Lepedat couple moved to Maribor. The latter is indicated to be true by my grandfather's diary, in which he noted who visited the office, and who wrote letters or telegrams for his birthday or name day. The Eckstein and Lepedat names are frequent entries. The last such entry is dated March 1, 1956. I can see my grandfather was sent a telegram for his eighty-ninth birthday from, among others, "Lilly Eckstein, Dusko, Maribor." Of the two letters sent to my father in 1951, one was written by Duško Lepedat in Serbian, and he wrote that they were delighted about the success concerning the house and give their congratulations. The other by Lili Lepedat/Eckstein was also written to my father from Maribor, on June 15, 1951, in Hungarian. She wrote that they were enjoying Maribor, and added: "May I please ask that you do all that you can, in case we do succeed in receiving the money from the leather factory. … Here [in Maribor] one really can live a good and pleasant life, and find anything as long as one has the money."

The matter of compensation for the nationalized property was never resolved. In 2011 the Serbian Parliament passed the Asset Recovery Act. I believe that in accordance with this, it would now be possible to make a claim in connection to the Becskerek leather factory. But I don't know whether there is anyone left to do so.

2. SOCKS ON THE CHANDELIER, LIVES BY A THREAD

File No. 12198

Many books that I have read start with the caveat that all actors and all events are fictitious, resemblance with true actors or true events can only be a coincidence. Trying to shape prose from the files in the family archive, I took the opposite approach. In this book, all actors and events are real. I added some reflections here and there, but I did not change the facts. The names are also real, with some exceptions. This case belongs to those exceptions. The facts remained unchanged, just as most names, but details of the divorce case prompted a change of the names of the main protagonists.

A Marriage and "Separation from Bed and Board"
Separatio a mensa et thoro

Karl Engel and Márta Kuzmin were married on January 28, 1938. Their daughter Judit was born about three and a half years later, on August 2, 1941. Karl was German, Márta Jewish. By January 1938, fascism had been gaining ground rapidly, but not yet to the point of stopping a mixed marriage in the town of Becskerek.

Apart from recording the cause for the divorce, the files say nothing about the marriage itself. People's memories lingered on, however. There was one episode I often heard about from my parents and their acquaintances. Sometime after the wedding ceremony, probably early in the spring of 1938, Márta and Karl invited guests over. Karl was the same generation as my parents, and quite possibly one of my mother's classmates. When the first guests arrived, including my parents, they were received by Márta. Karl, barefoot, showed up a few minutes later and with an irritable tone, enquired: "Márta, where are my socks?" "Why, on the *luszter*, where else?" Márta replied with a nonchalant smile. Some witnesses claim that the exchange transpired in German; others insist the couple spoke in Serbian. Whichever was the language, the words *zokni* [socks] and *luszter* [a type of chandelier], go roughly by the same name in the various *linguae francae* of Becskerek (Hungarian, German, and Serbian). In the various accounts of the incident, consternation mingled with sympathy, with frequent references to the Engels' household habits departing from middle-class towards bohemian. The stories I heard contained no trace of German–Jewish tension, nor of any grudge against history as it unfolded. This was not a Romeo-and-Juliet relationship.

At one point in the story, Karl's grammar school friends played an important role. Their names suggest it was a Serbian grammar school he went to, as did probably Márta herself. The stack of documents contains a number of letters written by the Engels to my parents. Some are in Hungarian, others in Serbian or German. After being enlisted in the German army, Karl wrote his letters to my father in German, logical given the censorship in place as well as his status as a German soldier. Márta herself also wrote in three languages. More often than not, there seemed no logic of any kind behind why a particular language was chosen, unless the apparent randomness or even indifference was a sort of logic in its own right.

Let me make a short tangent here. It goes without saying that Becskerek was not without its national identities and pride, of which mother tongue was a key part. Multilingualism was also important. When I went to elementary school in Becskerek, there was hardly a day when I only spoke in just one language. Exceptions were when I stayed home sick and received either no visitors or Hungarian-speaking visitors only. Outside the confines of the house, in the real world of neighbors, acquaintances and shops, trilingual communication was the norm. Then, during my grammar school years, the German language gradually faded out of public life. As a result, my German never reached the level of my grandparents and parents' knowledge, although my bilingualism survived unscathed. In fact, even after my Becskerek years, I can remember only a few occasions in my life when I spoke in just a single language throughout the day. In Belgrade, I had a Hungarian roommate, as I had in Aleksinac, where I did my military service, sharing digs with around eighty young conscripts in a huge warehouse of a barracks building. Our group included two Hungarian country boys (from around Subotica, the village of Kispiac, if memory serves), with whom I swapped a few daily words in Hungarian. I also had Hungarian and Serbian acquaintances in America as well, and often had my family around, and of course later the advent of email facilitated regular correspondence in the different languages. The trilingual way of life continued when I moved to Budapest, the Hungarian capital, where my wife and I alternated between Hungarian and Serbian, while I also taught in English at the university. Looking back, however, trilingual days are about all that was preserved from my Becskerek days, there is not much else.

Although the stack of documents begins with the divorce lawsuit papers (which began in 1943), many things had led up to the suit being filed, not least the occupation of Becskerek by Germany. The lawsuit I am writing about begins in 1943. An issue of the local daily newspaper *Torontál*, dated June 26, 1943, cropped up among the papers. I read it closely, but could not find a single reference to the case. The paper may have been stashed among the case file documents by accident, but it does have its uses: it shows a mix of news and perceptions, some shaped by the occupying authorities, others prompted by Becskerek events that managed to maintain relevance. The header reads "Becskerek," followed by the town's full name, "Nagybecskerek," in brackets. The address of the editorial office is listed as "Sepp Kraft (Zápolya) ucca 3." (Sepp Kraft, who gave the street its alternative name during the German occupation was an SS Sturmbandführer,) One full page of the paper's total of four pages is devoted to the funeral of Andor Marton. This is followed by a headline proclaiming that "Germany has drawn a reliable anti-aircraft shield over its territories to protect against the threat of Anglo-Saxon raids." Yet other headlines hinted at different direction of history. They told how Banjanin was appointed to head the exile Yugoslav government in London, and how Groll was the most likely candidate for foreign minister. Moscow meanwhile was calling for the transfer from London to Moscow of all exile governments "of states with a territory within the Soviet's desired zone of influence." On page four I read that the Lehel soccer team prevailed over Olympia 4 to 1. (The Lehel I know hails from the village of Muzslya, but what about Olympia? "Olympia of Torda" rings a bell, except I am not sure whether the coupling of these two words is the work of true recollection or of confused memories.) In another encounter between a local Hungarian and a local German team, the Hajrá team defeated the Schwäbischer by 4 to 2. Then there is this announcement on page three, the context of which I seem unable to recall or visualize. I leave it up to the reader:

The English translation:

ANNOUNCEMENT

At the airport only sheep (ewes) may graze. Grazing of other animals is strictly prohibited under threat of punishment.

District Commander
Amelung signed
Captain

This, then, was the state of affairs.

By then, Karl was no longer a merchant from Becskerek, had been enlisted in the Wehrmacht as a German national and sent as an Untersturmführer to the Russian front. As far as I know, such a fate was common among Germans of the Banat region. Like them, most of the Hungarian conscripts from Bácska were taken to the eastern front. The divorce itself, however, was not triggered by the ebbs and flows of history and the separations they caused. The causes listed were rather more conventional and timeless. Márta, drawing inspiration from her pulse of youth rather than global events, had been leading a life of verve, and word of her small-town secrets had leaked all the way to the Russian front, thanks to earnest neighbors. Life on the battlefront was not conducive to forgiveness.

The divorce suit was filed on "September 31, 1943," proof that official documents in those days were not immune to errors any less than they are today. The seal of the District Court of Becskerek shows the suit was officially registered on October 1, 1943. The explanation reads that, in the summer of 1943, after Karl had been conscripted and taken from Becskerek, Márta established intimate relations with a medical student named R. B. Moreover, during the month of August, in her residence she hosted a "bohemian company" of five or six, including R. B., with whom she spent the entire night drinking, playing cards and dancing, at times stripped down to her bathing suit. Three witnesses were recommended to take the stand for the plaintiff: the lawyer-candidate Ž. Slavko (whose son, of the same name, would later become an attorney himself), Erzsébet L. and Erzsébet P. Márta was defended by attorney-at-law Stojan Adamović. The Adamović family also had a line of lawyers running through generations.

Stojan was a few years younger than my father. I got to know him during the 1950s at an aquatic sports center called Brankovan. He was a noted swimming coach, among other things.

The first court date, scheduled for November 18, 1943, was for a reconciliation hearing, the summons from the Petrovgrad District Court were delivered to Karl Engel Becskerek and Márta Engel née Kuzmin of Becskerek. With all the changes of the name of the city there was never a chance that all the papers would be completely consistent. In any event, the reconciliation failed. Karl did not even show up for the hearing. My father wrote to him in German, informing him about the outcome and about the next hearing probably being scheduled for January 1944, and expressing his hope that Karl would be able to attend. The letter is postmarked from "Betschkerek" and addressed to a camp, Feldpostnummer 44609/A. On December 18, my father wrote another letter to the same postal address, wondering if Karl, from whom he received no reply, had received his November letter. This time, he informed Karl of the exact date and time of the hearing (9 a.m. on January 11, 1944), and that he intended to simplify the deposition and reduce details to a bare minimum. No reply is to be found among the documents.

Neither Karl nor Márta showed up for the second hearing. There is no sign of official minutes anywhere, although my father did make notes of witness testimony on the reverse of a document. Ž. Slavko stated that both Márta and R. B. had told him they had an affair. The charwoman Erzsébet L. testified that one day, as she brought water into the bedroom, she noticed Márta lying in bed with R. B. A cross-examination by the defense established that both had their clothes on. R.B., upset by Erzsébet's unexpected entry, was calmed down by Márta with the words, "It's all right, it's all right… It's just her, Erzsike." Erzsébet L. further recalled finding men's underwear in the laundry one day, when Karl had already left for military duty. The same day as the maid, Erzsébet P. also gave incriminating testimony. She said that, having been hired on August 5, 1943, she noticed R. B. spending entire days at Márta's. Prompted by the defense, she added that Márta slept in the bedroom with her little daughter, while R. B. stayed over in the dining room. She also recalled several visits by a company of men and "a lady from Pančevo." There was revelry, drinking and cards, and Márta would strip down to her bathing suit on occasion.

I am overcome by a sense of indecision as I quote from these testimonies. Admittedly, the case is far from egregious in the context of the international practice of divorce cases. Things like this do happen. Yet still vivid in our memories is the tempest of prejudice which instantly rounds up all unleashed ideas and comments and binds them to the pillory. Today the tempest has subsided, but the ingrained habit remains to look around and check if the brutish turbulence has really disappeared or just become petrified instead, and whether a story can remain in the simple human space between neighbors, friends or gossipers. Or, will the story painted by Slavko and the two Erzsikes drift away from us, and will the little crabby letters stiffen into an exclamation mark proclaiming that this is "how Jewish women are." (And Aryans not?) Drifted by the storm, Slavko, the two Erzsikes (and myself) may be caught up between two labels: looking from one or the other vantage point we shall either be qualified as outspoken Aryan visionaries or, alternatively, as scummy anti-Semites. Meanwhile, looking at things calmly, it becomes plain that the testimonies do not only fail to reveal what Jewish women—or women, period—are like, they also fail to make known what kind of person Márta actually was.

The verdict was delivered on January 29, 1944. Pursuant to the laws in force at the time, the judgement and any dissolution of the marriage were to be preceded by six months' of "separation from bed and board," imposed on the parties by a court order. The institution of *Separatio a mensa et thoro* had been a part of canonical law that survived in several European legal systems for a long time, superseding or preceding an actual divorce. During those six months, many things came to pass. A concentration camp, filled with mostly Gypsy prisoners, was set up at the end of our street. The German soldiers were fond of making the Gypsies fight against one another. The soldiers, above the fray, would watch over the melee, clearly enjoying the evidence of their superiority. Then afterwards, they would demonstrate their magnanimity by serving soup to the opponents. Decades later I recognized the same concept, albeit toned down for the milder tastes of a new civilization, when I watched *The Jerry Springer Show* in the USA. There, too, the main event consisted of real human beings embroiled in a real fight against each other, typically a love-triangle fracas or neighborly feud. Incited by the host, the arguments would develop into a spectacular verbal bout, sometimes spilling over the line into an all-out brawl. The participants at least reaped a more substantial reward than that camp soup, and were also then presumably free to go home. I watched those Jerry Springer shows in the company of a group of students in a dorm room. Most of them looked on smiling at the onscreen frays, with a smug glee not unlike that of the Übermensch. Some of us, instead of congratulating ourselves on rising above the filth, identified intimately with and rooted for one opponent or another. A few were outraged by the sheer humiliation of it all. Nowadays, you do not need to travel as far as the US for this kind of reality show entertainment. The paradigm of audience attitudes has remained unchanged. While I have no statistical data at hand to prove or disprove this, it seems to me that many continue to opt for the stance of the Übermensch, while a roughly equal number continue to somehow combine (or confuse) the superiority of the outsider with empathy for a participant. Yet the outrage has been marginalized, and the scheme divorced from the Fascist ethos. It has become natural.

March 19 fell within the six months of separation in bed and at table. Being the day of Joseph, my father's name-day, it was a day my family always looked forward to with relish. But in 1944, March 19 did not work out as usual. I quote from my grandfather's diary:

> *19/III 1944, Day of Joseph. At half past six in the morning, I hear footsteps and raised voices at the door. A little later—I was lying in bed—Józsi enters with a plaid blanket and a small pillow over his arm, and gives me a kiss. He came to say good-bye. Two German militia men had shown up at his place with orders for him to get dressed immediately, to take him and myself to the internment facility of the Messinger Institute. They said that militia had been dispatched around town to round up all the elders of the Hungarian minority. The argument in front of my door involved Józsi and Zorka who tried to explain to them I had been bedridden for two days and was unfit to be taken away. Thereupon one of the guards led Józsi away, while the other called his commander from the office and told him the old Várady was ill and lying in bed. What was he to do with a 77-year-old? At last, he left me alone. Meanwhile word came about those rounded up already. The entire known Hungarian leadership had been taken, along with our prelate; even the leaders of the women's camp, Saczi Mara and Vilma Végh had not been spared.*

The radio in Budapest aired no news at all. The word here is that the German army has occupied Hungary's borders and is pushing into the country from Serbia, Croatia and Romania. There is no resistance to talk about. The government resigned this morning. Some say that a military dictatorship under Henrik Werth has been declared; others report that Szálasi and his men have taken over the government. Confusion reigns everywhere. I have been at home. I have been lying here all day long.

This is how I spent Joseph's Day, for which we had such high hopes.

At half past seven, Pali returned home, and then Józsi a little later. They were all released. They were told it was just a routine security round-up. The German army was in the process of occupying Hungary, and they had to be stashed away for safety in case the local Hungarians began to conspire to stage a reckless movement. –Poor Hungary! Józsi and Pali tell us that, before being released, all detainees had to sign a statement agreeing not to leave town without a special permit. All political congregation and discussion were banned.

Becskerek had been under German occupation for a while, but the tense German–Hungarian relations and the occupation of Hungary ushered in a change in the streets of Becskerek as well. Here are another few lines from my grandfather's diary:

20–21 March 1944: It's all rumors, guesswork, total uncertainty. No radio news of the events in Hungary. Unpleasant incidents in the towns of the Banat. On Sunday (19 March) Hungarian students, both boys and girls, had their Bocskay hats knocked off their heads by the Hitler Jugend, and the ornamental cords of their suits torn off.

Also, some time during these six months, Márta was taken away to the camp in Csóka, then released after a while, possibly in part thanks to her soon-to-be-divorced husband. At least I recall hearing my parents say something like this later on, but I cannot be sure.

The six months of separation ended on July 11, 1944. The divorce suit carried on at its own pace. On July 17, 1944, Karl stated for the court that the matrimonial community has not been restored and no child has been born for the past six months. Citing the provisions of the Matrimony Act of 1894, he requested the court to dissolve the marriage. He laid no claim to a reimbursement of court costs (neither did the defendant). The verdict, passed on September 28, 1944, relied chiefly on the formerly established facts of the case, and was written in Serbian, in the Cyrillic script. I fail to see the imprint of history in its lines or arguments and findings. A verdict worded like this might have been handed down fifty years before or after. Having described the parties' positions and summarized witness testimonies, the judges concluded that they were unable to concede the claim that adultery had been perpetrated. Although they did perceive certain *signs* of adultery, they insisted that the *fact* thereof could not be established solely by inference, but that it must be demonstrated beyond a reasonable doubt. They added that adultery cannot be substantiated even by the circumstance that R. B. spent days in the defendant's home, often lying in bed with her (fully dressed, for that matter). At the same time, the judges allowed another grounds for divorce when they affirmed, in a language that strikes us as archaic today, that the defendant's way of life satisfied the definition of intractable, immoral conduct.

Next came an appeal against first-instance judgement, but from this point on things took a different turn. Márta was taken to Auschwitz; Karl deserted the German army; the three-year-old Judit came into the custody of family acquaintances. A year and a half later, on February 5, 1946, my father responded to the request of the Petrovgrad District Court dated January 29, stated for the record that the parties had moved to an unknown location. He would notify the court of any resumption as soon as he has established contact with his client. The court acknowledged that the process "has been stayed due to wartime events" and called on the parties to report to the court in fifteen days if they desired to continue the litigation. No such notice was ever received. At this point, I am concluding the first episode of the story.

Restoration?
Restitutio in integrum

Before my father notified the Becskerek court (at that time called Petrovgrad court) of the absence of the parties, and after the separation from bed and board was declared, many things transpired. Karl returned to Pančevo with the German troops, only to defect on September 30, 1944, two days after the divorce judgement was delivered, by which time Márta had been deported to Auschwitz.

One year later the war was over, but it is completely uncertain whether one could scrub off the stigmas stuck on during the past years—and whether one could return home. The stack of documents contains a letter by Karl, written from the town of Szeged on October 1, 1945, in which he recounted what befell him in the past year. This letter, which among other things, revealed that he managed to survive, is not simply a report but a statement of purpose—of his intention to return home. He wrote the letter to my father asking him to forward copies to Serbian schoolmates who joined the partisans. He asked the addressees for certified affidavits affirming that he had always been on the side of the partisans, despite his rank as Untersturmführer in the German army. Ostensibly, such affidavits could have allowed Karl to return to Becskerek and claim immunity from the laws imposing sanctions on German nationals and German-owned property. Naturally, the events recounted by Karl were selected and portrayed with this aim in mind. Nevertheless, subsequent correspondence and documents do substantiate Karl's version of events. A letter from October 1, 1945 is addressed to *Dragi Mišo* (Dear Mišo), a certain Miša Dragović who was assigned to the Yugoslav embassy in Tehran in the autumn of 1945. A copy was sent to Stanoje Županski, known as Bato by his friends (including Karl). My father tried to forward this copy via Bato's father, a lawyer in Becskerek. Another copy was sent to Nikola Škundrić, an official of the provincial authorities based in Novi Sad at the time. A further copy was addressed to Svetolik Popović, an instructor at the Trade Academy in Niš.

Karl related how he escaped from the German army on September 30, 1944. He had a tryst near Besni Fok with three partisans, to whom he promised that he would rally others for the partisan cause with the help of instructions from a priest named Božin. For the sake of credibility, Karl furnished Božin's address (Veršec, Zlatne grede 6) and reminded Miša Dragović of his recent meetings with him at the Local Committee of People's Liberation in Opovo. In Besni Fok, he asked for permission to enter armed combat on the side of the partisans, only to be dispatched from Besni Fok to Opovo so that his request may be decided by the local command there. Meanwhile, the Red Army was marching into Besni Fok, and Karl, along with a number of his mates who had joined the partisans after deserting from the German

Army, was taken prisoner on October 7. According to Karl's letter, they were treated better than those German soldiers who did not try to join the partisans. The prisoners were taken first to Timişoara (Temesvár), then to Debrecen, Jászberény, and finally to Brno. In the hectic coming and going, prisoner of war numbers varied widely, sometimes peaking at fifty or fifty-five thousand. The camp prisoners even formed a sort of anti-Fascist league, Karl being one of the leaders. He was released on September 12, 1945 in Brno, from where he somehow reached Szeged.

In the letter Karl, was bent on proving that he had planned to join the partisans long before the tide of war turned, and the German army's collapse became certain. He recalled making a proposal to Svetolik Popović as early as in May 1944, and even gave him information about German armories. Shortly afterwards he fell ill with malaria and remained bedridden for a long time. He asked Bato and Mišo to corroborate his delivery of intelligence for the partisan movement after his conscription in the German army. He added that he even sent winter clothes to the partisans via Márta.

The letters were mailed out of Becskerek as intended. There are copies of two cover letters among the documents, penned by my father to Nikola Škundrić and Svetolik Popović, to whom he was forwarding them. No reply to these letters was ever received.

My father wrote to Karl on October 31, 1945, informing him that he had delivered Karl's letters intended for Dragović to Županski's father, and sent the letters to Škundrić and Popović by registered mail. But this not how my father began his own letter. Karl's whereabouts had been unknown until his letter from Szeged arrived. The autumn of 1945 was a period of reckonings when news of surviving family and friends was received, and deaths were confirmed. Not until he received Karl's letter dated October 1—a letter Karl intended as a circular—did my father know he was alive and in good health. This is what my father dealt with first, "with immense and sincere joy," as he wrote. Then he proceeded to share some consequential news with Karl: Márta had survived the horrors of Auschwitz and sent word from the Netherlands. My father attached a copy of her telegram from Amsterdam. Before reading my father's letter (which spent additional time in the hands of the censors) Karl could not have been sure that Márta was alive. There was hardly any telephone service between Becskerek and Szeged in those days, which contributed greatly to the protracted interlude of both hopes and fears.

There was so much to say. In his letter, my father gave an account of mutual acquaintances, listing the survivors. He mentioned László Szerb, one of his fellow university students in Zagreb, whom Karl knew well. Szerb had been among the Jews deported to Bor. After being liberated from the camp there, he took a job in the foreign ministry in Belgrade. I was introduced to him by my father when I enrolled in the university in Belgrade. They lived a few blocks from my rented room, and I visited them every two or three weeks. He was born in Čakovec. His favorite poet was Árpád Tóth. He served as councilor for the Yugoslav Ministry of Foreign Affairs. He was always reticent about speaking of his experiences in Bor. One day, though, he spoke of meeting a Hungarian poet there, and even told me about the man's poems. That man was Miklós Radnóti. Szerb was unaware of Radnóti's fame and stature as a poet. I would often ask him to tell me everything he knew about Radnóti, or to write it down. He would not. He had a rather taciturn habit to begin with, and it was about a period of his life he opted not to recall, he only wanted to be done with it, once and for all. My father's letter to Karl touched on one more mutual friend, nicknamed Csicsi. "Two weeks ago, Csicsi showed up as well," he wrote. "He lost everything in the war. All he had left to his name was a shirt, a pair of trousers, and orders to travel to Nova Crnja, where he was mistaken for a German and taken to a camp. He has not been released yet."

The storm that had plucked Karl and Márta out of Gundulić street and swept them away in turns to Besni Fok, Auschwitz, Amsterdam, Timişoara (Temesvár), Debrecen, Jászberény and Brno, and which had more often than not reduced the chances of their survival virtually to nil, was slowly abating. Gusts of wind continued to gather, however, and to carry people away from Becskerek, and not only from Becskerek. The same thing happened to Csicsi, Uncle Csicsi to me, whose fate is worth another detour. His real name was Jenő Héger. He also attended university in Zagreb as a medical student. After the war, he was taken to a camp on account of his German name where he worked as a doctor. In his diary, my grandfather mentioned that he visited us in December 1945. The entry of December 31, 1945 reads as follows:

> *Toward the evening, we were paid a visit by Dr Jenő Héger, aka Csicsi, on his way from Rudolfsgnad to Mollyfalva. He had been employed—or, rather, starved, frozen, and tormented—as a physician in the lager in Ru-*

dolfsgnad, and has now been assigned to Mollyfalva as a therapist. Both he and the partisan accompanying him spent the night here. Everything he says reconfirms the rumors about the Rudolfsgnad camp. On average, 30 Germans perish of hunger, the cold, and sheer exhaustion each day. Yesterday, he says, there were 41 dead. The bodies are left lying there with the living, in the same rooms already overcrowded with miserable souls. – Csicsi and his companion left for the other camp this morning.

Having been liberated from the camp—I do not know exactly on what date—Csicsi emigrated to Venezuela. In a way, it is a typical story from Becskerek, a town that supplied Venezuela, and Caracas in particular, with quite a few new residents after the Second World War. Among them were my aunt Piroska with her husband, Pál Heklai, and a radio technician by the name of Halmai. Other people from Becskerek also wound up in Caracas. I am not sure how it all started. I do not even know whether Csicsi was a pioneer or a follower. Having arrived in the New World, Csicsi denied his profession as a physician, because in those days in the 1950s, Venezuela, allegedly bowing to pressure from the local medical chamber, was not admitting immigrant doctors. Csicsi succeeded in entering the country by passing himself off as a confectioner. Later, already in possession of his papers, he confessed to be a physician. They did not deport him but prohibited him from practicing in Caracas and other major cities, so he ended up in a tiny village in the middle of nowhere, called El Socorro, which means "succour" or "relief." In the summer of 1968, I visited the place myself by a twist of fate that had nothing to do with any intention of emigrating to Venezuela. What happened was that, in a pub on Harvard campus, I had befriended a Pole who was in the business of peddling the *Encyclopaedia Britannica*. After I made short work of convincing him of the impracticability of taking a series of heavy tomes with me to Yugoslavia, he told me the story of his life. He drank round after round, and I footed most of his bill. As a sign of his gratitude, he gave me a raffle ticket which he normally reserved for those who purchased the entire set of volumes from him. It was my lucky day. I won a bus ticket from Boston to Miami, and two nights' stay in a reasonable hotel there. The voucher had to be used early in the month of July. To break up the bus ride from Boston to Miami, which would have lasted several days in a row, I dropped by Bruno Draxlers's, a family from Becskerek who had settled in North Carolina.

The tourist season in Miami centers on the winter and early spring; July is muggy and hot. My aunt had been begging me for a visit to Caracas for some time. Knowing that in Miami I would already be halfway, I decided to take up the invitation..

In Caracas, I met several people hailing from Becskerek. Naturally, the conversation kept coming back to our hometown. That was when I realized that in exile or emigration it becomes suddenly clear from where the past begins. Mental images, like pictures at an exhibition, are fitted into frames and gain significance, just as the saltshaker on the dining table that was brought from home and carried over the ocean, and now no meal can be complete without it. I was astonished to find among these relics the last stanza of a limerick I penned at the age of twelve. (Even the folks in Caracas were unable to recall the rest of the lines.) I had written the poem on the occasion of my Uncle Pali's fortieth birthday, and he recited it to our audience by heart in Caracas. Uncle Pali was the tallest man in the family. I remember a wall clock in our dining room which no one else could wind up without standing on a chair. He was also well-known for his hobby of gardening as a source of respite from his work as a lawyer. These circumstances, along of course with poetic inspiration, shaped the conclusion of my poem:

Soft rain in the springtime
Falls on my sweet briar;
Uncle Pali dearest,
May you grow much higher!

Lo and behold, I seemed to have acquired a measure of fame in Caracas as the author of these lines.

Uncle Csicsi insisted that I visit them in El Socorro. In hindsight, as I type these words on my computer as a septuagenarian, that whole trip appears utterly implausible. The bus stopped a couple of times in order to get repaired. But the final bus-stop was not El Socorro. No paved road went as far as El Socorro, so in a village on the way I was met by a young American, a missionary in El Socorro, who was sent by Csicsi to pick me up. I was surprised to note he came with two horses. We covered the last stretch, a distance of some 15 or 20 kilometers, on horseback. The majority of El Socorro's inhabitants were native Indians who had received Csicsi among them almost as a sort of deity—or at least this is how Csicsi described the impression he created upon his arrival. His occupation as a healer probably played a part in this, as did the fact that he was an albino, whose white hair and pink eyes fit the local image of a god perfectly. Over the years that he spent among them, the miracle wore off, although it was plain to see that everyone in the village streets continued to greet him with the utmost respect.

Unle Csicsi with a fellow citizen in El Socorro

During the two or three days of my stay, we went to see a cock fight, and of course we talked a great deal about Becskerek and its residents. In fact, Csicsi was not born there, but from nearby in the same Banat region, yet most of his roots tied him in some way to Becskerek. He asked me about Karl and his wife. He knew that both had survived. Then the subject of sports inevitably came up. Csicsi was an ardent soccer fan. Ferencváros was his favorite team. I could hardly believe my eyes when he showed me a copy of the Budapest sports paper *Népsport*, boasting that he had a subscription! The paper would be delivered, often by a mailman riding a horse, with a time lag of about three months, which meant that there was a major phase shift between the conclusion of each game and Csicsi's elation or dismay, depending on the final score.

But let me return to Márta and Karl. Late November 1945 brought relief from another fear. On November 22, my father wrote briefly to Karl informing his "Dear Friend," among a few other terse details, of having "learned today that your little girl is in Kaposvár in the home of Ferenc Szikics at 48 Talián Gyula street."

Previously, in his letter of October 31, 1945, my father forwarded Márta's telegram in which she said she had survived Auschwitz. The telegram was in English. Censorship was still the order of the day everywhere, and I suppose that the Dutch authorities refused to accept telegrams in Hungarian or Serbian on account of the time it would take them to locate a competent censor. They probably understood German but pretended not to. Needless to say, incoming letters were equally subject to censorship. The authorities (obviously not just in the Netherlands) imposed restrictions where they could. As far as I know, Márta spoke no English; she must have had help with the text. The main reason why she addressed the telegram to my father was probably that she did not have Karl's address (or for that matter, any certainty that Karl had survived the war himself). Additionally, it is possible that she counted on my father's mediation in restoring their relationship. The papers include Karl's reply to Márta. It is undated, but the fact that he wrote about their daughter staying in Kaposvár makes it likely that he mailed it at the end of 1945. The letter is in Hungarian and reads as follows:

> Your letter gave me heartfelt joy. Congratulations to you for luckily surviving the horrors of the concentration camps. I did not understand everything you say in your telegram due to the poor English. I have located our daughter; she is staying with the Mariskas' in Kaposvár. We can rightly be proud of her in every way; you are going to be delighted by her. She recognizes you in the photos and speaks of you very gently. She is calm and soft-spoken in her habit, but everything interests Her. Although she is in good hands at present, I would like to see Her being taken care of by You, Her mother. Therefore I ask you to come to Budapest. You will find me under 5 Báthory Street, in District V, where I am staying at Dr Ferenc Lengyel's. You should ask for your travel documents to be sent to the town where you were born, for you will not be

> able to stay in Kaposvár longer than it will take for us to settle financial and other outstanding matters between us, and for our Little Girl to warm up to you again.
> I send you my sincere love and a warm embrace.XP. S. Hugs and kisses from our little Judit as well.

The word *congratulate* in the second sentence comes off as a tad constrained given the context. Evidently, Karl must have had a hard time figuring out how to begin this letter. It is quite understandable that the divorce litigation had been overshadowed and dwarfed by the war, but the communication block is still very much in evidence. Yet I feel he managed to overcome this block as he progresses with the letter.

The subtitle introducing this part of the text is the legal concept of *restitutio in integrum*, which means the restoration of original state of affairs (or original position). In that segment of society in Becskerek that I knew best, this concept provided the framework for much of people's longing for everything to be as it had been before the war: goods available in the shops; a lumberyard in lieu of the concentration camp; a resumption of city balls; a fresh produce market where it used to be; each religion and denomination restored to equality; a Messinger Institute as we had known it; Búza's stationery and book store and the Pentz confectionery shop reinstated in their antebellum splendor. The yearning for the restoration of the past was more likely than not informed by the selectivity of recollection. I grew up in this, although there were other desires around. Some would not seek to replace the war-torn years by what had been before, but by a whole new world. And these people prevailed.

Presumably, Márta and Karl, having survived all that horror, were also thinking along the lines of concepts and desires subsumed in the notion of *restitutio in integrum*. They set about the work of restoration by tackling their marriage first. Since they had survived, this was now all entirely within their own discretion, except for the issuance of travel documents. Following in the tracks of *restitutio*, the next step would have been their return to Becskerek, a plan easily gleaned from the case documents. On November 3, 1945, my father wrote to the Local People's Committee in Besni Fok, asking for an affidavit substantiating Karl's claim that he had intended to join the liberation army one year previously. The affidavit was solicited as a means of securing for Karl immunity from the restrictions of person and property applicable to all individuals of German extraction under a resolution passed by the AVNOJ (*Antifašističko veće naroda oslobođene Jugoslavije*, or Anti-Fascist Council of National Liberation of Yugoslavia). The resolution made an exception for those who undertook to fight in the liberation army or partisan outfits. The application was granted in a seal-embossed letter of January 16, 1946, from Besni Fok, addressed to "Drug Varadi Josif, advokat, Petrovgrad," i.e. Comrade József Várady, attorney at law, Petrovgrad. The sealed affidavit stated that Comrade Karl, former officer of the Wehrmacht, reported to the liberation forces on October 2, 1944, asking to join them.

Sometime later another affidavit was delivered from Besni Fok describing what happened to Karl following October 2: "He did not receive rank or orders on the date first mentioned above, but was removed from the location as a prisoner of war two days later by a contingent of the Red Army." The affidavit also mentioned Karl's claim upon arriving in Besni Fok that he had been in contact with the people's liberation movement prior to that date, and even supplied intelligence about the German army. Not only does the letter confirm that Karl made this deposition, but it certifies that his claims had been checked, verified and found to have been true to the facts. It goes without saying that the affidavit concludes with the customary slogan "Death to Fascism, Freedom to the People!"

A few days later, on January 22, 1946, my father wrote to Karl telling him that the affidavits have been delivered and enclosing a certified copy. He expressed his hope that Karl may be reinstated in his civil rights in Serbia (and Becskerek in particular) now that he had the affidavit from Besni Fok in hand. Now that I have mentioned Besni Fok so many times, let me tell you about this locality, the name of which probably does not ring a bell even for most of my readers in the Voivodina region. Here is everything I know about it: during the time that I drove often from Becskerek to Belgrade, just before the Danube came into view ahead of the turnoff to Pančevo, I would glimpse a road sign pointing the direction to Besni Fok to the right. That is all.

Next up in the stack of documents is a handwritten letter by Karl. It is undated, but it is no doubt a reply to my father's letter of January 22, 1946, to him. Karl thanked him for the affidavit from Besni Fok, adding that his former fellow students, now employed in the government, have not answered his letters. Then he proceeded to cite examples from his track record of anti-Fascist sympathies. For instance, Županski Bato left in his care (i.e., asked him to hide) certain books that would have constituted incriminating evidence against him under the German occupation, such as *The Capital* from Karl Marx and *Anti-Dühring* from Engels. Presumably, these volumes were safer in the keep of a German officer.

My father wrote on August 2, 1946, in reply to a letter received in June, which is nowhere to be found among the documents, about letters of baptism and other papers requested by Márta and Karl. They were also trying to locate Márta's valuables. My father established that, when Márta was deported to Auschwitz, Mariska (her first name is all I know about her) handed over some of Márta's possessions to a certain Nelli. My father remained pessimistic about the chances of a return to Becskerek. He said that even having Bato and other friends, in addition to the authorities in Besni Fok, corroborate Karl's anti-Fascist leanings would probably be of little help. "Exasperation with the Germans is rampant," he explains:

> Their property and assets have been confiscated and all, barring a select few, interned in camps. It is virtually out of the question for the authorities to make an exception for anyone who were involved with a German organization in any way. Of course, in your case, we have evidence for your record of actively supporting the movement. Nevertheless, we cannot ignore the general climate of public sentiment which, as I have suggested, is embittered.

On November 7, 1946, my father wrote again to Bato Županski and Svetolik Popović, reiterating his request of a certified affidavit from each affirming Karl's anti-Fascist conduct. Once again, no reply ever came. At this point, I see that my words are sliding towards the conclusion that these school buddies, whose fortunes had taken a turn for the better, simply turned their back on their old friend. But we cannot see from inside the position of Bato and Svetolik. Admittedly, no one could have been expected to make positive pronouncements about an Untersturmführer easily, even if that person had made an effort to collaborate with the partisans. Then again, I have no way of knowing exactly how much they knew. The Županskis were a well-regarded family in Becskerek; I had never heard anyone speak ill of them. But anyway, they could have put in a good word for Karl, or, at least, they could have responded to his letters.

Then comes an exchange of letters regarding registrar's certificates, followed by a hand-written, undated letter from Karl wishing a "belated Happy New Year." In this letter, Karl requested my father repeatedly to try and find "whatever remains of my wife's belongings." The letter was written in ink; at the bottom of the page, Márta added a note in pencil: "My deepest love to you and Zorka."

The last letter in the stack, again from my father, is dated February 10, 1948. It continued to address the registrar's certificates as well as family news of a personal nature. It ends with the overall conclusion that, "In my opinion, for you to return home within the foreseeable future will not be feasible." And, at this point, the "original state of affairs" fell short of being restored: Karl and Márta became Hungarian residents. I have often heard the cliché "starting a new life," I have probably used it myself on occasion, as a casual phrase without serious substance. Here, this is literally what happened: They started out anew, changed profession and became quite successful at applied arts and crafts. Their daughter Judit duly followed in their wake. She lives with her two daughters west of the Danube in Hungary.

3. THE FREUND/BARÁTH DOCUMENT

File No. 12432

Return

The protagonist of our third Becskerek story is Gyurka Freund, that's to say, Đura Frajnd, depending on whether it's into the Hungarian or the Serbian linguistic medium we wish to bundle this Jewish person's German name. I might add that a sales contract written up in Serbian is signed Đorđe-Đura Frajnd (most probably to be on the safe side, because in other documents the same name, György or Georg, must have been translated differently). Gyurka Freund also had a pen name: György Baráth. (Let me add that just as "Freund" in German, "barát" in Hungarian means "friend."). He published several poetry volumes under this pen name. Among the papers I found a cutting from the Hungarian-language newspaper published in Israel, *Hatikva*. In this issue is György Baráth's poem *Riadt félénk tekintetem* (My frightened, timid gaze). In the editor's note, it's stated that György Baráth:

> the writer of Hungarian poetry... is proud to be the descendent of the Freund family which settled in Nagybecskerek in 1760, with the Jaulusz and Guttmann families. György Baráth completed his schooling in the German-cultured town, before moving to Budapest where he continued his studies...

In his two poetry volumes which he sent from Israel "to Uncle Imre and Józsi" (my grandfather and father) is Gyurka Freund's/Baráth's picture. It occurred to me that he might have been the gentleman whom I'd met in our loft during the German occupation. Unfortunately, now there is no one to ask.

This is what the lion-hunter looked like—if it is him.

At the beginning of the dossier there is an authorization in which Đura Frajnd authorizes my father to recover his estates. The cases began in spring 1945, by which time the new powers had taken the German occupiers' place. They had also taken the estates seized by the German occupiers. A small number of these were empty in 1945, while many had already been allotted to new users. The people who had returned weren't able to immediately regain possession of their seized properties. They had to commence certain proceedings to reclaim them. In these proceedings, having Jewish descent wasn't a disadvantage, but the social judgement of wealth had also changed and so had become the tasks of the lawyers. Now the evasion, or the flexible application, of wealth restrictions was the goal, often unattainable. Providing evidence wasn't simple either. During the war and the changes of power many documents had disappeared or been destroyed, and often one couldn't even tell who was still alive among the owners and inheritors.

However, lurking in the background of this story, as in that of the previous two, is the disappearance of Jews and Germans from Becskerek. The first submission to be found in the dossier is dated May 8, 1945. It was typed up in the lawyer's office, the land register details and references to legislation are typical of standard legal work, but there is also a short summary of Gyurka Freund's life. It was clearly drafted with my father.

Four estates are involved. One of them is the family home and land at 7 Kraljice Marije. This street was previously known as Melencei Street, namely, Melenačka ulica. For a while it became Kraljice Marije, after Maria, Queen of Yugoslavia. I can see that in a 1948 document, the street's name is already Ivo Lola Ribar, and it hasn't changed since. Indeed, the street still leads towards the village of Melence. In the submission it is affirmed that this estate is partly owned by Gyurka Freund. The other owner is his brother, Tibor Freund, but—not uncommonly in 1945—"it was impossible to know whether he was alive, and if he was, where," and so the "absentee property" came under state management. Such judgements weren't always clear-cut or without error, sometimes properties which had been seized and used by the German occupiers were classified as "enemy property," others as "absentee property." This submission requests that Gyurka Freund may take possession of the family house, partly by his own right, partly as guardian to Tibor Freund's property until his brother's fate becomes clear.

Three other estates are also concerned. One is the company building of Sámuel Freund and Sons, which has or had many owners. Tibor Freund's fate is unknown. Gizella Freund and Ida Freund committed suicide in 1941 when the Germans arrived. Berta Kolos, née Freund, "fled to Budapest, it's impossible to know whether she is still alive." Two further buildings were the properties of the Steinitzer company, in which the Freunds had a half-share. The other half belonged to Manó Glück whose fate was similarly unknown.

In the submission it is stated that Gyurka Freund had gone to southern Serbia, but in Užice he had been caught by the Germans. He managed to escape, ended up in Zemun, then escaped through Syrmia to Novi Sad, and on to Budapest. It requests that the "absentee" classification be changed to "returning," and that the estates be returned in part to Gyurka Freund's possession, and the "absentee" family members' shares are to be placed under his guardianship.

The Melencei Street house had passed through many hands. First it had been seized by the German occupiers, then after the liberation it was claimed by the new communist power. It was used for public purposes.

From my grandfather's diary, I learn part of it was used for "Hungarian schools' purposes." Many varying demands cropped up during the war and under German occupation. The new power tried to take these into consideration as well as its own demands. Part of the house was allocated for Hungarian schools' purposes when the Freunds' fates were still unknown. In the fever of creating the new future and the new reality, their return was still well out of sight. However, Gyurka Freund did return. It was fair that some space was granted to the Hungarian schools and it was also fair, naturally, that the Freunds got their property back. But things had become complicated. There was no longer any kind of axiom that whoever held private property was indeed the master of that property. Nevertheless, my grandfather had some success here. Gyurka Freund once again became proprietor of the Melencei Street estate and Hungarian schools were founded, too.

I don't know whether Gyurka Freund and the rooms serving Hungarian education in the Melence Street building exchanged places or temporarily existed alongside one another. In my grandfather's diary it is revealed that it wasn't the whole building but "parts of the house" which were allocated for "school purposes." By all means, 7 Melencei Street was connected to the reorganization of the Hungarians. After the Second World War, the first Yugoslav Hungarian cultural society was founded in Becskerek. In my grandfather's diary I read, under April 25, 1945:

> *In the evening, at 7 Melencei St (in the Freunds' house) a meeting was held to debate the procedures of the newly authorized "Hungarian Public Education Community" general assembly. I also received an invitation. – I attended. The workers took the lead—in the name of the people. Both in the sphere of politics and in the sphere of culture. The guiding principle of the "Hungarian sense," however, was stressed as a reassurance.*

Soon after, a house barely one hundred meters from the Freunds' house was donated to the Petőfi Hungarian Public Education Community, which is still there to this day.

In the submission dated May 8, 1945, Gyurka Freund's address isn't featured. In a contract signed on March 9, 1948, it is: 7 Ivo Lole Ribara (namely, Melencei Street). So, by this point, the Melencei Street house (or at least a part of it) already belonged to Gyurka Freund again and he lived there. But then further sparring matches commenced with the new law and the new logic. In the contract signed in March 1948, Gyurka Freund sells half of the estate to a doctor named Veljko Popov, on the condition that beneficiary rights be reserved for Erna Freund, the widow to Tibor Freund. The purchase price is 250,000 dinars. It is revealed that the rights to dispose over the house should have returned to Gyurka Freund some time before. It is also revealed that Tibor did not survive the war.

I know the house, I knew it as a child, but I don't remember there being a Hungarian school. I would add that the school I attended from 1946 was much further from our home than 7 Melencei Street. This also seems to prove that there probably wasn't a Hungarian primary school at 7 Melencei Street. There certainly was no secondary school, as it remained in the Messinger Institute building. However, the house at 7 Melencei Street was divided up into several flats. My classmate, Jóska Könczöl, whose father taught in a Hungarian school, lived in one of them. It is possible that when my grandfather wrote "Hungarian schools' purposes," he wasn't referring to teaching, but perhaps to student or teacher's accommodation.

In the legal battle concerning the reacquisition of the estates, the new laws and new formulae of justice influenced not only the possibilities, but the goals, too. In the Freund cases it was a manageable task to avoid the "enemy property" classification, and to ensure that the "absentee property" classification, even if it had previously fitted the facts, was no longer applicable as the proprietor had returned. But the returned property—particularly where more than one estate was concerned—immediately became a possible target for nationalization. Too many things had changed. The boundaries between the rational and the irrational, as well as between the countries, were all redrawn—and those holding the pencil weren't limiting themselves to minor corrections. They drew a whole new world.

One potentially defensible reason for the new formulae of justice was that wealth had to be regulated so it could spread to more people. I try to think how this could have worked. In my family, and among our acquaintances, there were many who lost property and complained, perhaps with good reason, but in other circles there must have been many who made gains, too, who moved into the nationalized houses and flats. But what happened exactly? Who got the nationalized houses? And if low-income citizens received them, were they able to move upwards socially as a result? How much was poverty reduced? It is difficult to get any bearing, because at the time of course it was announced everywhere that justice had come to all and there was no more poverty, while today the popular view is there was nothing good under communism.

I remember that in school we hardly felt any class differences. Perhaps the fact we belonged to a minority strengthened the community. Of course, communist slogans were everywhere, but they didn't really get through to people. My own generation were witness to the change of slogans, and this made it easier for us to put a little distance between ourselves and the slogans; we could see they weren't permanent, and they weren't inseparable from life. In year one in primary school, when it was time to go home, we lined up in the classroom facing the door, to the right stood the tallest, Imre Réber, facing us, and he called out: "God bless..." and we responded in chorus: "our teacher, Sir!" Of course, the same was repeated every single day, whether we did feel the desire to bless Mr. Schwemmlein, our teacher, or not. We usually liked him. Then one spring the change came, but the ritual and the roles remained. Imre Réber continued to stand on the right, facing the line, but now he called out: "With Tito for the homeland...," and the chorus responded, "Forward!" Once, when Imre Réber had said "With Tito for the homeland," someone in the line who hadn't been paying attention, automatically started to say, "our teacher, Sir!" and the rest of us, returning to our old habits, followed suit. So: "With Tito for the homeland—our teacher, Sir!"

Disturbing signs also came from the most unexpected of places. I must have been in year three, when a young woman who was fulfilling some sort of "social function," took the "best students" to visit the mother of Mihály Szervó. Szervó was a partisan people's hero of Hungarian descent who had fallen in the Second World War. Our school was called Mihály Szervó Primary School. One of the biggest factories in the town also bore Mihály Szervó's name: Mihály Szervó Food Plant. His mother welcomed us with *kalács*, a typical, Hungarian sweet bread. She was a simple, kind woman in a dark dress. She recognized my name and even exchanged a few words with me in German. I don't know why exactly. Perhaps she herself was of German descent, perhaps she had been searching for someone to successfully exchange with and supposed that I might know some German. Otherwise we spoke in Hungarian. Then the young woman who had brought us said how immense the contributions of the people's heroes had been in building the new homeland and the new future, and she asked the mother of the people's hero a few questions. The mother told stories of her son. Answering a question, she uttered a sentence that our guide hadn't expected. When talking about her son's tragic fate she said: "I always said to my poor soon not to go off with the communists."

Who really was Mihály Szervó? He started off in a modest family who warned him against joining the communist movement. But he joined anyway. Was it to spite his family? Did he have convincing friends who he had trusted? Did he have any doubts? Doubts or none, he became a hero. The new power made him a symbol and from then on there were only ever figures, rather than people. Despite the later downfall or forgetting of those figures (the latter in Szervó's case), the real people behind them remained invisible. Perhaps I would never have been interested in who Mihály Szervó was, had I not happened to meet his mother.

In 1945, new laws develop concerning property. In the new system of principles, the ownership of flats and houses is correct and lawful, if the owner lives there; it is not, if the house or flat is to be used for the further acquisition of wealth, or if the individual wants both a house and a summer house, or perhaps it is the sort of house in which more than one family could reside. This is where the risk of eviction meets the threat of allocated shared housing. My own family has experience. Since we lived in a house larger than was permitted for one family, according to the post-war standards, my aunt Piroska and her husband moved to ours, followed by my uncle Lóri and the mother-in-law of our housekeeper, aunt Annau, so as to avoid strangers moving in. Property which "exceeded necessity" was cut back by nationalization or perhaps the enforced housing of others. Of course, when the new system had been consolidated, not for the first time we saw the creed of equality lose credibility, as it was no longer the temptations of others which the new powers had to manage, but their own. The new principles weren't discarded, but pretensions for comfort—for luxury, rather—found new means that bypassed private ownership. During communism, for a long time one's entitlement to luxury was disconnected from proprietary rights, and so one didn't feel the irritation of conscience. After all, it may well be a luxury villa where one is celebrating an important comrade's birthday, but the villa belongs to the state.

In 1897, a book was published in Budapest entitled *Luxury* by Geiza Farkas of the Becskerek locality. On page 5 of his book he writes that antipathy towards luxury is rational, "but it is a fact that antipathy cannot defeat the predisposition to luxury." Of course, one recurring question is: what qualifies as luxury? Though it may have been termed differently, the registration of the Freund-Popov sales contract was denied at the first stage because the authorities were trying to obstruct the occurrence of luxury. On December 30, 1950, the Zrenjanin City People's Committee decides not to grant permission to Veljko Popov and his wife, Danica, to write the 7 Ive Lole Ribara estate under their name because the Popovs already own a house in Aradac. In accordance with section 3/a of the Decree on Property Trade Control, in such circumstances, permission cannot be granted. In other words: why buy a property, if you've already got a house?

That is to say, the return wasn't easy. I find lawsuits and other legal processes in the Freund/Baráth file. Besides those already mentioned, there is another lawsuit against the older sister of his former wife, Ella Benedek née Goldschmidt. Here the question is who would inherit the property of his late wife (Klára Freund née Goldschmidt), who lost her life in 1944. This time the court accepted a fifty-fifty solution.

These lawsuits may have taken up a considerable amount of time in Gyurka Freund's life in the first years following his return. They also show his newly developing life. But then, all of this may simply have been part of facing a new Becskerek. The experience of survival most probably distanced him from those annoyances or part-victories resulting from the suits, and numbed him to them. I would suppose that in the first months nothing could have been more important than finding out who had survived and where they were. In the first years his exchange of letters with my father is seldom, perhaps because they regularly discussed his affairs in person. Later, when Gyurka Freund leaves Becskerek, the letters are more frequent and sometimes mention how others are doing. Earlier, though, it came to light that Gyurka Freund had a new partner and wrote poetry. My grandfather's diary also offers a few pieces of information. Allow me to quote a few notes:

> *8. XI. 1945: ...this afternoon Gyurka Freund recited for us in Piroska's room. He gave a reading.*
> *1. XII. 1945: This morning I paid a visit to Gyurka Freund-Baráth upon his invitation, and he read to me his poetic writings.*
> *23. X.1 946: I sought out Gyurka Freund Baráth. Insightful reflections.*

> *21. XI. 1946: On Monday I paid a visit to Jenő Grandjean for his name day and to Gyurka Freund Baráth for his birthday.*

On March 1, 1947, it is my grandfather's eightieth birthday. Among the guests is Gyurka Freund who recites a poem he wrote for the occasion. There is an entry referring to this in the diary, and the poem, too:

> *1 March 1947... Then Gyurka Freund-Baráth takes the floor and recites the following poem written for me – starting first with a few warm, spirited, amicable words.*

These are the opening lines of the poem:

For Dr. Imre Várady
One last thing remains...!

Today we gathered
To celebrate:
80 good long years
From which distance
Things shrink,
Mere dots!

One last thing remains
Which will never abate:
Friendly love...

Afterward, Gyurka Freund is mentioned in a few places. On December 1, 1947 my grandfather notes: "During the evening we were at the Hungarian Public Education Community literature night. After Józsi's subtle and quite beautiful opening speech, Gyuri Freund-Baráth also performed; a novice poet." In his diary my grandfather consistently noted who came to wish him well on New Year's Day, on his birthday, and on his name day. Gyurka Freund's name features regularly among the names of the well-wishers. In 1949, his name disappears. But an entry on September 19, 1949 informs of his departure: "I have taken care of my outstanding letters. Letter sent: ...Gyurka Freund-Baráth (Nathanya)."

And so, the return had lasted for four years. I suspect that the option of migrating to Israel arose early. I can't tell when the decision was made. My father and my grandfather ought to have known. Little attachment for Becskerek must have remained. Through his poems he may have been seeking new attachment beyond his new wife. And so, he performed, as a "novice," in my grandfather's words, for the Hungarian Public Education Community. The devastation of the Second World War and the erasure of the past empowered many with a new opportunity, the ability to choose hence where they belonged. Whether it had been an easy choice or not, Gyurka Freund chose Israel and became a Hungarian Israeli poet.

I know very little about the four years after he returned to Becskerek. It interested me and I tried to find some point of reference in his poems. I remembered that there were several of his poetry volumes in the family library. After searching I found only one. It is titled *History at Prayer* (Imádkozik a történelem), and it was published in Tel-Aviv. In it there is scarcely any trace of the Becskerek years. Then I tried the National Széchényi Library. There I discovered that he had published fifteen poetry volumes in Hungarian, and a couple of others in Hebrew and French. The title of his first volume is *Poems*, it was published in Nagybecskerek, but it isn't in the National Library either. The second volume is also called *Poems*, this was published in Budapest in 1942, after he had fled to Budapest ahead of the German occupiers, and of course before he could have returned to his hometown. The first poem of the volume is "I Came with New Poems!" The first stanza reads:

> ...An alarm ringing in my ear,
> I came with new poems, new deeds,
> I'm Hungarian, Hungarian-born.
> I came with new poems, new deeds.

The coming to Budapest of course could also be seen as adjusting to history. And there are other poems. One of them—presumably Budapest-inspired—is titled "The Strange Town!" In another poem ("False Courtesy") he contrasts himself with the city. The poem begins: "Outside lies petit-bourgeois false courtesy / Every word is a painful lie here." In the closing lines he says: "Softy city folk kowtowing brats, / to you I say, I'm a Peasant, and Proud!" Gyurka Freund wasn't a peasant, of course. His family had been among the Becskerek bourgeois for generations. But in this way, as a peasant rather than as a petit bourgeois, the contrast was starker and bolder.

In his volume titled *Crystal-songs*, on the first page (the collection was published in 1965 in Jerusalem) one can read the list of his earlier volumes, according to which he published two more books in Budapest: *Stubborn Adam* and *Woe My Word*. Beside the latter title is the note: "burned."

I wasn't able to look through every collection. In those I did, I found no reference as to how he managed the four years after he returned to Becskerek. Nor was I able to find in the poems the György Baráth whom I remember from my primary school years, from my grandfather's birthday or name day, enthralling the happy company with his words and his cadence.

Departure

Freund Gyurka sends his first letter from Israel on June 9, 1949. One can see his new address (and name): Georg Baráth, Nathanya, P.O.B. 45, Israel. The first lines of the letter read:

> Dear Uncle Imre and Jóska! I'm writing to you both because I would write the same to you both. We didn't want to get in touch until we had a flat and an address. Now, thank God, we have both. We live in Netanya. This small town lies between Tel-Aviv and Haifa. Its pleasant climate and coastal situation make it very inhabitable for us. There are plenty of Hungarians here and thus I can continue my literary interests. Hopefully in the near future I can write more! There are great possibilities, and great difficulties, too. Iby and I married officially, while still en route on the boat. Between a latitude of 34° and a longitude of 38°, a day's sail from Haifa! A whole horde of people joined in the festivities. More than 2500 people. The whole boat [illegible]. Afterwards we were invited for dinner with the captain…

On the other side of the page Ibi (Iby) writes that she is working: "I sew for different homes which pays very well." She says that a performance of Gyuri's in Tel-Aviv was a great success, at which "the great Hebrew-Hungarian poet, Avigdor Hameiri, who lives here welcomed him." She also writes that Hungarian is spoken on the street everywhere, "but we're still studying Ivrit (Hebrew), because naturally that's very important."

When he arrived in Israel, Gyuri/Gyurka was forty-seven years old, Ibi was most probably younger. I would add that Ibi was an actress, and later managed to continue her career.

In the meantime, the property suits carry on and the latest hindrance is that Gyurka Freund/Baráth has moved to Israel, taken Israeli citizenship and for that reason had to end his Yugoslav citizenship. At first there is minor progress: the Vojvodina provincial authorities did approve the contract made with Doctor Popov after all, as in the meantime Popov's village house had been sold. After, however, the property is nationalized because the owner was a foreigner, that is, had become a foreigner. Yet there is still a way out, my father argues that the sales contract concerning that half of the estate was concluded when the seller was still a Yugoslav citizen, that it is not the date of the approval of the contract which is decisive, but the date of the conclusion of the contract. As a lawyer, I can understand and follow these nuances, but I understand those non-lawyers too who might have based the decision of to whom a house belonged on much simpler terms. In any case, afterwards it was possible to claim the payment of the complete purchase price for that half of the building.

The rest of the properties were nationalized. Among them was the Main Street (Maršala Tita Street) property, half of which he had inherited from his wife. Regarding this address, the very most they could request was to not have to pay the inheritance tax. Here I would like to quote another of the letters from Nathanya (sent on December 1, 1952). In the letter, Gyurka Baráth asks my father to write from Becskerek. He says, "I'm interested in everything that's happening at home, even in the tarmacking of the pavement you wrote about." In this letter there are two sentences which explain to an extent another legal proceeding: "Here we have a slow life, but a safe one, and if there's a shortage of food, we hope it's only temporary. Most of all, meat is scarce." Allow me to stop here for a moment and note that understanding Gyurka Freund's handwriting is no easy task. My father must have experienced the same, because in a letter dated December 9, 1950, he praised Gyurka's poems, but regarding the handwriting, he adds: "... I say without praise, seldom have I seen such illegible handwriting as your own. I had some trouble struggling through the letter. Ibi's magnificent handwriting on the other hand was a truly refreshing respite. Why deny it, I do prefer to read in print." My own investigative work was aided by my father who had sometimes written in pencil the solution above undecipherable words.

In September 1945, yet another legal proceeding began. The Petrovgrad People's Court declare that Gyurka Freund can reclaim the personal property left inside the Melencei Street house. The decision lists the articles: a kitchen cupboard, a kitchen table, two stools, a refrigerator, a complete bathroom, a large dresser, a small dresser, a plain table, a glass table, a chandelier with 24 bulbs, 2 curtains, a pelmet, a china cabinet, and other pieces of furniture. The dining room furniture, however, remained in the possession of a tenant, Miloš Jovanović. On December 7, 1948 he confirms on record that the furniture is the property of Gyurka Freund. The signed record also confirms that Miloš Jovanović has buying preference, and that he may draw up the potential sales contract with my father. Gyurka Freund confirms this with a signature. This time he signs as "Frajnd Djura"; the Serbian version but with the Hungarian order, that is, surname preceding given name.

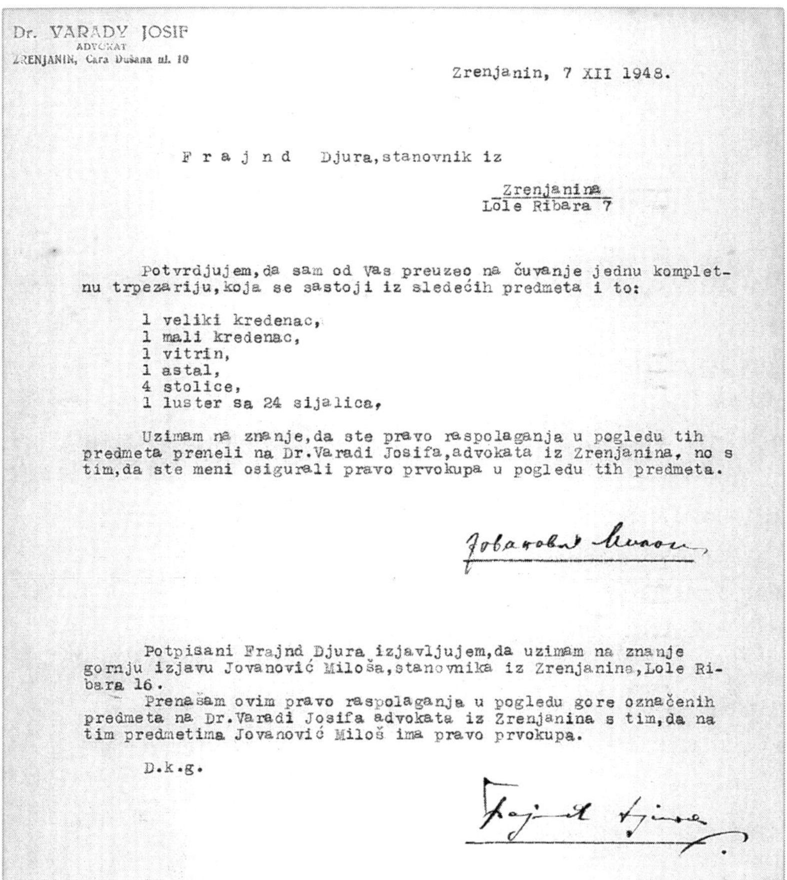

Dr. VARADY JOSIF
ADVOKAT
ZRENJANIN, Cara Dušana ul. 10

Zrenjanin, 7 XII 1948.

F r a j n d Djura, stanovnik iz

Zrenjanina
Lole Ribara 7

Potvrdjujem, da sam od Vas preuzeo na čuvanje jednu kompletnu trpezariju, koja se sastoji iz sledećih predmeta i to:

1 veliki kredenac,
1 mali kredenac,
1 vitrin,
1 astal,
4 stolice,
1 luster sa 24 sijalica,

Uzimam na znanje, da ste pravo raspolaganja u pogledu tih predmeta preneli na Dr. Varadi Josifa, advokata iz Zrenjanina, no s tim, da ste meni osigurali pravo prvokupa u pogledu tih predmeta.

Potpisani Frajnd Djura izjavljujem, da uzimam na znanje gornju izjavu Jovanović Miloša, stanovnika iz Zrenjanina, Lole Ribara 16.

Prenašam ovim pravo raspolaganja u pogledu gore označenih predmeta na Dr. Varadi Josifa advokata iz Zrenjanina s tim, da na tim predmetima Jovanović Miloš ima pravo prvokupa.

D.k.g.

While the negotiations concerning the price are still ongoing, Gyurka Freund moves to Israel. Jovanović offers 40,000 dinars, which Gyurka Freund claims is not enough in several letters, and then writes, if they can't do any better, then at least 50,000 dinars. In the end, with the help of my father's efforts they get a better price and manage to agree on 60,000. Now comes the next legal problem: one can't send money from Yugoslavia to Israel, particularly dinars. Sending parcels is a potential solution, at which point it becomes relevant that in Netanya "most of all, meat is scarce." First and foremost, Gyurka Baráth wants *szalonna,* fatty bacon, of which there is certainly little in Israel. On December 15, 1953 Ibi spells out the request: "Gyuri asks… that in place of the money, 3 parcels of bacon and salami be sent to us," (the underlining is in the original letter). The letter of December 15 was sent from Jerusalem.

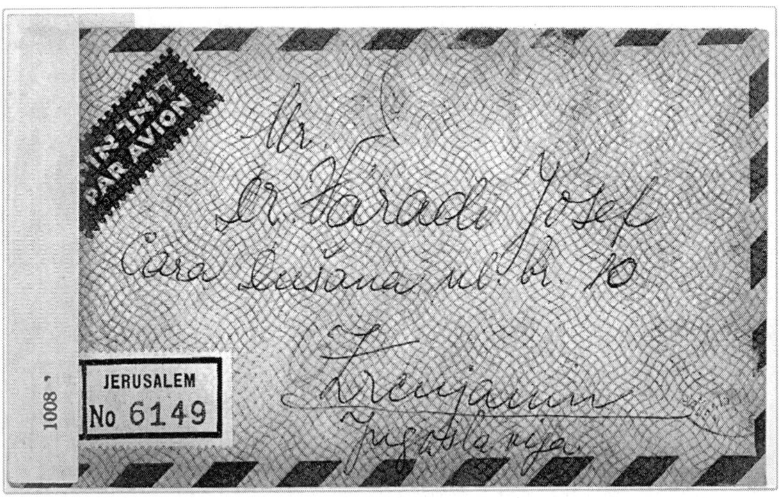

The new address: Georg Baráth, Jerusolajim, Herech-Bethlechem, 198/1, Israel. Ibi also writes: "We had to leave Netanya because of the climate. Unfortunately, in the whole country the climate is harsh, particularly for a cardiac patient." At the end of the letter Gyuri adds: "And I wish you a Merry Christmas and a happy new year. With God's grace, [illegible word] now we'll all be able to live a more peaceful life."

There are other setbacks regarding the shipment of the parcel. On December 23, 1953 my father returns the blessings, and among other things writes: "As far as I know, bacon can't be posted abroad, or at least not without special permission."

There were other challenges, too. They weren't living in the age of private businesses. It turned out that food parcels couldn't be sent to foreign countries by private individuals, but only state companies. And so, they would have to try via some form of state company. Matters were also made worse by the fact that customs could only be managed in Belgrade. All sorts of arrangements had to be made. My father got in touch with Albert Vajsz, the executive of the Association of Jewish Religious Communities of Yugoslavia. Incidentally, he taught me history of law at the Belgrade Law Faculty; his office was on the ground-floor in the corridor to the left.

I can see there is an exchange of letters with the Belgrade lawyer Avram Menorah, who suggests that the Dorćol company arrange the postage of the parcel. It is apparent from the papers that three companies got involved in the project. The Belgrade companies of Dorćol and Centar, as well as the Becskerek company Gra-Mag. There are handwritten records on large squared pages of ten parcels. It states what has been posted, and lists the costs exactly. In most of the parcels the salami is the most expensive item, the price ranging between 4000 and 4500 dinars. Then, among the expenses is the price of the box (35 dinars), the packaging paper (26 dinars), the string (10 dinars) and the customs tax (420 dinars). On the record in Serbian below, the word "salama" should even be clear to the English reader. All ten parcels were sent in 1954. In the end, mostly salami was sent to Jerusalem, but there is also ham, goose breast and goose leg, too. There is also mention made of a delivery made in 1956. This issue, it would seem, got resolved.

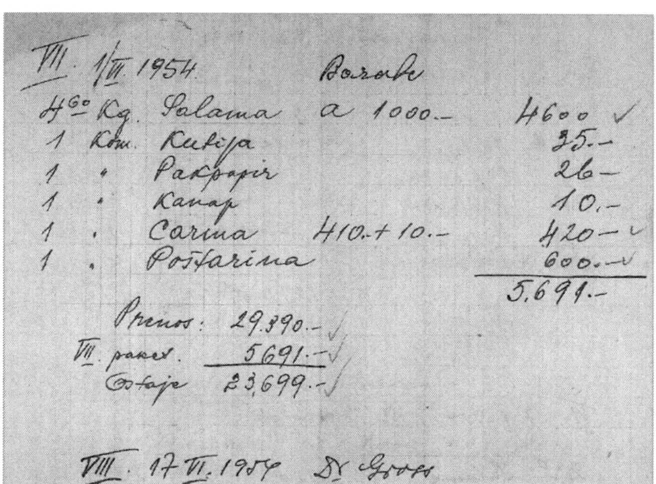
VII. 1/VII. 1954
4⁶⁰ Kg. Salama a 1000.- 4600 ✓
1 Kom. Kutija 35.-
1 " Pakpapir 26.-
1 " Kanap 10.-
1 " Carina 410.+10.- 420.-
1 " Poštarina 600.-
5.691.-
Prenos: 29.390.-
VII. paket. 5691.-
Ostaje 23.699.-
VIII. 17 VII. 1954 Dr Gross

There is evidence of one more legal proceeding in the file, but it isn't connected to any property. On September 23, 1951, Gyurka Baráth writes a letter from Netanya, here are the opening lines:

> Dear Uncle Imre and my Jóska!
>
> I received Uncle Imre's very kind, dear letter a good while ago, and straight away I wrote my reply but tore it up! It was a very sad, heart-stirring letter and perhaps I wasn't truly so wretched.
>
> In general, we're faring well, though getting by is difficult. 800 copies of my poetry collection have been sold, which is a tremendous result! Poetry is a nerve-wracking business! Especially if one has to make a living out of it!

Over the page he writes: "My Jóska, I would very much like you to look into an important matter." The important matter is that he would like to officially use the name György Baráth, and he asks that my father arrange it on his birth certificate "with a correction, and that's the crucial part." He requests that in the registry, in the "comment" column, the pen name György Baráth be entered, so he can refer to this in Israel.

While searching for any connections to Becskerek among the poems, I read the poem *Férfias fa* (Masculine tree) several times, which featured in the *Crystal-songs* volume in 1965. The poem opens: "Back in my childhood I ran out to the edge of the new forest and looked up at the slender trees." I don't know of any new forest, but there was a "wood." Might the Becskerek Wood have once been called the New Forest? The last two lines of the poem: "I thanked the tree for what it had told me and ran home. / But I never told it my name." There is no mention in the poem of which name he withheld, though it is clear his name is of importance.

The official registration of the pen name was unsuccessful, in Becskerek at least. On February 22, 1952 my father writes:

> I discussed the matter with the town registrar personally. Together we browsed through the registry law and the relevant provisions of the *Zakon o ličnim imenima* [Personal Names Act]. According to the Zakon o ličnim imenima writers, artists etc. have the right to use writer's or artist's names. The law, however, does not permit the writer's name to be added to the registry. Thus, much to my regret, your request can't be

> granted. I add that were the law to allow the registration of a pen name, there would still remain the tricky matter of how we would amend the entry in the registry… when the applicant is abroad and is not a Yugoslav citizen.

After the seizure of the properties, the compensation for them in part and the sale of the family furniture, there doesn't remain much material attachment. What remains is an interest in events in Becskerek (until the stage and the actors change utterly); the memories, though they are based less and less upon events, and more and more upon older stories. There remains the name, linked to Becskerek since 1760—in the Becskerek registry at least. It would be difficult to say whether the name change reinforces the departure. We might argue it does mark the departure, insomuch as he no longer looks to the Becskerek registry for a new identity, but to poetry. There is also the fact that taking the pen name of György Baráth was a decision made in Becskerek.

***

Finally, I would add that in the documents there are several blue envelopes, in which there are a few receipts for the delivery of parcels, notices of receipt, and customs transfers documents. In one of them I found a twenty-dinar note, the cost of string needed for two parcels.

It is a fairly worn, small red bank note, printed in 1944, with the picture of a partisan, toting a rifle on his shoulder. It had been placed in the envelope with care. Was it change from the postage costs? Or from the price of meat? Was it my father's money or did he put it away in the envelope (rather than his own pocket) because it was for someone else? Since then, any context of debt or claim is gone, along with its value. After diligence plunged to the past, what has remained is the act of forgetting, and with it, the twenty-dinar note in the envelope.

III.

HUNGARIAN STORIES OF BANAT

People and Formulae

I WOULD LIKE TO CONTINUE with three criminal trials. History hasn't taken note of the actors, but the actors have certainly taken note of history. In all three, the accused are Hungarians from Banat. There were similar cases involving Serbs, Romanians and Slovaks of Banat, too. The trials came about in the first years following the war, and this had a marked impression on the proceedings, the arguments and the judgements, too. Throughout the trials, a variety of people and formulae come up against one another.

* * *

1. AN EARLY ATTEMPT TO TOPPLE THE SOVIET POWER IN HUNGARY

File No. 12526

The Situation Analysis of Péter Kurunci

In File No. 12526 are the documents relating to the criminal proceedings of Zoltán Kelemen. When he was convicted, he was a pupil at the agricultural high school. His address is stated as being in the town of Vološinovo, and in other documents as Vranjevo-Vološinovo. Mention is also given of

Aracs, today a part of Törökbecse. Throughout history (especially during the years of the wars) the names were changed: Törökbecse (that is, Novi Bečej), Francisdorf, Vranjevo, Vološinovo. What remained unchanged was the designation of the region to which these small towns and villages belong: the region of Banat.

Zoltán Kelemen was sentenced for failing to denunciate his schoolmate, József Bleszkány, who, according to the judge, had the intention of going to Hungary where he would join an organization operating against the Red Army.

The file is incomplete. The reason may be that in May 1948, Jeremije Zlatar, a Vološinovo lawyer (but referred to as a Törökbecse lawyer in other letters), requested several documents, which my father delivered. However, the picture is still clear. Most of the information can be found in a request which my father submitted on September 21, 1951 to the Ministry of Agriculture of the Serbian People's Republic, Department of Cadre Training. In it, Zoltán Kelemen requests the ministry's permission to continue his third year at the agricultural high school, after serving his prison sentence and completing his military service. Zoltán Kelemen's sentence and crime are also described in the request, the details of which are illuminated by my father's notes and the letters of the convict's father, János Kelemen.

Among the documents are three original handwritten letters, which Péter Kurunci sent to his best friend, Zoltán Kelemen. How these letters relate to the criminal proceedings is not entirely clear. It occurred to me these may be letters sent to prison that weren't received, but when I checked the dates, it turned out the letters were written in 1945 when no proceedings had yet been instituted against Kelemen. The possibility arises that the sender, Péter Kurunci, had also been accused, and was also perhaps privy to the conspiracy, and the correspondence was evidence submitted by the prosecutor; in which case, it would be more logical that the original letters were in the prosecutor's files rather than my father's office. Or perhaps Zoltán Kelemen, before he was taken to prison, left a few personal documents, including letters, with my father. This seems to be the most likely explanation. Presumably I will never get a concrete answer to the question of how these letters ended up in the file. But since they are here, they can help me and the reader to get a better perspective of the accused—or as we say nowadays, the "terrorist." Even more so, as the accusation reflects an intense zealousness, and the defense could not ignore this while seeking counterarguments relevant in the world of the new formulae. This zealousness defined the procedure, and so one fact remains excluded from the criminal proceedings, namely, who Zoltán Kelemen actually was.

Péter Kurunci's letters draw into perspective the Banat environment where Zoltán Kelemen belonged. In chronological order, I'll quote the first letter whose envelope bears the date of September 1945. From the letter it becomes apparent the addressee was a soldier at the time. Here I would stop for a second, because in the documents we also learn that in the 1945/46 school year Zoltán Kelemen was a student of year three at the Becskerek (then Petrovgrad) agricultural high school. But he was born on September 24, 1926. The war had interfered with all sorts of things. In 1945 it wasn't rare for a nineteen-year-old to be in year three at secondary school, nor to be both studying at school and completing military service at the same time. We can find further explanation in the undated, handwritten letter of Zoltán Kelemen's father, János Kelemen. My father must have asked János Kelemen to write him information showing his son in a positive light with consideration to the new post-war values. János Kelemen wrote the following of his son:

> After liberation, following the army, he brought the ammunition by cart and by horse to St Becsej. Then, he ended up in the worker's battalion, where he enrolled as a soldier. As a student he was discharged from the military and he attended Zrenjanin Agricultural School where he took part in all forms of shock work: in the summer he worked the youth railway line and took part in the rebuilding of the new Yugoslavia.

So, he had already been a soldier before he attended the agricultural school in Becskerek, or before he continued at the agricultural secondary school after the war.

Returning to the letters, it is very difficult in another language—in this case in English—to reflect the poor quality of the spelling and grammar of the Hungarian letter. I shall just try not to change anything of what was said. I think it is still clear what sort of people those nineteen-year-old village youths were, who had allegedly made threats against the Red Army. In his first letter to Zoltán Kelemen, while completing his obligatory military service, Péter Kurunci writes:

Dear
Friend

I am thanks be to God healthy
Which with all my heart I wish for you too.
Dear friend I got your letter
Which filled me with joy.
But it's still not as though you had come
home yourself, in person!
I had not heard a thing from you,
Everyday I only hoped you would come home. ...
Dear friend. We are going
to a ball ...
Your Imre on Sunday was digging up
potatoes. For the *omladina*.
We are here at home still,
same as before.
Bözsi said to me, will
I still be here long?
And asked where are you.
...
Send my regards
To everyone.
Sincerely
Péter

Péter Kurunci and Zoltán Kelemen were classmates in their secondary school. Another of their classmates was József Bleszkány, the main accused and the main culprit. From the letter we can see that life found a way to continue after the world war. A means of getting by takes shape. There are village balls; habits hold on to their importance, for example, Bözsi's interest in Zoltán. In the Hungarian-written letter, there's one word in Serbian, the *omladina* (the youth), and here I would like to pause for a second. Imre (perhaps a brother of Zoltán's?) went to dig up potatoes for the *omladina*, that is to say he took part in some sort of locally organized youth operation. The fresh ideological markings on the word *omladina* are telling, and would have been lost with the simple Hungarian translation *ifjúsági* (youth). In these years of denying the past, "youth" did not merely signify an age group, but also symbolized an ideological and politically correct "direction." No matter what Péter Kurunci's view of that correct direction was, he certainly sensed that his own particular style of digging up potatoes could be expressed by adding the still fresh magic word. At the time, new symbols were being attached to the youth by the new powers, and *omladina* became a synonym for "positive." The word would pop up in railway-construction campaigns, and in the names of new dance spots, too. The minority languages didn't always follow suit according to the new connotations and attributed valuations in majority society. And so, the Banat Hungarians, Germans, Romanians and Slovaks also used *omladina*.

I would like to quote a few lines from the following letter that Péter Kurunci wrote to Zoltán Kelemen on November 3, 1945. He sent the letter to the Versec military lung sanatorium, where Zoltán was likely being treated at the time. The letter is addressed in the Cyrillic alphabet. Under "military lung sanatorium" (*sanatorium za grudne bolesti*) is written *streljan* (стрељан). This is confusing, because it means "shot to death." On another envelope I see Zoltán Kelemen served in the *streljački bataljon*, that is the "shooting battalion," or "rifle battalion." Therefore, with his shaky knowledge of Serbian, Péter Kurunci must have shortened *streljački bataljon* to *streljan*, but without much luck.

In this letter, Péter gives a summary of the "Apple Ball" in Aracs, and his romantic crusades, or rather, his much-anticipated crusades. Among others, he writes:

> Dear Friend,
> Dear Zoltán I am healthy which
> I wish for you too with all my heart.
> I thanks be to god passed a good time
> on Sunday. I accompan-
> ied just two girls home. It went well because
> one was a success And now on Mon-
> day there was a rehearsal, folk in Aracs are get-
> ting ready for the apple ball And then there
> I accompanied anna home But the problem
> is she's a bit serious but she'll soften up.
> ...
> Date: 3 XI 45
> Péter
> awaiting your reply

A terrible world war had barely ended, and the new powers were already applying harsh methods. The letters, however, seem to show a reality independent of history. The letter-writer is obviously influenced more by his own age than the current historical period. I don't know whether this was more possible at that time than today. Back then many communities came to be on the *korzó* or at dances. Today there is no *korzó*, there is dancing, but you can't really chat. There are TVs and the Internet. It would be interesting to know whether today it is any harder, or easier, for a community to form, and a world independent from history or ideology, like that shown in Péter's letters. Of course, the case may also be that the content of Péter's and Zoltán's correspondence was affected by the medium of letter writing, and by customs around what we write in letters. Most probably these letters recount what was most important to nineteen-year-olds at the time. And unlike in a court file, in these letters it was easier to recognize the "conspirators."

The Details of the Conspiracy

Now, however, I must write about the conspiracy on which the criminal proceedings were built. On October 8, 1947 Zoltán Kelemen was arrested. The reason charges were brought against him and he was shortly convicted was because he didn't denunciate his classmate, József Bleszkány. The limits to the punishability of such an omission have been debated in comparative criminal law. It also matters whether he could counteract such a serious crime via reporting/denunciation. And it matters how excited the society is, and how much scope for action is permitted by the demand for loyalty. In 1947, there was barely a free space on the map between those territories which were "with us" and which were "against us." Clearly this isn't only true in ideology-dependent states. A few years ago, a German court examined the expansion regulations for the German branches of the American chain store Walmart, in which it was discovered every working day was to be started with a company chant, dating within the company was forbidden, and employees were required to report (inform) if they noticed their colleague was meeting a coworker for a date. Whether it is to a zealous state or to a zealous major company, a requirement for loyalty assumes that one will report.

It is not entirely clear from the case contained inside File No. 12526 what form of unreported crime has been committed. József Bleszkány didn't reach the point of actually committing anything. I must add that all criminal law makes also punishable the attempt to commit a crime. According to the court, József Bleszkány was attempting to travel from Vološinovo, via an illegal border-crossing, to Hungary, with the intention of joining an organization, left unnamed in the documents. In the bill of indictment two alternative theories are given as to the organization's strategic goals. According to one, after the Red Army left, the organization intended to take power in Hungary with the help of some members from the village of Vološinovo. Considering that a Soviet withdrawal had already been planned for 1947, according to the other conception, the organization wouldn't have waited but would have confronted the Red Army. Unluckily for Bleszkány, the plans were made nearly two years before Tito split from Stalin, so when the Red Army was still the army of Yugoslavia's huge and loyal ally. The court found there was sufficient evidence of Bleszkány's intention to confront the Red Army. According to the judgement, this is the information which the guilty party had shared with Zoltán Kelemen (as is common for conspirators) and which he failed to report.

From my father's notes I can see that the one potential line of defense would have been that the accused deny he knew about Bleszkány's plans. There is a sentence suggesting as much in the notes, according to which Zoltán Kelemen said to my father that the UDBA (the secret police) had forced him to confess. The father of the accused meanwhile declared that Bleszkány had "dragged in" his son; perhaps true, perhaps information the Kelemens had got from the detectives. In any case, it wouldn't be easy to oppose the UDBA's recorded statement. I deem it likely the UDBA would have taken the statement they wanted. Yet it is also likely that Bleszkány really did share his notions of saving the world with his classmate, and Zoltán Kelemen did not subsequently dash to the police station.

Another line of defense might have been that the whole thing was ridiculous and blown out of proportion. It would seem this wasn't a viable route either. Bleszkány had already been convicted before the proceedings began against Kelemen, therefore the gravity of Bleszkány's act—more precisely his intention, his plans—had already been officially established. Furthermore, the qualities most typical of these feverish times were the dominance of the new formulae and the blindness to proportion. A Vološinovo initiative whose primary target was the Red Army couldn't be considered insignificant and laughable. Even the slightest step taken in a disfavored direction, or anything close, was a crime.

Consequently, attempts in the interest of Zoltán Kelemen could only be made within the extant formulae. The date of the trial was set for November 12, 1947. Beforehand, on November 4, my father recommended the hearing of a witness: Ilija Đakovački, a student of the Becskerek agricultural school, and a classmate of Zoltán Kelemen's. My father's submission also includes what evidence the witness ought to give. According to his suggestion, the witness ought to state that in Zoltán Kelemen's work for the people's youth (*narodna omladina*) he "performed with a genuine commitment, without any ulterior motives, and his contribution was consistently constructive." The goal was plainly that if one could not alter the UBDA's recorded facts and their gravity, then one ought to avoid at least a depiction which is completely negative. The chances of which are improved by stressing that someone is a member of the *omladina* "without any ulterior motives," is constructive, takes part in the construction of railway lines, and is a "shock worker."

To give a fuller picture, allow me to add that in those days, partaking in the construction of roads and railway lines may not have been the result of an absolutely altruistic, personal decision. Nor later, either. Barely more than ten years after the charge was brought against Zoltán Kelemen, I enrolled at the Belgrade law school, where we all knew that every summer it was advisable to spend at least one month helping to construct the so-called "Fraternity-Unity highway," while it was certainly expected of everyone to go at least once during our four years of study. One summer I took work on the construction of the Fraternity-Unity highway near the southeastern village of Džep. (It would seem džep is a word of Turkish origin, as well as the Hungarian word "zseb" of the same meaning; "pocket" in English.) If I wanted to brag, I could also say that of the roughly one-hundred people in the construction brigade only four or five received an honorary certificate, myself among them. It is also true that the others' services were recognized as "shock workers." Our brigade received special honors. The brigade's name was Kuzman Josipovski, whose name at the time I wasn't familiar with, and I'm still not; presumably he was a partisan hero of Macedonian descent. In fact, we were the winners of some sort of shock-work competition. All members of the brigade were law students, and there was some lawyer's guile in how we contributed to the construction of the myth around omladina and shock work. Success was measured by how much work we had completed. The work itself consisted of breaking up a hillside with pickaxes, and then transporting the boulders and gravel for the construction of the road. Our brigade commander knew the result would be judged by how much the hillside had reduced. Ten days before this was measured, we began putting in extra hours. But it was in the final days we found a more expedient solution: everybody worked on breaking up the hillside and nobody brought away the building materials, we just shoved it at the bottom of the hill, partly blocking off a stream. That was how the Kuzman Josipovski brigade won the work competition. And our brigade commander later became a renowned politician.

Zoltán Kelemen was a shock worker, too. I don't know how much this fact helped; his enthusiastic participation in omladina operations and Ilija Đakovački's statement. Zoltán's father writes in a letter that during the German occupation his son was taken for forced labor. János Kelemen adds that they have 11.5 hold (6.5 hectares), "paid my taxes, and satisfied my duty of compulsory delivery." My father must certainly have used this information, too.

The Red Army Gets Away Unscathed, Zoltán Kelemen Less So

The court sentenced Zoltán Kelemen to two years imprisonment and forced labor. After an appeal to a higher court, the sentence was not reduced. Today the judgement seems utterly absurd and unjust. In 1947, too, it was unjust, but in that climate it wasn't absurd. If something had been successfully forced into the shared formula of regimented passion (the partisans' and the Red Army's on the one hand, and the enemy's on the other), it was that the resultant judgements were more passionate than fairhanded. Perhaps even more draconian sentences were considered. Furthermore, one can only guess how much weight those lines of argument held which attempted to remove the convict's labelling as the enemy. After the sentencing, Zoltán Kelemen served two years in forced labor, and a further one and a half years in the army.

In the end, any attempts to force the Red Army to leave the territory of Hungary in 1947 were fruitless. Zoltán Kelemen's life began again in 1951, when he had completed the forced labor and military service, and when the Ministry of Agriculture of the Serbian People's Republic, Department of Cadre Training permitted him to continue at the Becskerek Agricultural School. At least one can hope, as there is no reply among the documents containing the ministry's decision. Zoltán Kelemen, Péter Kurunci and József Bleszkány are ninety-three today, or would be ninety-three if they were still alive.

2. THE CASE OF ISTVÁN BAKAI WITH VARIOUS ARMIES

File No. 12275

Inside File No. 12275, bearing István Bakai's name, is first a court order signed December 17, 1945, with which the Becskerek, then Petrovgrad, court officially assigned my father as the counsel for the defense of "Ištavan Bakaji" (viz. István Bakai).

At the beginning of the lawsuit István Bakai was thirty years old, my father was thirty-three. The following document is a citation for the court hearing scheduled for December 28, 1945. On December 28, not only was the hearing held, but a written judgement was also given, sentencing Ištavan Bakaji, "Pišta," to three years of forced labor.

As was common with known criminals, his nickname was included beside his given name in inverted commas, as a result of which he became known, notorious. Like, for example, Željko Ražnatović, "Arkan," or Milorad Ulemek, "Legija" (wellknown criminals who joined the por-Milošević paramilitary forces), or perhaps "Lucky" Luciano. Such names stick. A little more than half a century after István Bakai's judgement, the Belgrade prosecutor's office brought charges against those considered responsible for the NATO bombings, and among them the US president Clinton, more precisely against "William Clinton, also known as 'Bill,'" and the sentence was passed too. On September 21, 2000, the Belgrade District Court sentenced William Clinton to twenty years in high-security prison—along with Jacques Chirac, Anthony/Tony Blair and other defendants. In American court sentences, the "a.k.a." before a moniker adds emphasis. Thus, the inclusion of "Pista" was apt for stressing a criminal patina and a criminal classing. And we can assume it to be perfectly true that István Bakai was known as "Pista," just as William Clinton was known as "Bill."

In one section of the holding of the judgement it states that István Bakai was born in Lukácsfalva (Lukićevo in Serbian), he finished four years of primary school, he was Roman Catholic, he was a citizen of Yugoslavia, he was an agricultural laborer, he wasn't married and he had no property. In the folder are my father's handwritten notes and a copy of the appeal. There is no trace of the outcome of the appeal. The case may be that there is only one copy of the appeal court's decision, and this was forwarded to the condemned. It is also possible that my father received a copy, but it ended up in another related file. Now, seventy-three years later, it is difficult to follow up on this.

There are periods in history when there are attempts to force a blinding clarity or simplicity onto the law. Such formulae or trends always bear an effect on the judgement, as they do on every single individual's actions, but there are periods when we can talk of a dictatorship of formulae and trends. At such times everything is simple, and on the day of the proceedings even a written judgement may be passed. Everything depends on classing, and that classing isn't given a great deal of deliberation. There can be reductive consequences to deliberation when patriotism can be proven most convincingly through vigilance, and vigilance through the discovery of enemies. So, essentially, it was less risky to report an innocent as an enemy, than to fail to notice that someone was really on the side of the enemy. A false guilty verdict was much more patriotic than a debatable acquittal. Throughout history, such frenzied periods have come about again and again, and at such times the standard for suitable behavior becomes higher; it is not enough in a political speech to mention socialist self-governance, or maybe job creation, a mere five or six times, and it is not enough for a judge to convict only those who without any doubt did commit a crime, as then they would still be below the assessment and evaluation requirements.

A Digression Concerning a Baker-boy and Cominform

Another case comes to mind, which I still haven't found in the archive, but I remember the details my father told me over lunch. It must have been the fifties, and the dominant frenzy was directed against the Information Bureau (Cominform). In 1948 Tito took on Stalin, Cominform condemned Tito and Tito's politics, and our fate was somewhat improved. In politics, however, the keyword was "unity," as it had been before 1948, too, but unity softens easily, it becomes malleable when there is no one against which to be solid. A mood of unity can be crafted when we ruthlessly square off with the opposition. When there isn't any material with which we can craft—when there is no opposition—then material has to be created. There were people who really did go up against Tito, utterly convinced that in the end the enormous Soviet Union would come out the victor. It is difficult to believe that among them could be the baker-boy from Aradac to whom my father was the court-appointed defense counsel. I don't remember his name, thus it is difficult to find the file. He was Slovak. If I remember correctly, my father said he didn't have much schooling and he didn't speak fluent Serbian.

In the hearing, there was a dramatic turning point when the lawyer explained how much more humane, genuine and closer to Marx Yugoslav communism was than the mock-communism of Cominform. The judge asked the boy how he could possibly side with Cominform, at which the accused asked the judge—so convincingly that for a moment even the fiercest of critics hesitated—what on earth is this "Cominform" that they keep mentioning. And the judge begins to explain the difference between the Soviet, namely "Cominform's," communism, and "our" communism. Before long the boy interrupted, and excitedly said, with tears in his eyes: "But Comrade Judge, I don't even like our one, let alone that other one!" One would be hard-pressed to class this astonishing sentence as a declaration of patriotism, but more so to find any form of Cominform machinations. Yet they couldn't turn back. According to my father, the judge signaled that he recognized the person standing before him, but it could only affect the size of his sentence. He was sentenced to imprisonment for six months. But in the law circles of Becskerek the baker-boy's self-revelation was quoted for years to come: "But Comrade Judge, I don't even like our one, let alone that other one!" There were some who believed the boy had successfully courted girls whom others had also been attempting to court, and this circumstance spurred the denunciating patriot.

Lázárföld, Versec, Čačak, Leskovac, Mostar, Livno, Obersdorf, Armies and Narratives

Coming back to István Bakai, two completely divergent images are painted by the sentence, and the text of the appeal. In itself, this is not so surprising. The comparison of diverse narratives is a feature of the legal profession which has remained for centuries. I remember the first case entrusted to me, when at twenty-three I began working as a lawyer in the family office. The subject of the debate were two sheep from a small village called Melence in Hungarian and Melenci in Serbian. I was defending the sheep-owner who was claiming damages from the shepherd who hadn't taken care of the sheep; two had fallen into a ditch and couldn't be saved. I did my best to portray this as neglect of his duty, and I adduced proof of the value of the sheep. The shepherd's lawyer put forward a surprising narrative. He said what a good shepherd the defendant was, how well he knew the animals, and that actually the two sheep in question were reaching the ends of their lives, and sensing this, they withdrew to the ditch, because they wouldn't have made it through the day anyway. And so, in reality there was no damage, the sheep had lived as long as they would have, their wool could still be used, therefore the shepherd hadn't neglected his duty, but merely understood the sheep's fate. Smiling beneath his moustache, the judge asked, whether beyond their habits regarding passage into death, there were any other similarities between Melence sheep and African elephants.

Thus, narratives can form and do form even without any ideological compulsion. However, in heavily ideology-dependent eras—if there is some form of ideological relevance to legal disputes—it is not on the construction of a narrative and its provability that authenticity builds, but on how closely it relates to the reigning formula. Besides this, there is barely any crossover between reality and this or that mapped-out version, nor is there any mustachioed smile. In 1945 practically every other differentiation was ended by the divisions of the war. Those who served in the German army couldn't be easily extracted from the "fascist enemy" formula.

It isn't easy to read the judgement brought against István Bakai, and I'm not just thinking of its content. The accused must have received the original; in the office I found a bright-blue, pale, quite illegible copy. Back then more than one (often many) copies were typed up, carbon paper had to be spared, so often a sheet was reused, producing ever fainter results. The Petrovgrad People's Circuit Court established that on May 25, 1942 István Bakai, of his own will, joined the Prinz Eugen division, and remained in the German army until May 2, 1945, when he was taken prisoner by the allied forces. He served in Versec, Čačak, Kačarevó, Autovac (?), Kečaran (?), Mostar, Livnó and Bugajan, and so took part "in the fight against our partisans, and the Italian and Bulgarian partisans." (I don't know whether Autovac and Kečaran are spelled correctly, though I can't rule out that they may be smaller Serbian, or rather Bulgarian villages.) Therefore, Pista had intended to conquer these mostly southern-Serbian and Hercegovian territories. The judgement is based primarily upon the records of the OZNA after the accused's statement, and to some extent on the records from the hearing before the examining judge. Allow me to add that during the Second World War the OZNA (*Odeljenje za zaštitu naroda*), namely the Department of the People's Defense, was the first secret service in the developing Tito's Yugoslavia. It operated between 1944 and 1946. In 1946 it split into two parts: the military and the civil secret service. The latter became the UBDA (*Uprava državne bezbednosti*), the State Security Authority. Today, when these acronyms can be approached safely, one can examine them more closely, in fact, one might even ask quite disrespectfully why they jammed an "A" onto the ends of OZNA and UDBA, when only the OZN and UDB letters represent actual words. For example, the acronym of *Uprava državne bezbednosti* is UDB and ought not to be UDBA. Meanwhile everyone pronounced them OZNA and UDBA, and the same were used officially too. Now, as I'm etching these words, with slightly belated courage, I can't think of anything else, other than that in the Serbian language, it is uncommon to add vowel sounds between the consonants of an acronym, therefore one's speech isn't eased by an "udee-bee" or "ozee-en." It can't have been easy to enunciate OZN or UDB even for the hardened, veteran secret police, and it surely wouldn't have been elegant. By affixing an "A" the secret police acronyms were easier to say and more sonorous, and the deviation was fully legitimated. Today such things can be wondered on, at the time however, one could barely ask a question concerning OZNA, never mind OZNA's records. Hence the court rejected the defense's motions for a witness hearing, on the grounds that without one the facts were already clear.

It has been recorded in the judgement that the accused, before joining the Prinz Eugen division, lived in Lázárföld (Lazarevo in Serbian). The village was mostly inhabited by Hungarians and Germans, but after the world war Bosnian Serbs were resettled there, so it makes sense that in the autumn of 2011 Ratko Mladić was arrested there. Unlike Mladić, István Bakai wasn't in hiding but working at a farm. It is also mentioned in the judgement that at the beginning of the war he served in the "former Yugoslav army," and was then captured. The judgement doesn't mention who captured him, but since he served in the Yugoslav army, the German army must have taken him, highlighting this however would have complicated the depiction painted in the judgement. After he was released, he worked as a farmhand in Lazarevo, again at the same farm. The farmer's name isn't included. The court determines that on May 25, 1942 he joined the German army at his own will. It is of crucial importance to the judgement whether this really happened at his own will. The court's position is logical, but there is a palpable uncertainty, too, in the wording of sentences listing the arguments, the explanation runs into trouble at the utterance of "maybe." According to the judgement, he joined the German army at his own will, "maybe [*možda*] because his mother was German," and "maybe under the influence of the circumstances." His mother's name was Hartig. In Banat I knew many Hartigs, including a classmate, they considered themselves to be Hungarians. Of course, there may have been German Hartigs. I don't know whether beyond the surname Hartig there was any other support for the supposition that István Bakai's mother was German. As a supporting argument the court also exploits the fact that István Bakai was of Hungarian nationality, and under the German occupation it was only compulsory for the local Germans to enlist. Therefore, if the German occupying authorities had drafted him, he could have rejected it.

At this point the fates of the Banat Hungarians and the Bácska (Bačka) Hungarians differed greatly. (In 1941, Banat was occupied by Germany, Bácska was annexed to Hungary.) In Bácska, the Hungarians who were fit for service and drafted were posted mostly to the Russian and Ukrainian fronts. In Banat the Hungarians in principle weren't carried off to join the German army. Therefore, it wasn't without reason that the court saw an argument in the conditions that István Bakai was Hungarian. Yet it does give an unintentionally, slightly idyllic image of the fascist German drafting practices, supposing that all those who weren't German were allowed the freedom to choose.

It was also debated whether Bakai took part in any armed operations against the partisans. The accused denied this before the examining judge, and in the court proceedings (with my father's help), he explained that he hadn't taken part. The court, however, settled on the statement that the confession made before the OZNA "deserved absolute confidence," and the accused had not proven to the contrary. Looking at it with a modern legal eye it would be worthwhile asking whether, after the confession made before the OZNA, the burden of proof could really fall to the lot of the accused. And of course, it is also debatable how one could prove anything, when the court had ruled out all motions for proof by rejecting the defense's suggested hearing of a number of witnesses, "because the facts were sufficiently clear, and it would be extraneous to hear the suggested witnesses."

The appeal builds a second narrative. It was an undebatable fact that István Bakai served in the German army. His statement of defense attempts to call into relevance who István Bakai actually was, and tells how he ended up in the German army, and what he did there (or did not do). This thread of story sets out by stating that István Bakai was a poverty-stricken, exploited farmhand. This fact then, as now, might have caused for pity and sympathy. At the time, however, it also provided proof he was on the correct side. In the introductory sentences of the appeal, it is written the accused "belongs to the poorest levels of the people," "from sunup to sundown he worked on the properties of wealthier peasants," he didn't belong to any political or social organization, "his environment was formed purely by those who benefited from his labor."

My father also argues that while establishing the facts, the authorities had abused Pista's inability to express himself precisely. He indeed said that he had joined the German army "influenced by the environment," but he also said—and this the OZNA failed to record—that the fascist police had taken him to Versec, and when in Serbian he had awkwardly tried to say "uticaj okoline" (influenced by the environment), he was thinking of the fascist police. The "environment" therefore was the fascist police, and not like-minded friends. Pista wanted nothing less than to go to war in the German army, but he resisted in vain, and his Hungarian ethnicity was of no use. Debating whether Pista actually fought against the partisans, the appeal also mentions that since he didn't know German, he was assigned to guard duty. (Among his fellow soldiers many could speak to him, as primarily Banat Germans served in the Prinz Eugen, most of whom spoke Hungarian and Serbian too.) If there were no attacks, guards didn't fight.

The judgement in one sentence specified that Pista had fought against the Bulgarian partisans in Leskovac. According to the appeal, before the fighting Pista had been with a group of soldiers in the town (Leskovac), but when the Bulgarian attack began, he was injured by artillery fire. It was afterwards that the fighting really began, and instead of into battle, the defendant was taken into hospital, and afterwards was transferred from the local hospital to Germany. Therefore, nor was there grounds for the accusation that Pista had taken part in the fight against the partisans.

I would also add that in the military hospital in Germany, Pista was taken prisoner by the French army in Obersdorf on May 2, 1945. From there he was transported back to Yugoslavia. The appeal attempts to explain what Pista felt, and this explanation shows what had to be said at the time in such cases. The appeal found no grounds for the judgement that when Pista was taken prisoner by the French army he regarded this as liberation. This was probably an exaggeration of the truth. The defendant didn't speak German or French. He had four years of primary schooling, he knew Hungarian and broken Serbian. He hardly saw any solution in remaining in Germany, rather than in Lukácsfalva or Lázárföld, and taking orders from the French, rather than the Germans. He also couldn't have seen much point in him guarding the areas of Niš, Leskovac, Čačak, Mostar or Livno, regions he most likely hadn't heard of. It is also not certain whether he was able to make an exact distinction between the imprisoning and liberating "environments." He had formerly been enrolled in the Yugoslav army where he'd fought against Germans, but the Germans took him prisoner. Later he was able to return home to Lázárföld for a short while, then the "environment" dragged him off to the German army. When he was wounded, he ended up in Germany, and in the end there came the liberating "environment," via which he returned to Yugoslavia, and to prison. I believe we can confidently surmise that events didn't transpire owing to Pista Bakai's own choices. It simply wasn't Pista Bakai's war.

3. IS THERE A WINDOW TO SHOOT FROM?

File No. 12271 (The Case of Ferenc Nyihta)

Introduction

The subject of the third Banat Hungarian story is also a criminal case, and within it, the intent to decide without dispute who stood on which side. In August 1945, Moša Pijade announced that the new Yugoslav laws "express the desire that once the war has ended, the justice system too will leave behind the situation of war, and step into one of peace and into circumstances of normality." Moša Pijade was one of the closest allies of Tito, and was for a while the deputy head of State in Yugoslavia. After his death, the street where I lived in Novi Sad bore his name for a time. I'm not sure whether the announcement in 1945 was carefully considered and sincere; but if it was, the "desire" of which Pijade spoke was never fulfilled. Particularly not in those criminal cases which were linked to the divisions of the world war. A war can't truly be perpetuated outside of the "we're heroes, they're villains" coordinate system. Itis easier to shoot at the villains en masse. If we consider that on the other side perhaps there aren't only shady fascists (or shady communists), but also enlisted fathers of young children, dentists, orchard farmers, while on our side there are thieves too, or people who beat their wives—then it's much harder to fight a war. The situation is complicated even further, if—in Banat, for example—we recognize people who did both good, and bad, with Serbs, with Germans, with Hungarians, with Jews. During the climate of the world war a coordinate system that was beyond scrutiny developed, and stuck fast. There were no windows in it, not a crack to peek out of.

According to the formula of division "our side" was also the side of national honor, and the sentencing reinforced that national honor. The court's name was also styled to this formula. In July 1945 the Ferenc Nyitha was sentenced by the Judicial Council Acting in Cases of Crimes and Contraventions against the National Honor of the Peoples of Vojvodina (*Veće suda za suđenje zločina i prestupa protiv nacionalne časti naroda Vojvodine za Banat*). It is interesting here to pay attention to the relevant honor: "the National Honor of the Peoples of Vojvodina." In Croatia, the phrasing was somewhat more restricted; in April 1945 the "Court in Defense of the National Honor of Croats and Serbs of Croatia" was founded. The framework in Vojvodina was more flexible. In Ferenc Nyihta's case, on July 5, 1945 the prosecutor stated that the defendant had offended the Hungarian national honor, and therefore requested a harsh penalty. Consequently, from this example can also deduce that in Banat after the war, at least in principle, Hungarian national honor was a value worth protecting.

A Background: The Wisdom of János Gulyás

If we can only choose between hero and traitor, while relying on standards of national honor imbued with pathos, we greatly narrow the possibilities of classification. If someone were to denounce their communist or Jewish neighbor to the German police, expecting applause from the new authority, they would be the real traitors. If someone were to denounce their Jewish or communist neighbor, but not on their own initiative, or to appeal to the occupiers, but because they were forced to confess, because they had taken fright and they were scared what would happen if it turned out they'd been keeping something quiet, or perhaps in other words, because they were a coward, one could classify them as traitors. But it would be more humane to think in conceptual terms, in which one could distinguish between the two cases. The majority of people during the war saw fascism as twisted and inhumane, and they had every reason to.

After the war this image was flown from the flags of the victors, and flags tend to dictate passion, rather than nuance. The horrific crimes of fascism were certainly worthy of investigation, public knowledge and judgement, but consistently placing fascism and antifascism in contrast made it more difficult to notice imperfections in the developing antifascist power (for example, in the handling of the kulaks, among other issues).

Within this rhetorical straitjacket, it was difficult to avoid being classified as a fascist when criticizing the antifascist power. Besides this, following the flag's lead, many reconceived of their pasts, including those for whom it wasn't truly necessary. I remember that when I was a primary school child, there was an ice-cream seller who had been an ice-cream seller under the German occupation too, when he could have been 16 or 17 years old. He felt it necessary to retell over and over again how he had glared with rage and loathing at every fascist soldier he served ice cream. This most probably was not true. Was there any need for such explanation? Obviously, we couldn't venerate a seller who had a smile for everyone—including fascist soldiers—as he served them ice cream. But is heroic conduct the only humanly understandable conduct? Would someone be indisputably of the enemy if they, for example, invited a fascist neighbor to dinner? Leaving the post-war years for a moment to look at this dinner example: What happens if a shop manager accepts a dinner invitation from the CEO, who is known to mercilessly let people go, and to employ children in Indonesia on starvation wages under inhumane conditions? Is this utterly different? A classmate of mine once told me that his aunt had married a Becskerek German, who later joined the occupying army earnestly, of his own will. According to my friend's story, at a family dinner the German officer had asked where he should sit, at which the grandfather (the head of the family) said: "Sit where you like. Wherever it is, it'll be the lowest anyway." So, the grandfather stood on the side of heroism. It was a fact, however, that the aunt didn't file for divorce during the war. It was also a fact that the family dinner was still held with the fascist son-in-law present. Thus, were they traitors after all? There were people who must have seen it this way, because the aunt was arrested in 1944 as the wife of a German officer. Yet my grandfather managed to have her released relatively quickly.

In Banat, as in other places, there were some who would have liked to correct their own fates via the fever-dreams of Hitler, and also joined in on the heinous crimes. There were those who heroically stood in opposition. There were also those who merely wanted to stand by and wait for it all to pass over. There were those who tried to adapt to it all, who didn't join in, but gave a smile and a tip of the hat when necessary. This reality is difficult to place along the fascist/antifascist division. During the war, naturally the "hero vs. fascist" system of classification gave rise to a huge field of force. After the war, in political life, in criminal cases or simply in arguments, this field of force often consumed and transformed all other forms of differentiation. Any ties with fascism often suggested that the accused identified with the heinous crimes of fascism. On November 29, 1944, my grandfather writes in his diary:

> *The radio broadcasted, though it was also published in the Belgrade periodical Politika, that an established court sentenced 105 people to death, and the sentence has already been carried out. Among the executed were: six ministers, a few secretaries of state, a university teacher, a field officer, a journalist, a student and the writer Dr. Stefanovits Svetislav, who, if I'm not wrong, was the president of the PEN Club. His main crime was that he translated Mussolini's work entitled State.*

I looked into it, in 1937 Mussolini's book was published in Belgrade in Dr. Stefanović Svetislav's translation with the title *Korporativna država*, namely *The Corporate State*. This could indeed prove his ties to fascist ideologies. It is a fact, too, that under Nedić's government (remembered by history as the quisling government), Stefanović led the *Srpska književna zadruga* (Serbian Literary Cooperative) and other cultural institutions. Clearly then he wasn't on the correct side, but if his translation of Mussolini was really his major crime, then there would have been a more proportionate penalty than capital punishment. For example, he might have been removed from his position as president of the PEN Club, or perhaps expelled all together. But those suffering from such a blindness to proportions are incapable of perceiving boundaries within the formulae.

In the first of the three Becskerek stories I described how a young woman of Becskerek, who had returned after surviving the horrors of the war in Pest, needed "a certificate of moral-political conduct" to live again in the town where she was born, and to buy the necessary material for a print dress. Such certificates were also used to place people on either side of the fascist/antifascist dividing line. And here I might take the opportunity to explain the subtitle, namely, "The Wisdom of János Gulyás." János Gulyás was the chairman of the Local Liberation Commission in Torda in 1945, and he was required to sign the certificates proving one's moral-political suitability. In one of the office's files are Teréz Vertenbach's cases, and among them is her official certificate of moral-political conduct.

Two cases of Teréz Vertenbach (née Teréz Gábor) were taken care of by my father. One was her divorce. The husband (Vertenbach) was a German, he didn't return from the war, but the "German husband" imposed a status upon Teréz from which she had to escape. In the December 1944 entries of my grandfather's diary, I read that local Germans (including István Kaufmann, my grandfather's piano teacher, who was ninety years old at the time) had been taken off to mass P.O.W. camps. Hungarian and Serbian women with German husbands were also taken. Afterwards, news got around that if women filed for divorce, their fate would be better. For days in the office, from seven in the morning until late in the evening, divorce suits were written up, and there were queues upon queues of applicants. Teréz Vertenbach came to the office a few months later, on May 5, 1945, to sue for divorce against her German husband. I can see however that the court proceedings didn't start right away, the problem being that the courts who handled such matters weren't yet in operation. To prove to others that Teréz Vertenbach had done what she ought to, my father prepared a statement of proof with his own signature, in which he writes (in Serbian):

> To Teréz Vertenbach née Gábor, housewife, Vujićevo [Torda].
> I hereby certify that on this day, Teréz Vertenbach née Gábor gave authorization to commence a suit for divorce against her husband. I declare that I will do as requested as soon as the people's courts begin their work.

Teréz Vertenbach, however, had another case, which proves that after the war, it was no longer merely history, but also the young women and men of Torda who were able to create conflict.

From the documents I can see that my father recorded the facts first by hand in Hungarian, while later information was typed in Serbian. Teréz Vertenbach wanted to open a libel case against Ágota Makra. According to the victim, the following events required the court's intervention:

> Information:
> István Makra, a local drummer—with whom for a short time I have been cohabiting outside of marriage—was announcing the news by beat of the drum. Before the public present, who were listening to the announcements, Ágota Makra openly said to István Makra: "why not drum about Terka Pinke?"—referring to myself, since I'm known by this nickname in the community. Then in front of those present Ágota Makra loudly added: "the brothel's open, on the corner"—referring to and pointing to my own house.

> Evidence:
> Witnesses—István Maksai, official of the Municipal People's Committee Vujićevo and Katalin Varga, housewife, Vujićevo.

There is no court ruling among the documents, so I don't know how the people's court did justice in this case. Judging by the names of those mentioned it is possible there were deeper-running roots to the exchange. The name of the drummer was István Makra, the offender (or the alleged offender) was Ágota Makra née Rác. It is easily possible that Ágota was a previous (or current) wife of the drummer. I would add that Nikolaus Vertenbach, Teréz's husband, didn't return after the war; he most probably lost his life on the front as a German soldier.

In this complex situation the Local Liberation Commission of Torda had to size up Teréz Vertenbach's political and ethical suitability. The fascist/antifascist divide was necessarily in the focus, but the question was whether this could be amalgamated with local knowledge and local perspectives. With consideration to the historical background and the scope for action, I believe this amalgamation was successful. The certificate was written in Serbian, and signed by two persons: on the left the Local Liberation Committee's secretary, on the right the chairperson. The secretary's signature is illegible. The chairperson's signature is perfectly clear: János Gulyás. The certificate states:

> Subject: Certificate of moral and political conduct of Teréz Vertenbach née Gábor
> At the request of the 27-year-old citizen Teréz Vertenbach née Gábor, after thorough investigation, the Local Liberation Committee issues the following
> Certificate
> Under fascism, local citizen Teréz Vertenbach née Gábor was indifferent to the Liberation Movement, but made no efforts to help the fascists, nor did she get her hands dirty with the people's blood through any actions of her own. Nor does the named show any resentment towards the popular power now, after the Liberation.
> This certificate will be issued, after payment of the appropriate fee, for the named person's personal needs.
> DEATH TO FASCISM—FREEDOM TO THE PEOPLE!

Accordingly, morally and politically, Teréz Vertenbach wasn't perfect, but she was okay.

The Charge Against Ferenc Nyihta

Ferenc Nyihta was born in Kikinda in 1892, therefore at the time the charge was brought he was 53 years old. The charge notes that he was of Hungarian nationality, was a Roman Catholic, had no previous criminal record, was a farmer, married, the owner of half a house and seventy acres of land. He was the vice chairman in Kikinda of the Banat Hungarian Agricultural Association and Farmer's Circle. On April 14, 1945 he was taken into pre-trial detention. The hearing was scheduled for July 17, 1945. The hinges of the charge were the following:

1. According to the prosecutor during the German occupation Ferenc Nyihta had given accommodation to fascist officers in his own apartment, among them the notorious second-lieutenants Fischer and Richter.
2. From October 1942 until the occupiers' departure, "while our peoples fight tooth and nail against the occupiers," he organized lunches and dinners for the fascist officers, in particular on his name day and his wife's name day.
3. According to the last count, he had received a hunting rifle as a gift from one of the fascist occupiers, then in the summer of 1944, on two occasions he shot out the window of his farmstead "in the direction of the patriots" with the intention to "interfere with the patriots' operation," who had come to the farm to put an end to any threshing taking place at the occupiers' benefit. The indictment explains this point in greater detail. The prosecutor notes that the accused has acknowledged that there was a rifle shot, but according to him the shot was fired accidentally while he was searching for a match to light the lamp. The charge refers to the witness statement of Branko Sredojev, who was among those patriots intervening with the threshing and who believed the shot was not accidental, and that the accused had shot through the farmstead window at the patriots on purpose.

Besides the three counts, the charge also brings up other graver circumstances. According to the prosecutor, the accused helped the occupiers financially; in the terms that he paid the occupying officers to allow him to smuggle goods into Belgrade. Furthermore, the accused fled the farm in his shirtsleeves for Kikinda, and later fled Kikinda, too. According to the prosecutor's deduction, the accused committed a heinous crime against Hungarian national honor by maintaining intimate, friendly relations with the occupiers, and aiding them by force of arms.

The Defense

The defense didn't deny that fascist officers had stayed at Ferenc Nyihta's home in the town, but it explains that this wasn't a result of the accused's supposed fascistic sympathies, but the rooms were put into requisition by the German officers. On July 13, 1945, my father wrote a letter to Imre Palatinus, who was a member of the Hungarian Cultural Association of Banat (BMKSZ) board of directors in Kikinda. In the letter there is written among other things:

> After what's been heard, I kindly ask whether at the city hall you can attempt to establish if there are any documents relating to the military requisition which occurred during the occupation, if there are, please issue a statement… stating that in Ferenc Nyihta's apartment during the occupation, 3 rooms were put into requisition, the commandeered rooms were used for the accommodation of German officers. …

My father also requests that as a witness, Imre Palatinus confirm that on March 19, 1944, the Germans arrested the BMKSZ board of directors, including Ferenc Nyihta, "thereby wanting to prove that he did not maintain any class of friendly relations with the occupying Germans." The latter event is also confirmed by a certified statement, in which thirteen signators declared that on March 19, 1944, Ferenc Nyihta was arrested by the German occupiers.

There is one more certified statement in the file. It has six signators, and they bear witness to the fact that Ferenc Nyihta regularly complained about the German officers and their visitors quartered in the seized apartment, because they were constantly carousing, he had no peace in his own flat, and he had to stay in his farmstead outside town almost permanently. This declaration, similar to the one previously mentioned, naturally ends with the slogan: Death to fascism, freedom to the people!

The defense also requests a hearing of András Hegedűs, who is a laborer on the farm, and who is called on to confirm—countering Partisan Branko Sredojev's statement—that Nyihta couldn't have shot at the partisans out the window, because there was no window on the side of the farmstead that the partisans were attacking. My father also recommended Sava Savić's hearing, noting that his hearing wouldn't relate directly to the accusations made, but would confirm that the defendant "was on decent terms with his fellow Serbian citizens," therefore he could not have "stood, heart and soul, on the side of the occupiers." Sava Savić was requested to state that his wife had been saved by Nyihta, as once he'd arranged a car for her and drove her to Belgrade so she might get medical help there.

The Decision(s)

They didn't delay with the judgement. The trial was held on July 17, 1945, and ten days later, on July 27, my father wrote a letter to Géza Halbédl (a retired court official who was close to the accused's family, they may have even been relatives) and told him the result. During the proceedings my father maintained a constant correspondence with Géza Halbédl. It was he who sorted the legal expenses, and my father sent him the decisions. Since, after all, this wasn't an official correspondence, in spite of the stringent rules at the time my father addressed the letters to "the Honorable Géza T. Halbédl," rather than to "Comrade Géza T. Halbédl," who replies to "Dr József Várady, Esquire." In his letter dated July 27, my father informs Halbédl that Ferenc Nyihta has been sentenced to eighteen months of forced labor, and hastily charges were laid and a sentence brought against Mrs. Ferenc Nyihta, to the tune of one year of forced labor. Furthermore, Ferenc Nyihta and Mrs. Nyihta were sentenced to four years' loss of their national honor, and the confiscation of their property, except for fourteen acres and one house. It was also stated that the time Ferenc Nyihta had already spent in jail, since April, would be taken into consideration. My father forwarded Ferenc Nyihta's request that Mr. Halbédl send him "1 50x60cm suitcase, 1 set of underwear, 1 pillow,

1 blanket and 1 used pair size-41 shoes." Mrs.. Nyihta didn't live in the country at the time, and so didn't go to prison.

The letter also shares a few details. Several witnesses, on whom they'd counted, hadn't turned up, but the court hadn't ordered a new trial, rather it decided to deliver a judgement.

One of the recommended witnesses was Imre Palatinus, and I'll digress here for a second. Shortly after my father recommended him as a witness, charges were brought against him too for committing a crime "against the people and the state." He, too, was accused of collaborating with the fascists. My father defended him. One crucial point of the accusation is that in the Kikinda Farmers' Circle, once Palatinus had read out an anti-Bolshevist text. Looking at my father's notes, he lists the following potential counterarguments against the charge:

- The reading of a text does not equate to a heinous crime committed "against the people and state."
- Neither the prosecutor, nor any other, has mentioned what said text contained.
- Nobody ever spoke of the text since, the only trace that remains is the entry in the Farmers' Circle registry.
- Imre Palatinus did not write the text.
- István Tangl was supposed to read the text, but he lost his voice, and so asked Imre Palatinus to read.

According to the sentence passed on November 30, 1946, regardless of Tangl's role, the point was that Imre Palatinus "read aloud an anti-Bolshevist text," and thus "had proven his loyalty to the occupiers' ideologies." The court, of course, were of the idea that anyone who is opposed to Bolshevism can only be on the side of the fascists.

The court also took into consideration the certificate of moral-political conduct issued by the Kikinda internal affairs office at the request of the prosecution, in which the following is stated:

> The moral comportment of retired civil servant Imre Palatinus, son to Antal Palatinus, residing in Kikinda, is weak, unprincipled, which can be concluded from the fact that the aforementioned regularly meets and

fraternizes with immoral persons. In 1945, 2490 dinars were paid in tax, in 1946 no taxes were levied.

...

Death to fascism—freedom to the people!

One might suppose that the immoral people with whom Imre Palatinus met and fraternized were on the wrong side of the political ethics. He was sentenced to six months of forced labor.

Returning to Nyihta's case, it is noted by my father that Branko Sredojev recorded an "especially troublesome" statement. He supported the prosecutor's assertion, according to which Ferenc Nyihta had shot to "intervene with the patriots' operation." Had a witness been in the farmstead at the critical moment, they could have seen if Nyihta's rifle had really gone off by accident. Others in the building may also have known whether there was a window on the side the partisans came from. The attack occurred at night, so from outside it would have been difficult to see. Branko Sredojev seemingly said what he had assumed when he heard the rifle shot. But he was on the heroes' side. I must also add that in Yugoslavia, the communist movement had much more legitimacy than in Hungary, for example. Tito and the partisans truly did fight in arms against the German occupiers, and became a formidable enemy during the war. Rákosi, the communist leader in Hungary, didn't fight against fascism, he wasn't even in Hungary during the World War. Sredojev's statement may be the main reason my father wrote to Géza Halbédl that he feared there would be a harsher sentence.

Then follow the appeals and petitions for clemency. Attempts to have the sentenced somehow avoid the fascist/antifascist either/or straitjacket, during which certain facts and episodes from Nyihta's life come to light which, based on the relevant standards, namely 1945's standards, might place him on the correct side again. The new laws of clemency also present some support. The appeals and petitions for clemency are handled quickly. On August 24 my father writes a letter to Géza Halbédl, and explains: "I'm writing to inform you that Ferenc Nyihta's sentence has been halved under the Amnesty Regulation. According to which the penalty is nine months forced labor. Into which the time already spent in jail is included."

During this time Ferenc Nyihta is in the Sremska Mitrovica prison, the decision of clemency doesn't reach him in time, and new steps must be taken. In October 1945, my father writes a new request for clemency. A decision is made within days. On October 29, 1945 my father writes a letter to Géza Halbédl, and states: "I'm writing to inform you that the court has ordered for the immediate release of Ferenc Nyihta." The end result is seven months spent in prison.

Where Did Ferenc Nyihta Stand?

At the time, from a political viewpoint, the Nyihta case could have been labelled as a successful political trial, by which, I'm not saying it was a favorable or just result according to today's standards. A lot of questions were left unanswered. Among others was where he really stood, and who Ferenc Nyihta really was.

According to the charges he was on friendly terms with fascists, and he accommodated them gladly, "while our peoples fight tooth and nail against the occupiers," and he hosted fascist officers for dinner on his name day. According to the defense, the situation was quite the opposite. Nyihta was not at all happy about the German officers who lived in his rooms occupied by the authorities. He repeatedly complained to his neighbors, saying that the German officers and their guests were constantly carousing, while most of the time he was forced to spend his nights out of town on the farm, and he could hardly wait for the German residents to leave.

When I try to see a flesh-and-blood person, beyond the arguments and witnesses' statements, the question arises as to whether the two legal assertions rule each other out. In all likelihood, Ferenc Nyihta felt more comfortable at home *ohne* (without) German officers. It's also not unlikely that the German officers had guests and were loud—perhaps even so far as carousing. Celebrating name days was most probably a family tradition. Initially, there may have been a conventional guest list, but it is difficult not to invite those living where the name day is being celebrated. Of course, nor would it have been so dramatic to cancel the name day celebrations while the occupation continued, especially had they known in 1942 how long German rule would last. Ferenc Nyihta was a farmer. It is not at all unlikely that the Nyihta family strove to keep up friendly relations with the lodging officers who were representatives of the harsh, menacing German power. The Nyihtas invited them for name days, while complaining about them to their neighbors and those they knew. They really were forced to spend their nights on the farm, while the German officers caroused and earnestly desired them to leave.

I consider the accusations of bribery and smuggling which the prosecutor places into an utterly unusual and unexpected framework, from today's perspective. Nyihta's behavior is classified not as bribery and smuggling, but as "helping the occupiers financially." The explanation might be the following: If Nyihta was smuggling, then clearly it wasn't the occupiers he was delivering goods to in Belgrade. To the authorities one could only give, or rather one had to give, but not smuggle. Besides, if he was forced to bribe, then the goal was evidently to get around the current laws in place, that is, the laws of the fascist occupiers. And if he distributed goods (presumably grain) to Belgrade by evading German laws, then we can also assume that he wasn't supplying his buyers with produce as a priority of the occupiers. Therefore, in the fascist/antifascist dichotomy, he is not on the side the prosecutor sees him on, or would like him to be seen on. Evidently the German officers have to be paid off so Nyihta can deliver produce to somewhere prohibited by the occupying power, and to a buyer who wasn't supposed to be able to buy. Therefore, his trade, or his smuggling, wasn't so much colored with fascism as with antifascism. The scale is further tipped to the patriotic side by the fact that it was precisely Belgrade he was selling to despite the German prohibitions, though this may also have been influenced by the possibility that at the Belgrade markets, Banat grain sold for a good price.

Thus, the entire case could hardly be categorized simply as bribery or smuggling, because in the prosecutor's formula a window would have opened towards antifascism. Hence the prosecutor's construction in which the defendant aided the German army financially. But this wasn't truly convincing. According to the bill of indictment, Ferenc Nyihta paid the occupying authorities 500 or 1000 dinars per month to be able to smuggle. It would be difficult to convert this to today's money, but it may be of some help to know that according to the documents Géza Halbédl twice paid my father 1000 dinars and once 500 dinars in lawyer's fees. My father didn't charge high rates, especially not in criminal cases. In an earlier text I wrote about a twenty-dinar banknote, which during the first post-war years period bought enough string for tying two parcels. Therefore, 500 dinars would buy enough string to tie fifty parcels. A thousand dinars; twice as much. From the occupying forces perspective, this doesn't seem like a significant amount, not even if Nyihta paid 500 or 1000 dinars for several months. And if we move away from the formula towards what was concrete, the question remains as to where Ferenc Nyihta's money would have ended up. I'm not entirely sure, but it ought to be at least considered that those who accepted bribe money didn't put it towards the betterment of the German army. It is more likely that it was spent on drink or (if more came) perhaps on women of easy virtue. And so, in the end, this "financial help" didn't reach the fascist power, but went into the pockets of Kikinda pub owners and the purses of Kikinda ladies.

The indictment tries to prove that Ferenc Nyihta stood on the side of the fascists. According to the defense he did not. Hence the subtitle of this section asks where he actually did stand. Perhaps we ought to also think about whether the question is right during a period of forced categorization. Ferenc Nyihta was neither a fascist nor an antifascist, but a farmer and a trader. Neither the fascist years, nor the years that followed could truly be called golden years for farmers.

I would like to return to the question of what actually happened in the farm shed. The prosecutor leans on Branko Sredojev's statement, and says that Sredojev "and the other patriots" attacked the farm to "interfere with the threshing." In July 1945, in texts of all kinds the word "patriot" was an insignia, and represented an insignia to the court, too. But who had been threshing, or was preparing to thresh? According to the indictment's phrasing, the occupiers themselves were threshing, but it is more likely that the day laborers would have threshed, and the result collected by the occupiers. It is also possible that via the bribe money, Nyihta may have sold part of his yield in Belgrade. Whatever way it stood, the farm owner can't have been happy that on his own farm the Germans had control of the threshing (and the yield too). But he also wouldn't have been happy that those come to "interfere with the threshing" had attacked his farm, even if they were antifascist patriots.

Did he really shoot out the farmstead window at the patriots? I find the proposition quoted as the defendant's explanation unconvincing: that when the attack commenced during the night, the defendant got out of bed to light a match with which to light the lamp, and as he stumbled, the rifle went off by accident. The defendant also argued that there was no window in the farmstead wall facing the direction the attack came from. Therefore, he couldn't have shot from the building at the attacking patriots. This is very easy to check (which my father most probably told Nyihta), it is unlikely that the defense would put forward such an argument, were it not true. Since the attack happened at night, the partisan witness could hardly have seen, but of course afterwards it could be checked, and Nyihta did suggest a witness (a laborer), who could confirm where there was and was not a window. This matter was not cleared up either.

Ferenc Nyihta was stuck between the walls of the formulae. If there was no window, one could not shoot out, one couldn't even see out. As we can't see out of our own fates.

***

There were many such cases in the first years following the war. Then, as the years went by, slowly windows opened in the walls of the formulae, albeit often decorated with flags. At times belief surged, at time it simply sat there among us. It could also be examined up close and scrutinized with an ironic eye. Meanwhile there were other things too being swept among us. This period of progress is shown by a picture hanging on a pub wall in Vojvodina. The photo was taken by the photographer László Dormán, and was published in the *Új Symposion* literary journal.

I still don't know whether the pub landlord hung the picture in earnest or ironically. In it Marx, Engels, Lenin and Tito stand side by side, shoulder to shoulder (though they weren't really contemporaries). To the left of this ideology's great heroes there is a freshly arrived Coca Cola advert, to the right is a pheasant which had found its place on the wall long before but rode out both the German occupation and the arrival of communism.

IV.

A STORY FROM THE BORDER OF BANAT

FROM GOOSE-DOWN BUSINESS AND BORDER TRESPASSING TO A CONCENTRATION CAMP

File No. 12693/4

The OZNA

In the course of history, Banat belonged to many countries. Borders changed too, yet the land on Banat's left side (across the river Tisza), was always part of the same country. During the German occupation of Banat (between April 1941 and October 1944), this was not the case anymore, and this had an impact on the life of István Tóth.

This story is about the criminal trial of István Tóth. I found the mold-ridden case documents on a bottom shelf in the garage. They state that István Tóth, a farmer, was born in Hódegyháza (today Jazovo in Serbia), a village about 10 kilometers from the town of Csóka (Čoka in Serbian). The defendant's place of residence is identified as "Molin." I had to look this up. As I found, no village by that name survived, although it had existed since 1832 as a commune of German settlers, formed on the estate of Count Ferenc Zichy This village in the Banat region was called Mollyfalva in Hungarian, Molidorf in German. When István Tóth was brought to court in 1950, about a thousand people dwelled in that village. Then, as groundwater levels rose, the place became uninhabitable. In 1961, roughly ten years after Tóth had been charged, Mollyfalva ceased to exist, overgrown by woods and shrubs. Presumably, István Tóth himself, born in 1919, is now also dead.

In addition to usual criminal documents, the file contains an undated sheet, the relevance of which is a matter of conjecture rather than a clear fact. It was probably created in 1950, when the investigation started, and must be a copy several times removed from the original. My younger readers—and I can only hope there will be a few—will hardly recall that, in those days, copies would be made by inserting in the typewriter a number of blank papers, interleaved by carbon sheets. This meant that people well-versed in the mysteries of the typewriter had a certain power over copy legibility. If you wanted even the fifth copy legible, you simply banged harder on the keys! The first one or two copies in the row tended to read almost as easily as the original, as long as the carbon paper was fresh. This time, it was probably a well-worn carbon paper, and not a first copy at that, but it remains more or less legible. I will insert a scanned photo here, but before I do that, allow me to say a few words about the text. It's a list of assignments or groups of assignments, specifically seven by number, each marked by a Roman numeral. The first item, worded in flawed Hungarian, translates as follows:

> Gangs/groups—activities of various individuals and times when active

Nowhere in the text do we find a diacritically marked letter *á*, so frequent in Hungarian, presumably because the guilty typewriter, which must have been left behind by the German occupiers of Csóka, did not have a key for it. In the event, the letter was replaced by *ä*, with the umlaut. Apparently, nor did the apparatus have provisions for the otherwise rare letters *ő* and *ű*—or, if it did, they were happily ignored by the author. Another, particularly painful omission is that of the letter *é*, which yielded unfortunate words such as *kisebbseg* instead of the correct *kisebbség* (minority), easily misread, in the absence of the diacritical mark, for meaning "smaller asshole." The bottom of the page features a handwritten note identifying the true nature of the document:

> ÓZNA: Latest assignments.

Now it is really time to insert that scan:

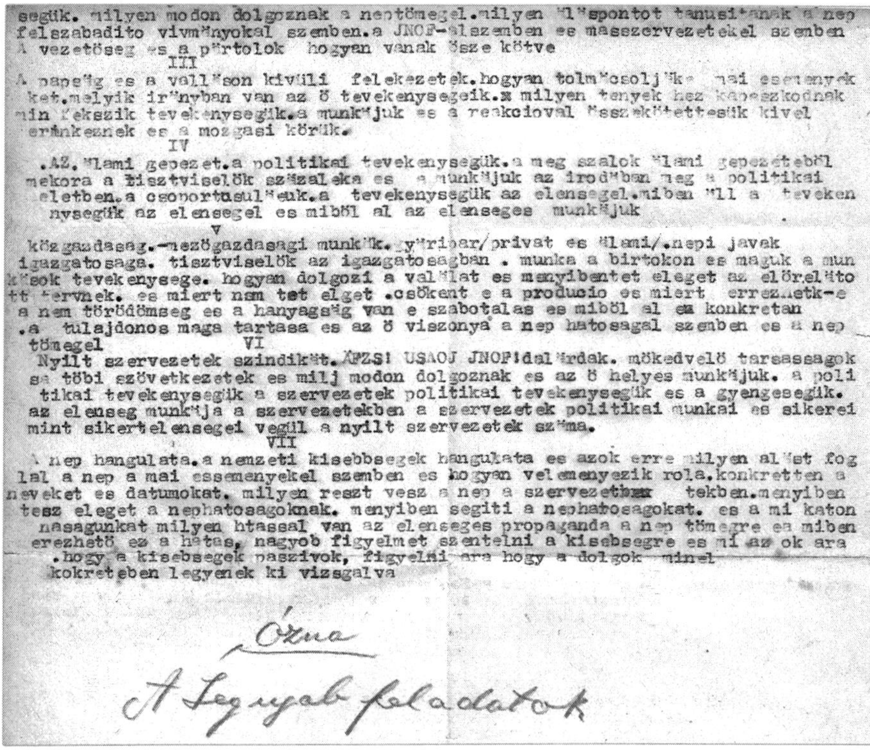
segük. milyen modon dolgoznak a neptömegel.milyen állaspontot tanusitanak a nep
felszabadito vivmányokal szemben.a JNOF-al szemben es masszervezetekel szemben
A vezetöseg es a pártolok hogyan vanak össze kötve
III
A papság es a vallason kivüli felekezetek.hogyan tolmácsolják a mai esemenyek
ket.melyik irányban van az ö tevekenysegeik.a milyen tenyek hez kapaszkodnak
min fekszik tevekenysegük.a munkájuk es a reakcioval összeköttettesük kivel
erinkeznek es a mozgasi körük.
IV
.AZ állami gepezet.a politikai tevekenysegük.a meg szalok állami gepezeteböl
mekora a tisztviselök százaleka es a munkájuk az irodában meg a politikai
eletben.a csoportusulásuk.a tevekenysegük az elensegel.miben áll a teveken
nysegük az elensegel es miböl al az elensegees munkájuk
V
közgazdaseg.-mezögazdasagi munkák. gyáripar/privat es állami/.nepi javak
igazgatosaga. tisztviselök az igazgatosagban . munka a birtokon es maguk a mun
kasok tevekenysege. hogyan dolgozi a vallálat es menyibentet eleget az elörelato
tt tervnek. es miert nem tet elget .csökent e a producio es miert errezhetk-e
a nem törödömseg es a hanyagság van e szabotalas es miböl al ez konkretan
.a tulajdonos maga tartasa es az ö viszonya a nep hatosagal szemben es a nep
tömegel VI
Nyilt szervezetek szindikát. AFZS! USAOJ JNOF!dalárdak. mökedvelö tarsasagok
sa töbi szövetkezetek es milj modon dolgoznak es az ö helyes munkájuk. a poli
tikai tevekenysegük a szervezetek politikai tevekenysegük es a gyengesegük.
az elenseg munkája a szervezetekben a szervezetek politikai munkai es sikerei
mint sikertelensegei vegül a nyilt szervezetek száma.
VII
A nep hangulata.a nemzeti kisebbsegek hangulata es azok erre milyen alást fog
lal a nep a mai essemenyekel szemben es hogyan velemenyezik rola.konkretten a
neveket es datumokat. milyen reszt vesz a nep a szervezetekben.menyiben
tesz eleget a nephatosagoknak. menyiben segiti a nephatosagokat. es a mi katon
nasagunkat milyen htassal van az elenseges propaganda a nep tömegre es miben
erezhetö ez a hatas, nagyob figyelmet szentelni a kisebsegre es mi az ok ara
.hogy a kisebsegek paszivok, figyelni ara hogy a dolgok minel
kokretben legyenek ki vizsgalva

Ózna

A Legnyobb feladatok

I have never seen a text like this among the case documents, or anywhere else, for that matter. In criminal cases the defendant's testimony before the OZNA was often recorded, but this particular piece of paper is completely different, resembling guidelines for internal use more than anything else. Does it suggest that István Tóth had been picked as a rat to report on others? Was it supposed to alert him to fields of action where he could distinguish himself by his services? Moreover, was it used by Tóth himself in an attempt to demonstrate that, rather than a hostile element, he was regarded by those wielding new-fangled power as a friend of the system, fit to perform certain patriotic tasks? I cannot say.

Like all my contemporaries, I have heard a lot about the OZN, or OZNA—the "People's Protection Bureau,": essentially, the secret police. These days, few people remember the distinction between the OZNA and the UDBA. (In Yugoslavia, the OZNA was the military secret service, and it preceded the formation of other secret services.) The trepidation associated with these acronyms has largely vaporized since those days, although here and there I still hear people revert to a hushed voice when mentioning the OZNA. In any case, back in 1950, there was certainly no other way you wanted to utter "OZNA" or "UDBA." It is also true that, as the secret services expanded their reach, an increasing number of local people were recruited to serve as informants. As we know, not all people are the same. Here and there, the OZNA was marked by some local touch. I do not imagine the CIA would ever set up, or would have ever maintained, an outpost in Csóka, as the OZNA apparently did. This consisted of OZNA recruits who happened to be from around Csóka or from the village itself. Some of them may have sworn more allegiance to the OZNA than to Csóka; others the other way around. The city of Becskerek (today Zrenjanin) had its own OZNA or UDBA informants. One of them was the protagonist of a story my friend Tibor Bencze told me a great many times. They lived on the same street; my friend in the middle, the UBDA sneak on the corner. This guy was good at sports, if memory serves, and even attended university briefly where he acted in plays, but he could not stick with anything long enough. Later, he worked as officer for a corporation while most of his friends graduated and became engineers or lawyers; one a famous athlete, another a noted actor. M. (as he went by the initial of his alias given to him by the UDBA) maintained these relations conscientiously, preferring to pen reports on his friends and acquaintances. One time he partied into the wee hours of the morning, drinking and playing cards with two pals, Ivan and Karcsi. M. and Ivan had attended the same Serbian secondary school, while Karcsi's alma mater was the Hungarian grammar school in town. They kept up the habit of playing cards together over the years. This time around, all in the company eschewed politically sensitive topics, keeping the conversation centered on women. Then, after a while, M. burst out: "C'mon, you guys, just tell me what the fuck I am supposed to report about you. They will know we played cards all night. I won't get away with saying nothing."

M.—unlike the UDBA itself—was regarded by my friends as amusing, if far from respectable. Would the UDBA have turned out differently if more fellows like M. had come its way? Perhaps not, but I cannot say for sure. Undoubtedly, the presence in one's life of an organization such as the OZNA or the UDBA alters human behavior, and to some extent the people themselves. The yardsticks of courage shift, more acts (or gestures of inaction) come under the influence of fear, infirmity reaps greater rewards, even the rivalry with one's neighbors discovers hitherto uncharted paths.

But was there a capacity of being influenced in another direction as well? One that may have rendered the local outpost of the OZNA cool in a funny way?

I catch myself smiling, perhaps with a measure of sympathy even, as my gaze lingers on the long *Ó* in the acronym (correctly OZNA) as spelled by the author of the handwritten note. In Becskerek, even Hungarians used to pronounce OZNA with a short initial vowel, whereas the good folks of Csóka apparently evolved a pronunciation favoring an elongated *ó*. In fact, the word sounds more toothsome this way, arguably even more *Hungarianesque*. As for those "latest assignments," they must have been drafted in the higher echelons of the organization, possibly at the Voivodina regional level of the OZNA, but the Hungarian translation, in both the typed and handwritten sections, bursts with local flavor. It is also obvious that the text was not created by members of the local intelligentsia. The imperfections of language and usage, along with the marked *couleur locale*, exude a sort of humanity—or at least something that could be confused with humanity.

I wonder how the tasks preceding these "latest assignments" could have been worded. Did they exist in Hungarian translation as well? Let me copy, the first three sentences of Assignment No. VII, or, to be precise, the first three sets of words, each followed by a period. It is difficult to mirror in another language the imperfections of a Hungarian from Csóka (probably a ploughman), who found himself in the OZNA and was charged with the task of translation. In English, his flawed sentences might sound like this: "The mood among the peeple. The mood of ethnyc mynoritys and there posicion and opynion on the ivents. with specyficc names and dates."

What must have been a novelty in 1950 (or perhaps at a slightly earlier date, when the document in question was delivered to István Tóth) was the requirement to supply specific names and dates. Quite possibly, some local "staff" may have formerly used in their reports phrases such as "the word is that..." or "many people say that..." or "it is rumored in the pubs that..." Meanwhile, the agents "reported" on what they had actually heard or what they thought would be received as valuable intelligence. Not infrequently, these reports coincided with their own opinions, as did the claim that the system of mandatory delivery of farm products was a cruel one. Now those in the high places wanted names and dates. It must have been hard times for the poor OZNA, as it certainly was for those named in the reports.

A Fray Between István Tóth and the Banater Finanzdirektion *During the Occupation*

So much for the OZNA; let me switch to the line of goose-down business mentioned in my title. The case documents incontrovertibly show that István Tóth sold goose feather down on several occasions while ignoring national borders—whatever those borders were between 1942 and 1944. In any case, the financial authorities of the occupying Germans determined, without specifying the exact location, that he had smuggled goose down into what was then Hungarian territory. What the papers do state is that Tóth's shipments invariably stemmed from Hódegyháza (today Jazovo), near Csóka. They possibly headed across the Tisza River to the town of Zenta, which belonged to Hungary at the time. One of the three penal orders mentions that Tóth was caught in the village of Gyála, on his way back from a delivery (in which particular case he cannot have returned from Zenta). In all three cases, he was apprehended by German border guards on his way back. The orders imposing a penalty were written in Serbian, except for a handful of as yet undigested bureaucratic terms in German, such as *Anzeige* (report). For instance, one Serbian sentence reads, "Anzeige No. 441 of 9/V-942 accuses three individuals of import smuggling..." One of them was István Tóth; his cohorts remain anonymous in the order. The official seal identifies the acting authority in German as "Banater Finanzdirektion, Betschkerek."

On the evidence of the order dated October 30, 1943, István Tóth confessed to have taken "the wrong path" (*stranputica* in Serbian) at 8 in the morning on May 7, 1942, as he delivered seven kilos of goose down to Hungary. The following day, still "on the wrong path," he traced his secret steps back into the Banat region, bringing with him a variety of merchandise from Hungary. The document provides a meticulous list of the goods found on the hands of István Tóth when he was apprehended at the post marking km 207:

- 5 and a half meters of shirting
- 12 small boxes of shoe polish
- 3 head scarves
- 2 meters of apron cotton
- 5 spoons

- 3 pairs of women's pantyhose
- 5 kg of lime
- 1 comb
- 100 cigarette papers
- 2 skeins of thread
- 1 lump of gum arabic
- 3 ribbons

This document (which features the longest list of all three) makes a mess of singulars and plurals, while it does not make it clear whether the given quantities were smuggled in by the three accomplices collectively, or by István Tóth alone.

The other two orders describe similar felonies. The one dated October 13, 1943 states that István Tóth was captured by German border guard precisely one year before, at 9 in the evening on October 13, 1942, when he had spirited away nine kilos of goose down to Hungary, according to his own testimony. On his way back, he brought a pair of women's pantyhose, some twine, a man's shirt, and fifteen and a half meters of tailor's cloth. The third order, dated February 24, 1944, establishes the offense as "crossing the border from Hungary into the Banat via officially unrecognized route," on December 8, 1943. This time the merchandise consisted of four kilos of goose down, and the administrators took the trouble to take down István Tóth's own deposition. In his defense, he cited the shaky livelihood of his household. He had crossed the border in an attempt to obtain medication for his ill wife, and paraffin for the lamps of his mother as this lighting fuel "was commercially unavailable in the Banat." He had been caught with twenty liters of paraffin at the kilometer post 208.

I am not quite sure, but I think it very likely that István Tóth made such exploits on several more occasions, although he was only caught three times. In all three cases, the *Finanzdirektion* determined a criminal offense on his part, seized the goods found on him, and imposed a fine which he could redeem by imprisonment if he was unable to pay—precisely, by one day behind bars for each ten golden dinars. Well, the cumulative amount of the fines came to about 50,000 dinars. I do not know whether these dinars were considered as "golden" dinars.

A closer look at the list of smuggled goods would seem to lend credence to István Tóth's claim that this whole goose-down business served the ends of a family household. He obviously looked across the river border to find articles they needed but which were "nowhere to be found for sale" in Csóka or the Banat region at the time. Let me pause at one of the articles for a second. According to the first list, István Tóth (acting alone or with his associates, but certainly in defiance of Hitlerian power) intended to bring in twelve small boxes of shoe polish, among other items. Was this considered a necessity just as vital as, say, spoons, shirting, lime, paraffin, or sewing thread? Perhaps it was, back in the day. As for me, I have for some time resigned myself to living the rest of my life in the absence of shoe polish, although a good few decades ago I did feel it inevitably necessary to have some around the house. Having read about István Tóth's categorizing shoe polish among the goods worth taking serious risks for possessing, even in times of war, I asked some friends, including a few my junior, whether they still used any, and whether they recalled that in the past this had been deemed an essential commodity. The answers were all but unanimous. None of them kept shoe polish anymore, although some felt mildly nostalgic upon hearing it mentioned, and all remembered having once used it themselves, if only as a nod to decorum. An acquaintance from Novi Sad said he had chanced upon a nearly empty box of shoe polish in the corner of the bottom drawer of his wardrobe, tucked away behind some old pairs of shoes, which made him feel like he was fumbling in a sort of "miniature museum" (his words).

Recently, I too found an archaic object in our family house in Becskerek. It was an old ice skate wrench. You see, not only thoughts but existence itself is often adrift between the shores of the nonsensical and what makes sense. The sheer existence of an ice skate wrench is a case in point. The years directly following World War Two permitted freer, I mean relatively freer, movement, so ice skating quickly came into view. At the same time, it would have been an inconceivable luxury, morally and financially, to keep a separate, purpose-made pair of skating boots that would have no other use whatsoever. Shoes represented serious value and were hard to come by in those days. To become eligible to purchase a pair, you had to collect points (the Serbian word for it, *tačkice*, was even adopted by many Hungarians as *tacskica*) before you could redeem them in the store. No wonder people did their best to make their shoes last as long as possible. A single pair would often go through several rounds of mending, even cobbling. There were still cobblers around. You had to fasten your skates onto the soles and heels of your shoes or boots using a special wrench to tighten the mounting bolts. When you took off the skate assembly, you could use the shoes as, well, ordinary shoes. Across the street from our house in Becskerek, there were stretches of land behind the back yards with large pools of stagnant groundwater throughout the year. City fathers might term them "sustainable groundwater" today. Our word for them was *bara*. We reaped their benefits in the winter, when for weeks, sometimes months, the bara froze over thick enough for skating. We would bring our skate wrenches, mount the skates, then remove them from the boots when we had had enough. With a little practice, we glided around with reasonable confidence. Some of us even ventured onto the thinner ice, but the risk was not all that great, with no more than 10 to 20 cm of water beneath. One of our German neighbors was the most skilled. His name was Gerhard. He could even do pirouettes. This was back then. Today, not a single bara remains. The fields beyond the back yards have been built on. We no longer have frost harsh enough for any ice to form over a bara or even a puddle, for that matter. In fact, we have no winters as such any more than we have cobblers. The Germans are long gone from Becskerek, and most Hungarians have left as well. I don't know what became of my skates. All I have is this skate wrench, without a context.

Could this be the fate awaiting bookmarks, too?

But What Happened in Macahalma?

The sources known to me tell a story of tragic and shameful events in Macahalma. The question that interests us here is whether, and to what degree, István Tóth had anything to do with them. Located in the vicinity of Csóka, Macahalma was home to a highly reputed model estate, particularly famous for its flower cultivation. The Lederer brothers also ran a distillery here. During the war, the place was converted by the German occupiers into a concentration camp filled with partisans, resistance fighters and others. The prisoners were routinely humiliated and tortured; some of them died in the camp. The guard was mostly supplied by the HIPO, short for *Hilfspolizei*, the German auxiliary police.

Among the background information on István Tóth (born in 1919 in Hódegyháza, a farmer by occupation, a citizen of Yugoslavia, of Hungarian ethnicity, knows how to read and write, married with one child, in detention awaiting trial since September 10, 1949), the indictment mentions that the accused is "reportedly without criminal record." It may be that the prosecutor would have found it less than patriotic to simply say "no criminal record" when referring to an individual he was apparently eager to categorize as a war criminal. Doing so might have even seemed like praise. The insertion of the word "reportedly" was obviously meant to distance the prosecutor from a semblance of positive characterization, when in fact, at this point, he was supposed to furnish objective data and formulate claims on behalf of the prosecution. Part of the prosecutor's job was to decide, within his own discretion, whether "criminal record" should be construed as including sanctions imposed by the German authorities during the occupation.

According to the prosecutor, from early 1944, István Tóth, "instead of joining the patriotic forces," served as a guard in the concentration camp, became a member of the HIPO, and committed a number of war crimes, effectively aiding a foreign power (Germany) "at war with our country." The indictment goes into specific detail, charging that Tóth, like any other HIPO servicemen on duty, dealt out blows, forced prisoners to run up and down, and tormented them with commands to "get down, now get up!"—all of which were found to satisfy the statutory elements of torture. In a specific instance cited by the prosecutor, Tóth is claimed to have beaten a certain Milan Kojičin and one Stevica Ostojin with a stick. The indictment also states that, when Csóka had been liberated, the defendant "first joined our army in order to hide his evil deeds, then moved to Mollyfalva, so it took a while before he could be apprehended." He was not charged with homicide, though, only with other categories of war crimes pursuant to Section 3, paragraph (3) of the Act on Crimes Against the People and the State.

In February 1950, when the prosecutor filed his plea, István Tóth was in detention in Becskerek, pending results of the investigation. My father spoke with him there as is apparent from a letter my father wrote to the defendant's wife the same month:

Zrenjanin, February 21, 1950

To: Erzsébet Tóth née Szemerédi
farmer

Jazovo
z.p. Ostojicevo
c/o István Lele

In connection with the criminal proceedings against your husband, please bring with you the next time you come to town the penal orders issued on your husband during the German occupation on charges of border trespassing.

I have talked with your husband today.

Yours sincerely,

The address of the recipient reveals that István Tóth's wife continued to reside in Hódegyháza (Jazovo), not in Mollyfalva. The couple had one child. István Tóth himself lived (or squatted down in hiding) in Mollyfalva (also located in the Banat region, close to Magyarcsernye), from where he probably ventured out from time to time to meet his wife. The address also suggests that Mrs. Tóth lived in the house of one István Lele. Presumably the Tóth family home had been seized and they had to move in with acquaintances.

The "penal orders" my father requested Mrs. Tóth to furnish were executed by the German-run *Finanzdirektion* in the matter of the illegal trading in goose down. In 1943, these documents demonstrated that István Tóth was on the wrong side. This time around, they served to show that he must not have been an evil man after all, since he was found guilty and sentenced by the German occupiers. For his part, my father needed to have the penal orders specifically for purposes of a submission he filed on behalf of István Tóth on February 22, 1950. In this he also stressed the fact that István Tóth, unlike other prison guards, never enlisted with the HIPO, nor did the role he played in the concentration camp have anything to do with the auxiliary police. He ended up in the camp because the occupying authorities had imposed a fine on him (as the penal orders demonstrate).

Since he was unable to pay the fine, German imprisonment and forced labor awaited him. Instead, István Tóth accepted, under duress, to serve as a guard in the concentration camp. The defendant admitted to having hit Milan Kojičin and Stevica Ostojin with a wooden stake, but only in order to stop a fight between them. The document underlines that, after the liberation of Csóka, the case of István Tóth, along with those of several other residents of Hódegyháza, was reviewed by the local People's Liberation Committee, which found him innocent of any serious offense and ordered his release from custody. Those found guilty by the committee were taken away and punished.

The submission continues by relating how István Tóth joined the People's Liberation Army after his release. This was possibly when the assignment from the OZNA reached him. He may have stashed it away among his other papers, which his wife would later bring into the office during his trial. After the war, he became a farmer-settler in Mollyfalva, and a member of the People's Front, as attested by Mihály Bicók.

The submission was filed with the attachment of a deposition signed on February 22, 1950, by one Lajos Vastag, who had served as chairman of the People's Liberation Committee at the time István Tóth's case was investigated after the liquidation of the concentration camp in Macahalma. The affidavit was also authenticated by József Tóth, chairman of the same committee in 1950. The document, written in (flawed) Serbian, states that the investigation of István Tóth's case proceeded with the participation of partisans who had been prisoners at the concentration camp. They confirm that Comrade Tóth was released on account of his good conduct. Moreover, as a candidate for membership in the Communist Party, he could be counted upon to support popular power in the future ("...će biti dobar radnik za izgradnju socijalizam"—loosely translated as "will good worker be to building socialism"). The text concludes with a recommendation by the local People's Liberation Committee to the People's Authority of the District Court (Narodna Vlast Okružnog Suda) to consider István Tóth an "asistiran." The Serbian version of another Latin word, *amnestiran*, would probably have better fitted the bill.

This is about all that the case documents divulge; the court itself could not have known much more than that. The trial was held on February 28, 1950. A hand-written note my father scribbled on the summons says that the verdict was delivered to the defendant's wife on March 11. No copy of this original verdict survives; there were no Xerox machines in those days. I tried the Municipal Archives of Becskerek, only to be told that no document of any kind had been kept regarding István Tóth's trial. Next, I contacted Csaba Majoros, a former student of mine, now a lawyer in Zenta. He did find a baptismal certificate, which states that István Tóth was born on December 14, 1919 in Hódegyháza, and married Erzsébet Szemerédi on April 29, 1942. Having served his sentence, he came back to Hódegyháza, but the exact date of his return remains unknown. Majoros also found out that István Tóth died in 2002, his wife in 2013. Their son Bálint lives in Hódegyháza.

Finally, remembering my father's habit of penning the verdict on the summons of each case, I gave the papers a last glance just in case. And it was there. He wrote it in Serbian, probably right after he had read the verdict and had not yet switched back to Hungarian in his mind: "3 godine!" "Three years," followed by an exclamation point. Now that the verdict has departed from the real world, leaving behind no more than pieces of a puzzle without a context, I wonder if that exclamation point was supposed to convey a sense of triumph or just the opposite: indignation.

I am also wondering what kind of verdict I would have handed down. István Tóth was twenty-five when he spent months in Macahalma. He had been in the business of smuggling goose down at the age of 23 to 24. Back in 1928, Kurt Tucholsky wrote that "he who is capable of witnessing a war without being disgusted is not a human being but a patriot." Well, with István Tóth, patriotism was not the problem. As far as I know—and I did experience some of this as a child—ethnic Hungarians in the Banat during the occupation generally preferred to steer clear of commitment rather than openly siding with either party to the conflict. Some did join the HIPO and a few volunteered to serve in the German army, but they were rare exceptions to the rule. And yes, some bonded with the partisans, a handful even attaining the status of "national hero," but this was not really typical, either. While a number of Hungarians received credit after the war for "championing the just cause," most of them did not cherish the cause itself so much as their friendship with a communist neighbor whom they were eager to help. That is how they came to be reckoned among the fighters. István Tóth himself tended to evade conflict, and if this was not possible, he simply drifted with the tide of events. He kept ducking checkpoints along the border, but he was busted three times. He also tip-toed around history. It was not by following this or that righteous idea or belief that he trespassed borders; he was driven by the need to procure pantyhose, gum arabic, and shoe polish for his family. What he took with him was not ardent conviction but goose down. Then, at one point, as no more byways and detours remained, he had to face the fact that the World War had come to Csóka and even to Hódegyháza. The restrictions of movement in space implied a restriction of ways in which one could move around. Essentially, you had to march from place to place. Anywhere. It was not feasible for István Tóth to simply stay put at home and continue to till his strip of land. The prosecutor was right in suggesting that he might as well have marched with the patriots, meaning the partisans. Joining them would presumably have been an act of escaping a prison sentence and forced labor. Instead, he chose to accept to serve in the Macahalma camp—which in essence amounted to the same act of fleeing something worse. In the absence of joining the partisans, the only option open to him was the penitentiary, in one of two versions: either as a prisoner (one day for each ten golden dinars of his debt) or as a prison guard in Macahalma.

In one case I am familiar with in Becskerek, these roles became jumbled within a single family. Karcsi, the preferans card-playing buddy of the UDBA informer whom I have mentioned, had a German surname. He considered himself Hungarian, though, as did his father, who held office in the Hungarian cultural association. On March 19, 1944, Karcsi's father was arrested by the Germans. According to my grandfather's diary, a group of German militia men, who also paid us a visit that day to bring in my father and grandfather, said that "the leaders of the local Hungarian community are being rounded up and taken to an internment facility." When they found that my grandfather was seventy-seven years old and bed-ridden with illness, they left him alone, but they did take my father away. The rounded-up leaders were held in custody for just one day. As the Germans later explained, the arrests served purposes of security only, and were carried out on the day Germany occupied Hungary, its ally in the war. Karcsi's father, too, was taken to an "internment facility." Among the guards he discovered his own father (Karcsi's grandfather), who landed this role as someone who had always embraced his German identity.

István Tóth also chose to be a guard. It was not a good decision, to be sure. But what exactly did he do or not do in Macahalma? Even if the People's Liberation Committee was correct in finding him "innocent of any serious offense," he was hardly to be regarded as a dissenter in his role as prison guard. What he joined under pressure was the staff of a concentration camp during what would be the last months of German occupation. It is not always easy to distinguish between drifting with the tide and movement by one's own volition. Indeed, it is a matter of dispute in criminal law whether such a distinction is necessary. The camp guards certainly beat and tormented the prisoners, and István Tóth could not afford to flout expectations. In hindsight, these acts proved to have been punishable offenses, regardless of whether he had dealt those blows with enthusiasm or loathing. And this cannot be a subject of debate. The context was gone; the sheer acts remained.

I am searching for an analogy by which to better comprehend István Tóth's situation, and I am having a hard time finding one. The best is example is the peer pressure I felt during my compulsory military service. Needless to say, it was in peace time, in 1965–1966. If we did something well, we were rewarded by thunderous praise. I do not remember what we did well. It may have been the whole squad succeeded in forming a proper line before the allotted deadline following the afternoon's nap time. We all tried hard, myself included. Sometimes we would tighten our belts around the waist without routing them through the loops to save time. "Vrlo dobro!" (very good!), came the thunderous praise. "Služimo narodu!" (we serve the people!), we roared in unison. We were unassuming, you see. We did not seek to distinguish ourselves out of ostentation; we only claimed to act for the benefit of the people. It was hardly possible to go against the tide by doing or not doing something based on one's personal decision.

I remember once venturing so far as to strike a casual tone of voice with an officer, of course making sure that this was not readily apparent from the outside. It happened at curfew time as the captain checked whether each of us placed his uniform on the chest in front of the bed according to regulation. The shirt had to be folded to a rectangle of the exact same dimensions as the pants, with the cap placed neatly on top of the pile. I was not exactly skilled at it, but I thought I had done a pretty decent job. There were about eighty of us in the sleeping quarters filled with bunks. When the captain entered, we got out of our beds and snapped to attention in our pajamas. The captain halted at my bed, his gaze on my folded pile. "I shall fuck this cap of yours!" he hollered. The captain could only be answered in one way: "Yes Sir, Comrade Captain!" In Serbian military code, "yes sir" was replaced with "razumem," meaning "understood." So, I duly replied, "razumem, druže kapetane!" (understood, comrade captain!) except that I did not enunciate "razumem" with the requisite firmness but mumbled it in a way that could be heard as "understandable," or "I understand you." The captain paused for a second, then moved on. Nothing happened. In any case, my cap was aligned perfectly with the edges of the folded shirt and pants. The only problem was that the five-pointed red star on the front piece faced the rear wall instead of the door as it was supposed to. I simply turned it in the right direction.

In a word, if you find yourself in a group, you will soon be under pressure to behave in a certain way, even if it's not a concentration camp. Of course, in a concentration camp all of this plays out in a far more cruel and inhumane fashion. For all intents and purposes, you don't have elbow room to act on your own. What could István Tóth have done? Was he supposed to pull fake punches? Or increase the intervals between his commands of "get down" and "get up"? Admittedly, it was his own decision to accept to serve in the camp. However, it so happened that the alternative was for him to become a prisoner in some German camp. All right, he might have joined the guerilla fight, except that he was not coerced to do so by the partisans themselves—and, apparently, he was not to be torn from his wife and newborn son, or the land he cultivated, except by coercion or force. Had I been his lawyer, I would have had no qualms about arguing that István Tóth, a farmer in Hódegyháza, had faced an extremely difficult predicament, although I would not go as far as to say that he made the right decision.

Let me pause at the single specific charge of the entire indictment: his use of a hardwood stake. The prosecutor pointed out that István Tóth wielded it so fiercely that the stake broke under the blows he meted out to the prisoners. István Tóth himself claimed that he brought the stake down to bear only "two or three times," and then only to separate Milan Kojičin and Stevica Ostojin, who had come to blows themselves. Then again, using a stick is hardly the proper way to break up a fight. It is not easy to tell the difference between what seems natural in a given situation and wrought-up state of mind from what is truly natural. And if you cannot make that distinction, you will be held responsible when the situation has changed.

It is conceivable that István Tóth treated the prisoners more leniently than the other guards did, perhaps even helping them here and there. At least this much is hinted at by the testimony of several former prisoners, based on which the local People's Committee determined that he had not committed any egregious offense. However, he did not, and could not, back out of all expectations, and for this he must be condemned with good reason. His guilt is compounded by the notoriety of the Macahalma camp. In 1950, it was virtually impossible to acquit anyone who had served as a guard there. True enough, István Tóth hastened to join the partisans after the liquidation of the camp, although the prosecutor argued, correctly by any reckoning, that he had not done so out of sincere conviction. One might add that it was not sincere conviction that had led him to agree to serve in the camp in the first place.

István Tóth, the defendant "reportedly without criminal record," was sentenced to three years in prison. I am not sure he comprehended everything that happened to him in his life. In his diary, Sándor Márai quotes a sentence by Lermontov's orderly. When asked by the poet whether he understood his poems, the orderly replied, "If I understood them, they would not be poems." For his part, István Tóth could have rightly said: "If I understood it, it would not be life."

V.

DIVORCES, NEAR DIVORCES, AND SHAM DIVORCES

1. A NEAR DIVORCE

After I graduated, and before I started into my academic career, I worked for roughly half a year in the family office. One of my first cases was a near divorce. I was in the larger office with windows that looked onto the street. My father worked there too. Between the windows there was a section of wall covered by a bookcase, in it were ornate volumes of Hungarian law books. By 1962 these were merely placeholders in Becskerek. There was also a huge *Corpus Juris Hungarici* in a brown leather binding. It was half a meter tall; it couldn't be put beside the others because it didn't fit on the shelf. It laid flat on top of the bookcase. It would have been treacherous if it was standing. My chair and my desk were in front of the bookcase. The desk wasn't entirely my own. The middle drawer was emptied for me, while in the others the earlier contents remained. Of course, I knew the office, it was in the same house I was born (in the strict sense of the word, at that time childbirth happened at home and not in the hospital). To the right of the office (if we were looking towards the street) was the living room, which we named the piano room. There was no need for me to leave or move elsewhere to begin work as a lawyer. I was twenty-three years old. The office had entered its seventieth year.

The goings-on in the office often reminded me of my own past experiences. This is how it was with the near divorce, too. A twenty-five or thirty-year-old, red-haired young man called Uroš sat opposite me. My father was at a hearing, Mr. Göttel sat at the typewriter, so there were three of us in the room. Rather embarrassed, and with a slight stammer, Uroš said that if it was possible, he would like to speak to me in private. Mr. Göttel had something to tend to in the filing room (inside the family we called it the "stable" because of its former role, though since I was born it was a filing room). I asked him to see to some matters before he carried on with his typing, and we were alone. Uroš began by telling me he and his wife had married in the summer of 1954. His story outlined some sexual concerns and a wavering self-confidence.

I was a fifteen-year-old teenage boy in 1954. Uroš may have been around twenty. One summer evening—perhaps the very day of Uroš's wedding—my father and I returned home from Little America (in Becskerek, there was a part of town called Little America, *Kisamerika*). I think we might have been coming from Bencze's home. A while before the Little Bridge and the reformed church, we headed along opposite the entrance of Plank Garden, when a group of singing and gesticulating young men came the other direction. They sang: "Više vredi tvoja mala pička / nego cela zemlja Američka," which in English means "There's more of worth in your small c*nt / than in the whole American land." In Serbian the rhyme was just right.

They sang with gusto, and repeated these two lines several times. Perhaps in the background of this striking value judgement, announced from street to street, was Tito's policy of non-alignment which valued neither America, nor the Soviet Union more than the other. It could even be understood as a mark of honor that it was America that was chosen as a parallel, because clearly they wanted to express that their female acquaintance was more important than even the most important. The case may also be that the rhyme played a role in America serving as a comparison (pička – američka). The young men also wielded two bottles of *pálinka* spirits.

When they had passed, there was an awkward silence between myself and my dad. Neither of us knew where we'd left the conversation. The singing young men had opened a door into a reality that was not a subject of discussion between us. And suddenly there it was. For a while neither of us spoke, but then my father must have seen that the conspiratorial silencing of what had occurred wouldn't resolve this ever so awkward shared experience, but only strengthen it, and so he spoke: "Those are some plain-spoken young men."

Of course, my father likely knew that as a fifteen-year-old I must have been curious about such subjects. And it was unlikely he would have been surprised to learn that amongst ourselves, my classmates and I dwelled on these questions. They often came up in the Proleter swimming and water polo club. As far as being informed goes, the expectations of the environment were indeed high. I tried not to give away that I knew less than I should. There are such situations in life, of course. At fifteen this was very unsettling. Only later, when I knew more, did it become clear that the others actual knowledge and experience hadn't reached the declared level either. But for this revelation I still had to wait. Once the older brother of a classmate broke things down for us—he must have been sixteen or seventeen years old. He acted as though he were ahead of us, and we didn't doubt him. I still remember one stylistically surprising sentence: "I've hoisted plenty of girls onto my root already." We laughed amicably of course. But the half-baked metaphor bothered me, that he made a cheap routine of the big event we still longed after, and had merely imagined. Had a similar sentence been said in a different context, then I likely would have thought it a mere laughable vulgarity, but I still felt too uncertain in that area to identify it as a vulgarity.

I also remember, in those days we remarked a lot on a certain sentence, albeit this time with a grin. Uncle Vili, who did odd jobs, was the one who said it. He was an unusual man. I vaguely remember his surname was Loch, but I might be mixing him up with the name of someone else who lived in the Becskerek scene at the time. Uncle Vili was a day-laborer, he was taken off to the camp as a German after the war. After he was released, he became a laborer, and acted a little oddly. He would stop adults and children alike on the street to ask something or say something, mostly in German. He often exchanged words with my friends and I. There were some who simply noted him down as being "not normal." Many people—a little cruelly—went along with the jape, and were amused. Once he was scrubbing a courtyard, and he asked the owner: "Sagen Sie mir Herr B..., ficken noch die Leute?," or "Tell me Mr. B., do people still f**k?" Many people spread this story like it was an honest question, with the explanation that he no longer did, and because the implicit gestures and behaviors had changed around him in the meantime, he'd become uncertain. Hence, he asked if they still do it. Of course, it's also possible Uncle Vili intended it to be a joke. I can also imagine that being released from the lager, paired with being regarded as a halfwit, posed a very unique opportunity. Our view of him provided him with a mask, from behind which perhaps he too was laughing at the people who, thinking him deranged, let go of their caution, and gave stupid answers. The case may also be that the reality was a mixture of all these.

Returning to my client Uroš, the point of the story follows. He thought he was living in a happy marriage with his wife, but one night he noticed that the bed was empty beside him, his wife had gone out somewhere. He searched the whole house. Their street was in the neighborhood where I went to school. More precisely, it was a little further along, towards Melence, where there were rows of village houses. When he found no one home, he went out to the courtyard, and there he saw his wife having sex with the neighbor in the haystack. I could see on Uroš that this was a recent event. It had happened three days before he came to the office. "Šta kažete, gospodine doktore?!" he asked, or "What do you say to that, Doctor?" (I would add that at the time I didn't have a doctorate. I was simply a graduated law student and legal apprentice, but I'd begun to get used to being called Doctor. The clients were less informed. My grandfather had been granted a doctor's title with his Budapest law degree, my father when he graduated in Zagreb. My degree from Belgrade did not grant me the title of doctor.) I avoided declaring my own opinion, and I asked him what he did when he found his wife in the act. He didn't respond immediately. He said about his wife that "[she] is the best lover. You must know, Doctor, what that means." It seemed Uroš respected the legal profession more than I did. Yet with my own education and experience I couldn't deduce precisely what it meant if someone were (in Becskerek, for example) the best lover. By all means, it was a strange feeling that eight years after I had heard the clear-cut standpoint of the "plain-spoken young men" as a curious outsider, lacking confidence in my own knowledge, I was now sitting in the wooden office chair of the all-knowing. I was the one who knew what her being "the best lover" meant. I would add that I was not entirely sure that I had understood the remark. My feeling was he hadn't expressed himself properly. What he'd said (that his wife was the best lover) amounted to a comparative appreciation, but his tone, and his eyes hinted at something else. They would have better fit a sentence such as "I found the woman for me."

I repeated my earlier question, as to what Uroš did after he saw what was happening in the haystack. It turned out he did nothing. Through tears he said that he was a clerk, but at home he tended to his garden and kept turkeys. He thought he had a happy life. He didn't want to tear this image to shreds. Peering from behind a second haystack, he watched until the end, then returned to bed. This way something was mixed into the pain: the tables had turned, and he knew more than his wife. "My wife doesn't know that I know," he said with a sort of bitter pride. He said nothing about the neighbor.

I turned the conversation in a direction as such a statement might naturally lead in the legal profession. I asked him whether anyone else knew about this breaking of their marriage, mentioning that if both the wife and the neighbor denied it, it would be difficult to prove reason for divorce. To my surprise he said he didn't want a divorce. "I'm asking, Doctor, that you prohibit her from doing this again."

Sometimes the profession is too narrow for life to fit within it. I told him that a lawyer can't prohibit such things, nor could anyone. He didn't believe me. He offered to pay more, as long as I took care of it. The conversation became more and more uncomfortable. I saw there was no chance I was going to convince him to believe that the law stopped at the threshold of his specific problem. In order to get out of the situation, I told him I would write to his wife, but I couldn't guarantee any result. He left in faith. Since I was prepared to fabricate a product of questionable ethics, I told him I couldn't accept money.

Then I wrote a letter to his wife with a letterhead, an official tone, and a stamp. I described what had come to my attention, that she had cheated on her husband. I included the date it had happened. I informed her that this could have grave legal consequences, and if the incident were to happen again, then proceedings would begin, as a result of which she would incur the aforementioned consequences. I didn't write that the "grave consequence" which I mentioned was in fact divorce. Yugoslav law knew no other consequence. And so, though my letter was not untrue, it was misleading.

That was all I could do. Roughly a month later, Uroš sought me out and brought me a bottle of homemade *pálinka* spirits in a wicker cover. He said my letter had been very effective. His wife was back on the right track. The case may also be that she was just more cautious, but I accepted the palinka, and so I became an adult.

2. DIVORCES AND SHAM DIVORCES IN THE WAKE OF WORLD WAR TWO

In life there are things able to limit the omnipotence of an ideology. This can of course cause irritation. The all-powerful do not want to recognize limits—or even to see them. At such times measures are taken against reality. Many times, marriages and divorces have formed the stage for the bouts of ideologies and life.

In his *Carnets*, Camus notes an anecdote of which a marriage stands at the center. Stalin was vexed that Krupskaya, Lenin's widow, often made critical comments regarding the Soviet reality. Sanctions were mentioned. Stalin threatened to name a new widow for Lenin. I don't know whether this would have resolved things. Krupskaya wasn't just a widow, but a legend, too—and not only in the Soviet Union. I saw the same in Atlanta, where I would often teach a semester at Emory University. Once in the '90s when I received the list of students, an unusual first name turned up: Krupsy. During the first class I learned that she was a black student from Jamaica. A year later, when she was no longer my student, I met her husband, an Indian doctor. Once they invited myself and my wife to dinner. Now that were speaking more freely, her name came up. Krupsy explained that her father was a communist (in Jamaica), her parents respected Lenin and Krupskaya, too. They were overjoyed when their daughter was born and wanted to give her an especially important name. Krupskaya seemed the best solution. (It's unclear whether they knew if "Krupskaya" was a surname or a Christian name.) Then there was only to make the legendary name fit into the Jamaican linguistic world, and so it became Krupsy. So, it can't have been easy for Stalin either. If he did replace Lenin's widow, he would still be powerless against the legend that had spread as far as Jamaica.

Besides Stalin's threats, other attempts were made to put an end to the reality-islands of marriages and divorces, to have them sink into the depths of the reigning ideologies. In Nazi Germany, there were attempts to produce marriages and divorces according to patriotic principles, and—just as with Stalin and Krupskaya—to place them above life and death. In his book *The Language of the Third Reich*, Klemperer writes of "post-fact marriages." Those women awaiting marriage, whose partners fell as German soldiers in the war, could still marry them afterwards, thus guaranteeing that Hitler's soldiers would be immortal. The girls who had post-fact marriages became greater patriots than those who merely learned their boyfriends had lost their lives. We can imagine there were girls who were inspired to take this symbolic step not only by patriotism, but also genuine love and pain. But it wasn't these girls who created the institutions of post-fact marriage. As a lawyer, I wonder what happened to those girls, those post-fact wives who later really did want to marry a man, and had the opportunity. Did they divorce their non-existent husband? Or did they lean on the fact that their husband was no longer living? The death of a husband changes the situation, and makes a new marriage possible. But what if the situation hadn't changed, because the husband wasn't alive at the time of marriage either?

In Becskerek, as far as I know, patriotism wasn't able to substitute for a living husband before the priest or the registry. Therefore, during the war too, marriages were genuine. As for divorces, things were more complicated. In many cases the reasons for divorce didn't occur between the married couple. The goal of the divorce wasn't to break a human relationship, but to hide it.

On December 9, 1944, my grandfather writes the following in his diary:

> *... For the last three days I have lent my room to Piros and Józsi, who alongside the clerk Ivkovics are receiving and hearing out complaints. Here they record the details in writing and prepare the petitions. Over the last three days the stream of complaints has been endless. Somehow news has spread that fate will be kinder to those women who file for divorce against their—German—husbands. These unfortunate women are lining up at the door. They are crammed into the corridor, and into my own room from seven in the morning until the evening. The complaints are being written; the divorce suits are being prepared. Everything of course is done on favor, pro bono. Today we accept money from nobody; one person, a woman who escaped from the camps, brought ten liters of wine into the kitchen out of gratitude.*

I already cited this entry in another text to give a sense of the general mood. Now I'd like to present the news and divorces mentioned in the entry in greater detail. Several letters show which news, scare-stories, experiences, and doubts the clients were attempting to navigate. On February 19, 1945, Mrs. Béla Bernauer (née Rozália Soós) writes to my grandfather from Szerbittabé (or Srpski Itebej):

> My husband, Béla Bernauer has been in a lager since the liberation. He is currently in Zemun. As a Hungarian woman, apparently I should be able to help my husband's release from the lager, but I don't know how. Though my husband is the child to German parents, he was raised as a Hungarian, as is supported by the affixed school certificate. During the occupation, due to his severe injury, he was only able to serve in the auxiliary services as a German soldier. ... Since news has spread that women of my age, and children will be relocated to Russia for 15 years, Your advice is crucial, as to how I can spare my children and myself this fate.
>
> The borough council advises urgent divorce, which I am only willing to undergo should there be no other means.
>
> Insofar as the relocation news is true, I would like it to be clarified whether it's possible that a Hungarian relative (perhaps my aunt) could adopt my children.

In the various sorts of democracies in which I've been, I often saw the following formula. The opposition learn that what can be seen or pointed out are the actual and alleged mistakes of those in power; what can be done is the denunciation of those actual and alleged mistakes. During an election campaign this consolidates in creeds and slogans, and beyond this point the visual angle can no longer be adjusted. After any potential change of power everything is guided by the same adversary, it becomes the solitary guiding principle: do the opposite of what the preceding government did. Is this what it was like after fascism, too? Yes, to a degree. Which of course brought a lot of good, but also bad. Particularly when that opposite was defined in the shallowest of terms, through the discrimination and exclusion of Germans. Whereas if we plunged a little deeper we might come to the exclusion of discrimination itself.

When the entry dated December 9, 1944 came into my hands and I read it, I was already a lawyer and the question arose for me on what grounds the wives filed for divorce. What was the presented reason? For a good time now, the law has addressed the question of when a wife can leave her husband, or a husband his wife. The Law Code of Hammurabi even specifies what a wife can expect should her husband be swept off by war. According to articles 133 and 134, if a man is taken prisoner of war, but there is food in his house, and in spite of that the wife "doesn't guard her own body and has gone to another house," then this wife is to be thrown in the water. But if there is not any food in the house, then a woman who goes to another house can't be punished. This law was passed two thousand years before Christ. In 1944, with regard to husbands taken to the lagers or reported missing, the same question arose differently, though parallels do remain.

A German Husband and a Hungarian Wife

File No. 12268

From among the documents I take out a petition for divorce, which was submitted on the very day off the diary entry, December 9, 1944. The petitioner is Anna Kraus, née Barna, her address is 11 Uroša Predića, Petrovgrad. The husband, or respondent, is Stevan Kraus, whose address is recorded as "place of residence unknown." (It would seem half a year earlier his name was still Stefan—and not Stevan—in official documents.)

Previously while reading the documents I was searching for an answer to the question of whether this case was genuine, or could be labelled a sham divorce. I heard from my father that a great number of the petitions submitted en masse weren't genuine divorce cases. Just as my grandfather writes in his diary, after news spread that "fate will be kinder" to those women who file for divorce against their husbands, many just did so to avoid the lager. There was also hope it might protect some of their money.

The other issue with mixed marriages was that it blurred the racial, national or class logic. If a woman who was one of us wedded someone of the other kind—instead of giving herself to us—it confused the "we're the hero kind, they're the lesser and or evil kind" formula. Though it doesn't null all stigmatization, it does ease the situation if the wife files for divorce. According to what I heard from my father and my grandfather, among the divorces filed against German husbands there were both genuine and sham divorces. There were marriages which truly had run aground. Yet in many cases, a divorce wasn't the wife's primary goal, but to escape a fate that had spread to her too. There were some cases when the husband and wife entered into a conspiracy to avoid fate, they discussed the divorce so as to spare something of their joint assets, with the hope that "if this passed," their married life could soon return. There were similar formulae under the German occupation, when divorcing one's Jewish spouse was at times desertion, at others the building of a joint future. When a law becomes inhumane, circumvention of the law becomes the human thing to do. During the German occupation there were sham property sales, too. The German term was *Scheinverkauf*, namely, a sham sale. Jewish property owners tried to have their estates put in non-Jewish friends' names to avoid the properties being seized, and so the real owner could get them back "if this passed." The occupying authorities, however, issued an order on April 24, 1941, which banned the sale of Jewish property, and threatened to court martial those who didn't respect the ban.

Divorces weren't prohibited, either under the German occupation, or afterwards. In December 1944, however, the new courts hadn't yet begun operating, and so Mrs.. Anna Kraus Barna didn't submit her request for a divorce to the court, but to the Petrovgrad Territorial Command (*Komanda područja Petrovgrad*). At the top of the request is a signed confirmation that the request was handed in, no. 1965/44. on December 9, 1944. (In this number, the 44 evidently represents the year, while the 1965 may represent the number of divorce claims filed in 1944.) It also states that Anna Barna Kraus received a separate official confirmation that she had handed in the claim. This official confirmation may have "made fate kinder to her." Otherwise, it would appear this wasn't a sham divorce, and so suggest the petitioners' statements, though those may have been altered for the circumstances. This much becomes clear in a written note, which my father apparently did not share with the court. Yet this case still belongs to a category in which an escape from a fate was the primary goal.

From a lawyer's perspective (but not just a lawyer's), it is interesting what kind of legal provision the petition for divorce relies upon. Nowadays, few people know that after World War One, when the province of Vojvodina (Vajdaság) had been annexed on to Serbia (that is, Yugoslavia), in two parts of Vojvodina, in Bánát and in Bácska, the 1894 Hungarian law no.

XXXI on the Marriage Act remained in force. This was one of the first European laws to place civil marriages in the foreground. Marriage in the church was still permitted, but a civil marriage was the one that had legal consequences. In the preamble for this law, it is stated: "Mixed marriages are an important element of Hungarian society and will continue to play a significant role in the future due to the country's demographic situation." It states that in 1889 there were 11,264 mixed marriages, and in 1890 there were 11,090, which amounts to 9.5% of all marriages. The preamble determines: "A unified marriage law, by its very nature, can only be of the State, and this implies a separation of powers between Church and State in matrimonial matters." In Vojvodina, mixed marriages were commonplace and natural, and this may have been one of the reasons that 1894 Hungarian law remained in force. To be more precise it remained in force in Bánát and Bácska. In the third part of Vojvodina, Syrmia, the Austrian Civil Code was applied, according to which marriage in the church was the only recognized form. In any case, in Becskerek the 1894 Hungarian law was in force in the '20s and '30s, under the fascist occupation too, and in the first two years of communism. On April 9, 1946 the new Yugoslav marriage law was put in force.

Anna Barna Kraus requested a divorce based on a rather uniquely extensive interpretation of the 1894 law paragraph 80(d). The laws were written in the previous century, but the atmosphere and the interpretation were new. The reason for the divorce was that the husband was German. The question was how to make the circumstances decisive. In paragraph 80, it states:

> A marriage may be dissolved at the request of one of the spouses if the other spouse: … (d) has after the marriage been sentenced to jail or to imprisonment for less than five years or to jail for an offence motivated by a desire for gain. [And] for one of the reasons listed above, the marriage is so distressed that, for the individual making the request to dissolve the marriage, further matrimony would be unbearable.

Stefan (Stevan) Kraus hadn't been convicted by any court. But on November 21, 1944, barely more than two weeks before the divorce claim was submitted, a new enactment stated that all German assets were enemy assets (unless the German in question had fought for the partisans). Most

Germans were taken to lagers, camps. In the divorce claim it is stated that "the new legislation regarding Germans has greatly worsened the legal position of ethnic Germans." It only takes another step of logic, or a leap, let's say, to deduce that the wife of a German would end up in similar circumstances as those wives whose husbands were sentenced to jail or to imprisonment "for less than five years." Therefore, a German husband was as much a burden on the wife as a husband serving a prison sentence, and the new social and legal judgement of the Germans "had distressed the marriage" and made "further matrimony unbearable."

Looking at the orders relating to the 1894 law, I can see that paragraph 79 may also have been taken into consideration, according to which one of the married couple may request the marriage be dissolved if their spouse was sentenced to death or at least five years in prison. In which case it is not necessary to prove that matrimony has become "unbearable." Curiously, at the time this cruel parallel was drawn, regarding ethnic Germans and convicts as equal, still, a handbrake appears: it was those sentenced to less than five years, not more than, who were equated with Germans. Even within absurdity there remains the desire for nuance.

Enforcing paragraph 80(d), which refers to comparable, or arguably comparable conditions, was not my father's own legal invention. I don't know on what consideration, but this became the standard practice. On the divorce claim I can see the markings of serial production. There is a basic text in blue ink (presumably Mr. Göttel typed up plenty of copies in advance with a blue typewriter ribbon), then the names and other precise details are added in grey. The whole thing is barely more than half a page. The sentence containing the broad interpretation of paragraph 80(d) was typed in blue, and to my knowledge, we weren't the only office to use this wording. A practice must have developed in which the husband's German status could be drawn (forced) within the scope of paragraph 80(d). At times life can be concealed by legal practice.

The sentence wasn't handed down by the Territorial Command, but by the Petrovgrad County Court. When the proceedings began, the first (then commonplace) problem was that the respondent's place of residence was "unknown." Given the apparatus of the law-based state had begun to be reinstated (especially in places where it didn't put more crucial interests at risk), the proceedings also attempted to guarantee, or at least show, hope for the husband, too. In October 1945 in the hall of the Petrovgrad court a notice was put up on the wooden noticeboard, calling on Stevan Kraus to attend the hearing. The call was also published in the Vojvodina Official Gazette. Stevan Krause didn't turn up at the hearing, and this caused no surprise. A court-appointed attorney stepped in, however, to represent his interests.

On December 5, 1945 the hearing took place. One witness was heard, I can see his name was János Dávid. He said that the respondent had joined the fascist army, later escaped, and his whereabouts were unknown. Both the husband and the wife had said to János Dávid before the liberation that they wouldn't be living together any longer, and they wanted to divorce.

It is not only from János Dávid's statement (maybe genuine, maybe he was on good terms with the wife) that I know this was not a sham divorce. Among the documents there is a handwritten reminder, in which my father wrote that according to Mrs. Kraus's own words, she had news of her husband. She heard he was living in Mauthausen with "some woman." Mrs. Kraus also said that she received a letter from him, in which he wrote that he, too, wanted a divorce and she could show it if need be.

I found the husband's letter, or part of it. It is written by hand, in German, from a page torn out of a notebook. The pages are marked with Roman numerals: a three, and a four on the back. It is possible Mrs. Kraus didn't bring the rest or it fell out of the file while being moved. In the documents I can't see what the husband's occupation was, but from the handwriting and the spelling it is apparent he wasn't in an intellectual line of work. The sentences are thrown together. In many places he writes "f" for "v" (for example: ferstanden and ferlassen, instead of verstanden and verlassen), which, I believe is a typical Bánát German error. In the letter, he writes: "you've changed, and now you think in a completely different way," and that is why "it's best if we divorce, and take no more notice of one another." He also requests she return to him his cloths and underwear.

There are no handwritten letters belonging to Anna Kraus Barna among the documents. Her occupation is recorded as housewife. During the case she receives a certificate of poverty, and so doesn't have to pay the cost of stamp duty.

Jewish Husbands, German and Hungarian Wives

A Jewish Husband and a German Wife
File No. 11933

Béni Grosschmid, one of the most prominent figures in the history of Hungarian civil law, was of German descent. He Hungarianized his name to Benő Zsögöd, and for a while he published under this name, then returned to his original name of Grosschmid. He was a close relative of Sándor Márai, the revered Hungarian writer, originally called Sándor Grosschmid, who mentioned him in a few of his writings. Béni Grosschmid wrote a book in 1908 about the 1894 Hungarian marriage law. He highlights the significance of the law's heeding of the importance of mixed marriages, and its consequent placement of civil marriages in the foreground. In 1941 in Becskerek this Hungarian law that respects mixed marriages is still in force. At the same time, we have German occupation. The pairing isn't harmonious. The occupying Germans aren't Béni Grosschmid's kind of Germans.

In the dossier there is a letter which shows the occupying authorities in a light different than how people (me included) might usually imagine them. I don't know how many other examples there are, but for me it is surprising that the German authorities hesitate, and confess as much in writing. The letter was written on July 15, 1941 addressed to my grandfather. My grandfather's name is written: Emmerich Varadi. The "i" at the end of the surname must have come from a Serbian document, as in German "y" is used. Emmerich from Imre however is undoubtedly a creation of the new German authority. The letter was written by the Judenamt (Jewish Office), a department within the Kreswirstcahftsamt (Circuit Economic Office). After all, if one divorced a Jew, there were economic consequences regarding the seizure of Jewish assets, hence in the divorce trial there was need for an economic office's stance. The German authority's letters signs off with a "Heil Hitler," and looks like this:

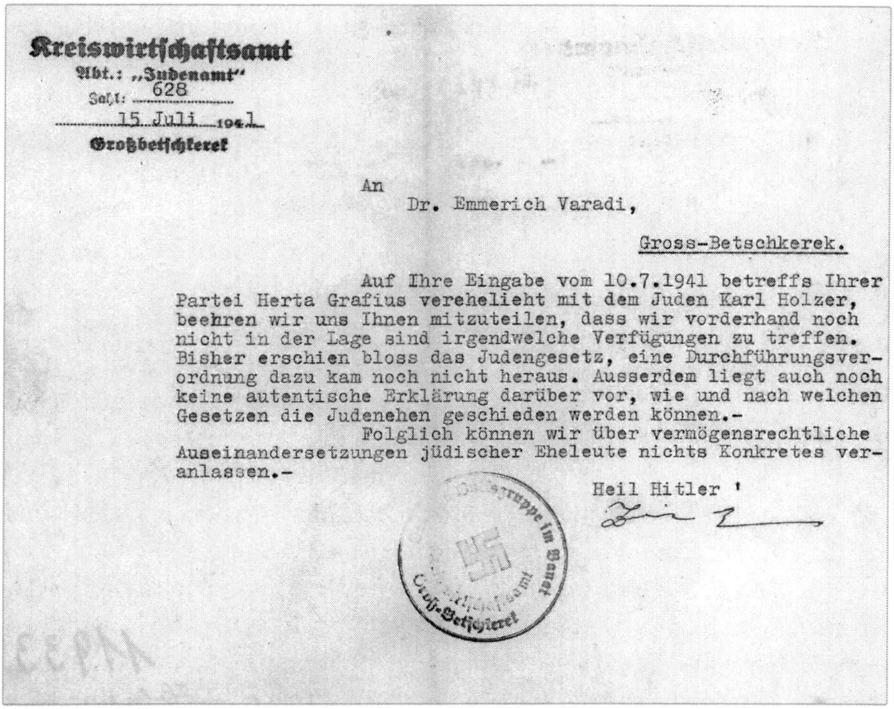

Kreiswirtschaftsamt
Abt.: „Judenamt"
Zahl: 628
15. Juli 1941
Großbetschkerek

An
Dr. Emmerich Varadi,
Gross-Betschkerek.

Auf Ihre Eingabe vom 10.7.1941 betreffs Ihrer Partei Herta Grafius verehelieht mit dem Juden Karl Holzer, beehren wir uns Ihnen mitzuteilen, dass wir vorderhand noch nicht in der Lage sind irgendwelche Verfügungen zu treffen. Bisher erschien bloss das Judengesetz, eine Durchführungsverordnung dazu kam noch nicht heraus. Ausserdem liegt auch noch keine autentische Erklärung darüber vor, wie und nach welchen Gesetzen die Judenehen geschieden werden können.-

Folglich können wir über vermögensrechtliche Auseinandersetzungen jüdischer Eheleute nichts Konkretes veranlassen.-

Heil Hitler!

The point of the letter is that the Jewish Office can't take a stance, because the Jewish law has been passed, but there are still no executive orders. Besides this, "there doesn't exist any official explanation as to how and on what legal basis Jewish marriages can be dissolved." According to the closing sentence, for the time being the Jewish Office cannot give any concrete response as to the legal financial consequences of Jewish marriages. This tentative, equivocating, "we still know nothing" stance of Becskerek fascism is intriguing. In this context, the closing "Heil Hitler!" is more of a stammer than a cheer, though this wasn't typical of the occupying powers, or in Becskerek.

The divorce was brought by Herta Holczer née Grafius against Karl Holczer, who was a Jew. From the papers it is not clear whether the husband really was a Karl, or whether he became Karl the same way my grandfather became Emmerich. He may have been known as Károly Holczer, or perhaps Karlo. In the attorney's register (presumably as a result of the wife's own information) it reads Károly. To the occupying powers, it is Karl. It is well-known that nations' mouthpieces rarely miss an opportunity to show their numbers. Following this traditional attitude, from a

German perspective, it was better if there was one more Karl, and one less Károly or Karlo. Meanwhile there was discrimination, and so things got confusing. It is not easy to follow the line if it comes to a fork. I don't know if the question ever arose among the German authorities as to whether these were still loyal Germans, if they could count one more Karl, over a Károly or a Karlo, thanks to a Jew.

The divorce suit begins on July 9, 1941, roughly three years before the Kraus divorce suit. In the Holczer case the German is the one who is escaping a Jewish husband, three years later it is the Germans being left by their spouses. In the divorce claim it states that Karl Holczer and Herta Grafius were married in 1927. From this marriage a daughter was born in 1928. They named her Klara-Herta, likely so as to keep her mother's Christian name in the amalgamation, and to resemble her father's too. In mixed marriages there is often some expression of a sense of balance. In 1941 this sense, if it even remained, no longer helped.

According to the claim, Herta was a housewife (previously a government clerk), while Karl was a dentist (in another document he is described as a dental technician). The original presented reason was that Karl had "broken the marriage," and paragraph 80(a) of the 1894 law justified the divorce, because he had "seriously violated the obligations of marriage through… his own deliberate behavior" and thereby "marring the matrimony." In the Kraus divorce suit, paragraph 80(a) is also mentioned besides 80(d), but it would seem 80(d) had become the template for proceedings against spouses of nationalities held in contempt. 80(a) speaks of "deliberate" violations of marriage obligations. Obviously it is absurd to talk about any "deliberate actions" of the husband when it was the Jewish laws and deportations which upset the marriage. In the original divorce claim it is stated that the husband left his wife in July 1941, a month and a half before the deportation. If that was the case, then there could have been talk of "the deliberate violation of marriage obligations," and the application of 80(a) wouldn't have been unreasonable. Later, however, nothing is said of him leaving her. It seems more likely the assertion was an attempt to find some way out, but the documents don't reveal the whole truth.

In November 1941 Herta hands in a new submission. In the meantime, one assumes certain standpoints of the authorities have become clear, the wife has honed her statement, and we have a better picture of what the situation really is. It states that she is a "pure Aryan," the husband a Jew. It continues:

> As a result of the orders of the German Military Command against Jews and Gypsies, there have been crucial changes in the respondent's situation. He has been stripped of the right to any assets, and taken away for forced labor; there he's been deprived of both his personal and financial freedom. This order has fundamentally altered the judgement of mixed marriages. The mixed marriage has become humiliating for the Aryan party.
>
> These far-reaching changes have put our marriage out of order to such an extent as further matrimony has been made unbearable. Hence I request the marriage be dissolved according to the analogous application of paragraph 80(d) of the Marriage Act.

And so, just like in the Kraus suit, a shelter was found under paragraph 80(d). In 1894, Hungarian legislation respects the reality of mixed marriages, and naturally such paragraphs weren't conceived of that would have regarded otherness as grounds for divorce. Then after humanity's half-century of development, it comes to the conclusion that if a husband is Jewish it is roughly equal to being sentenced to less than five years in prison, and consequently makes further matrimony unbearable.

In the divorce claim it is stated that Herta is a "pure Aryan," which at the time was necessary information, but it does sound a little arrogant. Yet I don't feel anti-Semitism in the cited part of the divorce claim, which states what sort of situation has been produced by the Military Command's order regarding to Jews and Gypsies, and how it has turned the marriage upside down. All that has been detailed here with an attorney's precision is how Jews were affected by the legislation at the time.

As I read the documents, the question arises within me whether this was a real or a sham divorce suit. Did Herta really become an anti-Semite? Or was she just afraid, and didn't want to stand alongside her husband? Did she have a chance to stand alongside him? Or did she mean to save her daughter and the family property, hoping that at some point in the future the marriage would come together again? In Herta's letters, she doesn't state that it was a sham divorce, but there would seem to be some amount of good-nature and understanding as regards her husband in her letters. Her letter dated August 16, 1941 ends with the sentence: "Unfortunately, as you probably already know, they're being taken away and I'll be in Belgrade on this matter."

If I was writing a novel, I would much more happily choose the storyline in which both Herta and Karl stand on the same side of history. It is quite likely they did, but I can't be absolutely certain. In novels we can know what happened much more precisely than in reality.

While guessing who Herta really was, it catches my eye that both she and her daughter claim alimony, for 500 dinars per month in total. This alimony was requested from the husband imprisoned in a concentration camp. At first glance this seems cruel and cynical. And following such a train of thought, it would be logical to pigeonhole Herta negatively—if there was scope for logic at the time. Were the coordinate system to suddenly shift, nothing would be in its place anymore. In the new situation it becomes illogical (what would otherwise be natural) that the husband should pay the alimony. This, however, is no longer natural, and in fact it seems an outrageous demand, because the husband is in a death camp. Yet the husband's property and money have been seized, and the alimony's debtor is therefore no longer the husband, but the occupying authorities who have taken and kept the Jewish husband's assets.

Therefore, if the alimony is passed, then a part of the seized money may return to Karl Holczer's thirteen-year-old girl and wife from the fascist authorities. This casts the demand in a totally new light. It also serves to explain why the occupying authorities were an interested party in the divorce suit. The fascist authorities take the side of the Jewish husband, against the German wife! Throughout the lawsuit, Herta's financial demands against her husband are disputed by the German authorities—presumably not to defend the Jewish husband against his German wife, but to defend the seized assets.

Another Example Along the Way

In several documents I see the choreography of the occupying authorities taking up the side of the Jewish party. The same happened in Mrs. Oswald's suit, which she brought against Béla Steiner in 1933 (File No. 12031). János Oswald was an employee of Béla Steiner's in Kikinda. One day at work, the car rolled, and János Oswald flew into a ditch and lost his life. The case began at a different attorney's office in Kikinda. Though it would be interesting, from the papers in the file I can't tell whether János Oswald tipped the car himself. The widow claimed damages from Béla

Steiner on the grounds that responsibility for the accident lied with the employer. At first instance, damages were awarded. Béla Steiner appealed, and the case went to the Becskerek Court, which is when my grandfather may have taken the Kikinda attorney József Hadik's place. Hearings were searching for agreement when the ongoing lawsuit and any potential agreement was interrupted by the German occupation, and this was not favorable for Mrs. Oswald either.

On March 1, 1942, the Becskerek Appellate Court notifies the plaintiff that proceedings cannot continue for two reasons. One reason is that the defendant is being represented by a Jewish attorney—proceedings can't continue with a Jewish attorney. The other is that the plaintiff lives in Zenta (or Senta, in Serbian). This is problematic because Zenta is on the other side of the River Tisza, in Bácska, where it is not German occupation, but Hungarian, and so the authority of the Becskerek Court doesn't extend to the claims of Mrs. Oswald. Since I was teaching conflicts of laws for many years, it occurs to me that there is an abundance of cases in which plaintiffs from one country have been suing defendants from another country. Allow me to add that Zenta (the plaintiff's place of residence), and Kikinda (the defendant's place of residence), were in the same country for centuries and still are. Just the country's name has changed. Previously it was Hungary, then it was the Kingdom of Serbs, Croats and Slovenes, then the Kingdom of Yugoslavia, finally the Socialist Federal Republic of Yugoslavia, and today, Serbia. The people were accustomed to living in the same country—hence the Zenta resident, János Oswald, worked in Kikinda. After World War Two, Banat came under German occupation, whereas Bácska (or Bačka) came under Hungarian. Miklós Horthy, Regent of Hungary, was an ally of the Germans, but the German occupiers in Becskerek saw Zenta to be unreachable (at least in terms of Mrs. Oswald's case). Yet Mrs. Oswald solved this problem. She moved from Zenta to Csóka (on the far side of the River Tisza, opposite Zenta). She moved to the home of János Mészáros, who she later married.

There was still the issue of the Jewish attorney, which was solved by the occupiers themselves, although not fully. They stepped into the shoes of the Jewish respondent. Béla Steiner's property had been seized as Jewish assets. Next they handled Steiner's property, and a non-Jewish attorney represented the German occupiers. However, so the proceedings could continue, the Kreiswirtschftsamt also had to join the suit as representative of the respondent by naming a commissar. Besides this, not only did Mrs. Oswald have to prove that responsibility lay with Béla Steiner's company for the accident, but also that neither herself, nor her two young children were Jewish or Gypsy. The certificate was issued, but the Kreiswirtschfts-amt didn't elect a commissar. My grandfather sped the matter up. In a submission dated April 2, 1942 he requested that the Jewish Office (Judenamt) of the Kreiswirtschftsamt elect a commissar within fifteen days.

This didn't happen, in fact things became even more complicated, the Jewish Office sold Steiner's property to a German shareholding company, Treuhand A.G. Afterwards, further steps could only be taken towards the Southeastern Military Command (Militärbefehlshaber Südost).

It is interesting that the fascists were being crafty, too. They played for time, and they didn't elect a commissar, so meanwhile the Jewish asset could be separated from not only the legal owner, but the creditors too. It is no easy question which way the dominators might suddenly want to go. Which would bring greater contentment, if they won by sweeping the rules aside, or by showing cunning superiority by bending them this way and that.

But Mrs. Oswald didn't give up. My grandfather got in touch with an attorney from Pancsova (Pančevo in Serbian), whose name was Nikolaus Bartosch (Nikola Bartoš in Serbian). He represented the German Military Command. At this name I have to stop. When I studied law in Belgrade, one of my most renowned teachers was Milan Bartoš. This isn't a common name. Could he have been a relative of Nikola Bartoš? Under the German occupation they were on different sides. I know that during the war Milan Bartoš was in captivity in Germany. It was a common story at university. According to one of the circulating stories, he had a photographic memory and used it to help his inmates. There was a newspaper in the P.O.W. camp, but only one or two copies were available very briefly. Milan Bartoš read the newspaper, memorized every word, and repeated all the articles to his inmates. For a while I thought that this was just a student legend, but then I realized there might be some truth in it when I took the comprehensive oral exam at the end of my master studies.

Milan Bartoš was a member of the board, his subject was international law. He was a corpulent man, he drank coffee from a huge cup, he was hard of breathing, and while I answered his questions he shut his eyes for some time. I wasn't sure what to make of it. His eyes were closed, and the labored breathing began to seem like snoring. Had he fallen asleep? I stopped. A brief agonizing moment passed, then Professor Bartoš opened his eyes, and said: "I know what you're thinking, but I'm listening." This eased my nerves a little, but I was ashamed. Bartoš, on the other hand continued: "I'll prove I was listening; I'll repeat what you said word for word." And he truly did repeat everything I'd said word for word for the past five minutes. He didn't leave out a single language error or unnecessary repetition. Everyone laughed, apart from myself. In the end, however, I passed.

But who was this other Bartoš, Nikola or Nikolaus Bartoš? I tried to find out something from my colleagues in Belgrade, they tried too, but without any result. And so, I don't even know if they were relatives. Nikola/ Nikolaus, the Southeastern Military Command representative, corresponded with my grandfather in German. I don't know what other cases he had. As concerned Mrs. Oswald, his letters appear to be those of a decent attorney. He recommended an agreement, and agreement then arrived, which. Mrs. Oswald accepted.

The occupying Circuit Economic Office's craft bore no results. Mrs. Oswald successfully brought the case before the Southeastern Military Command (Militärbefehlshaber Südost) and an agreement was reached. On May 24, 1944, Mrs. Oswald confirmed with her signature that in a lawsuit against "Béla Steiner a former trader in Kikinda, current location unknown," she took over 90,000 dinars "for the full settlement of the claim." Béla Steiner, if he was still alive, surely wouldn't have minded.

***

Returning to the Holczer case, in addition to the alimony, Herta asks for the return of her dowry. She claims that she contributed 50,000 dinars to her husband's dental laboratory. But first, a few things have to be cleared up. Fascism is in power, but there is still some amount of law. There is no roof over the stage, but the same steps and gestures resembling some form of etiquette walk the boards in the falling rain. Jews and Gypsies are taken to death camps because they're Jews or Gypsies. And yet, a divorce case can't continue if the defendant isn't properly informed, even if the defendant is Jewish.

The court asks my grandfather to disclose the defendant's address. To make things official, my grandfather turns to the German police authorities. The answer isn't a simple one. The Serbian letter states: "On 18.8.1941 the Jewish Karl Holcer was taken away with other Jews towards Belgrade." All that is disclosed is the direction he was taken in, but not where to. Mostly everyone knew where. Then a newer certificate shows that Karl Holczer's address is: Beograd, Topolska šupa Jevrejski logor (Jewish Camp). When I sent the first draft of this text to Ivan Ivanji—who not only is a well-known writer, but an old Becskerek local and an Auschwitz survivor, too—he wrote back, and brought to my attention that there was a mistake in the occupying authorities' certificate. The address of the Belgrade camp was Topovske šupe, and not Topolska šupa. Ivanji knows this as it was there his parents had been carted off, to later lose their lives. Two months after the certificate declares the Belgrade Jewish concentration camp to be Karl Holczer's address, the Becskerek police issue a new statement on November 24, 1941. In this it states that Karl's "current place of residence is unknown."

The solution was that Herta somehow managed to contact her husband, who from this point on was represented by an attorney. Karl's attorney, Stojan Adamović was a known attorney from Becskerek. To choose him, Karl signed a blank authorization to his wife, entrusting her to pick an attorney. I would suppose that my grandfather or my father recommended who to pick.

The hearing was fixed for December 24, 1941. The next move was Herta's. In her submission dated November 28, 1941 Herta asks that the hearing not take place on December 24, because it is Christmas Eve. The court postponed the hearing to December 29.

At the hearing on December 29, 1941 standing in for Adamović is János Székely, who was still a lawyer-candidate at the time. He was roughly the same age as my father, I remember him visiting our home many times. His son Jovica was friends with my younger brother. To my knowledge, János Székely was of Jewish extraction, but it would seem this was successfully hidden during the occupation.

Concerning Herta's financial demands, it is plain to see why Karl would have helped her. He didn't dispute either the alimony, or the dowry, or the proportion of Herta's contribution to the dental laboratory. It isn't clear how Stojan Adamović or János Székely got in contact with their client. For a while, there may have been some communication between Karl and his wife. That is when Karl may have signed the blank authorization and given it to his wife. One of my father's letters also shows there was some kind of contact. In August 1941, my father asks Herta to "please be so kind as to ask your husband to write a letter to Dr. Adamović, authorizing him to acknowledge the claims made in the statement, in particular that you gave him 50000 dinars in cash." The fact that Karl didn't dispute his wife's financial demands can perhaps be explained by a lasting good relationship with his wife. It is also possible that regardless of their relationship, he would rather see his money go to his wife and his daughter, than stay with the fascist Kreiswirtschaftsamt.

On December 29, 1941, at the hearing, it was only the German commissar who disputed Herta's claims. Several witnesses confirmed the value of the dental laboratory, among them were well-known people of Becskerek, such as the dentist Schwerer, and Mária Borál. The commissar requested the hearing of new witnesses to which my father objected. The transcript of the proceedings was written in Serbian, but had to be translated to German, too. The German version is in the file. The court declared the separation from bed and board, and ruled that the defendant (essentially the German Circuit Economic Office) must pay 300 dinars plus 200 dinars alimony monthly to Herta and her daughter. As for the question of the return of the dowry, the court's stance was that it was necessary to wait for the final divorce.

After the separation from bed and board, however, the suit came to a halt. The court wasn't willing to carry the divorce case any further, because the defendant had been "taken to an unknown location." Nor was the commissar willing to continue. Afterwards our office turned to the Kreiswirtschtsamt—Juden Abteilung directly. Earlier it had been called the Judenamt. Barely a year later it became the Juden Abteilung. Therefore, it went from Jewish Office, to Jewish Department. Bureaucracy whittled away at everything back then too. In Herta's name my father requests that from December 1941, they pay 500 dinars monthly, and return the 50000 dinars with which Herta had contributed to the dental laboratory. The result was heard in April 1942. The Jewish Department rejected the court's judgement to pay alimony, but conversely, was willing to give over the entire laboratory to Herta. On April 11, 1941, Herta wrote to my father or grandfather, the letter is addressed: "Most Honorable Doctor Sir": I have received notice that I have conclusively reobtained the laboratory..."

I can see (or I want to see) that the little human trick against history was successful. But I can't see from the documents whether Karl was still living or not when the occupying authorities gave back the laboratory. It is possible that at the time Herta didn't know either. Many Becskerek Jews were transported to the Belgrade Jewish camp, and most of them lost their lives there. Herta couldn't have expected much good to come, fearing that in the end, mixed marriages might be losers against history after all.

A Jewish Man and a Hungarian Wife
File No. 11924

The divorce suit is brought by Mrs. Margit Kálmán, née Margit Engel. My father represents her. The defendant, Dr. Ferenc Kálmán didn't take part in the proceedings. I do know something of what came of the actors in this divorce suit. The husband and wife pop up in my grandfather's diary on several occasions. Margit Kálmán submits her divorce claim on June 7, 1941. The proposed reason is that her husband has left her, in March 1941 he left Becskerek for Szabadka (or Subotica, in Serbian). In the claim of course it isn't apparent, but in all likelihood Ferenc Kálmán didn't leave Becskerek because of his wife. True, the German occupation only began in April 1941, but the dread may have already set in by March.

In the folder there is a printed case file, I can see that it was printed in Petrovgrad, therefore after World War One. Yet everything is in Hungarian. For internal use it remained the office language. With exception to "Judenamt," the German term for Jewish Office. This expression found no equivalent in the other languages of Becskerek. To keep us on the Becskerek stage, I will continue to use "Judenamt" in the English too.

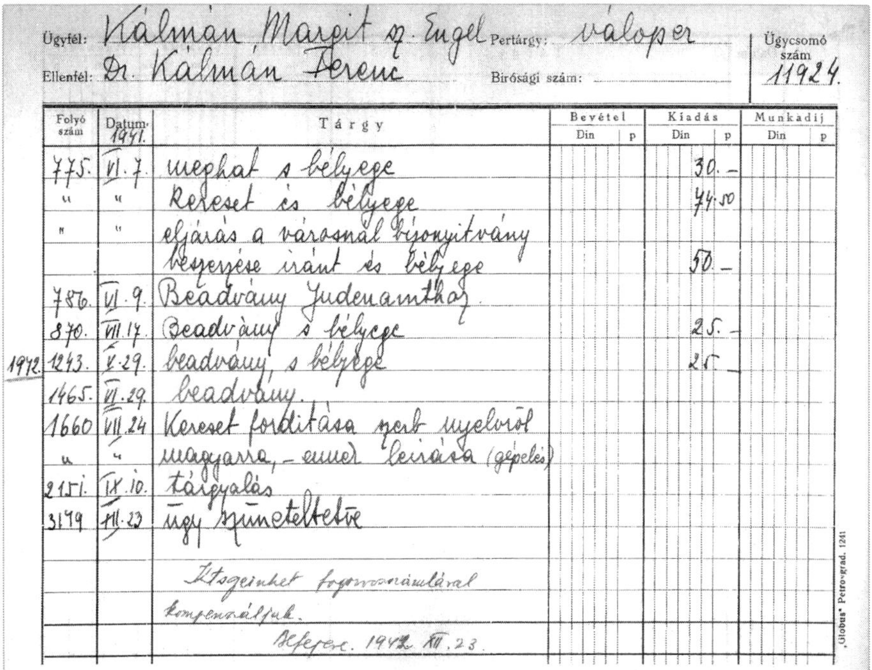

Ügyfél: Kálmán Margit sz. Engel Pertárgy: váloper
Ellenfél: Dr. Kálmán Ferenc Bírósági szám:
Ügycsomó szám 11924.

Folyó szám	Datum 1941.	Tárgy	Bevétel Din	Bevétel p	Kiadás Din	Kiadás p	Munkadij Din	Munkadij p
775.	VI. 7.	meghat. s bélyege			30.	–		
"	"	Kereset és bélyege			74.	50		
"	"	eljárás a városnál bizonyitvány						
		beszerzése iránt és bélyege			50.	–		
786.	VI. 9.	Beadvány Judenamthoz.						
870.	VII. 17.	Beadvány s bélyege			25.	–		
1942. 1243.	V. 29.	beadvány s bélyege			25.	–		
1465.	VI. 29.	beadvány.						
1660	VII. 24	Kereset forditása szerb nyelvről						
"	"	magyarra, – ennek leirása (gépelés)						
2151.	IX. 10.	tárgyalás						
3179	XII. 23	ügy szüneteltetve						
		Ktsgeinket fogorvosszámlával						
		kompenzáljuk.						
		Befejezve. 1942. XII. 23.						

„Globus" Petrovgrad. 1241

The date the claim was submitted is given, and it is also stated that two days later (on June 9, 1941) a submission was delivered to Judenamt.

Therefore, the Judenamt was immediately notified about the submission of the claim, but afterwards the suit simply dragged along. The submissions lagged. Procedural regulation was met, but it was as if the aim was obscured. On July 18, 1941 the certificate of the Becskerek authorities came before the court, showing that Ferenc Kálmán truly did leave his wife (and the town), and didn't come back. On July 22, 1941 the court halted proceedings, stating the reason that the "defendant is currently residing in a place with which contact cannot be made due to the war." Therefore, the situation is different from Karl Holczer's, who was transported to the Belgrade lager by the German occupiers. Becskerek was in Banat, where in July 1941 there was German occupation; in Bácska (ergo in Szabadka, too, where Ferenc Kálmán lived) Hungarian rule was in place.

Then in January 1942 proceedings began again, a hearing was scheduled for April 29, 1942. However, the defendant didn't show up at the hearing, which undoubtedly was no surprise to Margit Kálmán, or to my grandfather. Nor had he authorized an attorney to represent him. The court called on Margit Kálmán to share the defendant's address with the court. On May 29, 1942 Margit Kálmán answered the court that she didn't know her husband's address, she referred to the state of war, and asked for time to find out her husband's address.

If I read the documents closely, it seems this wasn't an honest answer. It might rather be called effective. This was confirmed by a message that probably didn't arrive in the post. It was written on Ferenc Kálmán's business card, which must have been brought from Szabadka. The message was written on March 13, 1942, "Dear Uncle Imre!" it begins. The following sentences are written: "As we're curious what's up with our divorce suit?! We hope it stretches like strudel pastry and never tears." It is also worth knowing that the message is written in plural, and is signed by both husband and wife (plaintiff and defendant), as "Maca and Franci," who send many kind regards.

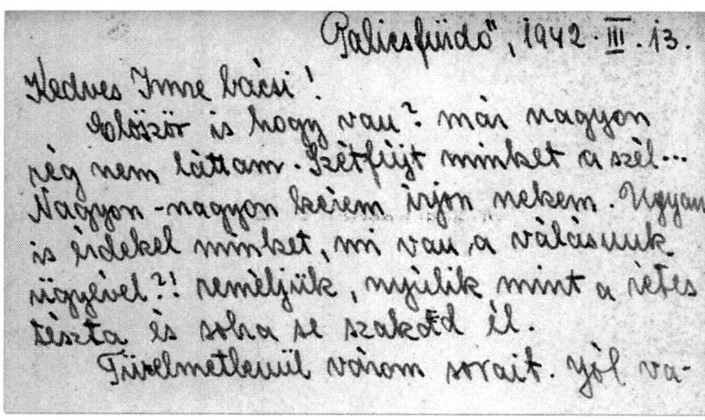

Palicsfürdő, 1942. III. 13.
Kedves Imre bácsi!
Először is hogy van? Már nagyon rég nem láttam. Szétfújt minket a szél... Nagyon-nagyon kérem írjon nekem. Ugyanis érdekel minket, mi van a válásunk ügyével?! Reméljük, nyúlik mint a rétes tészta és soha se szakad el.
Türelmetlenül várom sorait. Jól va-

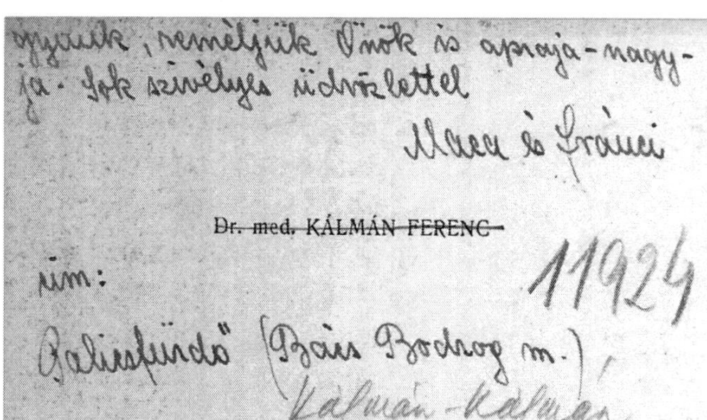

gyunk, reméljük Önök is apraja-nagyja. Sok szívélyes üdvözlettel
Maca és Franci

Dr. med. KÁLMÁN FERENC

cím: 11924

Palicsfürdő (Bács Bodrog m.)
Kálmán-Kálmán

Therefore, Margit Kálmán was in Palicsfürdő with her husband, and the two of them wrote this kind message together to my grandfather. There's no need for any complicated detective techniques to uncover that Margit Kálmán must have known where her husband was, as my grandfather must have too. It also becomes clear that the goal can't have been the divorce, but the divorce suit. Because even filing for divorce helped the situation of a Jew's wife.

At the end of the court deadline for the submission of the requested details, on July 29, 1942, Margit Kálmán states that she has established that her husband is in Palicsfürdő beside Szabadka. In 1942, Palicsfürdő and Becskerek weren't in the same country. Jews had better chances in Palicsfürdő than in Becskerek. At that time, the official languages were different (Hungarian in Szabadka, or Palicsfürdő, German and Serbian in Becskerek), the money was also different (the pengő in Szabadka and Palicsfürdő, the dinar in Becskerek). Since the divorce claim had to be forwarded to Palicsfürdő, it had to be translated from Serbian to Hungarian. The handwritten original of the translation is there among the documents. Pál Somogyi translated it.

Pál Somogyi was a contemporary of my grandfather's, they both studied law. I heard about him many times; I know that he had an unusual fate. I met him as a child, but I don't have any clear memories. Nor have any of his relatives remained in Becskerek.

The translation was forwarded on June 24, 1942, but it didn't speed things up much. Delivery wasn't successful. The next hearing was scheduled for December 23, 1942, but again the defendant didn't show. As Maca and Franci Kálmán would say, the strudel pastry was stretching, and it withstood every test. Maca Kálmán's classification was aided by her filing for divorce against her Jewish husband. She didn't really try to take any further steps.

In legal practice the accessibility of the defendant is often a crucial question. This time Becskerek and Szabadka had been swept far out of reach of one another, making delivery of documents impossible. Not long ago I was reading the documents of an American suit, in which the question of accessibility emerged in a philosophical environment. The plaintiff was Ernie Chambers, the Nebraska State Senator. The defendant was God. This is how the case was filed (you can see on the left side that

State Senator Ernie Chambers was the Plaintiff, and God was the Defendant):

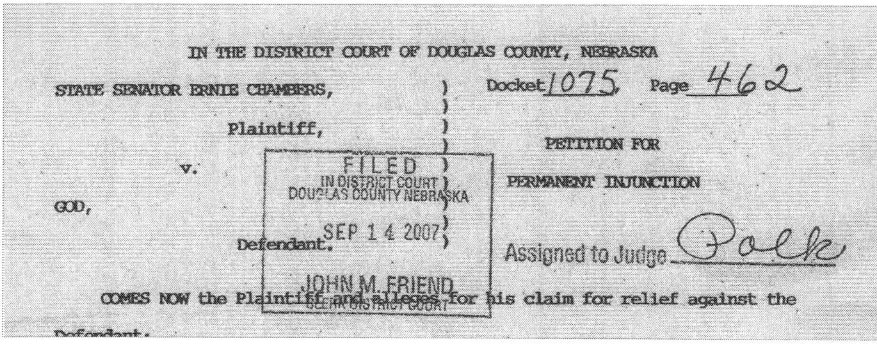
IN THE DISTRICT COURT OF DOUGLAS COUNTY, NEBRASKA

STATE SENATOR ERNIE CHAMBERS,) Docket 1075 Page 462

Plaintiff,)

v.) PETITION FOR

) PERMANENT INJUNCTION

GOD,)

Defendant.)

Assigned to Judge Polk

FILED IN DISTRICT COURT DOUGLAS COUNTY NEBRASKA SEP 14 2007 JOHN M. FRIEND CLERK DISTRICT COURT

COMES NOW the Plaintiff and alleges for his claim for relief against the Defendant:

What happened was that Senator Chambers concluded that enough was enough. On September 14, 2007, he started proceedings against God. He advanced a number of weighty claims. Count II appears to be particularly burdensome. It states: "Defendant directly and proximately has caused, inter alia, fearsome floods, egregious earthquakes, horrendous hurricanes, terrifying tornados, pestilential plagues, ferocious famines, devastating droughts, genocidal wars, birth defects, and the like."

The claim was submitted, but some procedural obstacles arose. First, the question was raised as to why he would sue God in Douglas County Nebraska of all places? In other words, did the District Court of Douglas County have jurisdiction? The plaintiff provided an answer. In the words of Senator Chambers: "This Honorable Court has jurisdiction by virtue of the fact that Defendant, being Omnipresent, is personally present in Douglas County." Hence, Douglas County may be regarded as his lawful residence (or one of his lawful residences).

Then came the procedural dilemma pertaining to postal address and proper notice. The District Court of Douglas County Nebraska noted dutifully that the accessibility of the Plaintiff is clear and unequivocal. He can be reached in the city of Lincoln, Nebraska, State Capitol Building room 1107, phone number: 1-402-471-2612. But how about the address of the Defendant (the God)? This represented a problem endangering the proceedings. It is well known that fair proceedings assume proper notice to the defendant. Proper notice normally supposes a valid postal address. Aware of the problem, Senator Chamber advanced several arguments. He respectfully requested the Honorable Court to take judicial notice of the fact that the Defendant— in addition to being Omnipresent— is also all-knowing ("Omniscient"). Hence, as stated by Senator Chambers, under the admittedly peculiar circumstances of this singular case, personal service may be waived, because the God should be deemed to have actual knowledge of this action, and this is sufficient to satisfy all requirements of law regarding notice.

With regard to service of proper notice, Senator Chambers pointed out an alternative solution as well. He stressed that in Douglas County (like everywhere else in the world) Defendant is present through agents of various religious denominations who publicly and notoriously hold themselves out to be agents of Defendant. What is also important, Defendant (God) "never publicly has disavowed explicitly any of said agents." Therefore, delivery of the claim to the address of any of these agents (priests) should be satisfactory.

I must say that as a lawyer, I enjoyed reading these arguments. Maybe Judge Polk did too, but he did not accept them. In mid-October 2008, he threw out the lawsuit against God, saying the defendant wasn't properly served due to his unlisted home address. In the words of Judge Polk: "Given that this court finds that there can never be service effectuated on the named defendant, this action will be dismissed with prejudice."

Some parallels may be drawn with the divorce case against Mr. Kálmán, although he was not a god, he was a dentist. His accessibility also represented a problem. Was he properly informed? Mr. Kálmán may not have been omniscient, but the fact is that even without court notice, he actually knew more about the case then an ordinary defendant would. But Mrs.. Kálmán and my grandfather did not use this argument. Instead, they submitted a postal address, what Senator Chambers was unable to submit. Yet, the court found that this address was "inoperative."

On December 23, 1942 the Becskerek court issued an order which suspends proceedings. The justification for such an order, written in Serbian in the Cyrillic alphabet, states: "With regard to the defendant currently residing abroad—in Hungary—a state with which the seat of the court cannot make contact due to events which occurred, for the aforementioned reasons the proceedings must be officially suspended, subject to the mentioned complications." The situations of Becskerek and Szabadka amidst "the events which occurred" (that is, in history) in

December 1942 are thus recorded in writing. Here the divorce case comes to end. The suspension of the trial became permanent.

I search for some form of continuation. The names of the principal actors are familiar to me. But on what grounds can one state that a name is a familiar name? It's difficult to say. I believe that I heard them plenty of times during card games. My parents held card parties, I myself didn't play but I joined them if there were pastries involved. My mother played cards right until her ninety-ninth year, in the last years she played alone with Maca Ormay, a previously well-known actress of Becskerek. I'm certain Maca Ormay mentioned the Kálmáns more than once, but I don't remember what she said. I know that she mentioned the husband by his nickname "Franci." It feels as though they talked about Franci Kálmán having curly hair, but perhaps the rippling sounds of "Franci" just naturally draw such an association. Had I got my hands on the Kálmán file sooner, I could have asked Maca Ormay, but she passed away a few years ago. I asked an acquaintance of mine from Becskerek, whose mother was also from a Kálmán family, but she didn't know. I asked others too, but nobody knew. And so, my only place of reference is my grandfather's diary, in which it turns out that after the war the Kálmáns ended up among the survivors, and it seems the marriage even survived the "events which occurred."

On April 14, 1945, the diary entry begins: "This afternoon I was contacted by Maca Kálmán who has now moved back from Bácska with her family for good..." Therefore, it is unlikely the plaintiff was paying the defendant a brief visit in Bácska, but they must have continued their married life there, while the German occupation carried on in Becskerek, and so did the sham divorce.

Later, in several diary entries I see Ferenc Kálmán's and Margit Kálmán's names among the birthday and name day visitors. In two cases, Ferenc Kálmán didn't come in person, but wrote a letter from Eszék (or Osijek). I can only guess what took him to Eszék. Perhaps a position, since they were no more private dental surgeries? Reserve military service? At my grandfather's eightieth birthday Mrs. Kálmán is in attendance, and she recites a poem. According to the diary: "I.III.1947. Saturday... Then Mrs. Engel Kálmán stood, and recited Gyula Juhász's poem entitled 'Mindig' (Always)..." The poem ends with these lines:

So life went on, I went on further,
Forever singing, forgetting forever.

After Mrs. Kálmán, there came Gyurka Freund-Baráth. His own bespoke poem is in this book too, in the section entitled The Freund/ Baráth File.

There is one more piece of information in the diary which could put us straight. It would seem the Kálmáns—presumably at the beginning of the fifties—moved to Novi Sad, as shown in the following entry:

> *24. VI. 1953. ...This afternoon the mother of Dr. Márgit Kálmán was buried, the widowed Mrs.. Engel. She lived for 92 years. The funeral, to which her daughter Margit and her son-in-law Franci had come over from Novi Sad, and though there had been no death notice, nor obituary carried in any paper, acquaintances had merely carried the news from one house to the next, was attended by a large part of the town's Hungarians.*

***

I would like to return to the printed case file, which features here as an illustration in this text. From the handwriting I see that Piroska, my great aunt, wrote the entry. She wasn't a lawyer, she just helped around the office. The last three lines, however, are my father's handwriting: "Our xpnses to be compensated with dentist's work. Ended, 23.XII.1942." The "xpnses" ("ktségeink" in Hungarian original) is an abbreviation of "expenses." It may serve as further explanation that in the folder are Dr. Ferenc Kálmán dentist's bills, for the treatment of my great aunt Piroska (the office entry writer), and my great uncles Tibor and Lori. There are also receipts of payments in 1940 and 1941, but I see there are some bills left unpaid. In 1942 when Ferenc Kálmán was a dentist in Szabadka and lived in Palicsfürdő, currency became a problem. In Szabadka payments were made in pengős, in Becskerek in dinars. But a citizen's solution was found: one tooth pulled for one divorce suit. Or maybe a few teeth filled for one sham divorce. The fact that compensation came through the defendant's (nominally, the adversary's) services, only strengthens supposition that in this divorce suit, the husband and the wife were on the same side.

3. A HUSBAND WHO VERY SELDOM VISITS PUBS AND ONLY IN THE PEOPLE'S INTEREST

An Almost Classic Divorce Suit

File No. 12325

During the world war, and in the first years afterwards, the stamp of the war was particularly strong (and harsh) if Jewish and German spouses were playing roles. But the proximity of the war can be felt in other divorce suits, too.

I would like to begin this case with a certificate which was at the top of the folder, under the cover. After reading this half page, I immediately put the file to one side with those I thought worthwhile working with. The certificate was issued by the Vrbica Local People's Committee on December 23, 1945. Vrbica (Egyházaskér), similar to Crna Bara (Feketető, the other setting in the story) was close to Csóka. The certificate is written in Serbian, and reads:

CERTIFICATE

> The hereby signed Vrbica Local People's Committee confirms, to the best of its knowledge, to all authorities, that Béla Nagy, 28, is currently residing as a village civil servant in Feketető, having previously (in 1937, in 1938 and in 1943) resided in this town. Formerly single, in 1943 with his wife, Irén Nagy, née Kocsis. He lived a very reclusive life, he didn't frequent any pubs, or only very seldom and only in the people's interest/ under the German occupation. Therefore he is not a drinker, he's not given to drinking, he doesn't smoke, he's not quarrelsome, he doesn't socialize.
>
> During the above mentioned years he was doing his job with industry. He worked a great deal after office hours, at night too, because at the time there remained a very large amount of unfinished tax affairs from 1940.
>
> Death to fascism, freedom to the people!
> György Hildenstab, /secretary/ Bertalan Puskás /president/

On the certificate is the stamp of the Vrbica Local People's Committee's, beside it are two ten-dinar deed stamps. One day before Christmas Eve, on December 23, the chief civil servants of the Vrbica local authorities try to confirm to all authorities (regardless of geographical and hierarchical limitations) that Béla Nagy, their former fellow civil servant, only visited the pub in the people's interest. In the sealed testimony of the authority of Vrbica came up with the following allocation: to fascism, death; to the people, freedom; and to Béla, an alibi.

Since, on the case file, beside the case number is the word "divorce," one can guess the basic connections before reading the rest of the papers. It was not uncommon that in divorce suits the wife would build her arguments on the husband's drinking, his time at the pub. The husband usually denied it. In this case, the local authorities (and the husband's former fellow civil servants) lent a hand.

Before I continue the story, I will mention that I did waver on whether or not I should keep the real names, or make an exception. In my legal prose I've made few exceptions. In this story there isn't anything which might show an actor in a really bad light, but there are more sensitive areas, and one can only guess how these might be received by the descendants. Which is why in March 2013 I called upon my similarly fated contemporary Kálmán Fehér, with whom I worked with at the Új Symposion journal. Kálmán is from Csóka, he knows the area, as well as Vrbica and Crna Bara, too. Kálmán said that I can keep the original names. He brought up that hardly any Hungarians remained in Egyházaskér/Vrbica or Feketető/Crna Bara, and not many others remained either. The world has changed, the economic situation has changed, these villages have emptied of people. All trace has been lost of the actors' descendants. Now there is an air of fiction even to real names. Kálmán must be right, but who knows! In the end I did change the names of the principle actors.

The picture of the husband/defendant painted by the certificate is one of a touchingly simple man, who not only does not drink, he doesn't smoke either, he lives a reclusive life and avoids company. I can also see that the certificate intends to serve as an alibi for the husband's nightly staying out: accumulated tax affairs serve as an explanation. But the typical system of arguments of divorces offers no guidance, when in the certificate I read that if Béla Nagy did visit a pub, it was only in the people's interest. I know of course that "in the people's interest" was a magic phrase that made anything positive (similar to "job creation" nowadays), but nevertheless.

The explanation is to be found in a second certificate, which was issued on December 23, 1945. This certificate contains the statements of István Fehér (former village president) and Frigyes Veres, while the authenticity is certified again by secretary György Hildenstab, and Bertalan Puskás, the president. Again, there is the stamp of the Vrbica Local People's Committee, and this time not two ten-dinar deed stamps, but one voided twenty-dinar deed stamp. István Fehér and Frigyes Veres write in their statement:

> In recognition of our moral, financial and punitive responsibility, we declare that once, in 1943, representatives of the Csóka Dairy Center came to our village, and entered reports in the books of our dairy farmers, filing complaints for failure to deliver milk. When at around 11 o'clock at night they had completed their entries, we went together with the representatives of the Dairy Center to Antal Ágoston's pub, with the intention of annulling the reports. With us was József Lászlófi the town-clerk at the time, Béla Nagy the civil servant, and another two or three people, among them Branko Krstić, the tax bailiff at the time. At around 12 o'clock when we had successfully annulled the entries, that is, accepted them, we went home completely sober.

In 1943 we had German occupation. One might not think the most fitting setting for the defiance of the German authorities, namely the conspiratorial annulling of reports and punitive proposals, to be a pub, rather than the loft of one of the conspirators' home. But I'm not so well-versed in old (or new) Vrbica relations. Reading the statement, I must also consider that the markers of patriotism often switched. First delivery to the state was the proof of one's patriotism, then (looking back) refusal, and then delivery again. In December 1945, any evasion of 1943's compulsory delivery (to the German occupiers) seemed patriotic. The statement's signators must have known that their own patriotism would also be preserved by the story, whose initial purpose was to prove that the defendant only ever visited a pub for patriotic reasons, in the people's interest. I don't believe that this is simply a made-up story. The reports, or their annulment, affected many people. In Vrbica, it must have been common knowledge whether there were consequences to evading delivery, and what the local civil servants did or didn't do. Most probably, István Fehér, Frigyes Veres, Béla Nagy, Branko Krstić and their associates—while taking advantage of the hospitality of Antal Ágoston's pub—got the upper hand against the fascist occupiers as regards delivery of milk to the state. What is less likely is that they would have returned home afterward "completely sober."

Béla Nagy and Irén Kocsis got married on May 25, 1942. Their daughter Aranka was born on May 28, 1943. The divorce suit was filed on July 8, 1944 by Mrs. Nagy. In the meantime, the war was raging on. In the divorce claim Mrs. Nagy states that her husband had abused her on numerous occasions, despite there being no reason to in her own behavior. Because of these abuses, Irén moved back to her parents. Afterwards her husband promised he wouldn't hurt her anymore, she believed him, and moved in with her husband again. The abuse continued. On June 23, 1944, Béla Nagy didn't come home for dinner, his wife looked for him, she found him in one of the pubs, but her husband didn't want to come home. Later when he did come home, he scolded his wife, because she'd put him in an uncomfortable position in the pub, and he beat her with a clog. In the claim she also requests property. Their pets are also listed under their property, and they ended up staying with the husband, though according to the claim they belonged to the wife. Also given are the wife's maintenance claim and child support claim.

In the beginning, Béla Nagy's attorney was Dr. László Rehák, an attorney from Kikinda. His submission begins that Béla Nagy acknowledges that their marriage "in truth wasn't the most fortunate." Yet he adds that it wasn't because he didn't take the marriage seriously, and its subsequent obligations, but because his wife wanted him to switch to the "new faith," and to refrain from all company. Another reason their marriage was less fortunate was because his wife made scenes if he didn't come home from work after one or two hours, she came for him to the pub and humiliated him in front of the company. Since he loved his wife, he tried to pacify her, hoping that Irén would see that her "extreme puritanism was unsustainable," but unfortunately that didn't happen. This submission is strictly speaking a counterclaim. So Béla Nagy doesn't resist the divorce, but suggests that it be granted on account of his wife's errors, and not his own.

Both spouses refer to the same paragraph when requesting that the marriage be dissolved. According to paragraph 80(a) of the 1894 law no. XXXI, still in force: "The marriage may be dissolved at the request of one of the spouses if the other spouse seriously violates their marriage obligations... through their own deliberate conduct." The question was whether the husband or the wife had deliberately or seriously violated the marriage obligations.

Over the course of the suit parallel narratives develop—and I believe, parallel convictions too. This is not uncommon. I've seen the same in other Banat suits, I've experienced it too in front of the International Court of Justice in The Hague.

Of course, the heatedness of the confrontations varies. In harsh divorce suits the narratives are often reducible to which between the two of them is the good person, and which isn't. The actors await the court's decision. The doubts, the feelings of guilt, the moments of forgiveness, of understanding, the details which don't fit the formula are often swept by the contest before the trial has begun. Knowledge adjusts to fit the formula. Memory too. Both litigating parties expect the court to see and to certify the image formed within them. And expectations are high too as regards the attorneys. I can see that first Béla Nagy took on László Rehák, then changed attorneys, and entrusted the case to my father. Most probably this happened due to the restructuring of the courts, and the case being moved from Kikinda to Becskerek. I can also see the names of other representatives.

The litigating parties see the totality of their husbandly being or wifely being (maybe the totality of their humanity) to be decisive. The court only sees the details which are set out. The parties explain these details differently, often editing them too. In this divorce suit, the parties are disputing several chains of events. I will choose three which are granted particular importance by both the husband and the wife: the demand to change religion, the explanation for the broken-in door, and an episode in a pub.

Did the Wife Demand that the Husband Change Religion?

This argument first came up in the submission/counterclaim of the defendant, presented by his attorney László Rehák, on November 30, 1944.

According to Béla Nagy's statement, his wife demanded that he should join the "new faith" because she (the wife) and her family belong to the new faith. There is no explanation as to which "new faith" she may have meant. First, it crossed my mind that "new faith" might be Christianity juxtaposed to Judaism, but then I saw that this was not the issue.

In her submission dated December 7, 1945, Irén Nagy denies the accusation, and says: "It never once crossed my mind to attempt to force the defendant to change religion. I am of the Reformed Church, as is the defendant. Thus, I had no reason, nor could have had any intention to change the defendant's religion. The defendant's claim is pure invention."

Next in the folder is Béla Nagy's letter (written on December 22, 1945), in which the defendant, now at my father's request, explains how they can deny the wife's various accusations. Here Béla Nagy says: "As for the question of religion, I stand by my arguments made in the counterclaim, because the plaintiff only converted to my faith after we argued, because she disrespected my faith. She agreed that she would convert for the sake of our children."

Probably my father had noticed that at this point Béla Nagy lacked coherence. In the counterclaim Béla Nagy says that his wife had demanded he (the husband) convert. Now he's writing that she converted. While the wife says that both were members of the Reformed (Calvinist) Church, therefore there was no sense in any alleged conversion.

It is difficult to get one's bearing in this question. Among the documents I found the marriage certificate, in which the religions are also stated. In this it states that Béla Nagy was born on June 23, 1918, and was of the Reformed Church, Irén Kocsis was born on September 30, 1923 and was Roman Catholic(!). The narratives remain blurred. If we suppose that Irén Kocsis really was Catholic, and later converted to the Reformed Church, then this still somehow agrees with what Béla Nagy writes to my father: that his wife converted to his faith (so converted from catholic to protestant). Irén Kocsis stresses that the religion wasn't the crux of the dispute, since they were both protestant (which might also be understandable, since at the time of the trial both were protestant, though the wording doesn't lean that way.) But if one or two details are matched up with some difficulty, there is still no explanation for the claim that the husband brought up regarding the question of faith. It is difficult to understand what he could have thought when he said that the wife was of the new faith ("novoverac"), and she was trying to force him to convert. It is difficult to suppose that Catholicism could be a new faith when compared to the Calvinist Reformed Church. And then, according to Béla Nagy's letter it was the wife who converted. In the end, there was a pulse there somewhere, but both parties had molded the story to the standards that might bring a better judgement, to the extent that now it is difficult to say what was the case exactly. Nor does the judgement tell us what the truth was. The justice system doesn't have an answer for everything either.

How and Why Was the Door Broken In?

In October 1943, the German occupation hadn't yet ended, but there were people who from time to time managed to slip out of history, and at the same time be left outside of their own home. This is what happened to Béla Nagy one October day when arriving home after midnight, around one o'clock he broke in the door. The fact in itself would suggest that Béla Nagy wasn't so sober and withdrawn as the official certificate had stressed. The question arises as whether he really did only visit pubs in the people's interest. It is interesting, however, that it was the husband who brought up this episode in his counterclaim filed with László Rehák's assistance, moreover with the aim of calling attention to his wife's intolerance. According to the submission:

> Once in October 1943 when I stayed out after midnight until 1 o'clock, after I got home all the doors were locked. After pounding on the door, my wife sent me back to where I'd come from, and declared she wouldn't be letting in the good-for-nothing, myself. And so I had to break in the door of my own apartment—but the things I still had to hear after…

On December 7, 1945 in her submission the wife didn't see things the same way. According to her: "There was no reason to break in the door when he came home from the pub. I had provided no reason for what he did. I didn't hear him pounding on the door because I was exhausted. I had to get up several times through the night to care for our child, and I fell into a deep sleep. But he believed it was an act of defiance and then made his malice known." In order to ascertain the truth, they needed witnesses. The hearing of witnesses was held in Törökkanizsa, presumably because it was easier to get there than to Becskerek from Feketető/Crna Bara.

Such circumstances had a different gravity at the time. I can see from my father's diary that in 1945 (or at least in the first six months of '45) one needed authorization to travel from Becskerek to a village in the Becskerek area. In 1946, at the time of the hearing of the witnesses, maybe one no longer needed authorization to travel within Banat, but it was still no easy task to get from Becskerek to Törökkanizsa (Novi Kneževac). There were no train connections, there are still none. There did exist buses, but they came very rarely, and it was hard for everyone to fit on. This is shown by an entry from my grandfather's diary:

> *5. I. 1946. Saturday. After much jostling, Józsi was finally able to fight his way onto the bus, and so at around 6 o'clock in the evening he arrived home from Novi Sad. There are bitter close-combat fights for a single seat, or a standing space on a bus. Many of those wanting to travel of course are left behind. They wait for another bus, and after a few unsuccessful attempts resign themselves to taking the railway. And then there the rush starts anew, the perilous shoving, and they're lucky if they eventually do fight their way on board. Coal shortages and train restrictions have both led to the cramped conditions for passengers.*

On route to Törökkanizsa, one had to change busses, and this would have made the outlook even more uncertain. One could barely (or only with some luck) make it from Becskerek for a hearing in Törökkanizsa, and back again, all in one day, despite the distance being less than 100 kilometers. Going by car would have been one solution, but this wasn't an option at the time. In 1946 not only did we not have a car, but no one in the family even had a license. Not including cycling licenses, which there were. I even found one among the documents. My Uncle Lóri's bicycle license issued in 1939. It was issued in Cyrillic script. The license is thirteen pages, and includes the entire text of an order concerning bicycle traffic. Here is how it looked:

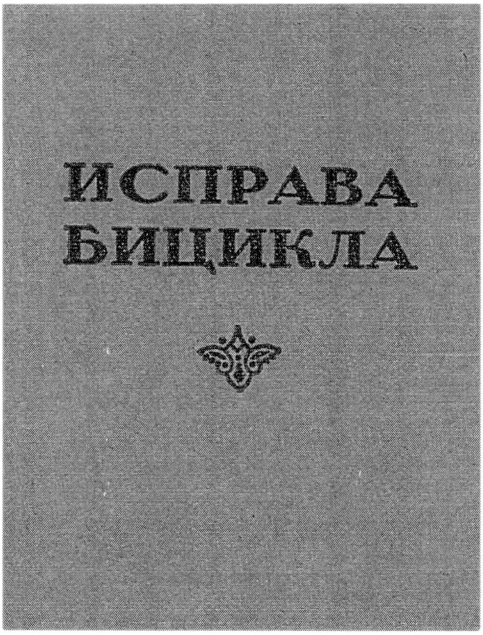

In the beginning of the sixties my father bought a car for the first time, and then followed the first driving test in our family. In the world of transport, the ages don't flow one after another. There were among them blank spots, especially looking at history from a family perspective. In the house where we lived for several generations, for a while there was a stable too. During my grandfather's lifetime travelling by horse and cart to somewhere outside the town was still a valid option. I missed out on this. And then for several decades we forgot about the possibility of travelling somewhere by household vehicle. We had to wait for the next age to come, the household car age. Such a novelty was a novelty for more generations. Things began to pile up. In the weeks we were still waiting for the purchased car (and we'd made a parking space for it in the yard), my father and I both began a driving course at the same time. At the time I was roughly twenty years old, and my father was almost fifty. We took the test on the same day. After the theory part was the practical exam. Conditions were rather favorable as there was hardly any traffic in the town. We left from in front of our house along Cara Dušana, towards Szentmihály/ Mihajlovo. In the car was the examiner, the teacher (called Géza), my father, and myself. I started. There were no cars in front. Maybe one or two cars might have come the other way. I overtook a cart, showing the correct use of the indicator (first left, then right). After two or three corners the examiner decided that my knowledge was satisfactory. My father was next. He drove for another half kilometer, also without a hitch, without even having to overtake a cart.

Later on, this became a foundation for many things. In America when I started teaching, I needed an American driver's license, and the Becskerek certificate helped a lot. It was recognized in part, I didn't have to prove my practical knowledge, but was limited to a written test. The questions that I had to answer in Atlanta didn't prove any particular challenge, for example:

> What do you do at a red light? (Circle the correct answer!)
> Drive on.
> Slow down and drive on.
> Stop.

I survived this test too. After the successful test a civil servant wanted to give me a timeslot for the practical, but I showed her my foreign license, so I only needed a written test. A week later I got my driving license. This has much more significance in America than it does in Europe. In America, people do not really use identity cards, and only very few people have passports. The driving license stands in for everything. Later I also got a driver's license in Hungary after showing my Yugoslav papers from Becskerek. And all this was based on evading a horse and cart on Cara Dušana Street, and for the correct use of an indicator.

Getting back to the trial, my father couldn't go to Törökkanizsa, and an attorney named Putnik had to stand in for him. Putnik however didn't turn up. The witnesses were still heard, and Béla Nagy gave my father an account in two letters dated March 17 and April 2, 1946. These letters were written in Hungarian. In his April letter, Béla Nagy goes into what the witnesses said with regard to the breaking in of the door and the wife's conduct:

> To my luck my witnesses stated that the first time when the whole thing started one night [the wife] declared beforehand that if I go to the pub she won't let me in, and when I got home not long after in the presence

> of my witness she talked for roughly 15 minutes just through the window and didn't open the door at which point I forced it in in anger.

***

In the plaintiff's submission dated December 7, 1945—in addition to distancing herself from the breaking in of the door—there is also a detail which tells of progress. In the claim, thirty-three valuable possessions are listed, which the wife (plaintiff) demands be returned. Somewhat more than a year later the wife acknowledged that she has received most of them, but not all. Béla Nagy didn't return the fifteen kilos of lard, the fifteen kilos of salo (cured fatback), three kilos of soap, or the can for lard. On December 22, 1945, Béla Nagy wrote to my father (mostly in Serbian) that he couldn't give any more: "I reject these demands, and I don't agree to them, because we never had enough lard to fill a can, and because at my wife's request I gave her a fattening piglet."

An Episode at the Pub on Béla Nagy's Birthday

Béla Nagy writes of the smashing in of the door in October 1943 that from this "the whole thing started." In the meantime, there were other exchanges and it would seem cases of assault and battery too, but the married life went on, or took a break but began again. After the incident of June 23, 1944, however, Irén moved out for good, and two weeks later on July 8, 1944 she filed her divorce claim.

On June 23, 1944, it was Béla Nagy's twenty-sixth birthday. In the claim the wife describes that she had been expecting him home for dinner, and when he didn't come she set off in search of him, found him in a pub and asked him to come home. The husband said he didn't want to come home. Afterwards, Irén went home alone, and when her husband got home, he abused her, beat her with a wooden shoe and caused her injury. Then Irén left her husband for good, and moved with her daughter to her parents.

The husband's counterclaim paints a different picture of the events on June 23. According to Béla Nagy:

> On 23 June, on my birthday, after official working hours I went to the pub to drink 1–2 glasses of wine, my wife came after me, she demanded

> I go home immediately, and gave me cruel reproach in front of those present. I reacted to these reproaches with one or two words, and so she might see her mistake. By no means did I attack her physically, let alone beat her, as she makes believe in her claim.

The episodes in the pub (or relating to the pub), and their accounts open greater and greater scope as the trial proceeds. It is not easy to orient oneself among the polished statements. In his letter dated March 17, 1946 Béla Nagy alerted my father that during the Törökkanizsa hearing of the witnesses, one of the witnesses confessed that on one occasion in the pub the wife had yanked on her husband's arm and pulled him out the door. The judge didn't dictate this into the minutes, but according to the witness, the wife, taking his arm, led her husband home from the pub. Béla Nagy suggested my father appeal for a second hearing of the witnesses. Of course if the question was whether Béla Nagy's dignity had been offended (and if he was the victim), then it was indeed important how he left the pub. Be it, Irén yanking on his arm, pulling him out in full view of everyone, or leaving arm-in-arm with his wife. Another witness statement also made for different interpretations. One night as Kálmán was coming home from the pub, inside a loud exchange was underway. The witness was stood beneath the window, and could confirm that they were shouting, he didn't understand what, only that the wife at one moment said: "Oh, Béla!"

Looking at the documents, I can also see that as new details came forward, it was as if patriotism had been forgotten—and the world war, too. With the help of his fellow civil servants (and by aligning himself with the trends at the time) Béla Nagy first tried to blend his own behavior into a background of the people's interest, and to highlight this. The explanations were embroidered onto a flag. But as they multiplied, they soon covered the flag, and the litigants only concentrated on the surface, on their own little lives.

***

The court did declare the divorce, and declared the husband to be in the wrong. The wife's request for maintenance was rejected. However, Béla Nagy was obligated to pay support for the child. The wife demanded 1000 dinars per month in child support. The court had already decided about this in an urgent proceeding, and settled upon a monthly 500 dinars. Béla Nagy appealed for it to be reduced to 300. The wife also appealed, asking for a larger sum. The judgement remained with a monthly 500 dinars. On June 5, 1946, my father wrote to his client that in his opinion the judgement was favorable, and there would be no point in appealing.

An Important Branch of the Story Involving a Croatian Woman

After my father requested that he write down what arguments could be raised to counter his wife's claims, Béla Nagy wrote a letter on December 22, 1945, in which he expressed himself half in Serbian, half in Hungarian. In the part written in Hungarian, another twist emerges. Béla expressed it as a theoretical question: "What would be needed for a Croatian woman to remarry, if the husband was German, and had been taken away at the time, and was allegedly no longer alive?"

This letter was, unexpectedly, followed by a telegram, in which Béla Nagy asked my father to "immediately reply with regards to the second case." The telegram is in a rather weathered condition, perhaps that is how it arrived. But this lends me a hand in showing the drama of these events.

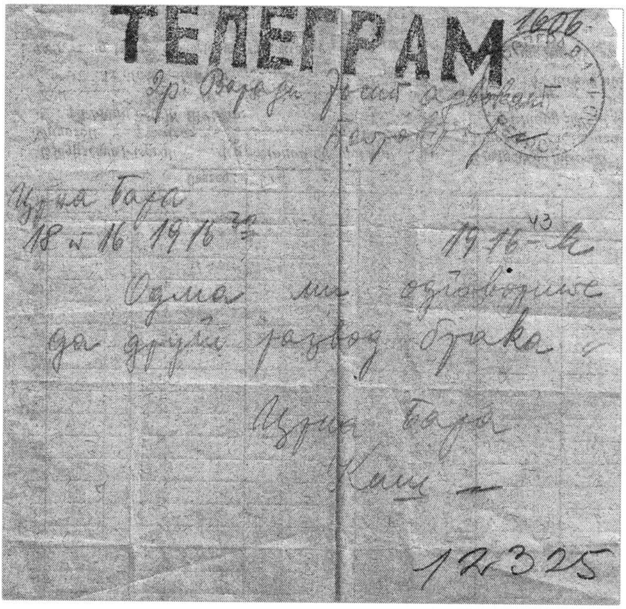

ТЕЛЕГРАМ

Црна Бара

Одма ми одговорите

да други развод брака

Црна Бара

12325

This telegram indicates, though it soon becomes clear, that Béla's interest concerning a Croatian woman and a potential divorce suit was not theoretical. On January 1, 1946, Béla Nagy began the new year by handwriting a letter to my father. It is possible he only had a typewriter in the office, and on January 1 he couldn't go into the office. In the letter he relates that the Croatian woman (whose husband was a German soldier) had spent some time in a concentration camp, but was released, and now the question was how she could divorce and how she could remarry. The letter closes: "Please, the matter is urgent."

On January 9, Béla Nagy writes a new letter. This time on a typewriter. Again, it is about the Croatian woman. Béla Nagy asks for an urgent response as to how she could divorce. He adds that his wife's attorney now also knows about the Croatian woman. But Kálmán believes it's of no importance, because indeed she has been living with him, though only for roughly a month. And so now the Croatian woman, too, (I can't find her name among the documents) is relevant to the case.

My father replies on January 16, 1946. He apologizes for his late reply. He explains that he has been travelling. He writes that the "circumstance in which you may have entered into extramarital relations with another will have an unfavorable effect on the divorce suit." In spite of Béla Nagy's theorizing, my father must have seen that the fact that the woman "was only recently" living with Béla, "roughly a month," wouldn't nullify the matter. It would hinder their efforts to have the divorce declared as a result of the wife's fault. Also, the date since which the Croatian woman had been living at Béla's was six months prior to the bringing of the judgement.

I'm particularly intrigued to read in my father's letter those sentences in which he explains that at the beginning of 1946, according to the legal practice in force, under what conditions could the Croatian woman divorce her German husband in order to remarry. My father informs Béla Nagy that if the husband served in the German armed forces, the wife could only ask for divorce if the husband had joined the German army "at the disapproval and protest of the wife." If, however, the "husband had fled with the occupying army," and the wife had remained, it had to be proven that during the occupation she did not enjoy any particular privilege. Her political conduct would have to be proven too. Since Béla Nagy didn't ask for legal help per se, but only advice, my father didn't elaborate on how the Croatian woman might prove her fulfilment of these conditions. Presumably, establishing whether or not the Croatian wife had opposed her husband's joining the German army, and her opinion of the German occupation, would be up to the neighbors and the civil servants of the people's committee.

In the case of Mrs. Kraus (and of those similarly fated), we can feel the first sweeping wave of changing power and changing fates. A divorce claim which is passed by the Regional People's Liberation Command is a chance for a spouse to break herself free from those swept along by the wave. It may help the plaintiffs to receive a less disadvantageous fate if they make efforts to divorce their spouse belonging to the rival cohort. I suppose, since often the goal was to protect their assets (perhaps the return of a dowry), that as the attempts increased, doubts may have arisen. Certainly, there were some who asked whether filing for divorce wasn't too simple a means to reduce the number of wealth and assets which qualified as being connected to the enemy, and could be used to enrich the state. And so, the question arises as to whether a woman who chose an enemy (a German, or formerly a Jew) as a husband deserves equality and another chance, if she hadn't previously shown any form of patriotic conduct countering the enemy. Meanwhile, following the same question, the divorce trial gets further and further from the matter of the relationship between the husband and the wife.

In another case I can see that not only was the divorce made dependent on (correct or incorrect) conduct, but the determination of death, too. On June 8, 1948 a Torontálvásárhely (Debeljača) woman came to our office, and asked for her husband to be declared dead. A record was filed; presumably the woman answered the questions with any essential information, then signed the text typed up by Uncle Göttel. The record reads:

> On 6 February 1942 I married the Jazovo resident Péter Pál Jaksa in Jazovo.
> In 1942 our son Endre was born of this marriage.
> My husband had a tendency to drink, and so in 1943 I was forced to separate from him.
> After this my husband joined the Hipo. ["Hipo" i.e. Hilfspolizei was an ill-reputed police unit of the German occupiers.]
> He died as such in the spring of 1944 in Serbia.

Four days later, on June 12, 1948, my father files a request, in which he asks for the death to be declared, and he supports the recorded facts. In the request he also mentions that the widow would like to begin settling the will, and to remarry. However, on August 30, 1948 the Törökkanizsa court rejects Margit Süli's request, with the justification that "before his death, her husband had shown enemy conduct in the face of our People and our Liberation Movement, that's to say he was an enemy of the people, who robbed and killed, and according to the court's practice the people's enemies cannot be declared deceased." The court therefore didn't dispute the death, but saw that any request which was linked to the enemy should be rejected. In the appeal my father argues that the court's position that enemies cannot be declared dead is incorrect. As a supporting argument he states that the wife had severed her marriage a long time before the husband joined the occupying armed forces. Therefore, the person asking for the death to be declared wasn't on the side of the enemy. The appeal was successful. On March 9, 1950 the Törökkanizsa district court took a decision. Péter Pál Jaksa was declared dead.

A range of things affected Béla Nagy's fate and chance. It became significant information that the Croatian woman of Feketetó was linked to a previously discriminatory ethnic group, now discriminated against. The legal logic was guided by the (yet) unwavering patriotic fever. In the divorce case of Béla Nagy and Irén Kocsis, the patriotic flag was flown, but then this was covered over by the details of their private life. If the husband was a German who had served in the German army, the flag hung over everything, nothing could be embroidered onto it, nothing could cover it, nothing could distract from it. The divorce didn't depend on the quality of the wife's relationship with her husband, but on the quality of her relationship with the world war and history.

I don't know whether the reader remembers Lili Eckstein's case, who in 1945 had to obtain a certificate of moral-political conduct in order to purchase a summer dress. In order to divorce, the Croatian woman had to prove that she was on the correct political side. If I simplify things a little, I can draw the following conclusion: summer dresses and free men are only available to women who prove the appropriate moral-political conduct. In other words, the situation was that for lack of an attitude that could be recognized as progressive, the Croatian woman couldn't divorce her husband, and Béla Nagy couldn't be held to be her lawful partner and companion—not even when Béla only went about his business in the interest of the people.

VI.

LEGENDS CHECKED IN LEGAL FILES

1. THE MESSINGER

Islanders

In our home in Becskerek there was a shed in the yard which we called "the garage." During World War Two when I saw if first, it was not a garage. It could not have served as one earlier either since the first time that the family would own a car was in the 1960s. There was some furniture in there, a boat, a tennis net and a stairway to the attic, made of wooden planks. When I was three or four, I also saw a woman there (Maška, our household help) a couple of times, stuffing geese. Moving away from the family rooms, by the garage there were the stables, already converted into archives when I first saw them. Next came a pigsty, then a stretch of the yard turned into a vegetable garden. After the war the garage was emptied. The furniture's owner was a Serbian friend of my father, a member of a distinguished, well-to-do family who, on departing from Becskerek during the war, left belongings in several homes for safekeeping. As far as I know he joined the partisans. Upon returning victorious from the war, he collected his boat and the furniture but left the tennis net, perhaps as a gesture of friendship. The Russians quartered with us took a lot of stuff, and several pieces of property had also been "requisitioned" by the Germans, but the net was definitely a gain, improving our post-war balance somewhat.

My dad actually wanted to make use of it too. The only question was where in our yard we should set up a tennis court. There was space, too, but the war had taught us that it was safest to leave things where they were.

The beds of tomato seemed important, but then so did the section covered with clover since the poultry had to be fed. To the right, when viewed from the street, there was the yard of the Bošnjaks. They also grew vegetables. However, in front of the of the back fence of the yard of the Bošnjaks there was another stretch of land which we owned but had no function. That was where the *bara* began. (We used this Serbian word to describe the spot because it implied a larger water surface than a puddle but did not have the sinister connotations of the Hungarian word *mocsár* meaning "marshes" or "mire"). The *bara* was at least 100 meters long and some 50 meters wide. At the end of our yard was a section which would remain dry for most of the year. The ground could be levelled by a roller, to a degree anyway, but not enough for the trajectory of the ball to be calculable on the bounce back, once it hit the ground. Tennis balls were sent by my aunt Bubus from the Netherlands. Tennis rackets were also found in the attic. Better still, the war was over. The time had come to play tennis. What was still missing, however, was genuine enthusiasm. My dad was busy all the time. At nine or ten, I made a few efforts to play tennis with a couple of my peers, very excited at the prospect of the extraordinary experience we would have, but in the end we did not really enjoy it. The rackets were too large for us, and other sports (like soccer, for instance) seemed far more accessible. The use of the tennis court fell mainly to my uncle Lori who played with a friend of his. I would watch them from high up, from a rather odd seat. There was a light grey wall running from the end of the garden right to where the *bara* ended. By the use of a pole in the ground, one could climb up to the top of the wall. I often sat there, facing the tennis court and watching my uncle Lori play. Sometimes I would walk along the flat top of the wall, about half a meter wide, watching the turtles in the *bara*, and then, at the end of the wall there was THE MESSINGER. Since I got there across the *bara*, the marshland, it appeared to me as a kind of island. In reality it was a *gymnasium,* a grammar school, and I knew I would be a pupil there once I completed the four years of elementary school. I also knew that "the Messinger" was also some sort of legend. The only thing I didn't know was what or whom the legend was about.

At any rate, I never really got enticed by tennis. I remained uninterested even after I had grown big enough for the rackets. I would play ping pong, however (maybe in lieu of tennis), which was the next best thing. I played even on the team *Željezničar* (Railwaymen). We had one genuinely gifted player (Melegi) among us, who could have gone really far, had he decided not to stay with us but go into the big leagues and play against the best players day after day. Even so, he made it to Champion of Serbia. As for me, I reached the zenith of my career as a ping pong player in 1963, by which time I hardly played anymore. By the end of December that year I travelled to France with the team of the Banat region. I no longer remember how this feat was managed by the sports managers, but I do know that the letter laying out the details was sent from Becskerek on December 6, 1963. I know because I was the one who translated it to French, and a copy survived in a drawer. The letter was written to a M. Bernard Sellier in the city of Toulouse. It described what a magnificent player Rudolf Melegi was, that he had been Champion of Serbia in 1961, that Milorad Živanov was the second most talented young player in Serbia after István Korpa, and a locksmith by trade (that is, a member of the working class). The letter also praises Nišavić and Granić and makes mention of the excellence of Vilmos Benkő as a trainer. There is information about me too, that I used to play myself, and am a referee ("arbitre") also. At the time there was no test or exam licensing people for refereeing in table tennis matches. The main reason for my presence in the team—namely that they needed someone who could speak French—was left unmentioned. There was also a social-political worker travelling with us.

We arrived in Nice by train after Christmas, following a journey of a day and a half across Italy. It was very hot in the train, but we could easily have had it much worse. Unheated trains were not infrequent in those times. The strong heat, however, had material consequences. The leader of our delegation, the socio-political sports leader, had the information that butter in France was far more expensive than in Yugoslavia, so it might be profitable business to carry butter to France and sell it. Thus, the smaller suitcases of our leader contained nothing but butter. The customs officers were not really bothered, but the butter arrived in Nice in a rather melted state. Gone were the regular cubes. The situation was only made worse when, after a considerably long time spent without a bathroom, our leader and also some others even took some pieces of the butter packaged in light paper in their hands.

In Nice there was bright sunshine, and since we had time to spare before the departure of the bus, we took a walk to the seaside. Despite it being December, people were sitting in the sand, some of them barefoot.

Our leader asked me to try and help to sell some butter along with him, because I knew French, but I refused. Instead, I undertook to teach him to ask in French: "would you like to buy butter?" ("voulez vous âchetez du beurre?"). But he failed to make business. The rough-hewn French did not inspire confidence, and nor did the plasticine-like pieces of butter displaying traces of the long trip. We didn't look too trustworthy either, unshaven, with our clothes crumpled after the long trip. But we didn't get into trouble. In the wonderful sunshine people saw our effort to make money not as an act of forbidden trade or an example of the profit-making instinct throbbing even in communist leaders, but rather as another source of laughter on a beautiful day. Not a single piece of butter was sold. The next destination was Tarbes, a small town in the Pyrenees barely larger than Becskerek, where we played against the local team (excluding myself who interpreted instead), and even won. Then followed a dance organized by the local communists for us, comrades from a communist country.

It was the first time ever that I saw a communist event organized by anyone other than the authorities. It was odd. I went to France in the hope that I would see a bourgeois world outside my own family. Our hosts, on the other hand, expected to meet real-life communists, the representatives of a genuine (and not only hoped-for) communism. Yet in the sentences of the enthusiastic communists of the Pyrenees, I often recognized the curves developing against the stream which, in my country, were characteristic of the ideas of the dissidents. The speeches, however, were dynamic. I waited for my turn to translate but the happy momentum gave not the slightest chance for translation. It was inconceivable that the speakers should stop and wait for their words to be translated into Serbian by me. The speeches frequently emphasized how inhuman capitalist exploitation was, but that this meeting—including the Serbian guests—was a happy little island of good people. To make everything clear even without translation, every speaker patted us on the shoulder and embraced every single member of our team.

Next day we performed in the town of Pau. There were speeches before the matches, this time with translation. All emphasized the friendship between heroic peoples. After one particular sentence of our team leader, I hesitantly stopped translating. However, he warned me that even if I was within my rights in refusing the butter-selling, I had no right to decline translating since this was why I had been brought along in the first place.

And he was right, too. The beginning of the sentence went something like "…. Similar to the ancient Slavs who, before battles, made the chivalrous gesture of donating butter to their opponents, so we…" I duly translated. This was followed by the traditional giving of butter to every French official and player on the team. The somewhat shapeless pieces of butter with fingerprints on the light-colored paper looked heavily worn— and maybe gave greater visual credibility to the historical parallel of the event. I was scared that there would be a scandal. What? Slav warriors in the Middle Ages (or before) giving butter to the enemy leaders before the fight? What will reasonable Frenchmen have to say about such nonsense? Well, not a word. They were deeply moved. They took over the modified-shaped pieces of butter and organized a "counter-gift" during the matches: we got a bottle of excellent Champagne each, and our leader (the owner of the butter) also received a small box with select wines. Thus, the butter export proved good business in the end. I have no idea, though, whether, on his return, our social-political sports leader made sure the party authorities were also properly informed of the diplomatic and financial success pertaining to the ancient Slav custom of donating butter to the enemy.

There was another thing that happened in Pau which did not exactly support the communist world view. We went to a restaurant after the successful ping pong battle. At the beginning I translated our conversations, but after several glasses of wine it became pointless. Having exhausted all possibilities of polite small talk, the French talked increasingly among themselves, and so did the members of our team. However, I exchanged a few words with the owner of the restaurant who let me know that I had a chance to receive a written diploma from King Henry IV of France. I wasn't sure in which century Henry IV had lived but I was fairly certain that it was a pretty long time ago (later I found out that he was King of Navarre in the sixteenth century, he was a Huguenot, and had had a castle in Pau). Anyway, I was definitely excited by the possibility. The following conditions had to be met: to eat a portion of goose liver with garlic, drink a bottle of white *Jurançon* wine—and pay for it. I managed to satisfy all conditions. The restaurant owner then hurried up to the attic, telling me that the King was staying there, and that is where he would sign my diploma. Which duly happened. My diploma is dated December 30, 1963, and declares that by the garlic and the *Jurançon*. I was baptized as a son the Béarn region, all of which took place for the purpose that "the above named gentleman, Tibor Várady… should always keep his gallant promises." I asked the owner what this really meant, but all he answered was that "this was completely obvious."

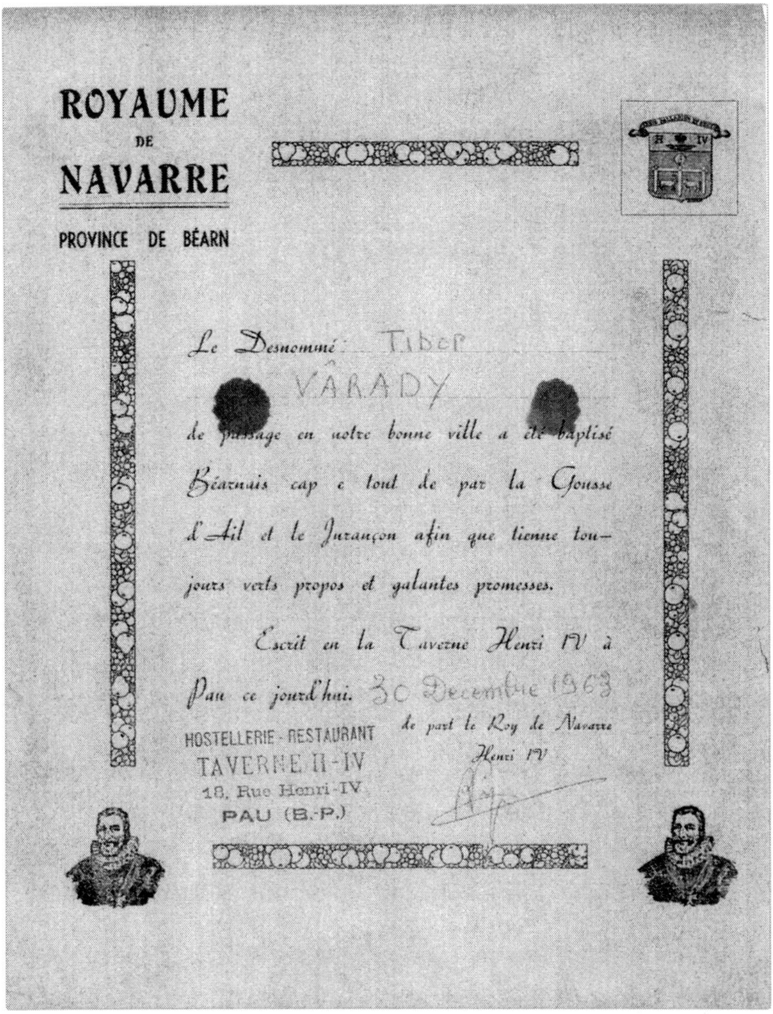

ROYAUME DE NAVARRE

PROVINCE DE BÉARN

Le Desnommé: TIBOR VÁRADY

de passage en notre bonne ville a été baptisé Béarnais cap e tout de par la Gousse d'Ail et le Jurançon afin que tienne toujours verts propos et galantes promesses.

Escrit en la Taverne Henri IV à Pau ce jourd'hui. 30 Decembre 1963

de part le Roy de Navarre Henri IV

HOSTELLERIE - RESTAURANT
TAVERNE H - IV
18, Rue Henri-IV
PAU (B.-P.)

So, this was the crown upon of my career as a table tennis player. But to return to the issue of tennis, the court built upon the *bara* did not survive long. The *bara* itself, however, did. So did the wall leading across the water to the Messinger.

At the same time that the tennis court was rolled flat, my father also took part in re-establishing the town's Hungarian schools after the war. Evidence of this is a dossier on the cover of which stands the word "School." The documents include a "guide" dated November 1, 1944. It contains the guidelines of the Bánát-Bácska-Baranya Military Command of the Yugoslav People's Liberation Army regarding the reopening of schools on the territory of BBB (i.e., Bánát-Bácska Baranya, or Banat-Bačka-Baranja in Serbian). It ruled that the teaching of history should be suspended until the new textbooks were completed. Until then, only the history of the people's liberation war could be taught, one class per week. The completion of the new textbooks took quite a while. In 1950, owing to a temporary measure, I learned universal history from a Soviet textbook. The book, by the way, had also been translated to Hungarian. It was also ordered that "honest teachers"—apart from the exceptions detailed—should use the curricula of the time previous to April 6, 1941 (that is, those from before the German occupation). Which teacher was "honest" was to be established from a *karakteristika*, the fill-in form which was issued by the Military Command of BBB on November 20, 1944. The following questions had to be answered: 1) Did the person involved cooperate with the People's Liberation Movement, assisted it or remained indifferent to it? 2) What is his character like, and what is his reputation among the townsfolk? 3) Was he inclined toward fascism, and if he was, how did he manifest that inclination? This is how the *karakteristika*, written in Serbian, looked:

Na osnovu raspisa Opšteg otseka Komande Vojne oblasti za Banat, pod Pov.Ibr.208 od 20.XI.1944 godine daje se sledeća:

K A R A K T E R I S T I K A

Za ______________________________ učitelj-ca /zabavilja/nastavnik iz ______________________________

1/ Da li je dotično lice saradjivalo sa Narodno-oslobodilačkim pokretom, pomagalo isti, samo simpatisalo isti, ili je bilo ravnodušno prema NOP.:

2/ Kakav je po karakteru kao čovek i kakav ugled uživa u gradjanstvu:

3/ Da li je naginjao fašizmu i ako jeste čime je manifestovao /pokaozivao/:

There was a fourth point on the backside of the form, which read: "Should this *karakteristika* be negative, it must be fully explained with appropriate evidence provided." Fair enough, or so it seems. It would be helpful to know, though, to know what explanations and evidence were accepted as appropriate. Naturally, the text ends with the slogans "Death to Fascism—Freedom to the People!" By the way, the BBB guidelines treat Slavic-language schools and the schools of the two non-Slavic minorities (Hungarian and Romanian) separately. Regarding the latter, article no. II/6 declares that they will open only "when suitable teaching staffs have been assembled," thus defining the task ahead. Along with that came the recognition of how this should be accomplished. The issue was raised in a handwritten letter by Ferenc Jeszenszky, written from Versec (Vršac in Serbian) to my grandfather on January 8, 1945. During the last years of the German occupation, Jeszenszky was head of the Hungarian Cultural Federation of the Danubean/Banat Region. The letter begins:

> My deeply respected Uncle Imre,
> The four-year Hungarian gymnasium in Versec, where teaching started in the last days of September, has naturally ceased its operation.

Upon reading this, one is immediately taken aback by the intimation that it could be "natural" for a school which barely began teaching at the end of September to cease already in October (October 1944, that is). Obviously, Jeszenszky's intention was not to give the impression that this was all right, only that the reasons were common knowledge, and this was bound to happen since it was happening everywhere. A new world and a new order were setting in, and all things would have to stop for a while to give time for the new power to think about how things should continue, provided they should continue at all. Then, as a result of all the thinking, on November 11, the BBB Military Command gave birth to the guidelines mentioned above. In their wake, others would have to do their share of thinking, too. Leaders and intellectuals of the Hungarian minority, for instance, would think about how to allocate a place for Hungarian schools within the new system of coordinates established by the guidelines. It is very likely that the same questions were raised also in connection with the other minorities of the Banat. Teaching in several languages had been an ongoing practice in the Voivodina (to which the Bánát and Bácska belonged) for many centuries, irrespective of who was in power and to which country, monarch or other authority the region happened to belong at the time. Jeszenszky inquired if any kind of decision had been made in Becskerek "from which one might draw conclusions on the ideas of the powers-that-be on the matter" and about the chances of having a Hungarian middle school in Versec. My grandfather's answer unfortunately cannot be found among the documents.

There are, however, quite a few letters dealing with the recruitment of teachers. I can see that there were proposals to make my father director of the Hungarian grammar school at Becskerek (the Messinger, that is). The proposal was supported by someone in the new power too. Maybe it was the same person who left the furniture, the boat and the tennis net in our house, but I'm not sure of that. The request was written by Zarko Božjak on February 10, 1945 on behalf of the Cultural Department of the Military Command, ending with the obligatory closing slogans "Smrt fašizmu—Sloboda narodu!" (Death to Fascism, Freedom to the People!). My father replied on February 12, that he lacked the necessary teacher's qualifications and suggested Mina Nestor or Béla Győrfi instead of himself. As far as I know, much more than the lack of qualifications, the real reason behind his refusal was that he did not want to give up his legal career. Then, between March and May 1945, some five or six letters were written (that is the number of those found in the batch of documents), proposals, recommendations, statements of support, and requests for András Fischer, Béla Győrfi and Fülöp Tordé to come to teach at the Hungarian grammar school in Becskerek. There is no indication on file that the requests were successful, not that I would need written proof, given the fact all three were among my teachers at the Messinger.

Returning to the situation in Versec, the file includes a letter written on June 24, 1945, that is, about five months after Ferenc Jeszenszky's letter. The subject is the same, the Hungarian schools, but the letterhead reads: UNITED PEOPLE'S LIBERATION FRONT, HUNGARIAN SECTION. The identification of the recipient still follows earlier customs: "To Dr. József Várady, Esq., Lawyer." I cannot make out the name of the author, but he addresses my father as "Dear Colleague," so he must have been a Hungarian lawyer in Versec. He invites my father (as well as my grandfather) to a meeting to discuss the issue of the Hungarian school, at ten o'clock on Sunday. The invitation, however, did not make it in time. From Versec, it travelled to Újvidék (Novi Sad) for the purpose of being duly censored, which would then be confirmed by another stamp in Becskerek. The backside of the letter bears the stamp of the "military censor supporting the post office of Petrovgrad" with a handwritten note by my grandfather underneath: "Sent to Újvidék for being censored. Delivered on 30. 6. 1945. Too late."

I must mention of another letter, its date missing but written in all likelihood in the first half of 1945. It shows what difficulties the school organizers were up against. I made a series of attempts to make out the name of the writer of the letter. It reads something like "Bély-Guiseppe" which seems a rather unlikely name for my town. Here is the bottom part with the signature. Maybe the reader will have more luck than me in finding out the actual name.

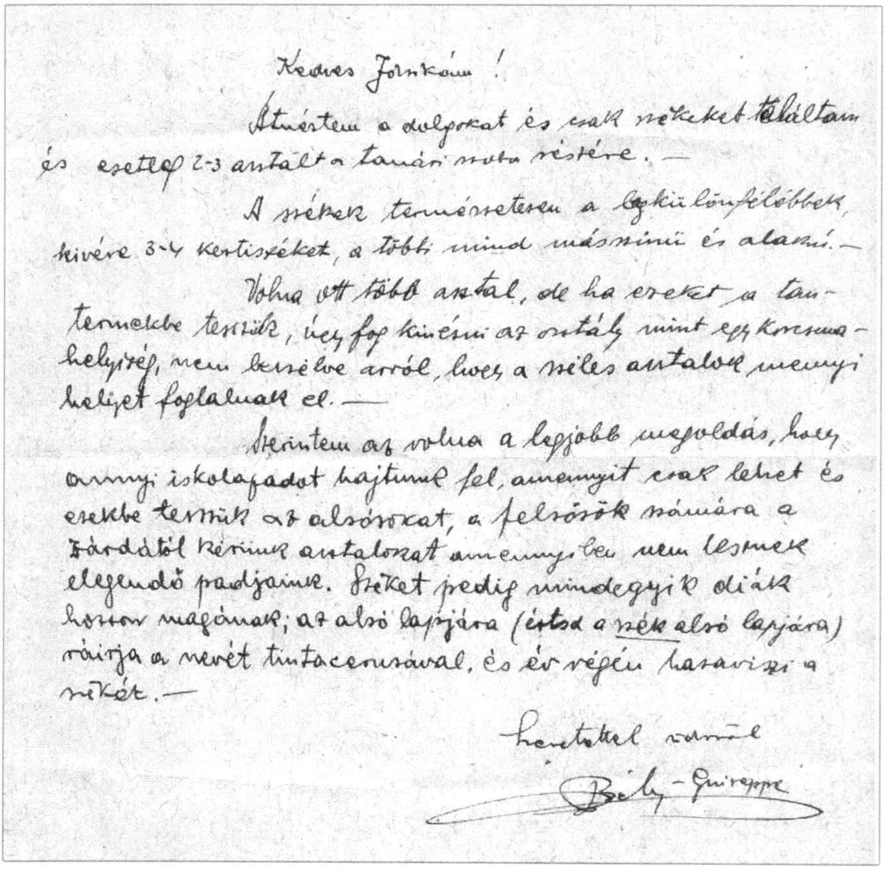

Kedves Jóskám!

Átnéztem a dolgokat és csak székeket találtam és esetleg 2-3 asztalt a tanári szoba részére. —

A székek természetesen a legkülönfélébbek, kivéve 3-4 kertiszéket, a többi mind másszínű és alakú. —

Volna ott több asztal, de ha ezeket a tantermekbe tesszük, úgy fog kinézni az osztály mint egy korcsmahelyiség, nem beszélve arról, hogy a széles asztalok mennyi helyet foglalnak el. —

Szerintem az volna a legjobb megoldás, hogy annyi iskolapadot hajtunk fel, amennyit csak lehet és ezekbe tesszük az alsósokat, a felsősök számára a zárdától kérünk asztalokat amennyiben nem lesznek elegendő padjaink. Széket pedig mindegyik diák hozzon magának; az alsó lapjára (értsd a szék alsó lapjára) ráírja a nevét tintaceruzával, és év végén hazaviszi a székét. —

[illegible]

Bély-Guiseppe

The letter was addressed to my father. Here is the text:

> My dear Józsi!
>
> I have looked things over and found nothing but chairs and maybe 2–3 desks for the teachers' room. The chairs are, of course, all different colors and shapes with the exception 3 or 4 garden chairs.
>
> There are a couple of tables too but if they were to be put into the classrooms, the latter will look like barrooms, not mentioning that they would take up a lot of space because of their width. The best solution might be to hunt up as many school benches as can be found and put juniors in them, while for the seniors we shall ask tables from the monastery in case we won't have enough benches. Students will be asked to bring chairs for themselves from home. Their names should be written in an ink pencil on their bottom (the bottom of the chairs, that is), and everyone will take home his own at the end of the term.
>
> Kind regards

Such were the conditions. I became a student of the Messinger in 1950, but by then it had proper chairs. I did not use the top of the wall to go to school but made a detour via Cara Dušana Street, and turned onto the street of the Messinger from there. I think it was called Masaryk Street at the time. Its name had been changed several times before and after that. Officially, the school bore the name of the heroic partisan girl Sonja Marinković, but students continued to call it "the Messinger." So did the teachers, more or less. Why precisely Messinger, few of us knew. Most of us felt some sort of concealed legend pulsating behind that name. But not everyone felt that way. I had a classmate who thought that "messinger" was some kind of synonym for "gymnasium." It is not only through correct information that things survive. At that time the Messinger was a Hungarian grammar school. It had been founded with proper regard to the guidelines of the BBB Military Command, and yet once it had been founded, it did not readily merge into the new world developing at the time. It was a kind of island in a new present. Minorities, unless they are targets, are not full-time players in mainstream history. Tito's portrait duly hung on the wall in every classroom behind the teacher's desk, yet—at a distance from the mainstream—our teachers would be addressed as "Sir" (*tanár úr* in Hungarian) instead of the newly obligatory "Comrade teacher." I started school in 1946, that is, precisely at the point in time when a new world began, yet our parents had prepared us for the kind of school that they used to know. Also, the teachers were people who had been teachers in the previous world too. By luck, while going to elementary school, we got a four-year reprieve from the dilemma between "Sir" and "Comrade" by saying "Uncle Teacher" or "Aunt Teacher." But once in grammar school (in the Messinger), there was no way to avoid the confrontation and the choice. In a minority environment, at some distance from the new streams, it was easier to continue to use *Tanár úr*, i.e., "Sir." The only person who gave us some pause was Mr. Đapić, our Serbian teacher. He taught us Serbian for a while, to be replaced by the teacher Fischer later. Fischer would remain "Tanár úr" even in the context of Serbian lessons. With Đapić this wasn't an option since, as opposed to "Tanár úr," "Gospodin profesor" (the Serbian equivalent) was unrelated to any tradition among us. It is not only because of their meaning that certain words are used, or not used. The solution that emerged was to call Đapić simply "professor" in Serbian. Otherwise we were on good terms with him. He was a decent man, if not exactly enthusiastic. Sometimes, toward the end of the class, when he had told and asked all that he wanted to tell and ask that day, yet there were still a couple of minutes remaining, he made no effort to force us to continue. He just stood there facing the door, holding his watch in his hand. And we began to chat with each other in relief, but no one stood up because the class was both finished and it did not yet end.

The school library was at the end of the schoolyard, quite close to the wall on top which one could get to the Messinger, also along the *bara*. I borrowed books by Karl May several times. Once, from a slot next to *Winnetou*, I pulled out a book by Dezső Szabó who was a politically objectionable Hungarian author at the time. There was a teacher there, too. She said: "That book shouldn't be there" but would not elaborate. Obviously, she was fully aware that reading Dezső Szabó was undesirable, but convictions and prohibitions reached us islanders with considerable delay, losing some of their edge on the way. I was intrigued by the fact that Dezső Szabó appeared suspicious and I checked out the book. At the age of eleven, however, I preferred Karl May to Dezső Szabó who was not included in the curriculum either. Most of the time we would study the Hungarian classics. This cautiously employed freedom of movement must have been helped by the circumstance that the guidelines of the Military Command had actually listed the Serbian and Croatian authors who qualified as "progressive," but there was no such list of similarly "progressive" minority writers. Which left some space for determining which minority authors were appropriate.

In December 1953, I wrote a ballad summing up a series of events at the Messinger. I used the nineteenth century Hungarian poet János Arany's *The Bards of Wales* as my model. This ballad was written about the incident when, as legend has it, King Edward I, having conquered Wales, ordered Welsh bards to be burned at the stakes because they refused to praise his glory. Well, my ballad had a slightly different background.

The Messinger counterpart of King Edward in my ballad would be our teacher, Mr. Fischer, who taught us German and Serbian. He was a very dynamic man full of ideas. Dynamism was what inspired by ballad too. It was Mr. Fischer's idea to turn the basketball field into a skating rink for the winter. Winters were longer then. There was also a well in the yard, from which we carried the water in pails. Unfortunately, we couldn't resist a bit of sliding on the surface before the ice got hard, which ruined the effort. We would never have a skating rink, on top of which we tried to craft explanations rather than displaying proper feelings of guilt and begging for forgiveness. That only made it worse. Mr. Fischer was furious, and our rule-breaking feeling of premature skating freedom drew grave punishment. Though avoiding the stakes, we were put to repetition. That much was the ground for the parallel between my class and the heroic martyrdom of the bards of Wales.

I was in the fourth form of grammar school at the time I wrote my New Years' Eve ballad. Grammar school began after four years of elementary school, which means I must have been about 15 years old. A couple of surviving notes show (and I also have some memories) that the year of Fourth Form (I went to IV/C) was exceptionally eventful. It was the year at the end of which we would sit for the "little finals" giving account of four years' study. We wrote a report on the year—which survived, too—containing that Form Four C "accomplished fine results in the field of sports and cultural work alike." It was added that "Our basketball title had been successfully defended" by Ferenc Turn, József Mosó and György Szöllőssy. Ferenc Turn moved to Germany before finishing grammar school. György Szöllőssy stayed in Becskerek and passed away a few years ago. I have no idea what became of György Mosó. According to the report, Miklós Fazekas excelled at target shooting and "even beat some gold medalists." Also, Tibor Várady "played successfully on both the table tennis team of the Gymnasium and in the colors of Željezničar."

The use of the term "cultural work" in the report shows that we were not quite the isolated island we may have seemed. This was an expression developed in the communist world. On the other hand, the biggest "cultural work achievement" of the year was the performance of, not a partisan drama, but a dramatized version of a contemporary classic, the novel *Abel in the Wilderness* by the Transylvanian author Áron Tamási. The report tells, and so does my memory, that "everything, from adapting the novel for the stage to producing most of the sets, was done by the students of Form IV/C." The chief role was played by Péter Kaslik. The sets were made mostly by Tibor Bencze. The organizer of the event was the Hungarian teacher István Víg. The "adaptation for the stage" was largely my work. The manuscript didn't survive. I had a vague feeling that it wasn't all that good. But the status of minority islanders did not only protect us (well, somewhat) from the ruling ideology but also from "quality control." Outside of us, there was not a single Hungarian grammar school, either in town or in the entire region to compare our work with. A major part of the Hungarian families in town attended the performance. Nearly everyone had relatives among the students. They were not exactly an impartial audience. Next year we performed "The Boys of Pál Street", (based on the novel written by Ferenc Molnár), in the gym hall of the school, also with great success. I was Nemecsek, the protagonist. Many people congratulated us after the show, praising all of us, only my father seemed to have some reservations. He said my performance was "reassuring." Later at home I asked what he meant by that. Why exactly "reassuring"? He said reassuring because it convinced him that I would never be an actor. Of course, he wanted to see me become a lawyer.

That was the Messinger at that time, or what I can remember of it.

Karolin Messinger and a Lawsuit from the Good Old Times before World War Two

Karolin

Who was the person after whom the school got the name by which we knew and still know it?

Her name was Karolin Messinger. She was born in 1868 in a well-to-do Jewish family in Becskerek. Practically everybody in town knows that she is a legend. They know little else. Part of the reason may be that Karolin never married and had no children, thus discontinuing the family. Then there was also the circumstance that, not only reality, but also the realm of rumors was shaken by the series of world changes (fascism, communism, Milošević's "Transition" along with the shift in the town's ethnic composition) that followed.

A few facts, however, did survive in the files. They show that her father was Jakab Messinger, and her mother Terézia Wippler, a renowned photographer. Karolin studied in Budapest, at the School of Higher Studies for Girls. She founded the Messinger Institute for the Education of Girls in 1903. She was thirty-five then. (Hitler still only fourteen.) The Institute became famous and gained high prestige. Several photographs have survived, showing spacious, well-appointed classrooms. There was a tennis court in the courtyard, serving as a skating rink in wintertime. I have just learned about this, as I am writing this text. Perhaps Mr. Fischer knew about it before. The institute could be seen in picture-postcards of Becskerek, too. One of these shows the open-air teaching court in the summer.

Karolin Messinger appears to have been inspired to found the school by a feeling of commitment. Her name appears several times on the program of the Lyceum Lectures as a speaker. On March 3, 1905, she gave a lecture on feminism. The topic of another lecture held on March 28, 1909 was "The Career Choice of Women." The institute also offered a special "extended course on commerce" for the girls. Karoline deemed it important to take on the teaching of physical exercise herself, as opposed to the tradition which held that this was exclusively male job. She became the first female teacher of physical exercise in 1894. The institute was founded partly to promote equal rights for women. Charity was another motive: the children of teachers whose fathers had fallen in World War One were entitled to stay and study in the institute free of charge. Making profitable business, however, was also one of the school's objectives. Which meant that those who did not belong to the charity group but failed to pay the fee would be sued. There are some files showing that, too. I can see that my grandfather claimed 15,701 dinars from a man named Đorđe Stefanović, a resident of Bóka, whose daughter Ivanka had stayed at the institute. The defendants of the lawsuits include a manager of the famous Belgrade restaurant *Ruski Tsar* (Russian Tzar), a man called Jovo Nikolić. It is hard not to make a brief detour when mentioning the name of the *Ruski Tsar.* The restaurant was much talked about even in the early years of communism. There was also a song about it, which may have been born after its name had been changed in the new world, which could have been the very starting point of the birth of the legend. The song was sung in Becskerek, too. We actually danced to it in the dance hall of the Commercial Middle School. There was also a Hungarian translation. Now as I am trying to recall it, it occurs to me that I may have been the translator myself, but I am not at all sure. It could be folk poetry, or folk translation, to be exact. Turned into English, it goes roughly something like this:

I am not a "mondain" fellow,
And I am penniless
Yet you'll see me dine each day
At the Ruski Tsar, no less

The word "mondain" was being used both in Serbian and Hungarian, and forgotten roughly at the same time. Mondain used to mean a fashionable, easy-going man of the world, a member of the "smart set" or high society. As far as I can remember, despite its first line, this was not an "anti-mondain" song. The melody was happy, the tone that of a cheerful man who couldn't care less about the worries of the world. At the dances it was sung by a trumpeter wearing trousers improbably wide at the ankles. The forms of expression of being mondain changed over time. A few years earlier it had been tight-fitting trousers that indicated revolt and political incorrectness. I remember having heard that some zealous builders of socialism went around carrying scissors so that ideologically inappropriate trouser legs could be slit right in the streets. In time, along with the passing of being mondain, the cult of the Ruski Tsar also faded. Under Tito, its name was changed to Zagreb as a symbol of brotherhood between the nations of Yugoslavia. Under Milošević, it obviously could not remain Zagreb, so Ruski Tsar was restored. Not completely, though. The old name was there all right, but people who still remembered the Ruski Tsar of the legends somehow saw that it was no longer the real thing. Not long ago, in 2015, another name change followed when the place was taken over by an international chain of Italian restaurants, and now it is called Vapiano. It is not really successful, or so they say.

Anyway, all that remained of the Ruski Tsar case is a postcard in which Mr. Nikolic pledges that he will pay his debt. The postcard bears the seal of the restaurant and beer hall Ruski Tsar. The addressee is *Mesinger Internat Veliki Bečkerek* (Messinger Boarding School, Veliki Bečkerek). It sufficed for the post.

***

Of all the cases involving non-payment of outstanding debts, the largest number of surviving documents are those concerning the legal action taken against Vaso Glavaški in September 1929. It is the story of that lawsuit that I am trying to summarize.

A Letter that is Somewhat out of Place Here

The Messinger file contains a number of letters sent to my grandfather by Karolin Messinger. There is something peculiar about these letters, something that makes them different from all others related to different cases or, for that matter, from any letter that I have written or received in all these years. They were written in a particularly beautiful hand in black ink, the strokes of the pen as perfect as anything I've seen in print. The signature at the bottom is strange too: "Headmistress and Paulanéni" in which the second name means "AuntPaula" written as a single word. The context makes it clear that the "Headmistress" is Karolin Messinger, the headmistress of the boarding school for girls in Nagybecskerek. The signature suggests shared letters, though the actual texts all concern Karolin alone. Karolin Messinger, it appears, was accompanied by "Paulanéni," on all her trips. The letters were written by her. Her real name was Paula Tóth, and she did not owe her "aunt's" status to being much older than Karolin, which she wasn't. She must have been addressed as "Aunt Paula" by the students, conferring on her a role she identified with so much that she turned it into an actual name by writing the two words as one, without a space. Since "Paulanéni" is found quite frequently among the documents, I tried to find out as much about Paula Tóth as I could. I inquired in Becskerek, and a retired parish priest, Father. Jenő Tietze was able to help. Towards the end of the 1940s, Aunt Paula was a regular visitor of the Tietze family, and Jenő saw her a few times too. He was about ten at the time, and now, almost seventy years later, he no longer remembered a thing. He knew, though, that Aunt Paula had been a Catholic nun but left the order and took on a job as a teacher and administrator at the Messinger. Father Jenő also said that Aunt Paula was buried in the Catholic cemetery of Nagybecskerek, but her tombstone no longer bears her name. The documents also indicate that Karolin and Aunt Paula travelled together everywhere, to Budapest, to medical treatment in Italy and to all other places. I think it is a safe to suppose that they were travelling companions in life too.

On October 17, 1932 "Headmistress and Paulanéni" sent a letter to my grandfather from Budapest. The letter did not directly concern the Glavaški Case but was related to it, so my grandfather wrote "Messinger c/ Glavaški" on it with a pencil. Let me show the handwriting also to my readers in English.

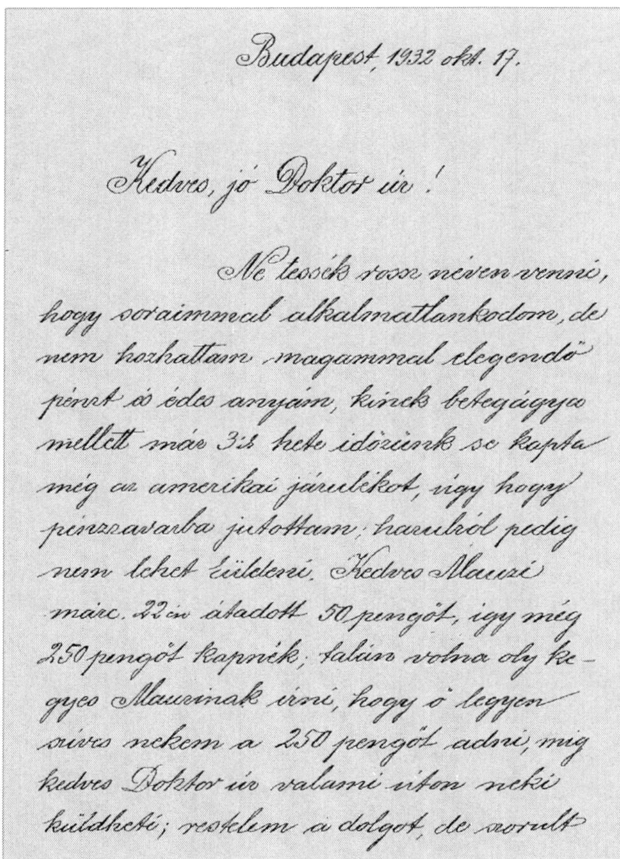

Budapest, 1932 okt. 17.

Kedves, jó Doktor úr!

Ne tessék rossz néven venni, hogy soraimmal alkalmatlankodom, de nem hozhattam magammal elegendő pénzt és édes anyám, kinek betegágya mellett már 3-ik hete időzünk se kapta még az amerikai járulékot, úgy hogy pénzzavarba jutottam; hazulról pedig nem lehet küldeni. Kedves Mauzi márc. 22-én átadott 50 pengőt, így még 250 pengőt kapnék; talán volna oly kegyes Mauzinak írni, hogy ő legyen szíves nekem a 250 pengőt adni, míg kedves Doktor úr valami úton neki küldheti; restelem a dolgot, de szorult

Translated, the letter reads:

> 17 October 1932
> Budapest
> My Dear Good Doctor,
> I apologize for the inconvenience this letter is causing you but I could not bring sufficient money along on this trip, and my dear mother, at whose sickbed we have already spent three weeks, has not yet received her American donation either, so I ended up short of money, and it is impossible to have some sent from home. Dear Mausie gave me 50 pengős on 22 March, so I still need 250. Would you be so generous as to write to Mausie that she should kindly give me those 250 pengős until you, dear Doctor can send it to her in some way. I am terribly ashamed but I am in an uncomfortable situation....

The letter is about being "short of money" but the shortness was in all probability limited to Budapest. Karolin Messinger was a lady of means, but at that time it was very hard to move money between Hungary and Serbia, or in other words, to return the sum borrowed straight from Becskerek to Budapest. That was why the scheme was adopted whereby Karolin should borrow money from my Aunt Mausie in Budapest, which she would then pay back to my grandfather once she has returned to Becskerek. The letter's connection to the Glavaški case was probably that repayment of the loan provided to Karolin was made in the form of it being deduced by my grandfather from the amount owed by Glavaški to Karolin Messinger.

Was there a Bench on the Corridor in front of the Headmistress's Office?

The issue turned out to have a crucial importance. Vaso Glavaški's daughter stayed at the boarding school for girls, for which he was supposed to pay a fee. He paid all right, but only for the days which his daughter had actually been in the school. He refused to pay for the days his daughter was away from the institute and spent at home because of illness or other causes.

The first item on file is a letter by my grandfather to Aleksije Bácsmegyei, a lawyer in Törökbecse (Novi Bečej in Serbian). It enlists the facts and arguments my grandfather regarded as relevant, then asks Attorney

Bácsmegyei to bring an action on the basis of those, and "kindly appear in court on the appointed trial day on my behalf as my substitute, and thereby seek satisfaction for the lawful claims of my client." The competent court was the one in Törökbecse, so a local lawyer was needed, and Bácsmegyei was there. As the facts were laid out, Vaso Glavaški's daughter (her name was Smilja), a student of the Messinger Institute for the Education of Girls, contracted for a full schoolyear (ten months' board), but Glavaški's wife asked that she should be exempt from payment for one or more months "for the days (the second half of the month) when she would not have her meals at the school." According to my grandfather, the request was not accepted by the Messinger Institute. It was made absolutely clear in the school's brochure that payment is due for the full period of the contract since food is not the only service for which remuneration is due, but the fees should cover entire upkeep of the school including maintenance and the salaries of the employees. Full information on these conditions had been provided well ahead of signing of the contract, and there were few exceptions "granted on humanitarian grounds" only. Glavaški, however, was a well-to-do man, so in his case there was no reason to make an exception.

The claim was for 1400 dinars with interest and costs. Glavaški did not really dispute that according to the brochure and the conditions the fee would have to be paid for full months. He was alleging, however, that his wife had seen Karolin Messinger, spoke with her, and they agreed that the days on which her daughter was not in the school would not be counted. A witness was also found. In a letter date January 22, 1931, Attorney Bácsmegyei informed my grandfather that at the trial held in Törökbecse, the hearing of Mrs. Glavaški:

> was followed by the testimony of the mechanic Rada Kurbanjev, a political comrade and good friend of the defendant. It supported the account by the defendant's wife. Kurbanjev testified that in the first days of September he visited the Messinger Institute and waited for the wife of the defendant. He was sitting in the corridor in front of the office when, since the door had been left open, he heard the wife of the defendant tell the headmistress that... of the monthly fee, only so much should be paid as conforms to her daughter's actual stay. To which the headmistress agreed, and said it was correct. The money covering a day can be calculated, and so can the amount to be paid. The conversation was conducted in Serbian.

It was these arguments and testimonies that had to be countered. Two days after the hearing, on January 24, Aleksije Bácsmegyei lays out a proposal for my grandfather as to the directions which the counterarguments should follow.

This is followed by a draft of a submission written by my grandfather for Karolin Messinger, whose name stands below the text as signatory. It can be assumed that the final typewritten version was actually signed by her. According to the submission, Karolin Messinger makes a deposition that she does not speak Serbian, so she could not have discussed any agreement with Mrs. Glavaški in Serbian. The truth is that the person who spoke to Mrs. Glavaški was Julkica Ilijević, a teacher of the school. Frankly, in the light of the conditions in Becskerek, it is unlikely that Karolin knew no Serbian at all. It is possible, however, that her Serbian was not good enough for her to negotiate with proper authority, so she asked someone to negotiate for her. According to the draft submission, Mrs. Glavaški's proposal was firmly rejected by Julkica Ilijević again and again. My grandfather proposes that Julkica Ilijević be asked to testify. Karolin Messinger herself took the witness stand later, but she asked to make her testimony before a court in Becskerek rather than Törökbecse.

The draft submission is written by hand on the backside of a flyleaf. The draft is followed by an additional argument written in a different hand, which is not incorporated in the text but must have been included in the final version. That different hand is my father's. As nineteen-year-old law student in 1931, he was already helping out at the office. My father found a weak spot in the testimony of the witness Kurbanjev who had said he was sitting in front of the office, listening to the discussion. According to the note, however, there is no bench in front of the office to sit on, so Kurbanjev cannot have told the truth when he said he heard the discussion from there. The sentence "Ilijević heard" is also added, meaning probably that Julkica Ilijević confirmed that there was no place to sit in front of the office. (Let me add that there was no bench in front of the office when I went to the Messinger either.) The case was won by Karolin Messinger. The sentence of the Törökbecse court awarded her the 1400 dinars with interests and costs. The file includes a few receipts confirming the payment of the instalments.

The conclusion I can draw from this story, now as I am sitting here contemplating it, is that history did not insert itself into everything all the time, and life was not always spent in a torrent of momentous events. There were times in Becskerek too when time held, and the days simply followed upon one another. So that Karolin could sit in her armchair in the courtyard in peace.

In those years Karolin regularly celebrated her name-day too. I could find that out from the diary of my grandfather. He recorded a memory about that on November 3, 1944. It reads:

> *Saturday, Károly's Day, 4. XI 1944. …There was a time when on Karoly's Day there would be a cheerful party held by Karolin Messinger, the owner of the highly reputed school and college who was driven to Budapest by the Germans' persecution of Jews where she died lonely, abandoned by everybody.*

Thus, in peacetime on Károly's (St. Charles's) Day, Karolin used to hold "cheerful parties." She would be joining the community of Charles's. I look up my diary which has all the name-days printed in it, sometimes several a day, but on the fourth of November I can see Károly (Charles) alone. But there are many kinds of diaries, and it doesn't take much legal brilliance to extend the day of St. Charles to cover the Karolins also.

Karolin and the German Occupation

Jewish Descent and Christianity

As I already said, Karolin Messinger came from a well-to-do Jewish family in Nagybecskerek. How much importance she attached to this circumstance I don't know. I can see from a submission addressed (in German) by my father to the economic officer of the German occupiers that Karolin Messinger "is of Jewish descent but she converted to the Christian faith already in her early childhood, about 70 years ago." The date is missing from the copy of the submission surviving among the documents, but, having been written in connection with a letter of foundation issued on July 12, 1942, it must have been sent to Belgrade sometime in the autumn of 1942. Karolin Messinger had been born in 1868, so seventy years before 1942 she was exactly four years old. But even if the "about" seventy years is taken to mean 65 rather than 70, it would still imply that she was a little girl under ten when she converted sometime in the 1870s. So, was she a Christian who did not consider herself Jewish? Well, maybe so, but it isn't certain. My father's submission does not concern itself with facts of family or personal history. It refers to her having converted only with the purpose of helping her evade the discriminative measures involving Jewish property. He obviously wouldn't have declared that Karolin had been baptized in her childhood if it hadn't been so. Everybody knew that this would be checked by the German authorities. The question, however, remains if this had any major importance. The decision by which Karolin became a Catholic had been made by her parents. Everything I know about her seems to support that she was a person who followed her own decisions throughout her life. Had she made her parents' decision her own? And if she had, how did she feel when she had to leave Becskerek because the persecution of Jews?

It reminds me of the protagonist of the novel *Daniel Stein, Interpreter* by the Russian author Lyudmilla Ulitskaya, a character based on a real-life person whose story made legal history and ended up at the Supreme Court of Israel. His real name was Oswald Rufeisen and lived from 1922 to 1998.

The real story is as if everything were written in capitals and in bold. Few things in Rufeisen's life happened of his own will or were civil decisions (as was in the case of the Messingers in the 1870s); every major turn was a consequence of cataclysmic historical events. He was dragged along by floodwaters breaking across barriers, carrying him towards various affiliations and identities, only to find later when the rivers had returned to their beds that he no longer belonged anywhere. Rufeisen was a Polish Jew who joined the Zionist organization Akiva in his youth. Then, before he became twenty, came the years of Nazi occupation. Since he spoke both perfect Polish and German, he passed himself off as an ethnic German living in Poland. After that he fled to Lithuania, then to Belorussia and became an interpreter of the German army in the town of Mir where, making use of his position and information, he saved the lives of hundreds of Jews and even smuggled weapons to the resistance. In the end he was forced to flee, then found refuge in a Catholic monastery and converted to Catholicism. As was established by the Supreme Court of Israel in 1961, he did not do so for opportunistic reasons but "out of sincere inner conviction." In a Carmelite monastery he first became Brother Daniel, and later Father Daniel. In the 1950s, he decided to move to Israel, but did not give up his Catholic faith. That was the juncture at which he became a character of legal history. In Israel, the Law of Return, passed in July 1950, was already in force. That law decreed that anyone who is Jewish is entitled to move to Israel, and when they move there, they will automatically be granted Israeli citizenship. The question was if Rufenstein fell under the law or not. He declared that he was not only of Jewish descent but also identified himself as Jewish—but his religion was Catholic. He added that he chose a specific Catholic Monastic Order because the Order had a chapter in Israel. The ultimate judgment was passed by the Supreme Court of Israel. In its justification of the sentence, the court quoted the opinion of Judge Cohen who pointed out that Rufeisen's feelings and statement were of crucial importance, and according to that statement "he was born a Jew, grew up as a Jew, suffered as a Jew and feels a Jew in the national sense." The majority of the judges, however, did not share Cohen's view. The court ruled that "a Jew who, by changing his religion, cuts himself off from the national past of his people ceases to be a Jew in the national sense to which the Law of Return gives expression." Still, Rufeisen did not give up. Since he was denied the simplified procedure ensured by the Law of Return, he took the longer route. He emigrated to Israel, and in time he did get Israeli citizenship. He went on to live in a Carmelite Monastery in Haifa.

There is a story I should link here as a parallel. When I was working on my PhD thesis in the US, my supervisor was Harold B., a famous law professor at Harvard, the author of several distinguished books on the relationship between law and religion, international trade law and other topics. He was the first legal scholar to go on a study tour in the Soviet Union where he spent a couple of years with his family. He wrote what was probably the best western book on Soviet law. He criticized it, of course, but unlike most other critics, he was genuinely interested in Soviet law. I think it was him who told me that you cannot make a good doctor if you only hate the disease. You can only have success at therapy if you are also interested in it. While he was in Moscow, he lent his house to Timothy Leary, one of the best-known figures of the LSD culture. When I was his guest for the first time (he invited me in 1967 to spend Christmas with his family), he made no mention of this. It would have been inappropriate to complain at Christmas. Another time, on another visit he told me how Leary left the house a complete mess when he moved out. He also invited me a few times to accompany him and his family to church. They were Episcopalians. Frankly, I was somewhat surprised at him displaying, apart from due dignity and respect, also a deeper bond with the church. His university lectures were full of interesting analyses, amusing examples and inspiring ideas. Each gesture and each movement or wave of the hand was in full harmony with that speaking style. In church I thought I saw a different man. Even his body language changed. Later we became even closer friends. In the seventies Harold visited me in Novi Sad, then for twenty years we taught together at Emory University in Atlanta, Georgia, he as a tenured professor and I as visiting lecturer. In the 1980s the state of Massachusetts legislated mandatory retirement at the age of sixty-five. In Georgia there was no such rule; that was why Harold left Harvard and came to Atlanta.

We often met, and I became convinced that religion was truly important for him. He told me that he was born in America, but his ancestors had come from Odessa. He grew up in a Jewish family, was raised and lived as a Jew until something very strange happened to him sometime in the mid-nineteen-thirties. He was in Germany on a scholarship, and Hitler was in power already. On one occasion he was travelling by train to France, alone in a compartment. He was burdened with heavy, ominous thoughts, and felt weighed down by the load on his shoulders. Then he saw a vision. While he was talking about it, I could see that he fully believed what he had seen, but he was also well aware that the whole thing was very, very strange, especially coming from a university professor talking to his former student. To ease the tension, he also made some philosophical remarks about the vagueness of the border between reality and fantasy. On the train he saw an apparition of Jesus Christ before him. His face had a dark color. He also spoke to him. He said, "don't worry. This is my problem." And then Harold felt sudden relief. I was close to looking for an explanation in dream or maybe hallucination, but I had little doubt that the experience was real. To get closer to all this somehow, I tried to ask questions—not really smartly, I guess. I asked him in what language had Jesus spoken to him. "You don't understand this at all, Tibor," Harold said. He was probably right. He told me that soon after that experience he converted to Christianity. On a different occasion, in a larger company, he was explaining that he was a Christian believer, but he continued to consider himself a Jew. This was disputed by a common Jewish acquaintance of ours. I did not want to intervene in their dispute but, listening to their arguments, in the end I thought I found myself on Harold's side, or close to it. I might add that Harold and his wife, who was Christian by birth, have four children. As far as their religious affiliation is concerned, life made a truly Solomonic decision. Their two daughters were brought up Christian. One married a religious Jew and converted to Judaism. The other remained a devoted Christian who even made her Muslim husband convert to Christianity. Of the sons, one is Christian, the other a rabbi.

The final thing to tell about the topic of Harold and religion, is that he strictly adhered to every religious rule including fasts. He pledged every year not to drink a drop of alcohol at the time of fasting. Once in the nineties, on the last day of the self-inflicted thirst, Harold and his wife gave a dinner party which I attended with my wife. There were some fifteen guests. The mood was great, only Harold mentioned once or twice that it was a pity midnight (and the end of the fast) were still hours away because he greatly missed having a drink or two with his friends, but well, rules were rules. I suggested a way out, bending those rules in a typical lawyerly fashion to free my former teacher. I asked him if Atlanta time or Jerusalem time should be applied. That argument, with the temptation added, won the day. Harold patted me on the shoulder, then we clinked our glasses.

Getting back to Karolin, I can find no trace of her keeping any remnants of Jewish identity along with her Christianity. Not everything can be brought back from oblivion. What I do see, however, is that "Paulanéni" was her companion also in Christianity. In the 1930s Karolin donated a bell to the Cathedral in Nagybecskerek. My friend in Becskerek, György Schön (whom I had asked to help find records on Karolin) discovered a website in which he found that the bell is called St. Stephen's Bell. More important, the inscription engraved on the bell reads "Paula Tóth et Karolin Messinger." All in all, I have no idea whether her Jewish ancestry remained important to Karolin or not. All I know is that by the time she fled to Budapest, what mattered was no longer what she thought of herself. In Ulitskaya's novel *Daniel Stein, Interpreter*, a character (Isaac Hantman) says: "No matter how Jews defined themselves, in the ultimate resort they were defined from the outside: a Jew is whom the non-Jews consider as one."

The documents are silent as to when exactly Karolin left Becskerek. My grandfather's diary says it was the persecution of Jews by the Germans that drove her to Budapest. Did she make her decision in the first days of the occupation? Or would it have been too late to flee by then, and she left a bit earlier? The Germans marched in in April 1941. They would have been naturally preceded by news, rumors and fears. The first fragments of new turns of speech and new attitudes coming from outside must have become apparent also in the streets, bars and cultural societies of Becskerek. Of course, the Germans of Becskerek were also concerned (and divided) by what was happening in Germany. The new kinds of tensions cropping among us are well shown by a registered letter written on September 17, 1940 by a Rudolf Wetzl to the leadership of the Hungarian Cultural Association. "In recent times," he writes, "I had to experience members of the association expressing… antipathy to my German race brothers and their leader." For that reason, he wants to leave the association. I hardly believe that a year or two earlier an expression like "race brother" would have been used by anyone in German, or in any other language for that matter, in Becskerek. Now it invaded the languages of my hometown. The Hungarian Cultural Association included German members with centuries-old bonds to other cultures. It appears that after so many years, at least for some, it became a problem.

At the bottom of the letter, there are notes handwritten by my grandfather. It was his habit to draft his reply right below the incoming letter, sometimes on its backside so as to make a clean copy of his reply later by hand or by typewriting, and then to send it. His reply stretches onto the backside. The closing sentence reads: "Our association holds every one of its members in high esteem. Yet, if anyone should feel that despite this, he no longer wishes to remain in our circle…we accept his resignation, if with pity, without unnecessary pretexts offered in explanation."

It appears that at that time (September 1940) world history was still manageable on a Becskerek level. Karolin may also have been in Becskerek still. But even if she was, she had to be painfully aware that she could not stay long.

I don't know if she was a reader of the Belgrade daily Novi Balkan. I found an issue among some other documents. It was the December 9, 1940 issue. In his lead article on the front page, Svetolik Cicvarić, co-director of the paper, declares first that he is a reasonable man. Then he tries to explain that the only person to assure the victory of reason these days is Adolf Hitler. Page two of the paper then goes on to discuss a pressing problem: "Can Jews be Firemen?" According to the author of the piece, they can, but only because it offers another chance for them to lay their hands on a lot of money, perhaps even on hundreds of thousands. This is how the big question—whether Jews can be firemen—appeared as a headline in the Cyrillic text:

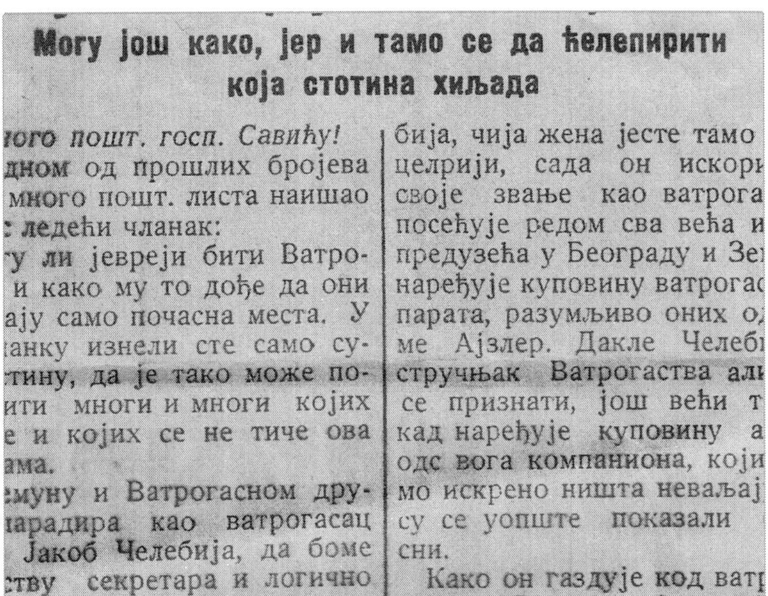

Могу још како, јер и тамо се да ћелепирити која стотина хиљада

іого пошт. госп. Савићу!
дном од прошлих бројева
много пошт. листа наишао
ледећи чланак:
у ли јевреји бити Ватро-
и како му то дође да они
ају само почасна места. У
анку изнели сте само су-
тину, да је тако може по-
ити многи и многи којих
е и којих се не тиче ова
ама.
муну и Ватрогасном дру-
арадира као ватрогасац
Јакоб Челебија, да боме
тву секретара и логично

бија, чија жена јесте тамо
целрији, сада он искор
своје звање као ватрога
посећује редом сва већа и
предузећа у Београду и Зе
нарећује куповину ватрога
парата, разумљиво оних о
ме Ајзлер. Дакле Челеб
стручњак Ватрогаства ал
се признати, још већи т
кад нарећује куповину а
одс вога компаниона, који
мо искрено ништа неваљај
су се уопште показали
сни.
Како он газдује код ват

Departure—From the Perspective of the Tax Authorities

After Karolin has gone to Budapest, legal proceedings continue in Becskerek, but these are no longer peacetime lawsuits of the Glavaški type. Neither does the kind of argument make a difference if there was a bench in front of the office or wasn't because waiting is no longer associated with benches anyway. People stand in queues everywhere, in front of bread shops, groceries and office corridors.

After little less than forty years, Karolin says goodbye to the daily worries, annoyances and successes that go with being owner and managing headmistress of her institute. In October 1941 she already is in Budapest and leases the entire Messinger Complex to the Hungarian Cultural Association of the Southern Region. Not for the first time. It was leased before (to the Serbian Ministry of Education) but as far as it can be established from the documents, that time it was only the school that was leased, while the students' living quarters were not. The new lease is not a genuine business deal. It is much more a last-ditch effort to stay in touch and not to lose all. Before her flight to Budapest, Karolin had been present and remained important for the Messinger. For a while, that is. Later on, they tried to obliterate that presence. Even her name was removed from the wall but in the public mind and speech it held on, perhaps out of defiance at the start, and later out of habit.

It is only the tax office that still fails to understand (or perhaps it both does and does not) what has been going on. As long as the institute was run by Karolin, it had a revenue after which income tax was paid. That was succeeded by the lease, and the tax levied on the rent. Then she left. A change in presence is not easy to comprehend, neither for the persons leaving their presence behind, nor for the tax authority. The tax office does keep track of the changes in the outside world but cannot break away from what became natural in its world of documents and paper trails. Tax procedures often show movements that outlive the reality. In this case the taxmen claim the tax on the lease, but they also demand the income tax from Karolin. Next follows a lawyer's submission addressed on April 10, 1942 to the Tax Office of Becskerek (called Petrovgrad just then). It contains that the levying of both taxes at the same time is contradictory and illegal. According to the submission, "the grammar school, finishing school and students' home, along with its furniture and teaching equipment" is on lease to the School Fund of the Hungarian Cultural Association of the Southern Regions, thus it is only the School Fund that might eventually be eligible for income tax payment. Karolin has taxable revenue only from the lease. On the same day, an appeal is also sent on behalf of Karolin to the Serbian Ministry of Finance. This one, too, mainly emphasizes that income tax might be levied only on the school fund (and not on Karolin), but it also includes the request that the school fund be exempted from this tax. According to the argumentation, the school fund is not a business enterprise, its revenues are sparse and come from voluntary donations only. Its aims are charitable, students do not pay, and the living expenses of children from families without means are being also covered by donations.

During World War Two, the Messinger operated by the school fund was indeed no longer a business venture. Neither had it any revenue. Karolin was due a rent payment, but the documents indicate that it was hardly more than symbolic. And it wasn't really possible to transfer money to Budapest. There was war. The tax levied on the rent was, as far as I can see, not paid by Karolin but by the school fund. Thus, the profitable business went on functioning only in the perception of the tax office.

I have no idea what became of the submissions requesting that Karolin should not pay two taxes and the school fund be exempt from the income tax. I can find no reply among the documents. Maybe none came. Those were not the days of bureaucratic meticulousness.

The Donation

Karolin arrived in Budapest not only as a persecuted Jew but as a very sick woman. Her days there were dominated mainly by her illness. She died on October 7, 1942 in cardiac arrest. She was laid to rest in the Farkasrét Cemetery. On her grave, on the same white marble slab, below Karolin's name, there is another name: Erzsébet Csoó, who died thirty years later. There is not a trace of that name in any of the documents. I tried to ask people in Becskerek, who I thought might know something. But I never found out who Erzsébet Csoó was.

A few months before her death, in the Weiss Manfred Sanatorium in Budakeszi, Karolin was facing the problem as to how the thing that was most important to her could continue into the future. She had no inheritors. What was close to her grew distant. In wartime, not only years change, but also eras, and even the recent past is separated quite sharply. That was probably the time Karolin started to grow into a legend in Becskerek. She was still looking for some kind of continuity in Budapest, and she saw that possibility in turning the Messinger into a Hungarian School House. That was also when her deed of donation was born. Karolin was a rightful owner, only in those years law and ownership were pretty volatile things. In order to implement the donation, on July 12, 1942, Karolin drafts a deed of foundation which reads "I am creating hereby a foundation out of the facilities of my educational institution and the boarding school attached to it including all its movables and other equipment." She designates the Danubian Hungarian Cultural Association (DMKSZ) as the trustee. Since at the time the survival of any current title, institution and even country in a few months was highly questionable, the deed of foundation adds that, should the DMKSZ cease to exist, the role should be filled by "the most prestigious Hungarian union active in Nagybecskerek at any given time." Page two of the document lays down that everything must be settled with proper attention paid to the "actual conditions and legal rules in force there" (whatever conditions and the rules of whichever country they may be), adding that "I only wish to emphasize that the school and the boarding establishment must exclusively serve the purpose of Hungarian schooling at all times." The document was written out in two copies. One remained with Karolin, while the other was passed on to the Danubian Hungarian Cultural Association. This second original copy went to the legal office where it stayed, and this is what I am holding in my hands at this moment.

The next problem was whether the donation of an owner of Jewish descent meant to serve "exclusively the purpose of Hungarian schooling at all times" had any chance of achieving its purpose in July 1942 in German-occupied Serbia. At that time, the occupying authorities wanted to deprive persons of Jewish descent, not only of their property, but even of the right of being mourned in the way anybody would deserve. My father (or maybe it was my grandfather) remembered that when Karolin died in Budapest, the Catholic Church in Becskerek was planning to have a memorial service for her, but the German authorities "warned" that Mass must not be said in memory of a Jewish woman. She nevertheless had her Mass. It was also announced in the paper *Torontál*. The church was crowded.

The "Sale," and a German Jail on Hungarian-Owned Grounds, for Hungarians

In the end, the grief could not be confiscated. The denial, however, went on. The tax office continued to demand that Karolin Messinger pay tax on the rent. My father wrote several appeals (on March 16, 1943, among others) asking the tax office to acknowledge that Karolin Messinger has passed away, no more rent is being paid to her, thus the tax claim is null and void. But what happened to the donation? I don't exactly know, but a number of things can be deduced from the documents.

For the Messinger Institute to end up in the hands it was meant to, first it had to be saved from being seized as Jewish property. A submission in German was the vehicle by which the effort was made. One lawyer's argument emphasizes that the objects in question are schools, and as such, badly needed by the community. According to the other, Karolin already converted to Christianity some seventy years ago. As far as I can see, the ploy was not completely successful. On August 12, 1943, DMKSZ petitioned the tax office to inform it of Karolin's eventual debts in taxes, pointing out that this is needed because it has to be presented to the Commissar of the (German) Military Command, so that "it can sell Karolin Messinger's properties to us." This more or less indicates what must have happened.

Thus, the Messinger is allowed to be the site of Hungarian schools, not as a donation by its owner, but as property sold for money by the Nazi Commissar (after he has confiscated it). There is also further evidence of the Hungarian character of the Messinger during the war. Here is a note from my grandfather's diary (one that I have already quoted in an earlier piece of writing):

> *19 March 1944, the day of St. Joseph. At half past five in the morning I hear loud talking and footsteps outside my door. Not long after that, in comes Józsi—I was in bed—with a blanket and a pillow on his arm. He kisses me, telling he came to say goodbye. Two German militiamen came to him with orders to get him dressed and take him along with me to the internment facility set up in the Messinger immediately. All the leaders of the Hungarian community here will be collected and kept in custody there, as the militiamen sent all over town to get them have said. The long discussion in front of my door was about me not being fit for being taken because, as Józsi and Zorka told them, I was sick in bed since the day before yesterday. At which one of the guards left, taking Józsi, while the other was phoning his commander from the office that the elder Várady is sick and in bed, and is 77 years old anyway (which, I indeed am, as I write this note), so what should he do? He left me home in the end. In the meantime, news kept coming in about the people who had been captured one by one. Our entire known Hungarian leadership is in custody there along with our prelate, even the leaders of the female camp: Saczi Mara and Irma Végh.*

So, when the German occupying authorities were confronted with the problem as to where to take the arrested Hungarians, or, using their terms, in what location should the "protective custody" take place, the answer was the Messinger. It seems even the German occupiers must have learned that when the Hungarians of Becskerek are involved, their place is the Messinger. This, by the way, was the day when the German army occupied Hungary (its ally), and this had repercussions in Becskerek, too.

The "protective custody" took a single day only, its memory dissolving fast in the quotidian reality of the war years. I still have some vague memory that at about noontime that day my mother left for the Messinger and took me along. She wanted to pass some sandwiches to my father and my uncle Pali, but we couldn't get past the German guards.

Karolin's Donation and the Liberation

I shall begin this section, which already takes us to the world that I came to know, with another diary note.

> *Thursday, 8. II. 1945. After a long pause, today we got a Russian quartered with us again. He is running the reparation works of damaged airplanes in a workshop set up in the classrooms of the former school in the Messinger. He is a young officer, 26 years old. He has been serving in the Russian army for 7 years, and he says he has fought in nearly every theatre of war. His mother was wounded several times and his brother was shot dead by the Germans.*

I remember the Russian soldiers assigned to and staying with us. I cannot recall a 26-year-old young officer among them, but of course the perspective from which I saw people at the time was quite different. It is quite obvious from my grandfather's lines that he did not dislike the fellow, but he did not envision his proper place to be in the Messinger (or in our house, for that matter). It was established two years earlier by Karolin in her deed of donation that the buildings donated must exclusively serve the purposes of Hungarian schools. Fate must have interpreted the "purposes of Hungarian schools" pretty broadly if they included the reparation of damaged Russian planes. I don't know, by the way, if the enthusiastic school supervisor who visited the Messinger sometimes in the early fifties knew anything about those airplanes. He delivered a rousing speech in the gym hall. There was one particular sentence I remember very clearly up to this day, especially as he repeated it three times: "The future is flying toward us!" From the safety of the back rows, a classmate and I objected that thus far we had been taught that we were advancing toward the future, not the other way around. Somehow we couldn't see the future galloping backwards to reach us. But that was a time when the optimistic dynamism of the word "flying" would trump everything. The right word at the right time could replace meaning. And not only then.

On May 7, 2013, I received a circular from the Dutch airline KLM. It informed me not only of the oft-repeated dream trip KLM is offering, but there were also the words "KLM takes new steps in sustainable flight." The magic word "sustainable" just had to be included. It made me think. When we mean that what we are doing is good and successful, then it has to be "sustainable." Words drawing applause join forces against pedestrian logic. How can a flight be sustained? Do the planes owned by KLM never land? When surrounded by vanguard words, nothing will be suspect. The committed school inspector lecturing us could easily have been a highly successful communications officer at KLM, had he been born a little later. This is, of course, sheer speculation. As is the question (and I would be sincerely curious to know) whether Margaret Thatcher and George Bush, had they grown up in the Soviet Union, would have become dissidents or party secretaries....

Continuing my search, now by computer, for items containing the name Messinger in my grandfather's diary, I read once again about the first days of liberation (or takeover of power).

> *Saturday, 12. V. 1945. I went to take a look inside the Messinger Institute of Education and boarding school. This was once an outstanding school and educational institution with a reputation far beyond the borders of the Banat. It had a modern, spacious gym hall which, after Trianon, when we were unwelcome everywhere, provided a home for the lectures of our Hungarian cultural association. With the possible exception of Lóri, all my children completed elementary school there. It had a well-kept, clean, tree-lined yard. Modern, airy, dormitories with running water for the children taking board there. All this was in the past. There is nothing today but ruins, litter, weeds, the walls separating it from the neighbors demolished, the trees uprooted, the school benches burnt up for heating, the entire equipment robbed, door handles broken, the floors, with visible traces of firewood having been chopped on it, scraped and cut up, stoves turned upside down; the whole place has been vandalized. It's sad. It was inhabited by Russians, then by partisans. –There is a possibility now that*

the entire building might be handed over to serve as the Hungarian grammar school. It is full of students, boys and girls busily trying to clean up the place and set things in some kind of order.

Read in this light, I have a much better understanding of the letter by Bély-Guiseppe (if that was indeed his name) which I quoted early on. When the school was reopened, the reason new school benches and chairs were needed was that the original furniture had been burned for firewood. There were no benches anymore, not only in front the headmistress's office but in the classrooms either.

As far as the "possibility" was concerned ("that the entire building might be handed over to serve as the Hungarian grammar school"), the battle between Karolin's final will and various authorities and policies continued. According to Paul Valéry "Politics is the art of preventing people from taking part in affairs which properly concern them."

In 1949, a suit is filed by the government agencies. The aim of the whole process is to prevent the Messinger from coming into the possession of those people to whom it was donated by Karolin, and to prevent them from being involved in its affairs. Identifying the opposing parties is not really easy. The petition is filed by the City Housing Assets Company of Zrenjanin on behalf of the Federal People's Republic of Yugoslavia. The respondent is named as "Hungarian Educational and Cultural Foundation in the representation of the Board of Directors represented by dr. József Várady, attorney at law in Zrenjanin." The petition was filed on June 16, 1949. The City Housing Assets Company (on behalf of the Federal People's Republic of Yugoslavia) demands that the district court bring a sentence declaring that the sales agreement made between the German commissar and the respondent is null and void because the property was seized by the occupiers against the will of the owner. The ownership of the property in the land registry must be restored (in favor of Karolin Messinger), but since she is no longer alive, it must be qualified as "abandoned property," the ownership of which is devolved on to the state. On March 23,1953, Serbian Deputy Minister of Education Jovo Grbović produces additional arguments in support of the ministry's claim. He points out that those who abandoned their property because of the occupation were entitled to reclaim it, something that Karolin Messinger failed to do; being dead, she could hardly do any such thing. Told in brief, since the Germans strove to take possession of the Messinger on the basis that it was the property (and donation) of a woman of Jewish descent, the cornerstone of the argument of the new people's liberation government is that the Messinger was appropriated by the Germans on invalid grounds. As a consequence, nothing is valid that has happened since, including the sales agreement. It follows that Messinger should go into the possession of the (new) state. The lawyers' counterarguments focus on Karolin's deed of foundation. That deed, they explain, is fully valid, so the facilities at issue do not constitute abandoned property. It was not Karolin from whom the property was seized by the occupiers, but the organizations to which she had donated it. And if the Messinger was taken illegally, then it must go to those from whom it was taken (the Hungarian foundation). The file includes the authorized Serbian translation of the deed. Earlier on it was translated also to German.

Exactly how and on what basis the decision was made is not entirely clear from the surviving documents. On the table of the decision-makers there lay a fragmented mosaic consisting of half-finished and half-destroyed pieces. For guidance, there was the momentum and the magic words. A Serbian lawyer of about my father's age remembered once that on one occasion in 1946 or 1947, in one of the people's liberation bodies there was a discussion of how competencies should be divided between the new town and county people's liberation authorities. The disagreement boiled down to which solution was bound up more closely with the word "antifascist." One participants of the dispute argued that it is more "antifascist" if the county has a broader responsibility. His opponent objected that the genuinely "antifascist" solution was if it was the town that had a greater competency. Lord Mansfield, the great eighteenth-century Scottish judge and legal scholar once said famously that "Most of the disputes of the world arise from words." It may be added that often the outcome of a dispute hinges on words also. In any case, once the real issue of a debate is which solution is more antifascist (or more communist, more liberal or illiberal for all I care), we will find ourselves in a much more comfortable position. We will no longer be hindered or slowed down by lengthy deliberations regarding the consequences, there will be no need to stop and examine the meaning of the words uttered. Pure momentum will help us over everything. Confucius said: "If I were to come to power, I would restore the meaning of words." But Confucius is still not in power anywhere.

The case was still open, and it had not yet been decided whether the Messinger was the property of The Hungarian Educational and Cultural Association of Becskerek or that of the state, when teaching in Hungarian began again. My grandfather's diary has this to say about the start of the schoolyear in 1950:

> *Sunday, 10. IX. 1950. Opening Ceremony of the new schoolyear announced for 8 o'clock today. Póji, and Tibi, dressed sharply, holding hands with Póji's little friend Lujza Lukics-Tunner, are waiting to leave for school. The 3 little schoolchildren are accompanied on their way by six adults: Zorka, Józsi, the Lukics Tunners, Dudy and László, but they are also joined by Imi in his little wheelchair, and me, watching from a block away. Big ones and little ones all enter the door of the Messinger Institute; me, I turn around and walk home.*

This was the day my little sister (Póji) entered first grade. I began earlier, in 1946, when the Messinger had not yet opened. My first school was about a half an hour's walking distance from our home, and walking was the only option. Except for the first couple of days, I would go to school alone, or at times together with some schoolmates from the neighborhood. We were only seven at the time but there was no car traffic in town, and when looked at from the perspective of a recent war that had just been finished, a peacetime walk like this did not seem particularly dangerous. We remembered much greater dangers and were accustomed to higher risks. I was transferred to the Messinger, almost next to our home, after four years of elementary school, in 1950. Conditions there were largely settled by then. There were school benches in sufficient numbers, and there were also all variety of chairs. We knew that there was a Soviet flag somewhere in the building, most likely in the attic. It was found by a school employee. In a sudden flash it comes to my mind that it was probably Mr. Kerekes, but I am not entirely sure. He did not dare to bring it down and was too afraid to dump it. This must have been right after Tito's break with Stalin. So, the Soviet flag stayed in the attic. The library stored mostly books from the past. Benches had been burned for heating, but the books weren't touched. True, they would have been lit more easily but they wouldn't warm you up. The benches produced more heat. There were instances when reason prevailed, even in the war years.

In practice the Messinger was no longer owned by the Hungarian Cultural and Educational Association, never mind that the lawsuit had not yet ended. The foundation did not go to whom it had been intended to go by Karolin Messinger, but, in the given circumstances and with reservations, it did serve the purposes of Hungarian schooling (just as it had been required by the deed of foundation). In hindsight, one might even argue that even though unjust, the takeover of the school by the state (first in practice, later also formally) may not have produced only bad things. As I mentioned earlier on, the Messinger was a kind of island in a world of new names, new titles, new forms of address, new beliefs and new drives. In the early years after war it was not impossible for a school to be owned by someone other than the state, but it was incompatible with the system even then. Had things developed differently, there could have been much bigger waves washing over the island, eventually running over it.

"The Messinger Possessions of the Hungarian Community"

The file includes a document which, if unintentionally and in a vaguely formulated manner, actually vindicates Karolin and the deed of foundation. On March 29, 1952, the land registry office of Becskerek (Zrenjanin) issued a formal summons regarding a new survey of property. The addressee is, in Serbian, "Mesinger dobro mađarske zajednice" (Messinger possessions of the Hungarian community). The confusion gained a fitting expression. The office seems not to be aware that the name of the establishment is no longer "Messinger," nor is it aware what exactly has happened. Not that it was easy to follow. The deed of foundation was not recognized by the German occupiers because it had been made by a Jewish woman. In line with the deed of donation, a foundation called "Corvineum" was duly established which, however, could not simply take possession of what it received as a gift because it had been donated by a Jewish woman. Instead, it had to buy the facilities from the German commissar. Liberation followed, but the way the new authorities saw it, property that had been confiscated by the Germans was tarnished German property, which could therefore not belong to those who bought it from them—not even if the property in question had actually been seized by the German authorities from the Hungarian foundation which was forced to buy it from them later. After the documents got mixed up or had burned, the office was unable to find the valid term, so it relied on what had been there in people's minds. The wording shows utter confusion, but the crucial fact, the connectedness between the Messinger and Hungarian schooling is there. That is how it became "The Messingers possessions of the Hungarian community."

Thus, Karolin's will had been acknowledged by the land registry, but the official view was different. One might draw the lesson that one of the ultimate means of the preservation of truth is well-intentioned lack of information drawing on public consciousness. In any case, the public consciousness on which the rather vague wording ("Messinger possessions of the Hungarian community") of the of the registry office relied on hung on after that too. When I was at grammar school, some initiatives (initiatives possible in the circumstances) were definitely inspired by Karolin's memory. All the teachers knew (we were not quite aware) that physical exercise had always been one of her priorities, and it remained one of their guiding principles in the post-war Messinger too. This may have been behind Mr. Fischer's skating-rink creating ambitions as well. Basketball and softball courts were also developed on the grounds. As opposed to every other school in Becskerek, the 10 o'clock "long intermission" took a full 30 minutes (in the others it was 20) so that we might run full circle around the nearby market square.

The Messinger today is a mixed-language school, both Hungarian and Serbian. Its name is Sonja Marinković School (her namesake was a Serbian partisan hero in World War Two: my sons also went to a school named after her in Novi Sad). The image living on in people's minds was reconfirmed recently when a tablet was placed on the school's wall in memory of Karolin Messinger. An even bolder initiative was launched at the end of January 2016 when the school board accepted the proposal that the school should officially retake the name "Messinger." This requires a decision on the level of Vojvodina province. That decision still hasn't come through. Getting back to the story of the registry office, it made me guess if the address was written correctly. On the envelope I read No. 3 Masarikova ulica. Turning the pages of the documents, I see that a pre-war submission has the address as No. 5 Masarikova ulica. In 1942, the year when Karolin Messinger made her deed of foundation, the same place was in 3 Nádor utca. In 1930 it was Slovenačka 8. But there was a time when it was Teplička 8. Today it is No. 7 Slobodana Bursaća. God knows, there may have been other addresses, sunken by now. Fortunately, the building has survived.

Street names and house numbers are not exempt from the various realities and visions of realities that succeed each other. There have been many different realities in recent years. Indeed, they seem to be stepping on each other's heels. And they include also the future. I do not think that the future is flying towards us. It rather waits for us. Hangs about, smiling. That smile is somewhat similar to that seen on the face of people standing on the front part of the platform, waiting for the arriving passengers, as the train draws up. When you are one of the arrivals you never know if the smile is meant for you or for someone coming up behind you. Maybe it is meant for no one on your particular train.

2. DUELING IN BECSKEREK

A World and the End of It

I have found nineteen dueling affairs in my grandfather's files. The majority of these took place between 1895 and 1920, but I found a duel case from even as late as 1944. In some of them, my grandfather was one of the dueling parties, in others a witness, a second, or a member of some duel court. Before I began browsing in these files, I only read about duels in works of fiction. Dueling was not a topic of conversation in my family either, not since I was old enough to take part in the conversation, that is. My grandfather did tell things, but only when asked. I was nineteen when he died at the age of ninety-two. I was aware that in sports, one of the fencing weapons, *épée* is called "dueling foil" in Hungarian but I never knew that real-life duels had been fought, usually by sword rather than by foil. Continuing the family tradition, I also took fencing lessons from Aunt Putsu, and I can even prove it by the photo below; I am seen squatting on the left.

I did not know, however, that earlier on, fencing had a different social role, a civilian reality beyond sport. Like most of my schoolmates, I was interested in a lot of things I was not supposed to be interested in, but dueling was not one of them. It never came to our minds since it did not have a specific purpose with which we could associate it with. Purposeless interest is something that makes its appearance only at later a later stage in life.

Dueling was prohibited but was also proper. It was often helpful in people's rise in society. Talking about the supporters of dueling, the famous nineteenth-century Hungarian novelist Kálmán Mikszáth has this to say in a 1892 piece titled "Romantic Raiders Reheated": "So sweet is the glory and the feat of being talked about! It is really worth having your skin scratched a little bit. More than that, it is worth seeking a chance for it."

Duels also drew the attention of the law to themselves. The best-known legislative act in Serbian legal history is the Code of Tsar Dušan, enacted in 1349. This act takes a somewhat hesitant approach to duels, concerning itself only with dueling between soldiers. According to Article 131, soldiers should not quarrel, and if they nevertheless do, they should fight a duel instead.

The same hesitation was still evident some 550 years later. In 1899 a law on military disciplinary courts was enacted in Serbia which permitted dueling between soldiers. The world of business, on the other hand, knew no hesitation and no bounds, and the Italian insurance company Assicurazioni Generali saw business. It published an ad in the official journal of the Serbian military (No. 32, 1904) proudly declaring what was most important for military officers. It was that the life insurance plan of Assicurazioni Generali also covered death in duel or war. Therefore, it was really worth his while for a military officer to sign up with Generali if he was the kind of man who preferred to take care of all eventualities.

Detailed dueling rules developed outside the boundaries of law but nevertheless in a legal language. In Montenegro, for instance, the rule was generally acknowledged that when someone challenges a person to duel, he is also obliged to send him an apple. In Hungary a detailed duel code was issued but it was put into words, not by a legislative body, but by Vilmos Clair. Clair was a descendant of one of Napoleon's soldiers; an ancestor of his halted in Hungary on the way home from Russia and started a family here. Vilmos Clair's Duel Code was first published in 1897 and saw twenty-nine editions. The one I found among my grandfather's books was the second edition, also published in 1897, the same year as the first. Well-worn, the copy must have been read very thoroughly, and maybe by more than one person. Some sections are underlined by pencil, others by blue or red ink. On page eighteen, for instance, the following sentences are underlined by blue ink: "In Greenland, song is being used as a weapon of duel. The opponents are mocking each other with songs, supported by their seconds. The party running out first of answers to the mocking is declared loser, and the winner is entitled to seize most of his possessions." Thus, as opposed to Becskerek (and the rest of the world), dueling in Greenland posed no danger to life, as no bodily harm was being done either. The seconds would fill the role of supporting poets. On the other hand, unlike in a traditional duel, it could have very severe financial consequences. The second edition of Vilmos Clair's Duel Code includes drawings by three painters, explaining the various kinds of dueling. The type "Duel by pistols with advancing" is illustrated by the drawing below.

Pisztolypárbaj közeledéssel (avance).

In Hungary, dueling was an offense punished by the courts (sometimes, that is), but judges also dueled quite often. At the time that Criminal Code of 1879, the problem of dueling provoked sharp disputes. In the end the problem was solved by the formula that dueling was forbidden and punishable—but under special rules. Which meant that if a person was to shoot his opponent dead or cause serious injury in a duel, he would not be charged with homicide or violence but with offenses described and specified in Paragraphs 293 to 300 of the Code. Punishments were much milder and prison sentences were spent in more favorable circumstances. There were four types of prison at the time. The mildest variety was the so-called "state penitentiary," which was where those sentenced for "duel offense" were sent. In these establishments, prisoners could spend the night in cells of their own, were allowed to wear their own clothes, have food brought in and even see lady visitors. According to György Ságvári, the author of the preface to the 2002 edition of the Vilmos Clair book, the guests of the state penitentiaries were allowed to have wine brought in and consume a maximum of five liters (!) a day. In Nagybecskerek there was no state penitentiary, so Becskerek duelists, in the rare cases when they were charged and sentenced, had to link serving their prison sentences with an excursion to Szeged.

If you allow me to digress a little, while leafing through the contemporary Nagybecskerek press, I found another example of the many ways in which the town of Szeged influenced the social life of my hometown. The August 11, 1904 issue of *Nagybecskereki Hírlap* (Nagybecskerek News) carried the following appeal:

> Who Wants to Marry?
>
> I have the good fortune to bring it to the notice of ladies and gentlemen, **local or regional**, that without any difference as to religion and nationality, **marriage** proposals appropriate to age, job, social standing and financial position are available at the highest degree of confidentiality.
>
> Requests from the countryside will be immediately answered in case a stamp in the value of 10 fillér is attached.
>
> With the highest respect
>
> **Béla Kövesi**
>
> Szeged, No. 18, Mérei utca

Returning to dueling, many were critical about the vogue of duels, which appeared to be spreading. Anti-duel leagues were even formed at the beginning of the nineteenth century, but to little or no avail. The first movement against dueling was established in Nagyvárad. Endre Ady, one of the most famous Hungarian poets, was among the organizers. After that, an organization was formed on the national level, too, but its chairman, István Rakovszky, himself continued dueling. The irony of something being both "prohibited and appropriate" was pointed out by Ady in a piece of journalism:

> Minister Fejérváry and Deputy Lengyel dueled unperturbed, and in Nagyvárad, the seat of the league, two journalists pointed pistols at each other, both of whom must have written frequently against dueling. Thus, the dueling epidemic seems to be more virulent than ever... With all its tragic overtones, this is a very ridiculous little matter. So long live dueling, this homeland of chivalry and honor, and goodnight!
> (Endre Ady: In Support of Dueling, *Nagyváradi Napló*, March 22, 1903.)

And dueling, this homeland of chivalry and honor, did live on for quite some time. Illegal though it was, in this forbidden little world rules and rituals had a key importance. The documents show that there were three kinds of courts active in the world of duels. *Courts of honor* were established mainly to determine if someone was qualified for dueling or not. It was the job of *duel courts* to decide on matters of principle regarding the peaceful or armed settlement of issues of honor (for instance on the question whether, in a given case, it was justified to demand full satisfaction in the form of armed combat, and who was obliged to provide it). And then there was the *court of weapons* to decide (if the parties were not able come to an agreement) on the weapon with which the duel was to be fought. There were other participants who helped directing the action taking place on the site. The various courts were picked by the parties themselves or by their seconds or other supporters. There were some cases (though rare) when the matter ended up in a regular court in the wake of information to the police. From then on, however, the focus shifted from the issue of the duel to the duel itself and its punishment. Nor was the court picked by the parties.

There were duels whose outcome was fatal. To remain in the Banat, in 1886 the novelist Ferenc Herczeg fought a duel with an officer in Versec. The events leading to the conflict were associated with the charity ball of the Versec Association for the Promotion of the Hungarian Language. At the ball, a girl, a relative of Herczeg, was offended by a military officer. After the event Herczeg, pointing at the officer, apologized to the crowd for having invited people of such behavior, who were obviously not gentlemen. It was the officer who challenged Herczeg to a duel. The duel was fought with swords, and the officer lost his life on the spot. Ferenc Herczeg was sentenced to four months in a state penitentiary. It was while in prison that he wrote the novel *Fenn és lenn* (Up and down).

Duels were expected most of the time to provide some kind of relief or an escape from the unending back-and-forth of heaping scorn at one another. They may have been actually helpful in the sense that by putting people in the way of genuine, deadly danger compared to which the silly "offense" provoking the affair (say, an ironic sentence of the type of "this coat hardly fits you, you must have stolen it") was dwarfed.

Beyond the Banat, the nineteenth century novelist Jókai tried to lend a more human face to dueling, or at least one kind, in the book *Egy magyar nábob* (A Hungarian tycoon).

> So, when the parties do not seek duel out of bloodthirst or pure rage but are forced to bring it about in order to demonstrate the strength of their heart of the firmness of their conviction even in the face of death, that is normally the time when their second put pistols in the hand of duelists. They will think in cold blood, both being exposed to the threat of being shot dead, but neither will shoot at his opponent. Thus the duel will be completed, nobly and befitting men. The demands of honor are satisfied and the issue of the offense buried deep, so much that it must not even be brought up again.

There were also authors who even attempted (though without the great talent of Mór Jókai) to claim that duels were above the law. Behind a row of books lined up neatly on my grandfather's bookshelf, I came upon a thin little booklet authored by Zoltán Cseresnyés de Felső-Eőr, first lieutenant of the hussars, published in a private edition in Budapest. According to the author, "The Duel, not the law, is the only means that keeps some people from giving way to the wild outbursts of their nature, to unjust attacks and offenses." The title of the book, *The Outcome and Possibilities of Dueling with Swords without Danger* is itself quite interesting.

The length to which some people were ready to go to be served proper satisfaction is illustrated by the celebrated affair of István Keglevich, who became my grandfather's fellow member of parliament in 1905 (Keglevich was a government supporter while my grandfather sat in the opposition). Before his election to Parliament, Keglevich had a duel in Paris which was famous enough to be included in Máté Eszes's bestseller *Famous Fights, Infamous Duels.* Keglevich stayed in Paris in the company of a Hungarian actress, and the actress was offended by a French aristocrat. What better occasion to prove a gentleman's virility and heroism than an incident like this! Keglevich instantly demanded satisfaction of honor. It turned out, however, that there was an obstacle. His French opponent, although he did come from a noble family, was not only in debt up to his chin but also suspected of bill forgery. This meant that he was not qualified for dueling, but worse, it seemed that Keglevich would be deprived of the opportunity to provide proof of his knightly honor. What does Keglevich do to overcome such a hindrance? Well, he paid the man's debts down to the last penny, in effect restoring his opponent's honor, so that he was qualified to duel again. The famous fight, now a celebrated affair in Paris too, duly took place. Not even the seconds were common men. One of them was a certain Colonel Pétain, ten years later the great hero of the French nation in World War One, and later still, in World War Two, its even greater traitor (by then known as Marshal Pétain). Anyway, Keglevich was able to stab his opponent in the shoulder. I cannot help wondering about the feelings and responses of the actress, then and later.

And what were these duels like in Becskerek? I think their time is so far gone that they no longer belong to the part of the past that still makes itself felt. No one remembers, and even the stories and rumors surrounding such events have been long forgotten. Of course, there are archives but documents involving duels, being not only confidential but actually illegal, would hardly find their way into such public repositories in Becskerek. I wonder if they would elsewhere. However, there were also news articles that reported only the outcome. There are somewhat more documents in the court archives—involving the few cases where charges were brought against the duelists. There are books, though, showing that dueling was important. I know from a writing by the cultural historian Ferenc Németh that in 1897 a fencing trainer, Vilmos Payka, published a handbook called *Fencing Duel*, which was printed in Nagybecskerek in the Pleitz printing house.

And then there are original documents, records, declarations, witness confessions, decisions by duel courts, and written notes by judges—where they survived. I found documents on nineteen dueling affairs. A few cases are fully documented from start to finish, from the offense requiring satisfaction of honor to the duel itself. In other cases, the documents fail to cover how things ended, but the shape of the world of dueling emerges clearly even from those. I do not know if duel documents survive in the houses of other Becskerek families among papers not yet thrown out. Under the circumstances, it is highly unlikely. What follows has been selected from the dueling documents that survived.

Relieving Oneself Followed by Defense of Honor with Special Regard to Qualification for Dueling

The first document among the ones I found is a handwritten testimony dated December 2, 1895. Its signatories, Ferenc Kirják, his younger brother D. Kirják, and Gyula Semsey first describe that on December 1, 1895 they were sitting in the restaurant of the Hungarian King Hotel with company. Baron Pachtenkirch was with them, too. D. Kirják also signed his full name on the document, but of his first name only the initial "D" is clearly legible. Completed with the rest, the name looks reminiscent mostly of "Dragan," which, however, is contradicted by the fact that in a subsequent letter, Mr. N. Kirják is mentioned by First Lieutenant of the Reserves György Emmanuel Jr., a member of the court of honor. On the other hand, an unsigned note, most probably by my grandfather (on the basis of the familiar handwriting), who must have been also a member of the court of honor, mentions Dezső Kirják. I wonder what historians do in cases like this, when forced to decipher handwritten documents. Would they drop the "N" version because it contradicts the "D" so clearly visible in the signature, and make their decision after that, choosing between Dragan and Dezső? What if others are reminded by the characters following the "D" rather of "Dénes" than Dezső? Do they write history with a switched protagonist after that? Or do they simply admit that the issue is unresolvable?

A hastily scribbled "N" or a couple of flourishes of the pen may have been accidental, of course. Like when you walk absently, and one of your feet steps accidently in the roadside mud. But is the accident itself not transient like everything else? The rhythm and direction of the walk vanishes in time, as does the absent-mindedness. But the footprint in the mud remains, its accidental character gone. In the same way, if the surviving signatures of Kirják Jr. did not contain the "D" so legibly, then the accidental character of the "N" would disappear. Having raised the issue, I looked at all three documents with the signature of D. Kirják written at the bottom in the hope of finding out what the accident deviates from, but I found nothing. So, I will stick to "D."

Ferenc Kirják was a resident of Temesvár. D. Kirják lived in Becskerek. Baron Pachtenkirch was in all probability also from Becskerek and, as it turns out from the documents, a retired army lieutenant. His first name was Oscar. At the time, Temesvár and Nagybecskerek both lay within the borders of the same country, as two towns in the Banat. They were not regarded as being particularly far from one another. There may come a time when this will be so once again. On July 1, 2015 I read in the Serbian press that the shipping route on the River Bega between Temesvár and Nagybecskerek may be restored with EU funding. There may even be a bicycle route connecting the towns. Temesvár and Nagybecskerek could be once again within the borders of a single community of nations, the EU. But it takes some waiting still.

Returning to 1895, the handwriting reveals that the testimony was written by Ferenc Kirják but signed—in inks of different color—also by D. Kirják and Gyula Semsey. The document relates that:

> ...at one o'clock after midnight a very mixed and loud company entered, which compelled us to leave the place. After we left, and were relieving ourselves in the street, a young man unknown to us materialized in front, and asked in a provocative voice: "Why are you gentlemen leaving?" To which the Baron replied in all calmness: "Because we feel like going home." Upon this answer, the man, allegedly called Naszke, said to Pachtenkirch: "It wasn't you I asked." Hearing this retort, Mr. Pachtenkirch, still quite calmly, said, "You don't call me 'you.'" To you I will always be 'Sir,'" to which the above-mentioned individual replied, "You may be a baron for all I care, but I am not afraid of you." —At this

> statement Pachtenkirch, very upset by now, said: "You are snotty kid and a slapped-faced rascal!"

This is followed by the record of further details, showing how things slipped in the direction of physical assault, but remained in the end within the confines of an exchange of words as the gentlemen ready to fall upon each other were restrained by their companions. Reading the statement, I was intrigued mostly by the use of the phrase "relieving ourselves" in this context and in a style conceived in 1895. The documents, however, include the handwritten statement of D. Kirják himself. The very first sentence describes clearly what exactly the baron and his friends were doing after having the left the Hungarian King Hotel:

> On the 1st of December of the year 1895 we were having a conversation with my brother Ferenc Kirják, a resident of Temesvár, and Oscar Baron von Pachtenkirch, a retired 1st lieutenant of the army, in then restaurant of the Hungarian King Hotel, and when we left, all three of us were relieving ourselves (urinating) and were about to leave for home…

This is how a handwritten statement looked like in 1895:

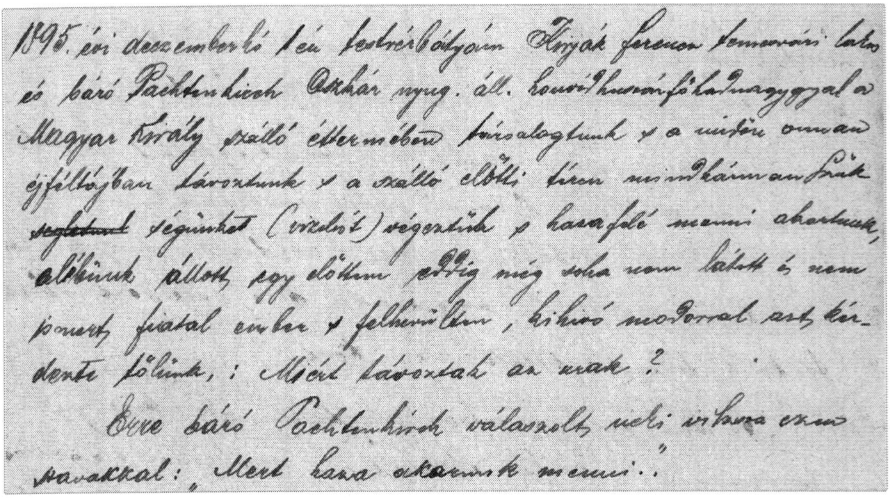

1895. évi deczember hó 1én testvérbátyám Kirják Ferencz temesvári lakos
és báró Pachtenkirch Oszkár nyug. áll. honvédhuszár főhadnagygyal a
Magyar Király szálló éttermében társalogtunk s a midőn onnan
éjféltájban távoztunk s a szálló előtti téren mindhárman szük-
~~szükségletünket~~ ségünket (vizelést) végeztük s haza felé menni akartunk,
előttünk állott egy előttem eddig még soha nem látott és nem
ismert fiatal ember s felhevülten, kihívó modorral azt kér-
dezte tőlünk,: Miért távoztak az urak?
Erre báró Pachtenkirch válaszolt, [illegible] ezen
szavakkal: „Mert haza akarunk menni".

The separate statement of D. Kirják clearly reveals that the baron and the Kirják brothers took a piss together. The quantity of drink consumed was probably one of the things urging them, but the historical circumstances also contributed: in December 1895 there was still no electric lighting in the streets, so the public nature of the action was less of an inhibiting factor. However, the same historical circumstances also prevented the conflict from turning physical. At that time, one couldn't zip up with a single motion and be ready to fight at once. One had to bottom up painstakingly. That gave time to intervene for those who wanted to prevent escalation.

These events in themselves hardly point in the direction of honor and chivalry. Maybe, though, the anger welling up in the participants grew past the events and raised things to the level of dignity of honor. Then there was also the anxiety not to be left out of the extended elite. For some time by then, the elite were no longer limited to the nobles (as opposed to the serfs) but included others as well, or they felt they could be included. That meant that there was a great deal of uncertainty too, since it could be clearly seen that the word "honor" written on the flag was a pretty volatile thing. Nevertheless, the duty of the defense of honor was an undoubted part of the deal. The men having drinks at the restaurant of the Hungarian King may have felt that they were inside, but the cost of staying in there was the protection of honor, at least within the community. This demand (or urge) to stay inside resulted in a way of settling disputes where the basic objectives known to the legal profession were absent. Who won, though not irrelevant, was not the point. Not every duel had a winner and a loser. It was not uncommon that the pistol of neither party hit its target. But whether there was a winner or loser or not, both parties were absolved. Nor was it important who was right and who was wrong, whether the statement provoking the disagreement was right or wrong. In a dispute where Mr. White declared that Mr. Black was a "liar and a thief," while Mr. Black called Mr. White a "libelous slanderer," the expected outcome was not to find out if Mr. White had lied and stole or Mr. Black had slandered. The point was the satisfaction of honor itself, which showed that Mr. Black and Mr. White were both gentlemen for whom honor was important and were ready to do what had to be done to prove it.

The events of December 1, 1895 were followed by other developments, and in the end the duty of giving chivalrous satisfaction fell not to Mr. Naszke and Baron Pachtenkirch but to Ernő Naszke and D. Kirják. In reaction to Baron Pachtenkirch's words, Ernő Naszke's wanted the matter solved by lodging a complaint with the Szeged military command rather than challenging the baron to duel. The command was in no hurry to return a verdict. In the meantime, life went on, and so did coffeehouse life. According to the documents, in April 1896, around Easter, Ernő Naszke and Baron Pachtenkirch ran into each other again in the restaurant of the Hotel Pest in Becskerek. D. Kirják was there, but so were some new characters: Dr. Lipót Pajor and Móricz Nessmann. According to D. Kirják's note, Ernő Naszke:

> ...made another rude attack on Baron Pachtenkirch who had been entertaining there, as a consequence of which he was beaten with a weapon by Mr. Pachtekirch.
> It was only thanks to the goodwill of the gentlemen intervening that he was able to escape uninjured, and at the same time forgiven by Pachtenkirch on the condition that he withdraws his unfounded complaint at the Szeged infantry brigade.

The documents include only a brief statement by Ernő Naszke which leaves the details unmentioned, so the picture is not quite complete, but he clearly emerges as a loser from this story rather than a winning hero. He was not only scorned but also beaten by a weapon by the baron. In all probability the weapon in question was a sword worn mainly as an elegant accessory for restaurants and coffeehouses, but sometimes used in a different way when needed. He was beaten probably with the flat of the sword and even made to apologize for having "rudely attacked" the baron (probably verbally only).

With that, Ernő Naszke slipped to the brink of losing his qualification for dueling. In a book titled *The Emergence of Duel and its Decreasing*, published in 1903 in Budapest, the law professor Mihály Herczegh makes an attempt to put dueling in the context of honor and morality. He complains (1903) that the border between what matters as honest and what does not is becoming increasingly blurred, that honor is losing ground, nevertheless the threat of becoming disqualified from dueling is still capable of commanding proper behavior. In Herczegh's view,

> The notions and borderlines of honor and decency have become rather blurred, and common delinquency is increasing even in the educated

> classes. So much so that today it is no longer the spell of honor and its creed that holds wrongdoers in check but their interest in benefits and their fear of being caught, and the keeping up of appearances, which suggests that anything can be done, only two things must be avoided at all costs: prison and loss of qualification for dueling.

It is safe to assume that Ernő Naszke had similar feelings. He had refrained from demanding a duel in his quarrel with Pachtenkirch, but when he came up against D. Kirják, he did not. They ran into each other in a coffeehouse again, and Kirják called him a "shameless brute." Naszke demanded that honor be satisfied. Kirják may have been a less of a dangerous dueling opponent than Pachtenkich. That was the point when, around Easter in 1896, the all-important question arose if Naszke was qualified for dueling or not. Kirják had several strong arguments against it. One was that in his disagreement with Pachtenkirch, "he evaded the satisfaction of honor, and worse, he even apologized, and by withdrawing his complaint, he set his character on such a low shelf at which <u>an open, manly character</u> cannot exist" (he underlining comes from the original text). As if this was not enough, Kirják adds, in a pub incident, a gentleman called Pál Végh "was hit from behind" by Naszke.

Once the qualification for dueling had been called into dispute, it became important to clarify who was right: the party alleging the other's disqualification from dueling or the party denying that any grounds for disqualification existed. The court of honor had to provide an unambiguous answer to two well-defined and interconnected questions:

> Do you deem Mr. Ernő Naszke qualified for dueling? Yes or no?
> Is Mr. Kirják obliged to provide satisfaction of honor? Yes or no?

With regard to the complexity of the issue, the court of honor held several sessions, as is known from a letter written by György Emmánuel, First Lieutenant of the Reserves of the Hungarian Royal Army. (This is the one containing the erroneous spelling "N. Kirják.") On June 14, 1896, György Emmánuel excuses himself that "I am being prevented by unforeseen events from participating in the next consecutive session. For this reason, I am asking the Court to kindly accept Sub-notary Bertalan Szilágyi as my substitute," which indicates that the first session was followed by a minimum of one "consecutive session."

The jurisdiction of the court of honor depended on the will of the parties to the dispute. The file includes the relevant statement of both parties on the issue. Ernő Naszke declares that "I subject myself fully to the sentence of the court of honor" while Dezső Kirják writes, "I will be unconditionally reconciled with the decision of the Esteemed Court." This was the order of things in those days.

And this is also where the story ends, unfortunately. The batch of documents includes three pages of notes by my grandfather recording some of the more important words and sentences of the witnesses heard by the court. I see that they include the testimony of a certain Balázs Kresztics. (It occurred to me that he may have been an ancestor of Vasilje Krestić, a Becskerek-born Serbian historian and member of the academy. I met Krestić a couple of months ago, and I asked him. It turned out that I was right. It was his grandfather.) The decision of the court of honor, however, is unfortunately missing from the documents so it is precisely the outcome that remains a secret. I have some pangs of conscience at this point. Maybe I ought to have admitted it right at the beginning.

I shall try to recompense the reader by offering another decision by the court of honor from the same year (1896), in which the same thing was at issue: qualification for dueling. The parties to the affair of honor were Miksa Eibeschitz and Mór Schlesinger, both of them lawyers. The scene this time was not a restaurant or a pub but the "lawsuit store" of the Becskerek courthouse. This was a room where trial documents, files or records were being taken in and handed over, basically the predecessor of what came to be the registry. In this "lawsuit store," Miksa Eibeschitz was reading a statement from a lawsuit's records in which Mór Schlesinger had characterized him in defamatory terms, complaining about his "revolting false accusations." Schlesinger was just about to leave the lawsuit store when he was caught up with by Eibeschitz who told him, "what you have done is despicable." Eibeschitz then returned to the lawsuit store but this time it was Schlesinger who caught up with him and slapped his face. After these events, Eibeschitz demanded satisfaction of honor.

None of these events were disputed by either of the two parties. Both parties appointed their seconds, and my grandfather was named as one of the seconds of Eibeschitz. The duelists and their seconds agreed on the course of action in case there were a duel. Three moves were fixed with high precision on February 12, 1896:

> 1. Time: 13th of March, 1896, 7 o'clock in the morning.
> 2. Meeting point: the space in front of the treasury forest.
> 3. Weapons: pistols, a single exchange of bullets. A distance of 25 steps with an advance (advancing on each other) of five steps each. Dr. Miksa Eibeschitz is entitled to the first shot; shooting at a clapping of hands. Should both parties remain unhurt, the duel continues with swords, applying bandages, until disability to disability to fight, but in any case, the fencing cannot last longer than half a minute, and with that, the fight is over.

Thus, every detail was settled except for the minute point if there would be a duel at all, since the qualification for dueling of Miksa Eibeschitz was called into doubt by Mór Schlesinger. This was left to the court of honor to decide, the members of which included the famous jurists Ede Alföldy and Ferenc Stassik who had no need for the world of dueling to build prestige and honor for themselves, yet this was a world of which was impossible to stay out. Ede Alföldy was a court judge and also the author of several books published in Nagybecskerek as well as in Budapest, including one on tort in 1905, and he also published over fifty papers in *Jogtudományi Közlöny* (Journal of Legal Science). Ferenc Stassik was a renowned lawyer, and also wrote scholarly books, for instance on the Hungarian expropriation law, which was published in Nagybecskerek in 1905. I just checked this, and having done so, I must step back for a moment and wait until I catch my breath, the shock passing. What? Hungarian legal books published in Nagybecskerek in 1905? Today you wouldn't find a single bookshop where Hungarian books could be bought. Stassik, by the way, also translated Rousseau's *Du contrat social* from French into Hungarian in 1875. It was in his legal office that my grandfather began his legal career as a clerk and lawyer candidate.

Two arguments were brought up by Schlesinger which, he thought, would rule out Eibeschitz's qualification for dueling. One was that Eibeschitz had used his legal title before he had obtained the proper qualification allowing it. The other was put in the following way:

> When he still served as the office manager of the lawyer Lázár Stern, he received 50 forints from his boss for the purpose of paying the fine that one of his clients was obliged to pay, but he used the money for his own purposes, repaying it only when, three weeks later, it was revealed that he had failed to fulfil his assignment.

These were the allegations with which the court of honor was faced. It handed down a verdict, too, but entirely without having investigated the objections. The wording of the decision shows that it is a work of outstanding legal professionals. I suspect that they had looked for a solution by which the tiring work of establishing the facts could be avoided. According to the members of the court of honor:

> The court of honor cannot engage in the factual investigation of the objections raised by Mór Schlesinger against the qualification of Miksa Eibeschitz for dueling. Objections may be subject to trial by court of honor only when maintained by the objector at all times and not only when the question of the satisfaction of honor is raised.

The court of honor explains that during the process it was revealed that "the parties used to be close friends before the affair" and had been on intimate terms. Thus, if Mr. Schlesinger had found the early use of law title and the treatment of the 50 forints by Miksa Eibeschitz objectionable, then he ought to have raised his objections earlier, and not only when the issue of his own duel came up. In other words, a person's qualification for duel can only be called into doubt by someone who is consistent in his honorable objections. The court also brought up another argument supporting its decision, explaining that it cannot examine the objections of Mór Schlesinger because "the committing of a physical attack also cancels the right for raising objections." Thus, once someone has slapped another man, then he cannot avoid dueling on the ground that the person hit is not qualified for dueling. These ideas were of precedent value. They are also convincing, as are other legal arguments in sentences, submissions, books and legal papers by Ede Alföldy and Ferenc Stassik. Elevated thinking, it seems, may have had a place in legal practice as well as in practices prohibited by the law. No matter what shape a specific world takes, there is always a chance inside, in its details, for both wisdom and foolishness. The court of honor made its decision on March 12, 1896. It ruled that the duel could go on as planned on the thirteenth.

I am pleased to let you know this time that both of the parties survived, probably without any serious injury. In the case of Schlesinger, I know because the next file in the batch regards another duel involving him. The opponent this time was Dr. Győző Pollák, the site an army barracks, and the date April 15, 1896, hardly more than a month after the Schlesinger-Eibeschitz duel. My grandfather now was a second to Schlesinger. That Eibeschitz also got off without serious trouble I found out from my grandfather's diary, where he is mentioned several times, especially in connection with the turbulent events associated with the Nagybecskerek carpet factory in 1903. Turning the pages of old newspapers of surviving Becskerek newspapers, I also found that Dr. Győző Pollák, too, must have remained unshaken by the duel. I found the following piece of news in the July 9, 1910 issue of *Délvidéki Újság* (Southern Region News): "Tomorrow morning at half 9 will be the wedding of Dr. Győző Pollák, lawyer in Nagybecskerek, and the gentle lady Miss Vilma Fein, the beloved daughter of Mr. Lipót Fein, a former hotel owner."

Returning to the Naszke-Kirják affair, I can only make guesses. The guidelines laid down in the Schlesinger-Eibeschitz affair are hardly applicable to the Naszke-Kirják issue. It may provide some help in guessing that the Schlesinger-Eibeschitz disagreement (as well as some others) show a distinct pro-qualification for dueling approach. I have no proof, but somehow I do not suppose that this approach was unique to Nagybecskerek. On any case, if I had been in the place of my grandfather I would have voted for Naszke. The poor fellow had not only been scorned but also beaten by the flat of the sword. I would at least have let him have his qualification for dueling.

An Everyday Affair

The preliminaries took place in the Promenade of Becskerek on the morning of July 14, 1906. My generation, just like the previous ones, grew up in the belief that the Promenade was and would always remain the most important street in town. Looking for things associated with the Promenade as it was then, I came upon a picture postcard sent in 1903. In it, the street does not look exactly as it does today or did when I was a child, but I can recognize it. It is still the same street, but back in July 1906 it must have looked exactly the same as in the 1903 postcard.

The Promenade was also a place where duels were regularly sparked off. The files pertaining to one such duel came to my hands because one of the protagonists was my grandfather's childhood friend and later university classmate, Samu Kardos. They also spent their compulsory military service together in Trieste in 1887–1888, two young Hungarians from Becskerek, receiving commands in German in the army. My grandfather told me about that when Trieste became the matter for street demonstrations in the early part of the 1950s. Large crowds were marching in the Promenade of Becskerek, chanting: "TRST JE NAŠ! ŽIVOT DAMO, TRST NE DAMO!" (Trieste is ours. We give our lives, but we don't give Trieste!). Things, however, turned out differently: Trieste went to Italy after all, but we nevertheless stayed alive. Moreover, in the '60s, Trieste somehow became part of our life again because people from all over Yugoslavia would go shopping in Trieste. Not only from the Croat and Slovene regions close to Trieste, but even from Serbia, spending a whole night on the train. I also remember that right after Trieste had failed to become ours, the great country-expanding drive switched over to a scapegoating drive. The windows of the Becskerek lawyer Boža Ankić (his house was near ours) were shattered because "he approved that Trieste should go to Italy." I couldn't imagine—and frankly can't even today—how the act of "approval" actually went. People in the Promenade, no longer the previous crowds but only their hard core, were chanting: "BOŽA IZDAJICA!" (Boža is a traitor!). Calling Ankić by his first name could have indicated some sort of personal relationship, but that was not the case. The name "Ankić" could in no way make up a rhyme when connected to "indicia." (It wasn't perfectly in rhyme with the first name either, but it worked.)

So, there were days when the mood was fiery on the Promenade of Becskerek. The event described in 1906, leading to the duel, however, lacked genuine passion. Let me continue chronicling the events. Since he was my grandfather's classmate, I know that Samu Kardos must have been thirty-nine years old at the time. The records have his name as Dr. Samu Kardos. He was a lawyer. His opponent also had a doctorate, presumably also legal. He was called Dr. Dezső Papp. I know nothing about him. Most likely he was another lawyer. The records were taken down by the duelists' seconds (including my grandfather) on the day of the event. Even the time of day is known, because, according to the first sentence, these records "were taken in Becskerek at 9 o'clock p.m. on July 14, 1906, in the affair of honor emerging between the gentlemen Dr. Dezső Pap and Dr. Samu Kardos." I assume it was taken in our office because it was near the Promenade.

What went down (had the affair happened these days) could be summed up in a single sentence: on the Promenade, a guy by the name of Dezső called over to another guy called Samu, to which Samu must have said, "who is this guy talking to?" The whole thing would hardly raise eyebrows, or rise above the level of an ordinary event on an ordinary day. Not much more than that happened in 1906 either, but in those days, a duel was also something within sight on a normal day. The seconds of the duel noted events as follows:

> This morning Mr. Samu Kardos, in the company of his friends, while walking down the main street, was just passing Mr. Dezső Papp when he heard the following remark: "shabby fellow." As Mr. Kardos had not personally known Mr. Dezső Papp at all, and the two of them never had the slightest personal contact, so there was no reason for him to think

> that the above-quoted derogatory expression had been meant for him; however, at the same time, while uttering these words, Mr. Dezső Papp was steadily gazing at Mr. Kardos, so the latter had no choice but to turn to him and ask, "who do you mean?"

That was all that happened, nothing more, nothing less. Following the incident, the representatives of Samu Kardos asked for satisfaction of honor, and the representatives of Dezső Pap (including Uncle Pista Demkó whom I knew well) said that they were "willing to provide the satisfaction demanded in an armed form." The conditions were set out in detail too:

> A sword duel until inability to fight, with neck, armpits and wrists bandaged, in the boathouse of the local regatta association, to be fought at 8:30 a.m. on July 15, 1906. Stabbing prohibited. The duel is to be directed by Imre Várady.

The outcome is also recorded on the backside of the sheet of paper. According to that note, the duel had been duly fought next day, on the of July 15, 1906 at 8:30 a.m. What happened was this:

> Sword duel was fought at the previously established time and place and ended with the wounding of Mr. Samu Kardos on the left side of his neck. With the ensuing inability to fight having been established by the doctors, the duel was declared over by the duel director. With that, in keeping with the rules of honor, the matter has become completed.

As far as I know, the notion of "inability to fight" was treated pretty loosely—one might even say, humanely—and probably not only in Becskerek. A few drops of blood would do. The notion of being "against the law" was also tolerantly interpreted when applied to dueling. Almost every one of those present at the duel in the regatta boathouse was a lawyer, with the exception of Uncle Pista Demkó. After the affair was over and done with, the prohibited action was also duly and legally finished, honor having been restored. The time was a little over nine o'clock, so the actors, the majority of them lawyers could walk over to the courthouse, which was couple of minutes away, also on the bank of the River Bega. It was, and still is, one of the finest buildings of the town of Becskerek.

Later that evening both duelists were able go for a walk on the Promenade with their heads held high. Thanks to the wound on the left side of his neck, now the manly honor of Samu Kardos became visible even on the outside for everyone to see.

Friendly Affairs

My grandfather had several dueling affairs. He was even sentenced in relation to one. That particular duel was fought on June 30, 1902. My grandfather's opponent was Géza Papp, a fellow member of parliament. My grandfather wounded him on his forehead. As established, the wound would heal within two days. Since the affair got some press too, the court also had to react. My grandfather was sentenced to five days in prison. Géza Papp got three days. The sentence had to be spent in the state penitentiary in Szeged (where, as we know, prisoners did not have to wear uniforms and were also allowed to have wine brought in—but no more than five liters per day). The arguments of the court are quite detailed. It provides a picture of the dueling world, including the fact that the territory was governed by the rule of law—but not really.

The statement explains that Géza Papp "turned to requesting satisfaction of honor by arms under the pressure of the oblique attitude of society." In the case of my grandfather, the same idea is expressed in the sentence

"He too acted under social pressure." With that, the court acknowledged that duels, while forbidden, were somehow unavoidable. It seems as if the law made no special effort to remove the intruders from the forbidden zone. It was only signaling its presence. I remember that when I was a schoolkid, we crawled under the fence over to our neighbor's yard where there were muddles and interesting turtles. Most of the time we were able to crawl back unnoticed, but once or twice we were caught in the act by the neighbor. He never chased us back. He only gave us a signal. "Hey, I'm here!" he shouted.

I also found some cases on file in which the idea of dueling came up as a solution, and everyone agreed—but in the end there was no duel. One of these was the Vinczehidy-Várady affair in 1907. Vinczehidy was one of my grandfather's friends and political brothers-in-arm. However, on January 6, 1907, the regional daily *Délvidéki Újság* carried an article harshly critical of Vinczehidy. In general, the paper treated things with minute precision, almost pedantically. The front page declared, for instance, that the paper "appears every afternoon at 5 o'clock," which it did. This time, however, the article had no by-line. The editor-in-chief, on the other hand, was my grandfather, and its responsible editor Béla Schröder, so that was that. In such a situation Vinczehidy had no choice but to challenge someone to a duel (so as not lose his honor). The only question was whom? The Duel Code composed by Vilmos Clair covers this type of situation too. According to Paragraph 16 (d), "the responsible editor may step in for his colleague." It is also specified that such substitution is possible only if the colleague (i.e., the author of the article) has been the offender, but there is no room for substitution if the colleague is the offended party. Simply put, if someone had cursed a journalist's mother, only the journalist himself was entitled to seek satisfaction, and not his responsible editor.

In our particular case, Paragraph 16 (d) did not yield an unequivocal solution since Imre Várady was not the responsible editor but the editor-in-chief. Once the choice was made, however, the only thing that mattered was that everything should go according to the rules, consequently all parties were emphasizing that they were keeping the protocol. As I see from the documents, Vinczehídy's seconds appeared in my grandfather's office "a few hours after the appearance of the article" already, that is, probably at seven or eight in the evening. (The office was right where I knew it, only I wasn't there, and neither was my father because he was born five years after the Vinczehídy duel affair). As the records show, aware of the problem, Vinczehídy's seconds were asking questions. It was clear who the offended party was (Vinczehídy) but who the offender was, was not so unambiguous. Vinczehídy's seconds asked if my grandfather "encouraged" the article in question, whether he "agrees with it or identifies with it," and if so, was he willing to provide satisfaction to Mr. Vinczehidy? Imre Várady did reply, but his answer failed to solve the problem. The sensitive issue came up if it was honorable for an editor-in-chief to dissociate himself from an article appearing in his own paper. There was honor involved also inside the editorial office of the daily. It is pretty disgraceful for an editor-in-chief to dissociate himself from an article published in his own paper—even if "the article was neither suggested by him, nor was he aware of its appearance." In the end, according to the records, "Dr. Imre Várady declared that he had neither suggested nor written the article, moreover, because of his absence, he had no idea about its appearance either. He holds Dr. Vinczehidy, his personality and his character in high esteem; still, when asked, he refused to sign a statement according to which he does not identify with the article in question... he is ready to serve satisfaction, and he declared that his second will make their appearance next morning at 10 o'clock in the morning at the apartment of Mr. Cornel Faur (Vinczehídy's second) for the purpose of negotiation."

This is the point where the seconds take over. When you have a full world that matters and is important, then it will naturally have other actors as well as the protagonists. In the dueling world, too, besides the parties fighting the duel (or not), there were parts available for seconds, various duel courts, witnesses, physicians keeping ready on the spot, fencing trainers and others. The seconds acted on the instructions of the duelists but had a role of their own and, of course, did their best to display their skillfulness. My grandfather's seconds were excellent jurists (one of the two, Ede Alföldy was more than that; he can justly be called famous). They raised the question as to whether "there is a causal relationship between the behavior of Imre Várady and the offense?" And then they continued: "even though Imre Várady, out of his high regard for the personality of Vinczehidy, would be pleased provide satisfaction, however, owing to the lack of the causal relationship, this satisfaction would not be suitable for the reparation of the offense."

The logic "I hold him in high esteem, so I would be pleased to fight a duel with him" is rather odd. A little more bluntly put, it would sound like "we are friends so we would be happy to shoot each other to demonstrate our appreciation." However, things are not all that simple. While the parties are being set on opposing sides by a quarrel, disagreement, slander or perceived slander, refusal to show proper respect, a scuffle or a metaphorical fight ("please consider your face having been being slapped, Sir"), there is also something keeping them together. They are together somewhere, within a social stratum or group which defines itself by the maintenance of what it calls honor (or so it declares). In that group it is a sign of appreciation to regard somebody worthy of dueling with, or in other words consider him one of those with whom I would be pleased to cross swords.

Anyway, honor is all-important to all those involved; they all belong to the circle of honorable men (and also among those who matter). The seconds are skilled at arguing, the rules are followed by all, nobody is against dueling on principle—still, will there be a duel in the end or will there not? Deciding it was left to the dueling court. The question that the court was obliged to answer was put to it by consent. It was as follows: "Considering all the facts on record, is Dr. Imre Várady duty-bound to provide satisfaction to Dr. Ernő Viczehidy?"

I would very much like to know if there was anyone who really wanted this duel to happen. I assume my grandfather did not. Maybe Ernő Vinczehidy was more inclined, but that is not at all certain either. The most important purpose of the whole exercise was that all participants should stand their ground in the field of honor. The offended party could achieve that by demanding satisfaction, and the offending one by not denying the giving of satisfaction. If, in the end, the duel was cancelled because the duel court ruled that for some reason or other it would be unjustified (for example because the parties confronting each other were not the right ones), it still meant that the basic purpose had been achieved. Vinczehidy would not put up with having and offensive article written about him, while Várady was ready to acquiesce in the decision of the duel court. All in all, the end of the matter was that there was no duel, yet honor remained intact.

In December 1907 my grandfather once again got close to dueling with another friend. This time the challenger was Lajos Brájjer. Brájjer was the president of the Hungarian journalists of the Banat, a long-time editor of the *Torontál*. When he lived in Fiume for a while (1908–1917), he edited the *Estilap of Fiume*. He was permanent correspondent of the *Staatszeitung*, a German newspaper published in America. He authored books too, translated German poetry into Hungarian and published several volumes of translated poetry.

As opposed to Vinczehidy, Brájjer was more of a political opponent of my grandfather than a comrade. He was pro-government whereas my grandfather was in opposition. On January 21, 1944 (two months after the death of Lajos Brájjer) my grandfather notes in his diary that they regularly saw each other at two tables. One gathered on Mondays at the Café Central—its members included Lajos Brájjer as well as, among other, the Serbian author Todor Manojlović, a translator of Hungarian poets, mainly Endre Ady, to Serbian and German. According to the diary:

> *At these meetings, when recalling old events and memories regarding the county, we complemented each other's account with Brájjer. He as a one-time faithful adherent of the government and the county, and I as a former oppositionist and pro-independence politician, cast light on the past gone by from two different angles.*

Today I feel Brájjer's loss acutely. There is no one left of our contemporaries. I have remained alone with my memories.

Lajos Brájjer was a frequent visitor in our house, but I don't remember him. I was four when he died at the end of November in 1943. However, I remember his wife very well, who lived till ninety-six or ninety-seven. Aunt Stefi came to see us regularly in the sixties, maybe even in the seventies. She would wear a high-collared black dress with a black umbrella as an accessory and was full of indomitable energy. Her sister Erna came sometimes to see her from Versec.

I would pick her up at the railway station, with my car from the sixties on. I was astonished to see that Aunt Erna brought along dictionaries in hatboxes, to be at hand while she is with her sister in Becskerek. (Though Aunt Stefi also had dictionaries; I knew that because I had visited her several times in her apartment at the Market Place.) The Brájjers had two daughters. One lived in Rome, the other in Canada. The one in Rome died in 1952. Aunt Stefi cared for her when she was gravely ill. She kept the apartment in Rome, and in 1960 she decided she wanted to watch the entire Rome Olympic Games (she was over 80 by then). At that time a special permit was required in Yugoslavia for people over 80 to travel by air. With the help of my father and some doctors, she got it. Later she told us many stories about the Games.

On occasion, Aunt Stefi provided help. On February 4, 1945 my grandfather noted in his diary that he had visited Mayor Zoltán Perisits along with a company. They had a problem on the way back, but Aunt Stefi had thought of it in advance and also offered the solution. "At about seven o'clock," so the diary says, "Stefi Brájjer lit the little lantern that she brought with herself, and by the light of which—having said farewell to our hosts—we set out in the darkness of the night. There has been no public lighting for months. The nights are pitch-dark."

I also met the Canadian daughter of the Brájjers. A sentence by her was repeated so often it became almost a proverb in Becskerek. Once when she came to visit her, Aunt Stefi confronted her with an extremely taxing agenda of things to do during her stay. By then she was over ninety, and her daughter must have been around seventy. She tried to follow her mother for a while, then gave up in desperation and exclaimed: "Mama please leave me alone! Can't you see I am an old woman?"

Lajos Brájjer also sought satisfaction of honor because of a newspaper article published in 1907 in *Nagybecskereki Hírlap* under the title "A Fake Farce." This time there was no waltzing around who wrote the article, who the responsible editor was and who could be challenged to a duel. The author was my grandfather without a doubt, and there was no dispute about it. What happened is recorded in a page-and-a-half-long protocol, half a page of which is taken up by the names and titles of the parties and their seconds. The outcome is unambiguously clear. According to a statement by my grandfather: "The article appearing in the…issue of Nagybecskereki Hírlap under the title "A Fake Farce" was written in the highly charged atmosphere that was due to the political tensions of the time… but I declare that I regard Dr. Lajos Brájjer a perfectly honorable gentleman in every respect." This is followed by Lajos Brájjer's statement: "This is acknowledged by Dr. Lajos Brájjer, who declares that he regards the matter closed."

There were cases that were easy to finish.

This Was Probably the Last One

I must begin this duel story too with a diary entry. On October 24, 1944 my grandfather recorded that the Messinger Institute had been raided by the new authority (the latest "new" one, this time the partisans), and furniture, bedclothes and clothing were taken. Lenke Magyar asked for legal help on behalf of the institute. The diary also reports on other house searches: "Allegedly they went to the house of Jenő Stagelschmidt too. There was also a big house search in the home of István Demkó. —There is no remedy for such outrages."

Jenő Stagelschmidt and István Demkó played a prominent role in the Hungarian institutions, including the dueling world. A mere five months earlier (May 1944), during the German occupation, Jenő Stagelschmidt was a participant in an affair of honor, which must have been the last one in Becskerek, or so I believe. István Demkó was also party to many duels. According to the documents found, already in 1906, he acted as a second in an affair of honor. I remember both Jenő Stagelschmidt and Istvan Demkó personally. I was a young adult in the 1970s when they still made their appearance in the streets occasionally. Uncle István (or Pista) lived ninety-six years. Even though they were only a few months apart, the last Becskerek duel and the house searches by the partisans were not of the same era and the same world. In the life of my generation, these worlds got often mixed up. In the last months of the German occupation and the arrival of the partisans were five years old. This mix-up reminds me of the case of a contemporary of mine, Zoltán. German soldiers were quartered in their house. His parents warned him to avoid them when he could, but it wasn't always possible. The German soldiers insisted that he should greet them with a "Heil Hitler!" This was how soldiers must be greeted, they said. Zoli obeyed. His pronunciation was not quite perfect so he said, "Hey Hitler!" His "hey" would have fit more into a "hey you, guy!" kind of phrase. Or maybe "Hello, Hitler!" But this was not deliberate and didn't bother the Germans either. The problem occurred when the partisan soldiers came to town, and my (then) five-year-old friend only saw them as soldiers, so he welcomed them, too, with a resounding "Hey Hitler." He got away with a (not too hard) slap in the face. It was not easy to get your bearings. By the way, in the photo at the start of this chapter showing Aunt Putsu's fencing trainees, Zoltan is standing in the upper row. He is third from left.

Coming back to Uncle Pista Demkó, he was a man of an earlier era, and he would always stay in the world of that era. He had a butler, and as everybody knew in Becskerek, he would always look for butlers with the same shoe size as his. He wore custom-made shoes only, and he was convinced that shoes need to be worn for a month or two before they would become really comfortable. He assigned this job to the butler. According to a well-known local historian (Vilmos Szigethy), in the Demkós' kitchen, food was always cooked for two or three extra persons, should guests turn up unexpectedly. Uncle Pista was present at the coronation of the last Hungarian king as a member of the Becskerek delegation. I think he walked along the Promenade of Becskerek throughout his life as someone visibly aware of the rank thus bestowed on him, irrespective of the currently ruling Serbian/Croatian/Slovenian government, the German occupation or the communists. He never strutted but strolled with a certain degree of leisurely elegance. Most of the time he wore a hunting hat and a walking stick. That would make the presence of the past in the center of Becskerek even more obvious. It was a past chosen by Uncle Pista, which he did his best to impersonate. As we all knew and spread, he was arrested at the end of October in 1944 without any specific charge or reason, perhaps only because it stood out so clearly that he did not belong (in the world envisioned by the partisans, that is). Part of this story was his butler (who, according to the rumors, he had been long unable to pay but, another captive of the past, he nevertheless continued to serve Uncle Pista). The butler brought him lunch to jail on a silver platter. It was cold pikeperch. This was so astonishing that he got permission for it, so Uncle Pista lunched from a silver platter in the Becskerek jail in the first days of communism. The next day he was set free. Then he landed in prison once again, sentenced to two years of hard labor between 1946 and 1948 on later on the charge that he had been a board member of the sugar factory which, during the occupation, had "shipped more than 25 percent of its production to the German army." Following the hard labor, he continued to behave as if nothing had happened. For instance, he stuck to his emphatic opinion, well known in Becskerek and beyond, that the car industry had no future because "where on earth could so many chauffeurs be found?" The evening strolls were resumed too, not neglecting the hunting hat and the walking stick. He was allowed to keep his house, originally built in the times of the Turkish occupation, with its entrance behind the Catholic church, next to the vicarage and one wall opposite to the Town Hall, one of the oldest houses in Becskerek. For a time, they moved forced co-habitants in with him, and he was pushed to the butler's room. After that he was once again able to take possession of the entire house. He lived alone and didn't have a job. It was rumored that he was trying to sell a piece or two of the family silver, but in the late forties and early fifties there were hardly any buyers. It took time for the new winners to feel safe enough not only from their enemies but also from their earlier principles to dare put some silver on the table when inviting a comrade or two for dinner. Transition lasted untill we got there.

Uncle Jenő Stagelschmidt was also sentenced to hard labor in 1946, and he too returned to his life in Becskerek, got a job as an architect at a state-owned business and also resumed walking in the Promenade. Sometimes the two would walk together. Uncle Jenő had graduated in Switzerland and took a prominent role in the Hungarian cultural associations of the inter-war years, and for a while he was President of the Hungarian cultural associations DMKSZ and later BMKSZ. (It was a disagreement at a session of the BMKSZ that brought on the last duel in Becskerek.) On one occasion they were together in Uncle Pista's house while I was marching in front of the house with my classmates in connection with some pioneer event. This must have been in 1948, maybe 1949, when us marchers were nine or ten years old. The wall of the house still bore the coat-of-arms of the ancient Demkó family. It was a pretty complicated coat-of-arms, the way I remember. Since I cannot precisely recall it, I looked it up in the book *Hungary's Counties and Towns*. I read that "in a blue field, on a green ground, a Hungarian warrior galloping toward the right, wearing red, gold-braided *atilla* and a red-feathered helmet, holding an unsheathed sword in his upraised hand, on the point of which there is cut-off Turk's head dripping blood." This was the coat-of-arms in front of which we were marching, singing a highly dynamic revolutionary song. It began by the declaration that if we remained true to Marshall Tito, the heroic son of our land, not even the gates of hell would stop us on our way. So, we should raise our brows and march courageously, our hands bunched in a fist. This was followed by a somewhat muddled verse about us not being of Gothic descent (meant probably to emphasize our being different from the Germans), which then shot us up to the top of the lyrical dynamic: "*Ko drukčije kaže / Kleveće, laže /Našu će osjetit pest*" (anybody who says otherwise / is a slanderer and a liar / and will feel the power of our fist.) That was what we sang. With red pioneer scarves in our necks. There were girls among us too.

Uncle Pista and Uncle Jenő waved to some of my classmates. If I correctly recall, they were Tibor Bencze (the grandson of the owner of the Bencze furniture factory), Zoli, the one who had said "Hey Hitler," and myself. And while singing, we waved back politely. This utter confusion of worlds was separated by only a few years from what had been most likely the last duel affair in Becskerek. It was still in the Nazi era (In Serbia, the preferred term was "fascist," and it still is), and a duel was as alien to fascism as it was to communism. Of course, there was the notion that "we are what we are" —but we do not remain the same forever either. According the diary of my grandfather:

> *[1944] 13. V. at 6 p.m. Session of the committee of DMKSZ, introduction of the newly elected committee. An unpleasant dispute between Acting President Jenő Stagelschmidt and Journalist László Dániel. From that, an affair of honor. I became a second to the latter. Today, in these crucial times when Hungarian soldiers are shedding rivers of blood at the foot of the Carpathians in defense of their country, when the terrible monster of destruction is trying to break through every frontier of Hungary, that these Hungarian heroes here have nothing better to do than play knights and armors.*

As is clearly visible, my grandfather was anything but enthusiastic about the whole honor affair. And it wasn't hot passion of youth that made him join. He was seventy-seven at the time. Nevertheless, he accepted the request to act as second in a duel. Even then it was too hard to escape the "social pressure." Despite the fact that the society which created the pressure had long gone. I must also add that to the best of my knowledge my grandfather was a much closer friend of Jenő Stagelschmidt than he was of László Gy. Dániel. Still, it was Dániel who asked him, and requests in affairs of honor were still too difficult to refuse.

There are some ten sheets of documents dealing with the details of the Stagelschmidt-Dániel affair. Unlike those regarding earlier duels, these are typewritten. Some records are found in both handwritten and typed versions. The documents include a certification written by the Hungarian Cultural Association of Torontál county, attesting to the honesty and respectability of László Gy. Dániel.

All things considered, this is the richest of all the duel files. However, even this one raises questions to which I can find no answer. On May 13, 1944, at the session of the Becskerek chapter of the BMKSZ (Banat Hungarian Cultural Association), a submission by László Dániel was to be discussed. László Dániel was not supposed to have come, but he changed his mind since "his planned excursion had been cancelled." It came to a heated dispute on whether Dániel should be allowed to put forward his submission verbally, or it should be simply recited. The president of the chapter, István Kovács, had resigned and did not even come. The meeting was chaired by the acting president, Jenő Stagelschmidt. Following a harsh exchange of words, Stagelschmidt refused to allow László Dániel "to put forth the contents of the petition in words." Instead, he recited it himself as acting president, rejecting it out of hand with an answer prepared well ahead. In his reply he pointed out that "Mr. Dániel believes the boat of the BMKSZ is sinking; he wants to flee and also use the oars to hit those clinging to the boat in the head." After that—according to Mr. Dániel—Jenő Stagelschmidt, "thumping on the table with his fist, raised his voiced even higher, and yelled over in a threatening tone: regarding his submission, Mr. Dániel will receive a proper answer from me!" The key sentences were recorded on a separate sheet of paper.

László Dániel's submission is unfortunately missing from the file. He was not a man of restraint, so there is little doubt that he would have made some radical points. Although, according to Dániel, he handed over the submission "out of common Hungarian interest." At this juncture, one may halt for a moment to lament over the incredible ease with which Hungarian public interest becomes mixed up with personal antipathy even in times when there would be a lot more important things to do than quarrel with each other. I thought about bringing up some parallels, but then it came to my mind that on this particular topic it would be hard to say anything new to my readers.

The initiator of the affair of honor was Jenő Stagelschmidt, and the trigger cause the submission by László Dániel. From this point on, things are on track, conforming to all the rules, even though the doubt does loom up whether this track leads anywhere at all. The sentences on record show the self-assurance of the participants ("we know exactly how these things are done"), but here and there some vague doubt also makes itself felt, if very cautiously ("what's the use of is this whole thing?")

The first record was taken in my father's office four days after the event, on May 15, 1944. That was where the four seconds to the duel, including my grandfather, held their meeting. The rest of the family including me must have had their evening meal at about the same time, only two rooms away. There were further meetings and further records taken (namely on May 17, 20 and 23.) There are letters exchanged as well. They contain a considerable amount of twists and turns, shades and hues, principles ingeniously linked with the facts, along with the consistent voicing of the view that it would be better to find a simpler way. An explication on record ponders the issue if Jenő Stagelschmidt can really be regarded as the offended party at all. According to László Dániel he cannot because he was not the addressee of the submission, and it wasn't meant for him personally either. In their exchange, Stagelschmidt thought to represent the BMKSZ, and he too said more than once that it was at the express wish of István Kovács, the (resigned) president that as acting president, he ordered the statement about his resignation not to be put on record. László Dániel's submission also attacks the errors of a record so it cannot involve Jenő Stagelschmidt who at this point "functioned as nothing but a medium passing on the measures taken by István Kovács." Trying to simplify the argument, since László Dániel's submission had targeted the leadership of the BMKSZ and Jenő Stagelschmidt was only acting president (who made certain procedural moves according to the intentions of István Kovács), it is questionable if he has the right to claim satisfaction of honor. This was indeed something special to be set on the luncheon table for the connoisseurs of lawsuit documents, but in the meantime there emerged also a possibility to avoid that table. For László Dániel declared that if Jenő Stagelschmidt should "stick to his decision and remain a challenging party," then he, László Dániel "is ready for the settling of the matter of honor at hand by arms."

In other words, both parties were now ready to duel. This ought to have cleared the way, just like in all similar situations before—still, matters refused to proceed as before. When the dynamic of long-accustomed old routines is confronted with a new social environment, things become problematic. Questions arise. Convention requires that the knightly carriage be driven out, but then there is the question whether, after all the recent re-buildings, the front gate is still wide enough for the carriage to get through, the carriage beam hasn't rotted, or the reins frayed? And, indeed, are there still any horses in the stables?

On the side of László Dániel, it was raised in argument that "the rules of the current Serbian law in this field strictly prohibit all types of dueling and, in accordance with the orders of the ruling German occupying forces, weapons of any kind had to be surrendered to the authorities." In other words, the will was there but the way wasn't. The whole exercise was forbidden, and there was nothing to fight it with anyway. Still, László Dániel and his seconds were willing to show flexibility and indicate a vague chance that the carriage might be driven out after all. In the record dated May 15 they declare:

> So if Mr. J. St's deputies, conscious of all this, were still to insist on armed satisfaction, then in that case they must acknowledge that it is their (or their client's) responsibility to proceed at the competent civilian and military authorities in such direction that proper permission is given and weapons provided for the duel to be fought.

Put in simpler terms, if Jenő Stagelschmidt and his seconds (Zoltán Ambrózy and Andor Benkovich) can achieve that, in spite of the Serbian and German laws to the contrary, permission is given for the duel, to which the occupying German authorities will provide the weapons, then there is no problem.

None of the previous documents shows the faintest trace of the illegality of dueling being seen as a problem. The illegality of dueling was of course nothing new. It existed at the end of the nineteenth century just as well as at the beginning of the twentieth—but things were not quite the same. At that time, the practice of dueling was flourishing. The introduction of Vilmos Clair's dueling code begins with the words, "There is not another nation in the world where as many matters of honor are settled in the way of duels as in our own Hungary." Becskerek was no exception, as is proven by a March 1899 issue the daily *Torontál* reporting on the "public state of duelmania" in town. According to *Torontál*, "this mania is fully developed in Becskerek where, it is fair to say, there is a duel or two a week." Yet they were forbidden by the Hungarian penal code in force also then. Maybe *Torontál* as well as Vilmos Clair exaggerated a bit. If I only think about how often I heard in Budapest that "there is no such thing anywhere else in the world" or "a thing like that can only happen in Hungary" (when a case of corruption is discovered or a tram fails to arrive on time), and how frequently I heard the same thing in Belgrade, only in relation to Serbia...

There is no doubt, however, that despite the prohibition, there were a lot of duels in Hungary, including Becskerek. The level of fear from the consequences of the violation of the law and of the possible physical consequences together did never reach the level of fear from becoming a social outcast. Part of the reason may have been that the state penitentiary was not exactly a terrifying perspective; most frequently it was evaded anyway and so was physical injury, while being shunned could not be escaped. Already at the beginning of the twentieth century, one of the declared aims of the anti-duel movements was to eliminate treating those who did not want to duel as outcasts. But they never succeeded. So, when challenged, the president of the national anti-duel movement (István Rakovszky) himself chose to duel rather than risk being shunned. If you wanted to stay in the company of those who mattered, you could not escape defending your honor with arms. No sign of change was on the horizon regarding the rules of society, or that the yardsticks or weight of belonging would at least be modified. At the end of the nineteenth century and the beginning of the twentieth, the experience of having been accepted among the "real ones" was still fairly new, the order of the world was envisioned to be lasting, and dueling seemed a stable part of that world. It seemed that sticking to that world was a good strategy for staying alive and well.

Then came the shifting of countries and the world wars. The proud feeling that "we are still the real ones" hung on—but what "real" meant was no longer certain. It had to be checked from time to time. Of course, it is much easier to continue to believe (again and again) that we are the real ones than to keep finding out (again and again) what "real" is. I think that many of the people involved in this last Becskerek duel asked themselves who they were and what was this all about. But whether they did or did not, the confrontation did happen, and without philosophizing. In 1944 it was impossible not to notice that staying inside—surviving, really—had some far more important conditions than one's qualification or readiness for dueling. In the duel documents of 1944, the moves, the manner and tone of the discussion follows all the steps of the old ritual, but the issues themselves already suggest new problems.

At this point I would like to return to the proposal of the Dániel party that the difficulty was that duels were forbidden and there were no weapons to fight them with anyway should be dealt with by Jenő Stagelschmidt and his seconds. Well, Stagelschmidt and his seconds made no attempt to apply either to the Serbian or the German authorities to ignore the laws and make an exception. Nor did they ask the Germans to provide weapons. They did try something else, though. They proposed that the site of duel be moved to Szeged, to the Hungarian army barracks there. By raising this idea, Jenő Stagelschmidt and his seconds, Károly Ambrózy and Andor Benkovich, suggested a strategic move that would gain a certain notoriety in international law a good deal later. This was the outplacement of a problem. Probably the clearest example for this procedure was provided by the United States at the beginning of the twenty-first century. (Of course, not as a party to a duel but in its role as "policeman of the world"). "Coercive interrogation," or less euphemistically speaking, the torture of terrorist suspects and jihadist combatants was suggested as a possibility, something that was prohibited not only by universal human rights but also US law. The secretary of defense, Donald Rumsfeld had the idea, supported by President Bush, that torture could be applied but the torturing of suspected terrorists or people aiding them should be carried out outside US jurisdiction. The Guantanamo detention camp was thus established, Guantanamo not being US territory and hence not under US jurisdiction, even though effectively ruled by the US. On the basis of a contract signed in 1938 with an earlier, docile rather than renegade, Cuban government, the United states has been paying 4085 US dollars annually for the possession of the naval base in Guantanamo Bay. So that the principles should be secure, on the gate in front of the prison camp, it is written: "Honor bound to defend freedom."

https://commons.wikimedia.org/wiki/File:Camp_Delta,_Guantanamo_Bay,_Cuba.jpg

By the way, while on the subject of world politics, it may be worthy of note that readers of Becskerek newspapers were aware already on November 28, 1942 (thanks to the daily *Torontál*) that the United States was getting ready "to take over police control of most part of the world."

Coming back to Stagelschmidt and his friends, they, too, thought that if the law in force in Becskerek at the moment was forbidding what was about to be done, then the scene could still be shifted. In Hungary also, dueling was forbidden by law but there were some exceptions. Continuing to follow the logic of the problem's outplacement, the record taken on May 23, 1944, contains the following question being asked by the seconds of Jenő Stagelschmidt: "Is Mr. László Gy. Dániel willing to provide our client Mr. Jenő Stagelschmidt satisfaction of honor when passports to Hungary are accessible, and it is possible to travel again?"

This suggestion may have been influenced by facing the present (if not the future still). The present was the German occupation, under which a prohibited armed battle could have been viewed easily as an armed revolt by the occupying authorities rather than an obsolete ritual, and would have resulted in sanctions. As for the future, it may have occurred to them too that the barracks in Szeged could just as well end up as a Soviet barracks as Hungarian army property. I don't know if such visions of the future were within sight in May 1944. The answer, worded by the seconds of László Dániel, was:

> While emphasizing all our sincerest respect owed to the Szeged Command of the Army Corps of the Hungarian Defense Forces, we declare that since to the best of our knowledge neither Mr. Jenő Stagelschmidt nor Mr. László Dániel is a member of the Hungarian army, and since Szeged today—woe betide!— is still in the territory of a different country lying over the border, therefore the military command seated in Szeged can have neither the jurisdiction nor the competence to settle— in such devious ways, by ignoring the laws in force here— affairs with which it has no concern. We ourselves would abstain from such deviations from the straight path, and neither could we suggest them to our opposing party with a clear conscience. For it cannot be the purpose either of opposing party and his seconds or of us to stray from the straight road of lawfulness only to perform a demonstration of a gentry-type, bygone practice.

It is apparent that the value and importance of the law are on the increase again, and—moving on—even the dissociation from devious ways is making is reappearance. What happened, I think, was not that the careful prohibition of dueling in defense of the physical health of people by thoughtful legislation gained ever wider recognition. The rules meant to prevent injury were not particularly credible when a world war was going on. Much rather than that, it was the world and the society in which people were forced to stay "inside" at all costs including illegal acts (dueling) was on the wane.

Since dueling and qualification for duel are no longer unquestionable rules, irony also makes its appearance. The seconds make mention of the fact that in Becskerek, the Stagelschmidt-Dániel affair became the butt of jokes. In a draft I found the sentence, "we seconds have heard too that this affair is talked about, and moreover, made jokes of as an obsolete, old-fashioned way of settling disputes."

In 1903 it took Ady's iconoclastic courage to have a (bitter) smile over the compulsion of dueling. By May 1944 the population of Becskerek managed to reach the same stage. After it had been recorded and recited by the seconds of László Dániel that the shifting of the scene over to Szeged was—"despite all our sincerest respect owed to the Szeged Command of the Army Corps of the Hungarian Defense Forces"—not practicable, things halted.

At the end of the bunch of documents there are two letters by the seconds to their clients. My grandfather and László Nagy wrote to László Dániel on May 23. Károly Ambrózy and Andor Benkovich wrote Jenő Stagelschmidt on May 24. The contents are roughly the same, and so is the gist of the conclusion. One of the letters makes mention of the fact that at the end of the negotiations "the usual honorable joint conclusion and the taking of the record" was abandoned, but it is obvious that this was end. After the Szeged option got rejected, no new proposals were tabled. The seconds notified their "masters" in proper single-page letters written in a courteous tone that the affair of honor was over. According to the closing words of my grandfather and László Nagy: "our assignment is thus finished." As Károly Ambrózy and Andor Belkovich put it, "After all that, on our part we consider the affair closed." To all intents and purposes this was the end of duels of honor in Becskerek.

P.S. At least I think so. Anybody who says otherwise is a slanderer and a liar (*kleveće, laže*), and will feel the power of our fist (*našu će osjetit pest*)!

VII.

THE DEVELOPMENT OF THE ECONOMIC SITUATION

Lawsuits in the Years of the First Five-Year Plan

SOME PERSPECTIVE IN INTRODUCTION

I SET ASIDE ABOUT A DOZEN FILES in a single bundle. They are all from the same period (1947–1952), they all involve economic matters in one way or another, and are mainly criminal cases. I meant to begin browsing on today, but before I set to it, I thought I'd read my email. Not only to read messages and news but also in the hope that some parallel might turn up. In my US email, I found interesting news about the famous criminal lawyer F. Lee Bailey.

It is most likely that I won't go to America again. Some things simply end. My contacts with the old scenes naturally live on. I am regularly getting the news sent to all professors (including the emeriti) of the Emory School of Law. Therefore, I know that today (on Saturday, July 2, 2016) the building will close at 2 p.m. and so it will remain until Tuesday because Monday, July 4, Independence Day, is a national holiday in the United States. I might nevertheless be able to enter even after 2:00 because I still have my Emory ID, a magnetic card opening the door by the parking lot. If I did, I could check how many familiar names can still be found over the mailboxes to the right of the entrance. But I am on a different continent now. And I am not certain that my magnetic card would still work. The last time I used it was in 2012.

The email news circular notifies me of upcoming lectures and debates to be held at Emory in the lecture hall on the first floor. After the lectures I was often encouraged along with my (former) colleagues in e-circulars to help ourselves to the cakes and sometimes also sandwiches left on the reception tables. We can have any that we want, the circulars said.

Another sign that we remain in touch is the newsletter of the American Bar Association that I am getting even though I stopped paying the membership fee a few years ago. I am not sent the printed version anymore, though. Unless for some reason it still continues to be sent to my address at Emory from where, as we agreed, they stopped forwarding mail to me. The most recent issue of the *American Bar Association (ABA) Journal* (this is being written in 2016) also starts with the story of F. Lee Bailey, and so does *The Washington Post* on June 27. I know the name, I have heard it frequently before, always pronounced like this, with the two first names sort of pressed together: "Eflee Bailey." If someone said "Lee Bailey," or added in full the very first name which is known by hardly anyone, only the initial "F," people probably wouldn't recognize him. I don't think there is anybody in the legal trade in the USA who doesn't know who F. Lee Bailey is. People outside the legal profession also know. Just about everybody does. He successfully defended the football star, O. J. Simpson, who was accused of murdering his wife. He defended Albert De Salvo, also known as the "Boston Strangler." In another prominent case he defended Captain Ernest Medina of the US Army, who was acquitted of charges regarding the My Lai massacre committed in the Vietnam War. He was the defense lawyer of Patty Hearst who, dissatisfied with being "only" the heir of a billionaire press magnate, wanted to get a taste of bank robbery to get more out of life. One of his cases inspired a movie. Sam Sheppard, an Ohio doctor, had been sentenced in 1954 for killing his wife. He then hired F. Lee Bailey who succeeded in obtaining a Supreme Court order for a retrial in 1966 on the strength of Bailey's argument that the original verdict, and especially the jury, had been heavily influenced by the media hullabaloo surrounding the trial. In the renewed trial, the doctor was acquitted. The Harrison Ford movie *The Fugitive* was based on that case.

I saw F. Lee Bailey in person briefly once, or I think it was him. In the mid-nineties I served as an expert witness in an interesting lawsuit before a Los Angeles court. It involved a dispute between two basketball clubs, the Los Angeles Lakers and Partisan of Belgrade. The issue was whether the player Vlade Divac could play for the Lakers on the basis of a contract signed on February 26, 1992. It was an NBA Uniform Player Contract.

NATIONAL BASKETBALL ASSOCIATION

UNIFORM PLAYER CONTRACT

THIS AGREEMENT made this 26th day of February, 1992 by and between THE LOS ANGELES LAKERS, INC. (hereinafter called the "Club"), a member of the National Basketball Association (hereinafter called the "Association") and VLADE DIVAC whose address is shown below (hereinafter called the "Player").

RECEIVED & RECORDED

WITNESSETH:

The dispute centered on another contract according to which Divac still would have to play in Partisan. Divac denied having signed any such contract.

The Lakers and Divac reasoned along two shared lines. According to one argument, the contract never existed. According to the other, even if it had, any such contract was invalid according to the applicable Yugoslav law. My job was to provide expert opinion on the validity of the contract. We began by an exchange over the telephone. The lawyers of the Lakers proposed in a fax to call me on Tuesday, September 27 or Wednesday, September 28 at 8:00 a.m. LA time (which was 4:00 p.m. Budapest time):

ENT BY:SANDERS BARNET et al ; 9-23-94 ; 15:57 ; (310)553-2435→ 361 1763016

SANDERS, BARNET, GOLDMAN, SIMONS & MOSK
A Professional Corporation
1901 Avenue of the Stars, Suite 850
Los Angeles, California 90067
Phone: (310) 553-8011
Fax: (310) 553-2435

FACSIMILE TRANSMITTAL

DATE: September 23, 1994	**FROM: Richard M. Mosk**
TO: Prof. Tibor Varady	**RE: Lakers/Partizan/Divac**
FAX NO: 011 36 1 176 3016	**FILE NO: 219712**
NO. OF PAGES: 1 (Incl. Cover Page)	**cc:**

MESSAGE

Dear Prof. Varady:

Could Mr. Divac's attorney and I call you on Tuesday, September 27 or Wednesday, September 28 at 8:00 a.m. our time (which I believe would be 5:00 p.m. your time -- unless daylight savings goes off in Hungary -- in which case it would be 4:00 p.m. your time)?

Please confirm. Thanks.

We agreed that I will be expert witness for the Lakers. In the US, experts are not appointed by the court but invited by the parties. In Los Angeles before the trial, we spent some time walking in the streets with Divac (mainly between parking lots and restaurants). He was recognized everywhere, which is small wonder in the case of a celebrity all of 2.10 meters tall. People yelled at him, "Hey, Vlade!" was the standard greeting. A few asked to take his photo, some even extending the request to me, once I was there too. There was no denying that Vlade Divac was a famous man in LA. Still, when we reached the courthouse, I was truly astonished. I saw a throng of several hundred people, all excited and shouting in front of the entrance. I asked one of the Lakers' lawyers if our case was really so famous. "No, not that much," he explained, adding that these people came, not because of our trial, but for the O.J. Simpson case, only there was not enough space in the courtroom to accommodate all of them, so they were rooting in front of the building. When we got inside the building, the members of the O.J. Simpson defense team were already standing there in their robes. As we passed by them, we exchanged greetings. F. Lee Bailey was very likely one of them. But I cannot be certain.

Due to such celebrated trials, F. Lee Bailey became one of the best-known lawyers in America, and very rich as well. Everybody knew he had no financial difficulties. He could even afford to buy private airplanes. Then things suddenly turned south, this lasted for a while, and on June 26, 2016, the *ABA Journal* reported that Bailey became insolvent and filed for private bankruptcy. The turnaround was due to a case involving economic offences. The lawsuit concerned the financial dealings of the French magnate Claude DeBoc connected with a pharmacological company and involving money laundering. This time F. Lee Bailey represented the state but was paid in Swiss pharma industry shares instead of money. Then, he was accused of improper treatment of these shares. He was expelled from the Bar Association, back taxes were demanded from him which he refused to pay, deeming the demand unlawful. So, the interest on the taxes owed kept growing. A decade or two went by. In 2016 he got to the point where his accrued debts were more than 5 million dollars, which he was unable to pay. In an interview he said it was too late for him to start raising money again at the age of 83. He also owed money on his home. There came private bankruptcy as a last resort. And the obstinacy of F. Lee Bailey. "This is not yet over," he told the journalists.

1. CORN OR CORN FLOUR

The American world, about which I tried to tell some information and personal memories, is a world I think I know to some extent. I know because I spent considerable time there. I visited the US regularly, first to learn and then to teach. I had and still have a number of personal contacts over there, and I also followed things which were followed by many. Yet the more familiar it became, the clearer it was to me that it was not really my world. I feel more at home in the world of documents. The question is, do I really know that world? Names, scenes are familiar. Looking at the succession of moves or trying to guess the elements of which a certain mood is made up, I have the feeling that I am in home territory. This is the world I come from. But do I know it?

Now, having got over the difficulties of the introduction—and also in the hope that it will also provide some points and parallels I will be using later—I am going to proceed to a discussion of the economic situation. The period concerned is the years after World War Two. The designation "economic situation" turns up in many documents, especially prosecutor's submissions. The context varies. For instance, "the economic situation is very difficult…and still, the defendant…" Or the other way around. "Now that everything is fine, and the economic situation is promising, the defendant still continues to spread reactionary criticism." Even today, I often hear the magic words "economic situation" very often, and the somber tone in which those words are said intimates that we are looking at things from a special vantage point, a perspective which gives us genuine knowledge of what the situation really is.

While shuffling the documents I came upon the April 20, 1947 issue of the daily *Magyar Szó*. The huge headline on the front page reads: "The First Five-Year Plan of Yugoslavia." Above that, in somewhat smaller letters but fully capitalized and underlined, comes the slogan: "DEATH TO FASCISM–FREEDOM TO THE PEOPLE." Beside it, still above the main headline and also in capital letters: POŠTARINA PLAĆENA" (i.e., Post Paid). Thus, everything was settled, and we had all the important information at hand.

HALÁL A FASIZMUSRA — SZABADSÁG A NÉPNEK

POŠTARINA PLAĆENA

MAGYAR SZÓ

IV. ÉVFOLYAM 107. SZÁM — NOVISZÁD, SZOMBAT 1947 ÁPRILIS 26. — ÁRA 2 DINÁR

Jugoszlávia első ötéves terve

gazdasági és technikai elmaradottságnak felszámolását, az ország gazdasági és véderejének megszilárdítását, a népgazdaság szocialista szektorának továbbfejlesztését és minden dolgozó általános jólétének emelését

tűzi ki célul

By the way, that was when the first Five-Year Plan was passed by the People's Parliament of Yugoslavia, and you could read all the basic principles on the front page of the April 26, 1947 issue of the *Magyar Szó*. I have actually read it now—with the slight delay of 70 years— in order to see the economic situation, or at least its perception. The principles declare that many things have been restored in the two years that have passed since the war, and what comes next is "the raising of the general welfare of all the working people." There was also a more detailed explanation of what went on: "by abolishing the exploitative character of industrial production and the financial system, the preconditions have been established for removing the blind, mechanical operation of the laws of economy, and the work dynamic of the workers helped to realize the conditions for a methodical transition into planned economy instead."

The first Five-Year Plan shows a bright future. Just like every economic plan ever since, all the time. The use of the word "reform" also continues, having survived all regime changes. Maybe the difference is that these days the increasing absence of euphoria must also be dealt with. It is risky to say that well-being is to begin right now, because there is the threat that people might look around. For this reason, the way things are phrased is that "some last austerity measures will have to be taken just for now," but only because they are going to open the way for the next steps toward happiness. Back in 1947 there was less caution, and the rhetoric of "these last restrictions just now" before the general well-being was not yet present. Welfare, justice, equality and happiness were direct, declared, objectives of the reforms. "From now on—or in a maximum of five years—everything will be fine." When making more comparisons, you will realize that reforms back then really produced radical change (whether the direction was right or not is open for debate, though.) Reforms today, on the other hand, can always be contemplated; you can try to decide for yourself whether they brought genuine change or not. Perhaps we should make a count of all the reforms carried out in recent decades, all warning us that they would hurt a little but only to make things much, much better after that. Has the great transformation really taken place? Or is it only that the amalgam of justices and injustices actually became more sustainable through the reforms? I don't know. There is no consensus among economists either.

Anyone who tries to get a picture of the economic situation these days will learn how important the two major tools ensuring economic rationality are: budget cuts and competition (and along with that, the competitiveness that is to be increased). On July 1, 2016, I read in *The New York Times* that the wave of budget cuts had reached the army too. It was established that the United States had one hundred and thirty marching bands employing six thousand and five hundred musicians. That figure was going to be reduced in the interest of rationality and future-building. It brings up the thought that maybe future building would make even greater strides forward if the road of reduction took a different direction, and the United States Army kept its marching bands and their musicians only, scrapping the rest. And of course, the same would be done in every other army and armed unit in the world. (Police may be allowed to remain.) Then, say, the bands of NATO and the Russian army could blow their horns at each other with no reservation. We would just sit back with ears plugged or listening. However, this seems an unlikely direction for things to proceed.

At the time of the five-year-plans there were no budget cuts, or you wouldn't hear about them. As for the competition; well, there always was competition and there always will be. It was a recurrent topic at the time of the five-year-plans too. The term proved to be enduring as well as flexible, taken on by many ideologies. True, who competes with whom and for what was made somewhat murky at times. Shall we, for instance, compete for applause from the consumers or from the party? Or, to take another example, are salaries more competitive when they are high or, quite to the contrary, when they are low, since in that case the goods produced will be cheaper? And what does a more competitive nation mean?

I am learning from *Magyar Szó* that in 1947, competition was important not only in the Five-Year Plan but also in everyday life. On page five there is a somewhat lecture-style piece under the title *In Debelyacsa There is Competition but it is Incomplete* (Debelyacsa, Debeljača in Serbian, was a small town in the region). On reading the article it turns out that it is the Debelyacsa purchase and consumption co-operative, which had a thousand and six-hundred forty-five members, that is organizing a competition in ten events. All ten are noted in *Magyar Szó*. Let me quote a few:

1. Who will be manager of the best-arranged shop?
4. Which shop is going to be the cleanliest?
5. Who will issue more wall newspapers?
9. Which shop will have more parola (slogans) in it?

Still, this was not enough. In an attached editorial note printed in italics we read "*we see no trace of the contracting of garden vegetables, nor do we see an item on procurement.*" So, the race was on. Today you can hardly suppress a smile upon reading about the slogan contest. You might even ask in astonishment—if not altogether without irony—whether the world of the first Five-Year Plan was such an astoundingly free society? So free that you were allowed to say loud and clear that there was a sloganeering contest?

There had to be competition in culture, too, of course. This was seen by *Magyar Szó*. On page five of the April 28, 1947 issue one finds the inspiring title: "Hungarian Amateurs Must Compete Too." The last sentence points out that, not only a socialist but also a national minority issue, is at stake. "It is a point of national pride that the working people of our nation should not be left out of the race either."

The Five-Year Plan itself laid down general welfare undetailed. The files, on the other hand, show that the legal cases often force a detailing of principles. This is demonstrated by several lawsuits tried in the period of the first Five-Year Plan. One of them hinges upon the difference between corn and corn flour.

It can be noted that in many sentences between 1947 and 1952, and also later, the court establishes that a party should pay (for instance, to cover the court expenses), but then it is followed by the observation that it should not because the party does not have the funds to pay with. That is the kind of final outcome that F. Lee Bailey also aimed for. It is not exactly a sign of affluence bursting at the seams. But I'll rein in my irony because there is a kind of understanding pulsating behind some of the wordings of the sentences of the Becskerek court for the situation of poor people. Also, the war was still recent. It also makes you think whether the motives of the regulation of private bankruptcy include empathy, and how much, if any.

I don't know if there was such a "he should pay but there is nothing to pay from" detour in the final outcome of the corn flour case. As in several other cases, the sentence is missing from the file. The single copy was taken by the client. And it has not survived in the court archives either. What remained is the indictment and a memo of what the accused said and what the defense could be built upon. Even so, the economic situation got a bit closer.

The case in point is that of one Pera Vukov who ran the shop providing for railway men under 11 Tsara Dushana (Cara Dušana) Street (opposite to our house and the office). He was charged on October 27, 1947. According to the prosecutor, Pera Vukov committed an act "not motivated by the interests of the service but by a sabotaging behavior causing the violation of the rights of citizens." The Serbian original is not an iota less complicated. On reading this, I became instantly curious about what could have happened opposite to us, on the other side of the street, and what it was that Pera Vukov did. The facts enlisted in the verdict are not really different from what my father recorded in his memorandum after having spoken to the accused. There is no similarity, however, in the representation of those facts.

Vukov's job was to distribute flour supplies. Wheat and corn. The problem originated from the distribution. Lots of things were distributed at the time. Sometimes, however—though not for the first time in history—before distributing them, those things had to be taken away from someone so that they could be given to others. This was especially characteristic in the distribution of homes. It was the job of the Town People's Liberation

Committee to establish the number and location of "surplus" rooms, that is, in which apartment (or house) they could be found. Then they were distributed. Surplus rooms were donated mainly to the needy. And the needy who had better contacts with the powers-that-be had a chance of getting better, and maybe more, surplus rooms than others. I know, and I found the signs also in the documents, that a bit of maneuvering was necessary in my family too. People have tried to defend their property against many kinds of attackers. This time (in 1946, a little before the enacting of the first Five-Year Plan) the most threatening attacker was the image "surplus." In our case the ploy meant to repulse the attack from "surplus-ness" was that my aunt Piroska and her husband moved in with us. But that proved insufficient. The Committee found that we still had surplus rooms. So, we also registered our cook/household helper, Maška and her mother-in-law as residents of our home. Tthey had actually lived there for a long time anyway. The form in which Maška (Anau Marija) was registered as a resident was still the form printed by the German occupation authorities (in German and Serbian) but the stamp already belongs to the People's Liberation Committee. It even has a five-pointed star in the middle.

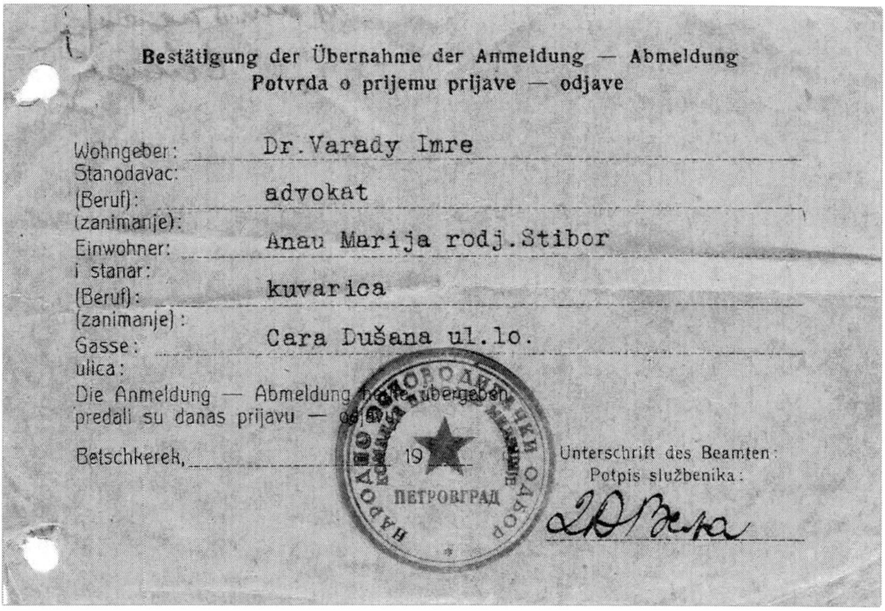

Bestätigung der Übernahme der Anmeldung — Abmeldung
Potvrda o prijemu prijave — odjave

Wohngeber: Stanodavac: Dr.Varady Imre
(Beruf): (zanimanje): advokat
Einwohner: i stanar: Anau Marija rodj.Stibor
(Beruf): (zanimanje): kuvarica
Gasse: ulica: Cara Dušana ul.lo.
Die Anmeldung — Abmeldung habe übergeben
predali su danas prijavu — odjavu
Betschkerek, ... 19...
Unterschrift des Beamten: Potpis službenika:

With that, "surplus-ness" was overcome. On September 28, 1946, the Town People's Committee (reduced in the meantime to People's Committee, with Liberation having been removed from its name) established that contrary to its earlier findings, the house of Dr. Imre Várady had no surplus room in it.

Returning to the affair involving Pera Vukov, things went fine for a while, but in June 1949 a problem emerged because the mills failed to produce enough corn flour. Measures were taken, however, to fill the need. Vukov's shop was shipped corn instead of corn flour, and the corn came with the (centrally established) rule that people entitled to 1 kilo of corn flour should receive 1.10 kilo of corn instead. Vukov said that this was written on the wall of the shop with a crayon. Still, only a part of the corn was taken, which was duly reported to the management by Vukov. Something had to be done about the remaining corn. Then, Kosta Mikalački from the management instructed Vukov to give 377 kilos of corn to the Žitopromet company. The key issue was whether Mikalački, who gave the instruction, and Vukov, who carried it out, deviated from the plan? The prosecutor thought that they did. According to Vukov, and my father, this was merely reasonable since Žitopromet, in return for the corn, got reduced-price vouchers to exchange for hoes for the cultivation of the company's vegetable garden, which was to the benefit of the people. Still, the prosecutor insisted that this was a deviation from the plan, which constituted a crime. Charges were raised also against Kosta Mikalački as an accessory. (He was not defended by my father but by another lawyer.) The crucial question was if the corn had become "surplus" (because if it had, then it was legal to give it to Žitopromet). The prosecutor objected that there was a party interested in the corn among those entitled to have it according to the plan. Namely, the Railway Industry School. The 337 kilos of corn could have been given to the Railway Industry School. In other words, it was not "surplus," and Vukov violated the plan. According to Vukov, however, it was he who kept the plan since The Railway Industry School asked for supplies, not for June, but for July, by which time there already was corn flour. By the rules of the planned economy, only corn flour was eligible for distribution, not corn.

The prosecutor stood by his position that the behavior of the two defendants constituted "a sabotaging behavior causing the violation of the rights of citizens." Not even the prosecutor said, though, that either Vukov or

Mikalački had personally benefited from their "behavior." All in all, as I see from a note made in pencil, Pera Vukov got a suspended prison sentence of two months.

Such was the economic situation. However, not everything was uniform and colorless even then. On Cara Dušana Street there was also a vegetable market in the years of the first Five-Year Plan and even a couple of years after, or so I remember. Mainly vegetables and fruit were sold by local farmers, but you could also buy trouser belts, which must have been against the law. On the even number side (our side), a vendor proudly put up her name. She was "Erzsike." She also wrote "watermelon" on a noticeboard. The spelling of the Hungarian word was flawed, which may or may not have impaired her sales, but in any case, it was in Hungarian. She also had it in flawed Serbian, to continue the hair-splitting, since the Serbian word she used meant muskmelon rather than watermelon. But such things troubled no one in the multiculturalism of Becskerek, and the green watermelons stood there in a pile.

On the opposite side of the street, where the shop of Vukov was also located, many were taken aback by the proud sign post in Serbian in front of a stall: IMAM SVE. SAMO PITAJTE (I have everything. Just ask me). Which shows there was optimism in those years too.

I am trying to remember the shop at number 11. I am almost sure that there wasn't any with a street front. It may have been inside the yard of the house. But I don't recall any inhabitants either. I remember, of course, that the Tunners lived a house or two past no. 11, but they no longer do. People in our street changed. As did the logic of life.

2. EVEN IF THE MONEY IS MADE AVAILABLE, I CANNOT TRANSFER IT...

The issues involved in this particular case (File No. 12683) are not all economic. The time is between 1947 and 1950. On June 20, 1947 Erzsébet Vértes, née Löwy, gives power of attorney to my father in Romanian with Serbian translation attached. The letter itself is in Hungarian. Erzsébet Vértes lives in Tarnaveni, Romania. The Hungarian name of the small town in Transylvania where she lives is Dicsőszentmárton. In the letters sent from Transylvania, the name of the place is written Tãrnãveni in correct Romanian (and similarly on the backside of the envelope), but the character "a" with the curved little line on top could hardly be reproduced in the letters and appeals typewritten in Becskerek, let alone the Cyrillic script used by the authorities. Here is the backside of one of the letters sent from Romania:

Erzsébet Vértes requests to inherit the property of Margit Reinitz, her younger sister murdered in a death camp. In the inheritance cases after the war, the heaviest part of the lawyers' job was to establish who was alive and who was not. Could the decedent still be alive? And who, if anybody, is alive of the possible inheritors? This was especially difficult when Jewish families were concerned. Mrs. Albert Vértes, née Erzsébet Löwy, was (or should have been) the heir of the house at 2 Takovska in Becskerek.

Takovska ran parallel to our Cara Dušana. A classmate of mine of German descent lived where Takovska began in an apartment overlooking the yard. Now that I know that the Reinitz family lived in No. 2 Takovska, I also know that they lived opposite to my classmate's home. My aunt Piroska had also lived for a while on Takovska, on the same side as the Reinitz's. Also, on the same side was the house of an elderly lady with a Serbian name who we visited several times with my parents and spoke Hungarian. My friend Laza Stankov, who I completed the military service with, lived two blocks from the Reinitz's. He made corporal, while I remained a *vojnik*, a private, the lowest of the low. Laza now lives in Australia. A block or two after the Stankovs' house there began the village-like part of Becskerek with several yards overlooking the street, some with haystacks.

When did the Decedents Die?

The house had been owned by Béla Reinitz and his wife. The wife was Margit Löwy, the younger sister of the client, Erzsébet Vértes/Löwy. The Reinitz's had a son, Gregor, born in 1924. They had been the inhabitants of the house at 2 Takovska. All three died in the Jewish concentration camp in Belgrade. Reinitz was fifty-four years old, his wife forty-six, and their son seventeen. Yet it was not easy to get a decree of presumption of death. There was little doubt that they had been killed. A legal process, however, requires facts and dates.

For a while the fate of the Jews stayed within sight in Becskerek. While leafing through other documents I came upon a newspaper page cut out from the May 16, 194 issue of *Torontál*. This was a social page recording who was born to whom, who married and who died since April 13. Among the dead, ten names were marked with red ink by my grandfather. He wrote on the bottom of the page by hand: "the [above] named are suicide victims of the German persecution of Jews." They included Mór Iványi, a classmate of my grandfather, and his wife Felicia. Ten Jewish people committed suicide in Becskerek between the of April 13 and May 16. Five names are marked in the bottom part of the newspaper page (they can be seen here) and five more higher up.

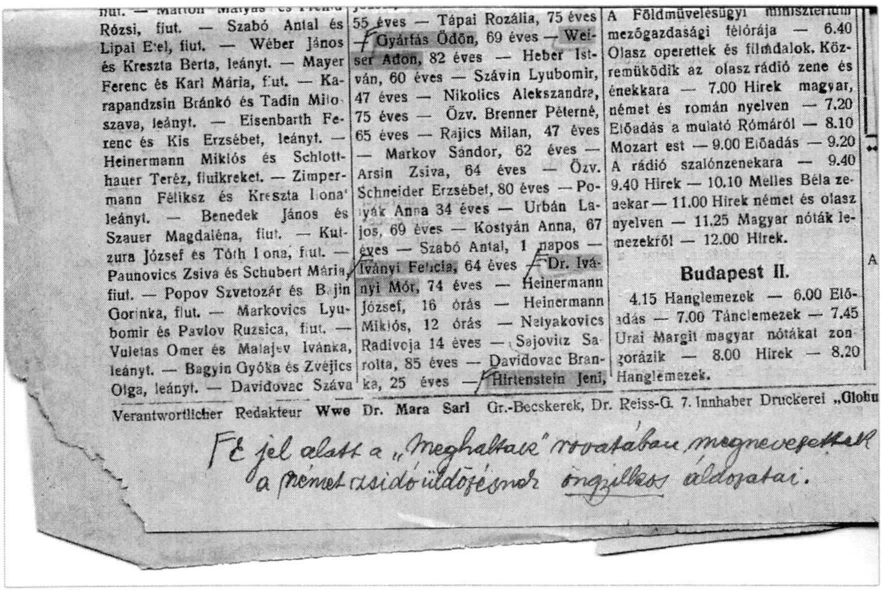
Rózsi, fiut. — Szabó Antal és Lipai E'el, fiut. — Wéber János és Kreszta Berta, leányt. — Mayer Ferenc és Karl Mária, fiut. — Karapandzsin Bránkó és Tadin Milo-szava, leányt. — Eisenbarth Ferenc és Kis Erzsébet, leányt. — Heinermann Miklós és Schlotthauer Teréz, fiuikreket. — Zimpermann Féliksz és Kreszta Ilona' leányt. — Benedek János és Szauer Magdaléna, fiut. — Kutzura József és Tóth Ilona, fiut. — Paunovics Zsiva és Schubert Mária, fiut. — Popov Szvetozár és Bajin Gorinka, fiut. — Markovics Lyubomir és Pavlov Ruzsica, fiut. — Vuletas Omer és Malajev Ivánka, leányt. — Bagyin Gyóka és Zvéjics Olga, leányt. — Daviđovac Száva

55 éves — Tápai Rozália, 75 éves — Gyárfás Ödön, 69 éves — Weiser Adon, 82 éves — Heber István, 60 éves — Szávin Lyubomir, 47 éves — Nikolics Alekszandra, 75 éves — Özv. Brenner Péterné, 65 éves — Rajics Milan, 47 éves — Markov Sándor, 62 éves — Arsin Zsiva, 64 éves — Özv. Schneider Erzsébet, 80 éves — Polyák Anna 34 éves — Urbán Lajos, 69 éves — Kostyán Anna, 67 éves — Szabó Antal, 1 napos — Iványi Felicia, 64 éves — Dr. Iványi Mór, 74 éves — Heinermann József, 16 órás — Heinermann Miklós, 12 órás — Nelyakovics Radivoja 14 éves — Sajovitz Sarolta, 85 éves — Daviđovac Branka, 25 éves — Hirtenstein Jeni,

A Földmüvelésügyi minisztérium mezőgazdasági félórája — 6.40 Olasz operettek és filmdalok. Közremüködik az olasz rádió zene és énekkara — 7.00 Hirek magyar, német és román nyelven — 7.20 Előadás a mulató Rómáról — 8.10 Mozart est — 9.00 Előadás — 9.20 A rádió szalónzenekara — 9.40 9.40 Hirek — 10.10 Melles Béla zenekar — 11.00 Hirek német és olasz nyelven — 11.25 Magyar nóták lemezekről — 12.00 Hirek.

Budapest II.

4.15 Hanglemezek — 6.00 Előadás — 7.00 Tánclemezek — 7.45 Urai Margit magyar nótákat zongorázik — 8.00 Hirek — 8.20 Hanglemezek.

Verantwortlicher Redakteur **Wwe Dr. Mara Sarl** Gr.-Becskerek, Dr. Reiss-G. 7. Innhaber Druckerei „Globu

F£ jel alatt a „Meghaltak" rovatában megneveztettek a német zsidóüldözésnek öngyilkos áldozatai.

This was the first month of the German occupation. Soon came the deportations, and what was left in Becskerek was rumor and guesswork. The Reinitz's were deported too. Later on, in the inheritance proceedings, exact facts were required. Evidence was needed on who died when. On March 10, 1948 my father tried to solve the problem in a submission to the Town People's Committee. It was common knowledge, he writes, that in the Jewish camp in Belgrade, the men were killed first, at the end of 1941, followed by the women in the spring of 1942. He attaches a certification by the Jewish community of Becskerek according to which Béla Reinitz and his son Gregor did not survive October 30, 1941 and Mrs. Reinitz did not survive March 31, 1942. That, however, did not suffice. On April 8, 1948, the People's Committee rejects the request for a decree of presumption of death. The decision refers to the decree issued by the Ministry of the Interior on February 1, 1947 according to which in the case of mass executions, evidence of the exact day of execution is required. But there was no evidence.

There was one more chance. According to the instructions of the Ministry of the Interior, the presumed date of death could be established by court procedure. The procedure was launched, and on July 16, 1948 my father was called upon by Judge Šoklovački to hand over the birth certificates of Béla Reinitz, Mrs. Reinitz and their son Gregor to the court, and also produce evidence that "these persons were threatened and probably lost their lives." Gregor's birth certificate was easy to secure but his father's and mother's were not. Maybe they were not born in Becskerek, and their birthplace could well have been outside Serbia in 1947. There may have been other problems as well. My father decided to locate the marriage certificate which normally shows the dates of birth. The wedding had been held in Versec. This complicated things a bit but was not impossible to solve. At my father's request the marriage certificate was obtained by Aladár Menczer, a lawyer in Versec, who sent it to him "with best collegial greetings." The court accepted the argument that the birth dates registered in the marriage certificate could substitute for the birth certificates. What was left to prove was that "these persons were in danger and probably lost their lives." On September 30, 1948 my father suggests Rózsa Tajti as witness to the circumstance that "the above named were deported and killed." I made efforts to find out who Rózsa Tajti was. Had she also been deported but survived? Or did she only see the Reinitz's being taken, and the rest was common knowledge? I couldn't find out.

The last attempt turned out to be successful. I use the word "successful" hesitantly. What I call success was getting a decree of presumption of death for the Renitz family, murdered in a concentration camp. But the new obstacles rising before us, especially when surmounted, indicate that at least things still go on, there is some kind of continuation. As I see from the correspondence, Mrs. Vértes, the elder sister of the murdered woman, was also glad that there was at least some partial result in the process that she had started.

The court verdict was signed by Judge Ivan Veljača on April 12, 1949. I actually knew him. His wife Hajnalka Veljača was my geography teacher. The verdict states that the District Court of Becskerek acknowledges the request of Mrs. Vértes and declares Béla Reinitz, Margit Reinitz and Gregor Reinitz "who, as Jews, were seized and taken to the Belgrade concentration camp" dead. The date of the death is determined for Béla and Gregor Reinitz as December 31, 1941, and for Margit Reinitz as April 30, 1942. The court followed a directive according to which, when there is no evidence of a different date, the day of death should be December 31, 1941 for men, and for women, April 30, 1942. I don't think anyone, including Ivan Veljača, could have found out exactly when they lost their lives. The law can get along somehow without reality but not without facts. And having mentioned the struggles of the law, or more precisely, the struggles of men against the law, let me return once again to the Ivanji family. As I said, my grandfather marked ten names in red ink in the daily *Torontál*, noting that they were victims of the "the German persecution of Jews." They included Mór Iványi and his wife. Mór Iványi had been a classmate and a friend of my grandfather. His grandson, Ivan Ivanji, Tito's translator and a noted writer, once told me that his grandparents took morphine. Mór Iványi was a physician, so he had access. Ivan's parents had been taken to the concentration camp in Belgrade and killed there. The survivors can't tell when. But legally they died on December 31, 1941 and April 30, 1942, respectively.

I have found a batch of files on a case in which my father represented Ivan and his younger sister Ildi, who survived Auschwitz, Buchenwald and Bergen-Belsen as children. They had to do with a life insurance. According to the contract, in case the father died, the sum of the insurance would be received by the children, Ivan and Ildi. The claim was launched by my father in 1948. At the time, Ivan was 19 and Ildi a few years younger. The process was simple to begin with, but turned out to be complicated. There are situations separated by a gulf from reality, and it isn't easy to fabricate a bridge. The new authorities (the antifascists, of course) noticed that in the last few months before the death of Ivan's father, the insurance premium was not paid. It could not be, since by then Ivan's father was in the death camp. The authorities maintained that the request could be rejected if the premium had not been paid. Normally this makes sense—only the world in which this sense took shape was suspended for a while.

I remember a signpost in Pest on the Danube quayside showing in which direction you were not allowed to drive. When facing the Danube, driving toward the left was allowed, and to the right was not. Then the flood came, and the quay was overrun. The water level rose by at least a meter and a half, covering everything on the quay. Only the "forbidden" sign stayed visible. The rule was of course still in force, only it made no sense. In the case of Ivan and Ildi, my father tried and tried. In the end a compromise was arrived at between the one-time sense and the new reality.

On September 3, 1948 a court decree was born, according to which, instead of the 15,000 dinars due, Ildi would get 13,271 dinars in Becskerek. The unpaid premiums were deducted. At the end of the same sentence it is mentioned that Iván would get the same amount, only he would be paid in Belgrade.

This is what happened, and here is the decree:

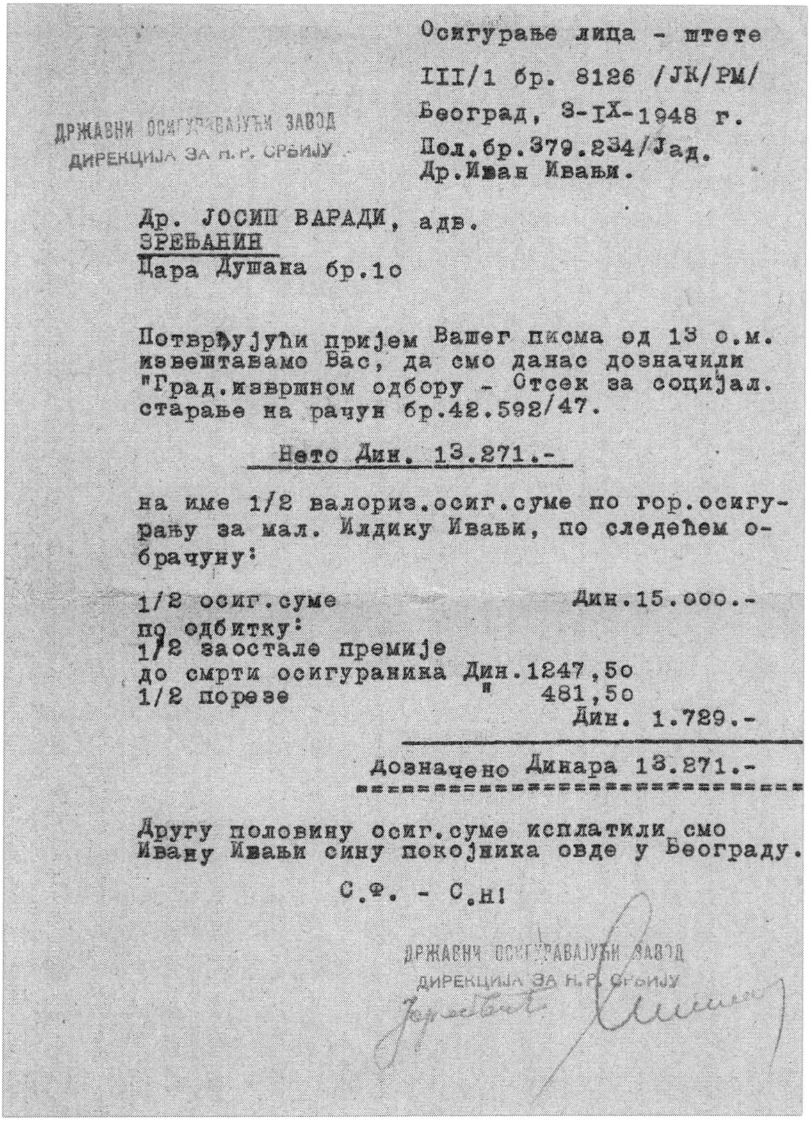

Осигурање лица - штете
III/1 бр. 8126 /JK/PM/
Београд, 3-IX-1948 г.
Пол.бр.379.234/Јад.
Др.Иван Ивањи.

ДРЖАВНИ ОСИГУРАВАЈУЋИ ЗАВОД
ДИРЕКЦИЈА ЗА Н.Р. СРБИЈУ

Др. ЈОСИП ВАРАДИ, адв.
ЗРЕЊАНИН
Цара Душана бр.1о

Потврђујући пријем Вашег писма од 13 о.м. извештавамо Вас, да смо данас дозначили "Град.извршном одбору - Отсек за социјал. старање на рачун бр.42.592/47.

Нето Дин. 13.271.-

на име 1/2 валориз.осиг.суме по гор.осигурању за мал. Илдику Ивањи, по следећем обрачуну:

1/2 осиг.суме Дин.15.000.-
по одбитку:
1/2 заостале премије
до смрти осигураника Дин.1247,5о
1/2 порезе " 481,5о
Дин. 1.729.-

Дозначено Динара 13.271.-

Другу половину осиг.суме исплатили смо Ивану Ивањи сину покојника овде у Београду.

С.Ф. - С.Н!

ДРЖАВНИ ОСИГУРАВАЈУЋИ ЗАВОД
ДИРЕКЦИЈА ЗА Н.Р. СРБИЈУ

Is There Another Heir Alive?

It followed from the court verdict that Margit actually survived her husband (and son), so the ownership of the entire house descended on her. What was thus involved was the heritage of Mrs. Reinitz. However, the question still remained if there might be other inheritors. My father wrote to Mrs. Vértes in September 1949. In his letter he asks facts about other possible inheritors, maybe parents, other siblings; "who is alive, and do the deceased lawful inheritors have descendants?" This was not an easy task at a time when, not only archives and data, but also the facts themselves were scattered around.

Mrs. Vértes replied on October 20, 1949, and she made an effort to summarize things precisely. She wrote in fine, clear characters, underlining in several places what she thought was most important. Among other things, the letter declares:

> Aside from my late brother-in-law, Béla Reinitz's younger brother who also fell victim, Mr. Reinitz has not a single relative. His late Father and Mother both died well before the war in Becskerek. –His younger brother Miklós Reinitz was single, a resident of Becskerek who, as I already mentioned, died because of having been taken to a concentration camp.
>
> The wife of Béla Reinitz, née Margit Löwy, was my younger sister whose only son, Gregor, also died. The Father of Mrs. Béla Reinitz was a resident of Becskerek, who died in 1939, and our Mother, Hermina Löwy, also perished in consequence of having been seized and taken from Becskerek in 1941–1942. I am the only survivor of all the relatives of my late brother in law and my sister.

Most of the required death certificates could be obtained with the help of Mrs. Vértes. It was more difficult to find documents on the parents of Béla Reinitz because all Mrs. Vértes knew about them was that they had died "well before the war," and the name of Béla Reinitz's father was József Reinitz. Our office tried three lines of inquiry: the Town People's Committee, the Becskerek Jewish Community, and Irma Berger, a hairdresser in Becskerek who must have been a good friend of the Reinitz family. The file includes a piece of paper with what is in all probability a note from Irma

Berger on when József Reinitz and his wife had died. The note is in German, either because of the three languages of Becskerek, this was the one she knew best, or perhaps because she had copied the data from a German source. By the name of Mrs. Reinitz there is the full date (4/10/1921) but by Béla Reinitz, there is nothing but the year of death (1917).

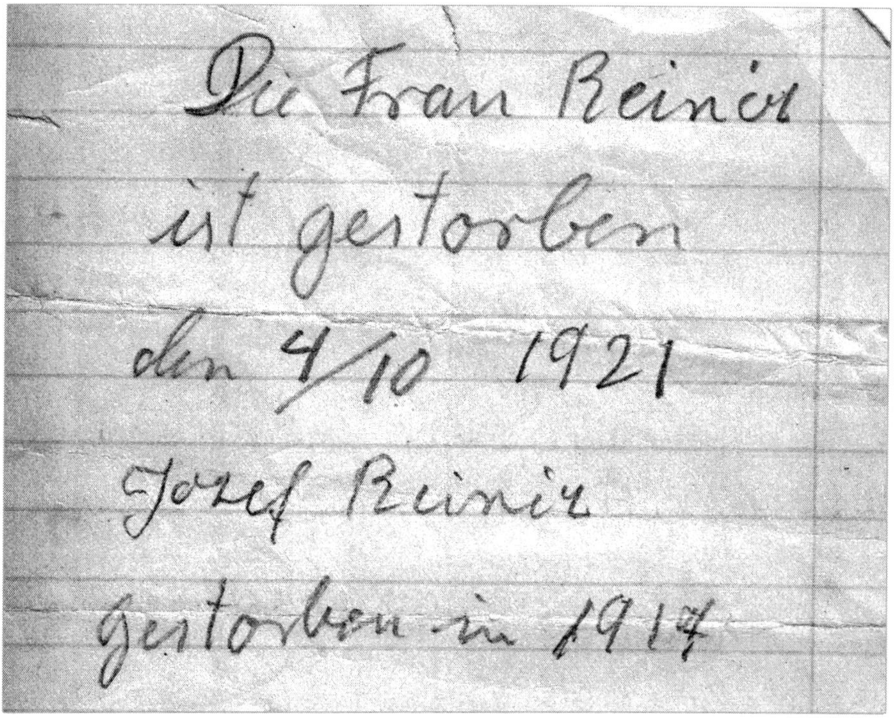

Die Frau Reinitz
ist gestorben
den 4/10 1921
Josef Reinitz
gestorben in 1917

In the end, the whole puzzle had been assembled, and all of the evidence was submitted to the court. It was proven that Erzsébet Löwy was the only inheritor.

Can the Heir Inherit?

The verdict was handed down on November 30, 1950. Judge Vujasinović decided to reject the inheritance claim. In the reasoning part he confirms that the claim was handed in on time. He also confirms the date when the Reinitz's lost their lives, that Mrs. Reinitz survived her husband, thus inheriting his part of the property, that Mrs. Vértes is the sister of Mrs.

Reinitz, and there is no other inheritor. The argumentation also covers that the house of the Reinitz's was confiscated as Jewish property by the German occupying authorities, that it was held by Treuhand A. G. of Germany, and after the war it changed from German property to the people's property. Then follows the key sentence of the whole reasoning: "The court finally established that returning the property (the building in question) would adversely affect the people's economy and the restoration of the country." Such was the economic situation, or the perception of that situation.

In principle there remained one more possibility. On the basis of the law of expropriation, financial compensation could have been claimed, though not much. However, the money eventually acquired could not have been transferred to Romania. The last document in the batch is the copy of a letter from my father:

> You are entitled to start an expropriation process and claim the countervalue of the house. In my view, however, it would be inadvisable to launch such a process. The reason is that in the course of the expropriation process, the value of the property to be expropriated is determined according to a value assessment rate fixed by special decree, and the value that can be achieved is unfortunately very low. And then, even if that value is actually made available, I cannot transfer it.
>
> It is my view that any further proceedings in this case should be suspended.

As far as I know, there is no continuation.

3. COOPERATIVE DENIAL

In the introductory principles of the Five-Year Plan, several mentions are made of the cooperatives. According to the principles, they rely on a voluntary initiative that deserves support:

> Similarly, it is necessary to provide effective support to the already existing agricultural cooperatives and to the voluntary initiative enjoying increasing popularity with the small and middle farmers for the establishing of cooperatives so that the land be cultivated together and common animal husbandry is organized.

It is not exactly my discovery that there was a lot more "effective support" than "voluntary initiative" around. Some lawsuits offer a closer view of this. I can also see the kind of treatment people got when they did not support joining the co-operatives. On May 9, 1950, the district prosecutor of Becskerek brought charges against eight "cooperative deniers" from Udvarnok (Banatski Dvor in Serbian). After some hesitation, I decided to publish only the initials of their surnames: Lajos Cs., András T., Vince Cs., Mihály B., József K., Vince Ó. and Miklós K. All of them were farmers. The prosecutor charged that "when the agricultural co-operative in the village was taking on a massive size, they took a hostile position, wanting to prevent their fellow citizens from joining the cooperative." The name of the cooperative was "Prvoborac Stanko" (Vanguard Fighter Stanko). Mainly Hungarians were warned by the accused not to enter the cooperatives. This was put by the prosecutor in the form: "They directed a destructive attitude especially at the Hungarian minority." There was one among the accused who even said, "this will not stay like this for long, everything is going to change." According to the prosecutor, none of this was accidental but done in an organized manner. The defendants met several times, "discussing the work and the massive increase of the co-operative." To add insult to injury, during the occupation, "more than one among the accused was close to the occupiers," proving that they remained hostile. The list of charges included some concrete facts as well. For instance, that József Cs. (a member of the cooperative) was attacked in the street by Lajos Cs., who scolded his mother, "like that of every member of the cooperative." András T. seized István K. by the neck in a pub, and told that he had betrayed the Hungarians, and also said bad things about his mother, and the mother of every member of the cooperative. "Vince O. attacked those who joined the co-operative, alleging that the cooperative has a debt of 400,000 dinars and is bound to go broke.

Mihály B. also attacked József Cs. (as did Lajos Cs.), and shouted, "hit him, God punish him and his mother!" A number of similar incidents are listed. It was, however, not specified which of the accused "was close to the occupiers," and in what way. Three of the accused were defended by my father. The power of attorney was signed not by the defendants but by their wives. In one case the signature was a fingerprint.

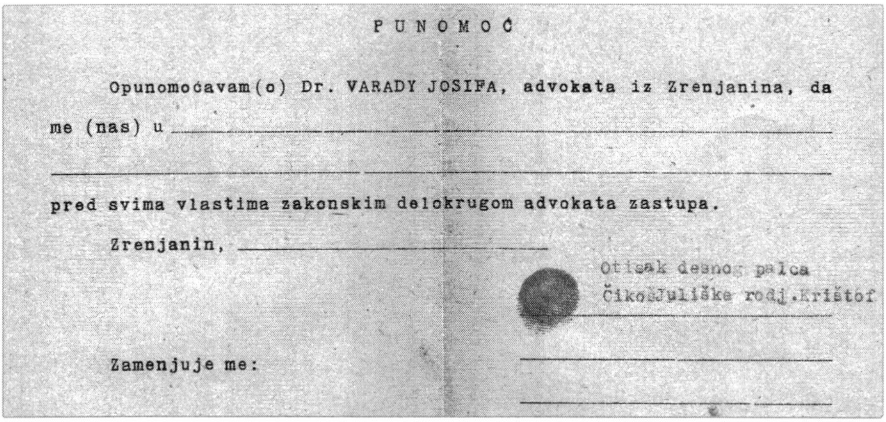

PUNOMOĆ

Opunomoćavam(o) Dr. VARADY JOSIFA, advokata iz Zrenjanina, da me (nas) u ______________________

pred svima vlastima zakonskim delokrugom advokata zastupa.

Zrenjanin, ______________

Otisak desnog palca
ČikošJuliške rodj.Krištóf

Zamenjuje me: ______________

That the signatories were not the defendants is explained by the fact that they were in preliminary detention and were not allowed to see their lawyers while the interrogation lasted. According to the indictment, they confessed to all the charges, saying only that they were drunk. But, according to the prosecutor, this could not be true, since it was not only in the pub that they did what they did. At which point my lawyer's sense whispers in my ear that the pub is by far not the only place where people can be drunk.

Then I see a handwritten note. My father was probably able to visit the defendants in jail later on, and he noted what they told him. According to the note, they did not at all admit to everything alleged by the prosecutor. Vince Ó. actually said not a word was true of what the prosecutor was alleging. The paper contains thoughts about things that could be used in the defense. I suppose a lot more was told by the accused to my father, and he probably knew what they did and what they did not. Just as, I suppose, F. Lee Bailey knew whether O.J. Simpson had killed his wife or not.

The parents of several of my classmates in grammar school were members of cooperatives. What I remember best was attempting to decipher a rather odd sentence that gave me a lot of headache. A classmate, his name was Antal, said to me: "zadruga people don't fuck." Antal used the official Serbian *zadruga*, instead of the Hungarian word for "cooperative." In this way his declaration sounded even stranger. Judging from its tone, the statement was succinct and to the point. He was unwilling to give a more extensive explanation. We were fourteen or fifteen. I was old enough to be more or less certain that Antal could not have meant his maxim literally, but I was intrigued for quite a while by what my classmate had meant. I thought I would understand when grow older, but I still don't, so I give up. Maybe here and now I can connect it with File No. 12718/7 which, although its approach is different, still shows some kind of relationship between couples and *zadruga*. Even though the consequences drawn from the case seem to point precisely in the opposite direction. The gist of the matter was that Ilona S. wanted to be married. It was also clear that Sándor B. wanted to marry Ilona, but they needed license from the district court since Ilona was still a minor. She was 17, to be exact. The missing year had to be made up for by legal arguments. My father wrote the submission on behalf of Ilona on October 3, 1950. It tells that Ilona has known Sándor B. since her childhood, they are in love, and at Easter they decided to become husband and wife. The earnestness of the marriage is also shown by the fact that Sándor has a trade (he is a baker) and he is a member of the agricultural workers' cooperative (SRZ, seljačka radna zadruga) in Torda. Moreover, Ilona herself and her parents are also members of the co-operative. Thus, Sándor and Ilona absolutely deserve the license to be married, because they are *zadruga* people.

Anyway, my grammar school classmates talking about family experiences kept repeating that "we had to join." Still, I heard not only bad things. A boy, perhaps the class's best soccer player, said his father had been reluctant to join, but now he's in, things are, after all, not that bad in the cooperative. Others told a different story. One thing I heard from everybody who was willing to talk was the constant compulsion to celebrate achievements, whether there were any or not. When I looked for a parallel, the first thing that came to my mind was closing time at the New York Stock Exchange where the bell and the applause are an obligatory ritual, whether share prices have gone up or dropped that day. There are even more extreme examples. I read in the *New Yorker* magazine on July 27, 2009 (and I made a note of it too) that when the giant Bear Stern company crashed during the last depression, Jim Cayne, the CEO, gave speeches at several company meetings, getting a standing ovation everywhere. The rituals of celebrating success which appear to be sustained, and sustainable, on all occasions might be a worthy subject for research by anthropologists.

The documents also show that one of the major crimes of the eight cooperative-resistant farmers was that they had been delaying the rate of the "massive increase." This was a much more serious matter than the question of whether András T. had slurred the mother of István K. (which he probably did). The Five-Year Plan had etched dates and deadlines into the public mind, and after that, the sense of loyalty had to adjust to them. These dates would make heroes and traitors too. The real heroes, of course, were the people who did not at all delay but actually overtook the dates, fulfilling the objectives ahead of time. A month after it published the fundamental principles of the first Five-Year Plan, *Magyar Szó* devoted the May 25, 1947 issue to the birthday of Marshal Tito. Page two displays the greetings from various organizations, mainly People's Fronts and cultural organizations. The greeting of the AFŽ (Antifašistički Front Žena, Women's Antifascist Front) is the only one specifying which birthday is being celebrated. It was the fifty-fifth. The second of the greetings' two sentences reads: "We commit ourselves to contribute with all our might to the realization of the Five-Year Plan ahead of time." A real patriotic woman, or man, is not the one who fulfils in time but the one who fulfils ahead of time.

The sentence is unfortunately missing again. Sensing the public mood surrounding the case, I have a feeling that the Udvarnok farmers delaying the "massive increase" languished in prison for a considerable time. I am trying to guess whether, if somewhat later, the eight defendants became cooperative members in the end. Who knows? Maybe they did.

4. A CALF-KILLING AGAINST THE PEOPLE'S INTERESTS

This was the criminal suit against Péter Balgó, a worker in Becskerek. The trial was on February 5, 1946 and the sentence was handed down the very same day by the Becskerek people's county court, sentencing the defendant to one year in prison and hard labor. The judgment was brought still before the first Five-Year Plan, but reflects the developing order of values and the general mood of the times. And also, that the creation of the plan was under way.

The file contains eight sheets of documents. I am going to follow their order. The first is an announcement of appeal. This submission was sent by our office on behalf of Péter Balgó three days after the sentencing. There was a hurry. According to the submission, the wife of Péter Balgó was seven months pregnant so she could not sustain herself if her husband was taken to prison. The documents include one from the district advisory body of expectant women which certifies that "Erzsi Balgó is in the 7th month of her pregnancy."

The announced appeal did not survive among the documents. I can see, though, that it was not successful. On March 16 the county court informs my father that the appeal was rejected. The justification consists of a single sentence. The appeal is rejected "because it is on record (taken on 5.2) that the defendant declared that he is content with the sentence."

I think it is pretty unlikely that Péter Balgó was content with the sentence. Nor am I certain that the keeper of the court minutes exactly recorded what he said. At that time, he did not even have a lawyer. His wife saw my father only after the sentencing. It is even conceivable that when the judge asked, "are you content with the sentence?" he simply said yes because he just wanted to conform. That was the direction in which all the roads slanted; everything and everybody were moving that way. Who was he to say no when everybody else was marching downhill? The time was February 1946. Péter Balgó was a simple day laborer. The inevitability of joining was more clear than the specifics of just what was being joined.

In the international economic suits that I had the opportunity to take a closer look at, I often saw that following a negative decision, lawyers still have options. Complex corporation setups often make it possible for another actor (legal person) to enter the picture. Efforts can also be made in the direction of a different decision-maker. I see a somewhat similar approach emerging in this trial.

The other person entering the scene this time is the wife, Erzsébet Balgó, née Kis. The request submitted on April 9, 1946 is written in her name. Erzsébet tells that she is in the ninth month of pregnancy, and asks that her husband's sentence be reduced or at least postponed by six months. She also adds "Death to Fascism and Freedom to the People." There is no real success this time either, but at least three months' postponement was approved by the court.

Turning the pages in the top batch, it was still unclear to me what sort of a criminal act it was all about, and whether it was worth writing about. The next submission answers both questions. The crime, it turns out, was "the unallowed killing of a calf," violating the rules specified in The Law on Speculation and Economic Sabotage. So, I went on turning the pages. The context also clarifies that the unlucky beast in question was not a different owner's calf, neither the people's calf but it was the culprit's own. What was appropriated by Péter Balgó was not the calf but the right of decision about the economic reasonability of killing it. The people's interests were violated by anyone who himself decided about whether he should kill his own calf. It was for the people to determine whether there was sufficient reason to abandon that source of milk.

At this point, another actor enters the scene, unexpected to me too. His name is Milan Brusin, and he is a butcher in Becskerek. I suspect he was found by the defendant and my father after the rejection of the appeal. The submission must have been put into words by my father, and it was written on our typewriter in the recognizable clerk's style of Uncle Göttle. Brusin is turning to the Town Court and asks for Péter Balgó to be sent to work in his butcher shop in Becskerek instead of prison in Mitrovica. In that way he could stay close to his wife. The most effective argument, however, is not the condition of the wife. Brusin is a supplier of the military, so helping him in this endeavor is a patriotic act. The court also acts patriotically if it sends an unskilled laborer to help him. The effort turned out to be successful. Then came another attempt. This time, on July 22, 1946, my father appeals to the Serbian Ministry of Interior for the release on probation of Péter Balgó. His arguments are as follows:

- Péter Balgó has a clean record
- He has no fortune; his only source of income is work on hire
- His wife gave birth to a baby May 29, 1946, so she is currently unable to work, and there is no one to assist her
- He killed the calf due to dire need, and he promises to refrain from any such act in the future.

Now that I am beginning to have some kind of view of Péter Balgó. I would be happy if I could attach his picture here, if there were any. As in quite a few other cases, I took a walk to see the site specified in the documents as their place of residence (32 Gundulićeva). There is no longer any trace of the Balgós over there. I had little hope anyway. As far as I know people's movements in Becskerek, there is just about as much chance that they moved to Australia as that they stayed in Becskerek. The likeliest, though, is that they moved to Germany. The Balgós' son was born on May 29, 1946, which means he is younger than I am. Has he kept picture of his parents? Does he know about this trial? Are their remnants surviving somewhere? Or are those eight sheets of paper all there is left?

To return to the process for a moment, I can also see that one more appeal reached the Supreme Court of the Voivodina, but this was not kept in the files. The arguments were probably the same as in the other documents.

The last piece on file is a copy of a letter, actually the only text in Hungarian in the whole file. It is addressed to Peter Balgó by my father on September 18, 1946 and reads: "I wish to inform you that in reaction to our request, the Supreme Court in Novi Sad has reduced your sentence to 3 months. Please come to see me in my office tomorrow for a discussion of the rest."

With that, the case was closed. The three months were over, and Péter Balgó could go home to his wife and newborn son. In a few months there would be another birth: that of the first Five Year's Plan.

5. MAFIA-TYPE ACTIVITY IN THE YEARS OF THE FIRST FIVE-YEAR PLAN

In various economic situations, the mafia usually turns up, if in different forms. I want to write a bit about how organized crime worked in the Becskerek area during the years of the first Five-Year Plan. It is a cliché scene of many a crime movie that criminals are lying in wait to ambush the money van, most frequently before a curve in the road where it has to slow down. That is where they would stop it. Sometimes by enacting a mock road incident, at others in a more straightforward manner, standing in the middle of the road and spraying the van with machine gun bullets. It was the prosecutor's view that an ambush of a similar kind was committed by Pál H., János H. and József R. Pál and János must have been brothers because their parents are of the same name. According to the verdict, Pál H., the principle defendant, could read and write, having completed four years of elementary school, while János was illiterate. József R. was also literate with four years of elementary school accomplished. The latter even had a nickname. According to the verdict it was "Popori," while in the sentence it is "Kanan." Neither appears too convincing. I asked an acquaintance in Szentmihály (Mihajlovo in Serbian), and he also regards both variants unlikely. It seems the prosecutor or the judge (possibly both) were wrong where this topic is concerned.

The operative part of the judgement established that the three perpetrators "appropriated a part of the people's total assets." The ambush, however, did not happen quite like in the crime thrillers. Luka Surla was driving, not a van, but a horse-drawn wagon towards Elemér (Elemir, in Serbian). The target, according to the prosecutor, was the cargo of this wagon.

Elemér is some 10 kilometers from Becskerek. I am trying to find some connection with the village. I have driven through it by car several times but never stopped. Elemér won a spot for itself in Hungarian history. One of the heroes of the 1848 war of liberation, General Ernő Kiss, had his estate here. After the Habsburgs and their Russian allies had crushed the revolution, Kiss was executed in Arad along with other generals. Geiza Farkas, a big landowner in Elemér, was a great-grandson of Ernő Kiss on the maternal side. Farkas was a brilliant intellectual, and a close friend of the well-known social scientist Oszkár Jászi. He was born in Budapest, lived there for several years, and died there, but he was nevertheless mainly an Elemér man. He was also associated with Becskerek. When I was going to school, I still met people who knew him. He was always spoken about with respect. Only my mother said a few times that she was also annoyed by him. When they were honeymooning with my father in Vienna, they met Geiza Farkas, who made efforts to organize too many appointments. Geiza Farkas published ten-something books and pamphlets, several of which discussed questions of social psychology. Among the papers I found a book which he had dedicated to my father. I learned form it that Farkas was the sponsor of my father at his confirmation.

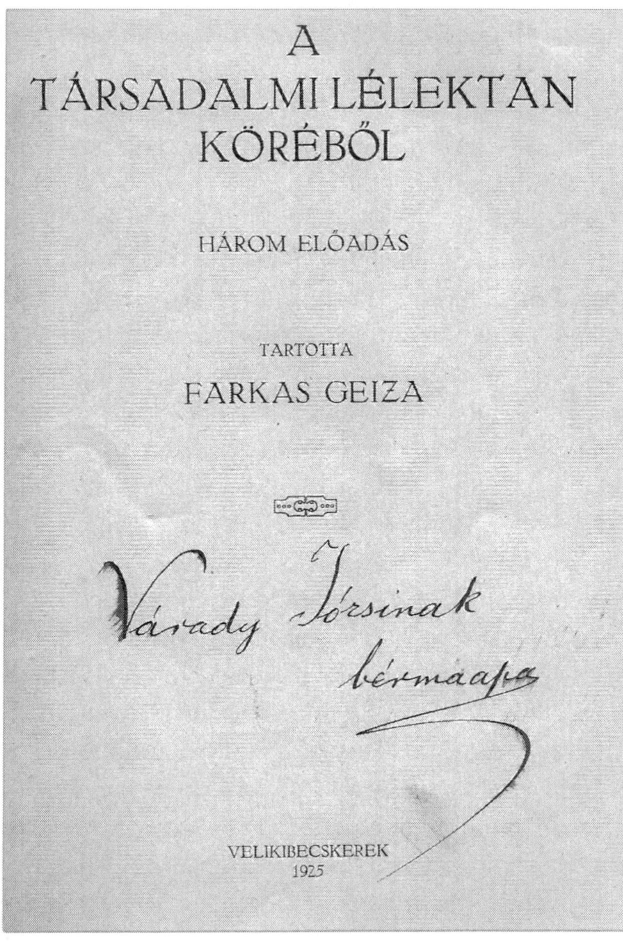
A
TÁRSADALMI LÉLEKTAN
KÖRÉBŐL

HÁROM ELŐADÁS

TARTOTTA
FARKAS GEIZA

Várady Józsinak
bérmaapja

VELIKIBECSKEREK
1925

He had some literary publications too. And he discussed topics which would come today under the heading "terrorism" or "struggle against terrorism." In September 1928 he wrote in the *S. H. S. Királyság Országos Magyar Pártjának Havi Értesítője*, the monthly bulletin of the Hungarian Party of the Kingdom of Serbs, Croats: "Political murder atrocities—regardless of whether they succeed or fail, whether they are retaliated and condemned, or rewarded and glorified—have one result that is absolutely certain: people will get used to the idea of murder along with which the threat of more assassinations will grow." The closing sentence is the call to "Arise for the fight to destroy this thousand-year-old monster, the superstition of the permissibility of political murder!"

Common sense was and is on the side of Geiza Farkas; history, well, not quite. The new dangers also brought new chances for spreading various beliefs, for selling arms, and a lot of other things.

Geiza Farkas also had a wealthy library which he left to the Petőfi Cultural Association in Becskerek. While inspecting the documents, I have so far set aside six Farkas files, including the one on the donation of the books. The Farkas files also include manuscripts, mostly of books and booklets that have been published. The title of one manuscript is *My Bad Little Friends* and is subtitled "Notes of an Amateur Pedagogue." It has two variants among the documents: one in Hungarian (typewritten) and another in German (written by hand). I have no idea if the German variant was ever published. The Hungarian was, and appeared in *Pozsony* in 1931. In this book, or more exactly, a pamphlet, he writes with great sympathy about the children playing in his garden in Elemér. Each child gets a few pages, most of them Serbian kids, but there are other nationalities, too. The names are Mišo, Branko, Aleksa, Luka, Sima, Ilona, Gyula, Milenko, Desanka, Pali and Lazo. A German child of French descent is also mentioned. The whole book is forty-five pages altogether. Yet it is the one from which I learned the most about the village of Elemér. What I don't really know is how much of what I learned is still valid. Geiza Farkas, by the way, was also a university professor. It was always his quest for knowledge that lead him on to the various stages and stations of his life, much rather than any effort at career-building or a desire to rise. Not only in Elemér was he an "amateur pedagogue." When *My Bad Little Friends* was written in the interwar years, Elemér was inhabited mostly by Serbian settlers. I would also have classmates from Elemér later, who went to the Serbian classes running parallel with ours. Luka Surla must have also lived in Elemér. A strange name, by the way. Surla means "trunk" as in "elephant's trunk."

The act took place on the road to Elemér. The culprits were from Szentmihály. Elemér is less than 10 kilometers from Becskerek, Szentmihály is at a distance of 13. Today's highways leading from Becskerek to Elemér and Szentmihály run nearly parallel to each other. A teacher from the Messinger told me that there is a 6 or 7-kilometer-long carriageway too. That one must have been the scene. When interrogated by the court, Luka Surla said he had been "dead drunk." The horses somehow broke free from the shaft, and the wagon ground to a halt on the road to Elemér. Which means no one had to stop it by pretending an accident or by machine gun fire. It stopped all by itself. That was when the three criminals went into action. There were three barrels of rum on the wagon, owned by the catering company of Elemér. They lifted one of the three barrels with 96 liters of 40 proof rum in it, put it on their own wagon and took it to Szentmihály. Those 96 liters of 40 proof rum constituted "a part of the people's total assets" (the People's Rum?). The narratives of the defendants and the witness coincide up to this point.

Later on, they deviate from each other. According to the indictment, one of the accused "stuffed 1,000 dinars into Luka's pocket." Luka Surla does not remember this but confirms that next morning he found 1000 dinars in his coat pocket. According to the principle defendant, however, things happened quite differently. He offered 1,000 dinars to Luka Surla for one barrel. Luka accepted the offer as well as the money, and then they took the barrel. In other words, it was a deal. At this juncture the problem looms up how delicate and uncertain the dividing line between organized crime and market trade can be at times.

The context of the economic situation at the time, however, put the defendants' arguments into a difficult position. There was such a thing as legal trade, but the people's property could not be sold and bought at a discounted price picked out of thin air. Everyone knew that a barrel of rum was worth a lot more than 1,000 dinars. The defendants were probably aware of that, too. That is why they confessed that they too had been dead drunk and had no idea what was in the barrel. They only realized it the next day. When they did, the secondary defendant (János H.) actually went to the municipal hall where he told Secretary Dezső Tót that they wanted to return the rum because they knew they had paid too little for it.

It is hard to make heads or tail of this. I am catching myself at rooting for the culprits but I'm not sure their statements reveal the complete truth. At any rate, Judge Jovan Ateljevic decided not to believe them. In his view it did not seem too likely that all three were equally drunk because "a man who is totally drunk would not be able to take 1,000 dinars from his wallet, stuff it into the pocket of a drunken man, then carry the barrel over to his wagon, load it and drive it home."

It was also questionable if they returned the rum of their own free will. It was not what the evidence of Dezső Tót confirmed, although it did not completely run against it. Dezső Tót said the authorities in Elemér had informed him of the rum rubbery instantly, and he suspected the perpetrators. János H. did go to his office next day, but when asked, he denied any knowledge of the barrel of rum. It was only a day later when an official had been sent to the principal defendant that János H. went to the office again, admitting that they had taken the barrel and promising that they would return it. Which meant that he went to the office of his own will, but only after he saw that they would be caught.

Weighing all this in the scales, the court concluded that the defendants had "appropriated a part of the people's total assets with the intention of obtaining unlawful material gain for themselves." All this had been done in an organized manner. Pál H. got a prison sentence of two months, and János H. and József R. got one month each.

Compensation for the Purchase Price and the Out-of-Pocket Expenses of the Criminal Organization

According to the sentence, the authorities took the 1,000 dinars from Luka Surla, who was not accused. This means there was no reason to do anything about the 1,000 dinars, and there was no need to tinker with this thing, which was no doubt comfortable for the judge.)

But how did 1,000 dinars get into the pocket of Luka Surla at all? If this was a case of mafia action, then the three Szentmihály men certainly deviated from the globally developed pattern. In the case of robbery, it is definitely unusual for the robber to stuff money into the pocket of the victim. Was there some kind of a business negotiation between them? If there was, why did Luka Surla accept such a low price? True, the rum was not his but the people's, and he would have got 1,000 dinars free. But if that line of action had been followed, he would certainly have tried to hide the money. It is of course possible that even though none of them were as completely drunk as they had said (neither the defendants nor Luka Surla), still everybody was highly drunk, and it was this state of general intoxication which made the whole baffling story hard to classify.

And who got the 1,000 dinars in the end? The fate of the money is documented accurately in the file. On June 21, 1950 my father wrote a letter to the police station in Elemér, declaring the defendants had bought a barrel of rum for 1,000 dinars. I can see that the defense stuck to the story of a "sale." The letter also states that the rum has been returned to the catering company of Elemér, and the "buyers" have been sentenced. That being the situation, my father claims that the purchase price should be returned. Earlier on, the court did not accept the reasoning that the incident was a sale, but it did not try to qualify it, and did not put the 1,000 dinars on the trial table, but left it in the pocket of Luka Surla, from where it got to the police. But if it wasn't a price paid for a sale, then what was it? Should it be classified as the out-of-pocket expenses of the criminal organization?

The police replied on July 10. Since the court avoided specifying the position of the 1,000 dinars, the police would not specify it either, but informed the lawyer that the money had been transferred to the prosecution's office and from there to the court. Thus, it is the court that it should be claimed from. Which was exactly the lawyer's next move, made on July 13. And the money was returned. It was transferred, if with some delay. Its reception by the office is not on the file but it can be seen that on December 19, 1950 it was received from my father by Pál H., the principal defendant. He duly signed a receipt. All of which meant that as far as the economic aspects of the case were concerned, the balance was restored. The total assets of the people were complete once again and the purchase price was returned. Or, if you like, the out-of-pocket expenses of the criminal organization were recovered.

Wrapping it All Up

Following the World War, it took until the 1950s (still at the time of the first Five-Year Plan) for us to be able to have guests from abroad once again. My aunt Bubus came to Becskerek from the Netherlands. She was accompanied by her Dutch husband, Uncle Jan. One day during their visit I was playing in the yard, I must have been eleven or twelve, when I overheard Uncle Jan and my uncle Lóri speaking in German. Uncle Jan asked politely about the members of the family. He also asked if it was still nice to swim in the Bega River. Lóri answered obligingly. Then Uncle Jan also asked about how the economic situation was shaping up in our part of the world. "Danke gut." Fine, thank you, my uncle Lóri replied.

VIII.
EXPLOITING FASCISM AND ANTI-FASCISM IN DISPUTES BETWEEN NEIGHBORS AND CHURCHES

1. FASCISM FOR HOUSEHOLD USE IN BECSKEREK

Jemricsnéni, a.k.a Adolf Fichtner

THE PROTAGONIST'S NAME in this lawsuit was "Jemricsnéni," pronounced "Jemrichnaynee" and meaning "Auntie Jemrics." The name, however, was always written and pronounced as a single word. That was the name by which she was known and called by everyone, even when she was spoken to in German. This is also what I see in my grandfather's letter written in German on December 8, 1942 and addressed to her: "Liebe Jemrichnéni!"

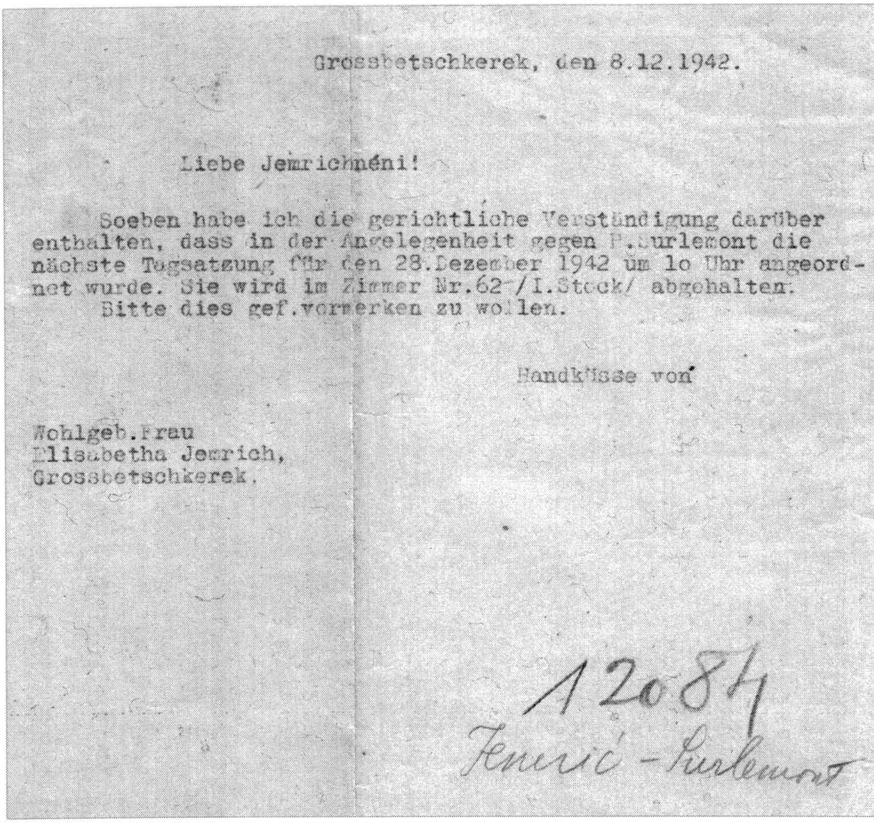

Grossbetschkerek, den 8.12.1942.

Liebe Jemrichnéni!

Soeben habe ich die gerichtliche Verständigung darüber enthalten, dass in der Angelegenheit gegen P.[illegible]urlemont die nächste Tagsatzung für den 28.Dezember 1942 um lo Uhr angeordnet wurde. Sie wird im Zimmer Nr.62 /I.Stock/ abgehalten.
Bitte dies gef.vormerken zu wollen.

Handküsse von

Wohlgeb.Frau
Elisabetha Jemrich,
Grossbetschkerek.

12084

Thus, no *Liebe Frau* Jemriics or *Lieber Tante* Jemrich, despite the letter being in German. Even though the word for "Dear" is used in German (*Liebe*), *néni*, (auntie), is nevertheless written in Hungarian, glued together into a single word with the name Jemrich (or Jemrics in Hungarian writing). By the way, "néni," implied no difference in generations. Jemricsnéni was born in 1860, my grandfather in 1867, so she was somewhat older, but by no means as distant in years where a lady is seen as an "aunt". All it meant was that this was the name by which she was known, and it stuck with her. All acquaintances in Becskerek called her that, Hungarians, Serbs and Germans alike. According to the file, her maiden name was Schultz. The court sentence also designates her nationality as German. I have no idea what her husband, with his obvious Slavic name, may have regarded himself to be. In 1942 she was already a widow, as is indicated by another letter. It is also evidenced by the abbreviation "Wve" (*Witwe*, i.e., widow) attached to her name.

Now that I am trying to remember her, the name definitely rings familiar. I seem to recall that she lived at the Bega riverside, which was either really so, or could be just a vague, confused memory. There is, however, no address on file (probably because everything was sent straight to the lawyer). I cannot see an address on the court summons either. All I can see in the printed forms is that all persons summoned by the court were "entitled to use the state railways free of charge." In this particular case, however, the free trip was not needed. All those involved were residents of Becskerek (Petrovgrad according to the form, since that was the town's name for a while, although my grandfather had used the name Grossbecskerek in his German letter to Jemricsnéni.) Without the address I have no means to check if she really lived at the riverside. I am trying to dig up some kind of personal memory, and there is actually a faint recollection that I saw her once, but I am not so sure.

A day or two before I began to write the story of Jemricsnéni, an interesting letter turned up in even older sheaf of documents. It was written by Ede Alföldy to my grandfather on October 28, 1918 in Budapest. Alföldy told him of having received the information from someone "yesterday, on Sunday" (on October 27, 1918, that is) that he would be offered the job of Justice Minister in Count Mihály Károlyi's cabinet. The end of World War One was followed by a series of rapid shifts in power. The Károlyi government was a liberal attempt that survived for a mere two months. Ede Alföldy was a highly reputed lawyer, so the idea would not have been entirely without logic. The letter, however, is as carefully worded as it is witty. Rumors abound, Alföldy writes, and he is considering if it might be worthwhile accept such an invitation, should he ever get one. He even wonders about the chances of the Károlyi government, "in case I lacked the power to resist the temptation of joining it," because "at this time this government could hardly offer more than an adventure and some excitement." He cites an anecdote to illustrate how real his encounter with the minister's job was: "Maybe my position is like that of the anecdotal Hungarian who, when asked if he ever saw the Emperor, replied, 'Certainly. I did see his Majesty, but only once, and it wasn't him.'" I, as the anecdotal author, have a somewhat similar feeling about my own position when I write about Jemricsnéni, wondering whether I ever saw her.

As a small boy, I used to know many Germans in Becskerek, and Jemricsnéni could easily have been one of them. German proverbs and sayings were still used, some of which I understood, and some I did not. One was for instance "Gottes schönste Gabe ist der Schwabe," which translates as "God's finest gift is the Swabian," and it rhymes, of course. Before Hitler, the joke was funny, good-humored, even benevolent. Local Germans used it too in a sort of self-mocking way, rather than in seriously. Later on, however, even the space reserved for jokes became filled with convictions, in the midst of which the proverb became paralyzed. It could have lived on, if literally meant, to emphasize racial superiority ("there is no one finer than a Swabian") but then it simply didn't work. The saying continued to wear its garb made of smiles, and the smile is not the kind of uniform in which you march around swaggering. Even to move was inadvisable anyway.

Jemricsnéni had no part in the arrival of Hitler. She probably wasn't even very happy about it, but then she saw her chance, because she had a bad quarrel with her neighbor. The neighbor was called Arthur Sürlemon. There was a time when they used to drink together, swap rumors, and would occasionally disagree. But then the disagreements grew increasingly bitter, reaching a point where Sürlemon banned Jemricsnéni from entering his house. That happened at about the same time as the Germans invaded the Banat region. Jemricsnéni was already eighty-one years old. Something had to be done. From the available options of warfare, the war of rumors seemed most suitable both as a medium and a theatre of operations. Earlier on, rumors would win power and stature when they rose up to become marketplace topics. Now there was a possibility that they might to turn into topics for fascism. The proper term would probably be "Nazi," but in Serbia, including the Banat, locals were using the words "fascism" and "antifascism" all the time. Anyway, some of the rumors surrounding her neighbor Sürlemon, if selected with care and with some extra added for good measure, so Jemrichnéni thought, may find appreciation in the upcoming world of Hitlerian thinking, and help her hit back at the neighbor who so rudely banned her from his house.

Accordingly, on April 21, two weeks after Hitler's soldiers took power in Becskerek, Jemricsnéni wrote a letter under a false name to the brand-new German military authorities. The choice of the assumed identity was meant to give added weight to the document. For a surname she picked the very Germanic "Fichtner," an ingenious move taking her instantly closer to the new authority, while the first name chosen was the downright irresistible "Adolf," nothing less. A letter signed "Adolf Fichtner" could in no way be ignored in the year 1941. Adolf Fichtner (a.k.a., Jemricsnéni) informed the German military authorities that Sürlemon was falsely claiming to have been an officer (or NCO) of the German army in World War One. He had been nothing of the kind. Quite to the contrary, he guided various enemy troops into Germany across the border (which border was not specified). After the war, his wife got him a fake Belgian passport which he used to into Serbia under an assumed Belgian identity. On top of it all there were "all sorts of things to be found in his home, including perhaps even files and money owned by the Jew Gyárfás." It is also added that Sürlemon used to be an employee of Gyárfás. All this combined sufficed for the Wehrmacht to arrest Herr Sürlemon.

The files indicate that Sürlemon spent only four days in detention. The charges turned out to be sheer fabrication, or at least that was what the Wehrmacht found. According to the Becskerek Prosecutor's Office, "all allegations had been investigated by the German armed forces," including the charge that there were "all sorts of things to be found in his home." Jemricsnéni was also exposed as the author of the letter. That possibility was probably raised by Sürlemon himself during the interrogation. Proving her authorship was easy since the letter was handwritten. Jemrichnéni never used a typewriter.

Who Sürlemon was is not entirely clear. The Christian names (Arthur Friedrich) are obviously German. The surname less so. It is most often written as "Sürlemon" but "Surlemon" also occurs a couple of times, and there is one instance of Sũrlemon too. In the prosecutor's submission, written in Cyrillic letters, the name is Сирлемон. The surname suggests French origins ("Surlemont," perhaps? A Huguenot?). In the procedure he identified himself as German. Then there were those Belgian ties. Can anyone establish an indubitable identity with full certainty in such circumstances? At this point, Wittgenstein comes to mind, who devoted a book to the problem of certainty (*Über Gewissheit*, 1969). The book consists of numbered notes. In Note 470, Wittgenstein writes:

> Why is there no doubt that I am called L.W.? It does not seem at all like something that one could establish at once beyond doubt. One would not think that it is one of the indubitable truths.

Had Wittgenstein lived in Becskerek, he would have seen all this even more precisely and in a broader perspective. The problem of certainty here got even more confused by the movement of people to and fro over Hungarian, German, Serb and Jewish identities for generations. Even the names lost their certainty. Had he lived in Becskerek, Wittgenstein would have known that (over or above the doubts) beside L.W., Ludwig Wittgenstein, he could just as easily be W. L., Wittgenstein Lajos in Hungarian, Lj. V. (Ljudevit Vitgenstajn) or even Витгенштајн, thus the essence of the problem of doubtful identity would have gained an even clearer form in his mind.

As for Sürlemon, what he had actually done in World War One could not be fully established either. Had he really been a German officer (or NCO) or just lied that he had? The Serbian prosecutor handling the case later on surmised that he had served in the French army as a lieutenant.

In any case, Sürlemon was cleared by the Wehrmacht, and Jemricsnéni was sentenced by the district military commander, Captain Rentsch, to a fine of 200 reichsmark, convertible to 20 days in prison, should she fail to pay. But Jemricsnéni paid up. The decision had to be published in the daily *Torontál* in the form of a "notice":

1941 julius 12

Értesités

Jemrics Erzsébetet büntető rendészeti itélettel **1941. jul. 10. névtelen** levélirásért és hamis **vádaskodásért** 20 napi elzárásra **változtatható** 200 birodalmi márka **pénzbüntetésre** itélték.

Nagybecskerek, 1941 jul. 10-én.

Rentsch s. k.
százados kerületi
katonai parancsnok

I can see here that the newspaper turned Jemricsnéni into an Erzsébet (Hungarian for Elisabeth). The documents, however, have her as Elisabeth.

The affair, though, was not over yet. Once upset, Mr. Sürlemon could not be calmed down so easily and was not content with the sanctions meted out to Jemricsnéni by the Wehrmacht. He pressed charges against Jemricsnéni at the court. Unlike the Wehrmacht, the court procedure required the involvement of lawyers, and Jemricsnéni asked my grandfather to represent her, while Mr. Sürlemon's lawyer was Pál Heklai (the husband of my aunt Piroska, thus Uncle Pali to me). In consequence of the accusations, in July 1942 charges were brought against Jemricsnéni by Prosecutor Ivan Markov.

A Parallel Case

Parallel with this one, another case, somewhat similar in nature, was in progress in the summer of 1942. Eighty-one-year-old Jemricsnéni was not the only one who saw a chance in fascism to settle her private score. Ilona V., 23, insulted by her boss, Emil N., must have felt much in the same way. What happened to Ilona V. is attested to by the medical certification of Dr. A Heinermann. My old acquaintance Péter Heinermann, who now works in at the archives of the Matica Srpska, the historic cultural institution of Serbs, in Újvidék (Novi Sad) but was born and raised in Becskerek, says the abbreviation "A." signifies the name Alois. Doctor Heinemann's deposition, written in German, begins with the information provided by Ilona N. herself. According to Ilona, at about 5 p.m. on May 1, 1942, her superior, Emil N. "hit her with his hand and fist, pulled her hair, and also kicked her with his foot." This is followed by a precise description of the injuries, and then by the diagnosis that these injuries are expected to heal within ten days and are not assumed to have enduring consequences. Far more dramatic harm was being done all over the place at that time (May 1942), but personal offenses are hard to put into perspective.

In June, Ilona turned to my grandfather, but previously she "gave information to the authorities," that is, she effectively denounced the pharmacist Emil N. Ilona must have felt, or so the letter of accusation shows, that she needed, and could have, a bit of extra push provided by fascism to be able to kick back more successfully. So, she alleged that in addition to hitting and kicking Ilona, the pharmacist had been listening to forbidden radio stations and "made derogatory remarks about prominent personalities including the Führer Adolf Hitler."

As regards forbidden radio stations, I have some personal memories myself. I distinctly remember that my father also listened to all kinds of radio stations in various languages during the German occupation. I was too young to know what he was listening to, I was five only even toward the end of the occupation, in 1944, but I remember him turning the dial, moving the finder somewhere else when someone knocked at the door. Most of the time it turned out to be a late client arriving after office hours who, having failed at the office entrance, came to knock on the home door.

On inspection of the list of the lawyer's moves (and their costs) it turns out that things did not proceed along the traditional trajectory of lawsuits this time. Most items are of the type of "several lengthy consultations with client," "discussions with opponent," "composition of settlement," "repeated consultations with client and opponent."

The result of all this was a statement of which several variants are found in the batch of documents relating to the case. Ilona's declaration was first drafted in Hungarian, then in Serbian. It was this Serbian version which, after several modifications, was signed. The heart of the matter was established already in the first version and remained unchanged, only some minor details and nuances were modified. Among other things, the handwritten declaration in Hungarian contains the following:

> I have authorized the lawyer Dr. Imre Várady to seek proper compensation for me for the injuries suffered as a result of the assault committed by Emil N. against my person.
>
> At the time of reporting my information, since this was immediately after and under the effect of the injuries suffered, when I was quite understandably in a state of shock, I made the complaint that... had listened to forbidden radio stations and abused leading personalities including Adolf Hitler...
>
> Having regained my composure, I declare today in a fully calm state of mind, that these statements were made only due to my aggravated state. I am sorry to have made them, and I am renouncing them hereby as unfounded and untrue.

The declaration also includes that since Emil N. apologized for the bodily harm done and paid 65,000 dinars in damages, Ilona considers the matter settled. The lawyer's fee paid to my grandfather (10,000 dinars) was also covered by Emil N.

The procedure was terminated on July 13, 1942, after fascism had been dropped from the case by Ilona and Emil after all with the assistance of my grandfather.

Back to Jemricsnéni

In the same month, July 1942, the prosecutor charged Jemricsnéni with libel. Early in August my grandfather raised procedural objections. He disputed the legality of seeking punishment for actions that the defendant had already been punished for. (Sentenced by the Wehrmacht, that is). The court saw things differently, and the trial continued. Jemricsnéni attempted to explain the situation. Part of the evidence of that effort can be found in the file, including a four-page text written in German by hand on squared paper, which is quite difficult to read. In the manuscript, Jemricsnéni was trying to clarify to her lawyer what actually happened. I suppose my grandfather was better equipped to read the near-illegible German handwriting in which Roman letters are mixed with Gothic script than I am. And if he failed to understand, he could also ask. I only managed to make out some sentences and half sentences here and there. But I did not stop there. I thought someone with deeper ties to the German language and also more experience in using Gothic script could do a better job. Even at dusk when there is poor lighting, you can easily move about in your own home, avoid bumping into pieces of furniture, and even notice what is missing. So maybe somebody very much at home with a language can just as easily establish what belongs to where and find the missing pieces. That is why I asked Erzsébet von Kontz (the German translator of my first book of documentary prose) to help, which she generously did, and succeeded in reading, and transcribing, the whole text with the exception of a word or two.

Jemricsnéni's narrative begins by recounting that she made the acquaintance of Mr. and Mrs. Sürlemon, "a few years ago" (i.e., a few years before 1942) through the Niederbachers. Mr. and Mrs. Niederbacher made a trip to Graz in Austria once, and there was a lady travelling with them, who "called herself Mrs. Sürlemon." The wording hints at a feeling of vague suspicion which is verified by the rest of the text. Months after the trip to Graz, at the beginning of April 1939, Jemricsnéni heard the rumor that Mr. Sürlemon was about to marry the lady whom the Niederbachers had travelled with. This meant that the claim that they were already married had been a lie. She went to the registry office to make sure, but the young woman working there said it was illegal to give personal information. Jemricsnéni told her that she wanted to surprise the new couple at the wedding, so in the end the woman told her that the wedding day is set to be on April 12, 1939. Thus, the information that they were already married was a lie, which was extremely suspicious.

The Niederbachers held *Bowleabend*s (punch bowl evenings) "almost every Saturday" at which the Sürlemons were present, and so was Jemricsnéni. According to the note, there were times when Mr. Sürlemon told things which he would not normally tell. Once, for instance, his wife had had 12 shots of "Slivovitz und Likör" already on an afternoon visit (the Serbian word for plum brandy, "Sljivovica" was used also by the local Germans. As for what "Likör" meant, the word must have a familiar ring for English readers as well). The *Bowleabend* came only after that, from which Mrs. Sürlemon went home earlier. At about 11 p.m. the others left too. Sürlemon accompanied Jemricsnéni almost all the way home, and it was then that he told her how, during the first World War, despite being a German soldier, one night he guided foreign troops across the border into Germany. Jemricsnéni also tells that the suggestion that Sürlemon was keeping the money and jewelry of Gyárfás (who was Jewish) for him was not her idea but she heard it from others. It is also described in the document that on one occasion, meaning well, Jemricsnéni suggested to Sürlemon that "he should go to bed and sleep it all off." Another thing that she thought she must inform my grandfather about was that the Wehrmacht's men visited her three times in connection with the letter written under the name "Adolf Fichtner," which was terribly uncomfortable since the neighbors all stood there in front of the house watching what was going on.

On reading the note, the text now fully recovered and typed, I am convinced now that that I was right when I thought Jemricsnéni had lived at the Bega riverside. In one place there is a reference to a butcher who also gave her information about Mr. Sürlemon, and the butcher's shop is "here in Little America." I remember that Little America is a part of town surrounded by the river Bega in a U-shaped bend, hence it seems more than likely that she lived on the bank.

Occasionally, emotions also emerge from Jemricsnéni's lines, for instance when telling about the shock she felt upon hearing Sürlemon's revelations about his behavior in World War One. "Oh my God, I said to myself, there is a danger that he might do something evil to Germany again!" Her emotions rise to their highest where she exclaims "Um Gotteswillen!" (for God' sake!) more than once, indicating how shocking it all was.

In his *Sketch for a Theory of Emotions*, Jean-Paul Sartre maintains that emotion may be viewed as a breach in accommodation. I wonder if, in Jemricsnéni's case, it is the other way around. Cannot be emotion itself a way of accommodation? At a time when there is so much turbulence, so much noise out there in town (and in history), perhaps it is precisely emotions that provide the opportunity for accommodation. Or a display of emotions. Crying out with feeling (more than once), "Mein Gott! (my God!) and "Um Gotteswillen!" (for God's sake!) might make the people believe that she belongs to the main act (and rise above Mr. Sürlemon). True, the feelings of distress as enacted by Jemricsnéni show something of the accent of the amateur actress as well as that of the eighty-one-year-old lady. Which might be one of the reasons why the ploy went awry, the attempt at accommodation failed, and Jemricsnéni was exposed behind the mask of "Adolf Fichtner."

Before the court, however, it was not Jemricsnéni's script that set the tone of the defense. My grandfather chose not to not emphasize how worried Jemricsnéni was about the fate of Germany or that Germany was in danger, on account of Neighbor Sürlemon who had banned her from his home. Instead, the defense attempted to explain that she did not describe (under a false name) things she invented out of ill will, but rather information that she had heard in the street and things that the neighbor himself had said in a drunken state, not excluding the possibility of misunderstanding either. Even so, the court ruled, the act committed (libel) was illegal because she ought to have checked what she had been alleging, and because the circumstances indicated that the libel had been deliberate, which was essentially correct. It could be that Jemricsnéni had actually believed much of what she had written as "Adolf Fichtner," but the act of deliberate smearing can hardly be denied. What was left to be decided was the punishment she deserved.

The original of the sentence is missing from the file. There is, however, a German translation written in my grandfather's handwriting. I think it is pretty unlikely that Jemricsnéni did not speak Serbian. It is quite feasible, though, that the text in Cyrillic made her uncertain, and that is why she needed my grandfather's help. The sentence is a mere page and a half long even in manuscript. I suppose it got typed by our clerk, Uncle Göttel, then the typewritten copy was taken home by Jemricsnéni, while the manuscript remained on file. Jemricsnéni was sentenced to one year in prison, but suspended for a year, which meant she did not have to go to jail, granted she would not commit any other criminal act during that year. One might say she got away with it.

***

Reading through the files pertaining to the two cases, I am inclined to conclude that fascism was not really a success in Becskerek, not even for home use.

Setting the documents aside for a while and taking a look around, I see a great deal of evidence for efforts to employ world shaking zealous convictions for private gain or for settling private scores. Attempts abound to appropriate the magic words invoked in the age of terrorism and the struggle against it. Not long ago in Russia, a passenger caught up in a traffic jam on his way to the airport, on seeing he would miss his flight, simply called the airport to report that there was a bomb on board. All flights were delayed. The same tactics were used by a woman in Switzerland whose husband was about to board a plane in order to visit another lady. She also reported a bomb, thereby successfully preventing the husband from flying to see her rival. This also shows ordinary people and their ordinary affairs cannot be completely ignored when it comes to word-shaking events.

Meditating on, I am tempted to step out of the literary genre of documentary prose and write about the things that are missing from the file. And, even as I manage to conquer the temptation, I cannot resist at least considering the questions I would like to see answered.

A novelist would quite certainly tell the reason why Ilona was so severely beaten by Emil N. There are innumerable possibilities. Maybe he caught the laboratory assistant at stealing. But there would have been preliminaries to that which would also have to be told. Another possible path is that it all happened in the wake of a failed courtship, and it was an unwanted amorous advance that escalated to the point of physical mistreatment. It would be also interesting to know if Emil N. had really been listening to forbidden radio stations and made abusive remarks about Hitler. Ilona did take back this allegation with the explanation that it was her shock-induced instability following her injuries that led her to deviate from reality in the first place. This, however, was probably not so. True, she may have really been motivated by anger and irritation rather than by a compulsion to tell the truth, but she very probably did, or at least the gist of it was true. I am, however, familiar enough with the typical wordings of lawyers to recognize them, so I would say, or rather write, if I were a novelist, that her renunciation of the original charges was not a return to what was really true. It was, however, part of the settlement, and made the payment of the hefty sum of 65,000 dinars justified. Which means Emil N. did listen to forbidden radio stations and did say bad things about Hitler, but that was not his crime.

It would be good to have a closer look at Sürlemon too. Was he really hiding Jewish properties? I don't know. My Uncle Pali, who represented him in the lawsuit, may have known. The evidence in the file is not sufficient even for guessing. I think I would leave it entirely up to chance which line to follow if I were writing fiction.

I wonder what happened to Gyárfás? Was he lucky enough to get away after having left a couple of possessions with Sürlemon? Or he did not leave anything but took with him everything he could? Or he failed to escape and was murdered in the Belgrade death camp as were most Jews from Becskerek? If it was up to me, I would favor a storyline in which the Germans leave, Gyárfás returns, and invites both Jemricsnéni and Sürlemon for coffee at the Rózsa restaurant.

And was anti-Semitism the motive of Jemricsnéni when, as "Adolf Fichtner" she also included the money, possessions and documents of Gyárfás in her denunciation? I consider it more likely that the really important thing for her was her disagreement with her neighbor, not the Jewish question. While doing my guessing regarding Jemricsnéni, I am also trying to recall if there was anything hidden in our home by Jewish friends and acquaintances in those days. As regards possessions, I am not so sure, but I definitely remember that for a few weeks a man was hiding in our attic. Jemricsnéni probably never knew about it. Had she known, would she have given him up? If this were fiction, I would probably write no, because she had no personal quarrel with either the unknown man or my grandfather. This is also closest to what I sense from the file.

Jemricsnéni's texts and the way my grandfather treats her conjures up the memory of someone, and a kind of vague image is beginning to take shape. The person I see was thin, dark-haired, perhaps with a big nose, wearing black dresses, an avid reader of romantic novels by Courts-Mahler, someone whose life is controlled by personal acquaintances, friendships and conflicts. I called someone my age and asked him if the name "Jemricsnéni" rings a bell for him. He said he remembered that she was a somewhat nutty old lady. While trying to fit together the pieces carved out by myself, I recognize that the assumption would fit the picture nicely that Hitler lost his value in the eyes of Jemricsnéni as soon as it became clear that the Führer was of no use to her in her battle with Sürlemon.

The final question, of course, is what became of Jemricsnéni herself. At this point I can at last turn back to my documentary prose. Leafing through the pages of my grandfather's diary, I can see that November 19, 1944 was an eventful day. There were no more Germans in Becskerek, and power had gone to the partisans. For short while, a People's Liberation Committee operated in town, the members of which, beside the partisans and communists, included a few Becskerek citizens who did not belong to the movement. My grandfather was a member too. On November 19, 1944 the recently established People's Liberation Committee (Narodnooslobodilački odbor) held its last meeting. According to the diary, Secretary Kiselički "reported on the actions of the odbor in the last few weeks, then he announced that administrative authority in the Banat, thus in Becskerek too, had been taken over the military, and the operation of the odbor had ended." However, the entry for the day of November 19, 1944 did not end there. The day was Sunday, and also the day of Erzsébet. My grandfather notes that after the meeting of the People's Liberation Committee he visited Erzsike Liptay and Jemricsnéni to congratulate them.

The diary contains two more entries referring to Jemricsnéni. According to entry of January 19, 1946, my grandfather took part in a card game that day. That was not a rare occasion. My parents played cards regularly, and sometimes the scene of the session was our home. When the game was held in our house, I would also make my brief appearance in the room when the cake was being served, along with my younger sister and later also my younger brother. My father arrived usually late or left before the end of the game. He was always busy. My mother was never late and never left early, either. When the session was held in the house of the Benczes, I was taken along several times because the Bencze's son was a classmate of mine. My grandfather never played; he was content with just observing the game. Or he would just sit around and occasionally take part in the conversation. I have no idea where the game was on January 19, 1946. That is not recorded in the diary. What is noted, though, is that during the game "the women said" that Jemricsnéni had died at the age of 86.

The last piece of information on Jemricsnéni, entered on January 20, is that her funeral was on that day. It was announced to be held at 3 o'clock in the afternoon.

2. A CYNICAL ANTI-PEOPLE SMILE (FROM BEHIND THE WINDOW)

Pupsi

Pupsi (pronounced "Poopshee") lived at the next street corner, about 150 meters from our home. The word "púp" means "hump" in Hungarian, but he wasn't a humpback. Maybe the nickname originated from the German word "bub" (boy). Hungarians, at least in the Banat region, also used it in the form "bubi" or more often "pubi." This could have been twisted by the family and friends somehow into "Pupsi." All of which is pure guesswork, of course. I can't recall if the nickname was used in the family too or only among the playmates. Actually, his name was István, István Csepcsányi. That was also his father's name.

I remember he wore glasses. He was a year older than me. We were more or less of the same height. I went to his home a few times. At the corner on the way towards their house, on our side of the street, there was a well before the crossing. We would go there with a pail to fetch water. Past the crossing there was a church. We called it Tóttemplom (Slovak Church).

After the church there came a churchyard, and next, a house, part of which served as the vicarage. Pupsi's father was a Lutheran minister. The house had three windows overlooking the street, then a front yard, which was actually a meter and a half wide grassy strip bordered by a wire fence; next came the pavement, then a mostly mud-covered two- or three-meter wide area, and finally, there was the carriage road. When I was in their home, Pupsi suggested several times that we try to guess the next vehicle to appear before the window, whether it would be a one-horse or two-horse carriage. Sometimes we pulled the curtain aside, sometimes we did not. It hardly mattered since the curtains were transparent anyway. Pupsi was better at the guessing game, he made more hits than I did. We were watching the horse-drawn carriages go by at the end of the 1940s or in the early 1950s. Pupsi had just moved from the single-digit to the double-digit age group, while I was somewhere at the threshold between the two. At that time, it was not mentioned, and I wasn't aware either, that those front windows had played a major part in a criminal case a couple of years earlier. It is highly uncertain if Pupsi himself knew about it at all.

I also remember that we went to the market together once, sent to fetch something by our parents, and on another occasion, I accompanied him to the Lutheran church. These details have drifted to the brink of oblivion in my mind since then. Nor am I certain any more about the language in which the ceremony was held, Hungarian, German or Slovak. It could be any one of the three. Maybe if it had been in Slovak, it would have stuck in my memory better. Things we understand or which do not strike us as strange or surprising are more readily forgotten. We are stunned much more by things that we do not understand at all, or only a little, or even though understood, appear unusual. In the same way, if you stumble while taking a routine walk, that walk will be much more memorable than all the others when nothing unusual happened. So—even through this much "evidence" would surely be less than sufficient to serve as the basis of a court sentence—I am ready to assume that the service was not in Slovak because then I would remember it. German is also unlikely, since as far as I can remember, Lutheran Church events were no longer held in German at the Tóttemplom in the early fifties. It must have been in Hungarian. I am trying to recall something beyond that, but I am uncertain. And I cannot afford to be inaccurate because Pupsi may still be around (there is a fifty per cent chance that he is), and he would accuse me of spreading lies or fabrications. I know that they moved to Verbász a very long time ago, I was still living in Becskerek then. It suddenly springs to my mind that Pupsi played ping pong, just as I did. Still, somehow, he doesn't fit him into my memories of the sites where I played. Maybe ping pong brought us together when he already lived in Verbász.

I met Pupsi's dad once or twice in their home. I remember him as a skinny man in a priest's robe—I must have seen him directly before or after service—and as a very withdrawn man. A classmate who also lived nearby even suggested an explanation. He said the reason Pupsi's dad hardly ever smiled and spoke so little was that he had done something bad during the war. What it was, was never discussed. The realization was just dawning on us that beside the obviously ugly, cruel and outrageous things (of which there had been many), the notion "having done something bad" may cover some vague and undefinable things as well. This was not exactly helpful. The war was still recent, and we were all aware that there are things we'd better not talk about. We knew much less about what those things were, and why we should not speak about them. In any case, whenever somebody halted at one point, then the others stopped too. Another boy in our class had an explanation for the cause of the silence: "it's one of those things," he said. All in all, we made no effort to find out about the "bad things" Pupsi's father may have done during the war.

It was not easy to see the events of the world war just on the threshold of school age. Also, our parents' generation was just undergoing a change regarding its past. As for us, we still had no past, only fragments of memories in our minds, which we didn't know where to fit. And then there were the things which remained unexplained. Like when there was shooting in the streets, and I remember seeing an arc of light, maybe a thin firebrand, with an object at its end which landed in our bed of clover. Its shape was like that of a small-size canteen. I ran into the next room and told my parents. They suspected a bomb, and we waited for some time for it to explode but nothing happened. Nevertheless, afterwards I was forbidden to go near our clover garden for a day or two. Later on, when we did go there, we found nothing. The only evidence confirming what I saw or thought to have seen was that in one spot the grass was slightly burnt. Nevertheless, I was sure that something fell in our garden in a brightly lit arc. My parents were inclined not to believe it. I must have been five years old. Later, when I was already going to grammar school, it occurred to me that perhaps we found nothing because our neighbor came into our garden (that had happened before) and took it. At any rate, that event (or hallucination) has been one of my most enduring memories of World War Two.

I also remember that some fears eased after a while. There was a bunker nearby which we carefully avoided for a year or two after the war. Then one of the boys got up his courage and entered it. He was followed by the rest of us. We went collectively, including Pupsi. After that we often played there. We separated it from the world war. The same kind of separation, however, failed to work where the story of Pastor István Csepcsányi was concerned. As long as we still kept seeing each other with Pupsi, it remained a kind of given between us that the war (which had not yet become history at that time, and its hold was still palpable) forbade bringing up the subject. It was a bunker we were afraid to enter. Later on, I learned that the line between forbidding and forgetting may become blurred.

And then, half a century later, a file turned up with faint letters on the cover.

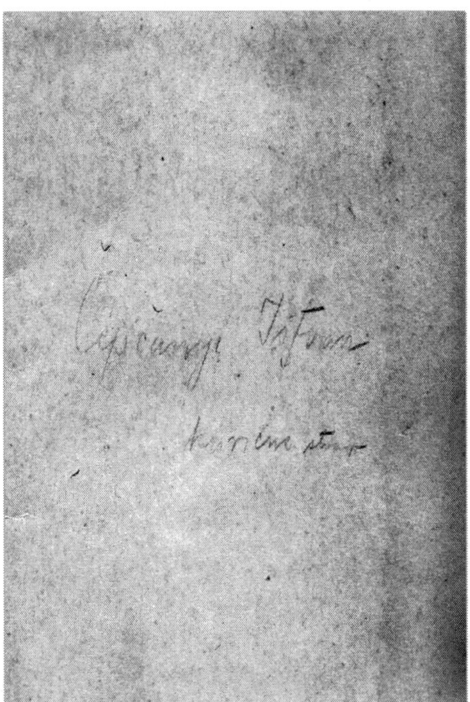

Here is a translation from illegible to legible:

Čepčanji Ištvan (Csepcsányi István, in Hungarian)
Krivična stvar (criminal case)
12536

The subject of the file is precisely what Pastor István Csepcsányi (Pupsi's dad) was supposed to have done wrong, if it really was wrong at all, during the war. The indictment has "krivično delo protiv naroda I države" (crime against the state and the people) as the charge, meaning that according to the prosecutor, István Csepcsányi committed a criminal act against the people and the state during World War Two. I was of course interested. I wanted to know what he did and how.

What the Next-door Neighbor Said

Criminal proceedings began in the summer of the year 1945. Several witnesses were interrogated by the prosecution in August. The first testimony that got into my hands came from a neighbor, more precisely a next-door neighbor. He testifies that even though he has no "close knowledge" about the life of István Csepcsányi during the war, he nevertheless saw some "important things." I thought that these things were really important from the viewpoint of my narrative, so I translated the whole testimony.

> TESTIMONY
>
> Taken before the Prosecutor of the Petrovgrad District on August 20, 1945
> Witness: BOŽOVIC, Sava
>
> I know the accused Istvan Csepcsányi from sight as my next-door neighbor. During the occupation, as soon as word came that Horthy's soldiers are about to enter the town, the accused and his wife bought flowers together and went to wait for them. I have no close knowledge of his life during the occupation.
>
> Right after the liberation, when the Red Army was marching in, the accused stood by the window in his priest's apartment and watched them marching with a cynical, derisive, smile on his face, then in a moment

> he closed every window with the exception of one from which the march of the Red Army was being watched by a young man standing there, whom I do not know. The accused waved a hand, and after lowering the blinds, went into the room. I have nothing else to say concerning the case.
>
> This record has been read out to me and I recognize it as my own testimony.
>
> *Božovič Sava*

Neighbor Božović's insights appear to match not only the expectations of the times but also our historical knowledge. I may say they are in sync with one another. There really were rumors afoot that the Banat would be annexed to Hungary. A little over twenty years earlier both Bácska and the Banat had belonged to the Austro-Hungarian Monarchy, and within it, to the Kingdom of Hungary. During World War Two, the Banat was invaded by Hitler's army, while Bácska saw Hungarians (the soldiers of Admiral Horthy) marching in. The inhabitants, Serbs, Hungarians, Germans and Jews alike, kept guessing. Looking for information to supplement the documents of the "Csepcsányi Criminal Case," I found a report (*Bericht*) dated June 20, 1941 by a Dr. Bornikoel for the KKA (*Kirchliche Aussenamt*), the Office for External Church Affairs of Germany. Translated into English, the title of the report reads "Report on the Situation of the German Lutheran Community in Bácska Following the Collapse of Yugoslavia." Dr. Bornikoel visited Bácska from June 13–17, 1941. He reports that the repressive behavior of the Hungarian authorities created "tensions" between the local Germans and Hungarians. An example of that repression was that the Führer's birthday was not allowed to be celebrated in the Újvidék Center of Germans in Yugoslavia, so the celebration had to be held in the Lutheran church. (Which reminds me that we would also have a family dinner on the Führer's birthdays. Not to celebrate Hitler, of course, but because it coincided with the birthday of my grandmother on my mother's side. Ironically, we would also have a family dinner on the birthdays of Marshall Tito because it was on the same day as my own birthday.) Bernikoel also noted that the German inhabitants of Bácska were disappointed, because instead of the expected invasion by the Wehrmacht, the province was occupied by the Hungarians. So, a lot of hopes, disappointments and guessing went on among the Hungarians of the Banat and the Germans of Bácska alike. There really were rumors in the Banat that the Germans would be withdrawn and replaced by Hungarians, but such concrete action as buying flowers and going out to wait for them would have required more specific information, or at least firm belief, than sheer rumor. Something like "they are coming sometime," would not suffice. When would they come? Tomorrow or next Wednesday? And where would one go, flowers in hand, to meet them? To the edge of town? Say, to Baglyas, to the road from Aradác? Or rather the other side of town, to the road coming from Écska? The latter would have been given more credence, since according to local legend, "Écska" got its name after one of the wives of King Attila the Hun who was called that. Yes, it would seem logical for Horthy to come from that direction, thus using the occasion to show his support for the theory of Hunnish-Hungarian kinship. Or perhaps the right place to wait for them would have been in the center of town rather than the edges, in front of the railway station? But then those coming with flowers would have surely noticed that standing guard there were still German soldiers. Still, as far as I know, the rumors never went beyond the "they will come someday" or "they are sure to come" stage. At the same time, some of the local Serbs (and also the Germans and others) kept telling each other with a smile on their face that those silly Hungarians really went crazy this time with their constant flower-buying and cake-baking in expectation of Horthy. And after that, whatever the real cause of the flower-buying or cake-baking, it would be treated as evidence.

And there is more. István Csepcsányi himself also testified on August 20, 1941, and I can see he was questioned by the prosecutor about the bunch of flowers meant for Horthy quite specifically. It turns out he was confronted with the allegation that the bunches had been made by the Lutheran Women's Association (the Serbian text has "Zenska zadruga," that is, "women's collective"). This was denied by Csepcsányi. The charge, however, was aggravated by the fact that the name of the women's union was "Gustav Adolf," evidence that it was still Hitler ("Adolf," you see?) lurking behind the whole thing. This was countered by István Göttel in his testimony. In all likelihood it was the same István Göttel whom I knew as "Uncle Göttel." He had worked for over half a century at the family law office as a clerk. I just learned that he was Lutheran. Göttel testified, "István Csepcsányi did found a woman's union called "Gustav Adolf," but it was named after a Swedish king who died in the war (the Thirty Years' War, in 1632) as the champion of Protestantism." Uncle Göttel was quite certainly right, yet the serious suspicion hovered on. On January 20, 2018, I read a story on the Belgrade news portal *B 92* which suggests that today this heavy suspicion may be on the wane at long last. A person called Adolf Stadler told that early on during the war his parents had been taken from Romania to Germany so that his father could join the German army. A group of the Romanian Germans were put up in a camp at the Austrian-German border (Hohenschwang). The camp and the Germans taken there got high praise from Hitler who also promised that he would be godfather to the first child born there. It happened to be Adolf Ernst Stadler (born on April 25, 1941). With regard to his godfather, he was given the name "Adolf," beside the originally planned first name which was Ernst. After the war the family returned to Romania, to the village Voivodeasa in Bucovina where the only name ever used was "Ernst" while the other one remained a closely guarded secret for the next decades. In the end, the explosive, lethally dangerous secret fizzled out as an anecdote. But it took 77 years of waiting. Well, after having written this down, I waited just a little more, and I came to read in the *New York Times* of March 14, 2018 that in Afghanistan, a baby was given the name Donald Trump, hoping for some advantages. The boy was born already in September 3, 2016 (in Daikundi province) but the *New York Times* only learned about it later. The full name of the boy is Donald Trump Assadullah. I'm wondering what his fate will be once the US really leaves Afghanistan.

Coming back to the Csepcsányi case, the file also shows that the women's union had been a constant source of trouble. The documents include a letter dated January 19, 1943, written in German from Ferenchalma (the German name was Franzfeld; it is called today *Kačarevo* by the Serbs), by the Lutheran bishop. It is addressed to a "Lieber Amstbruder," best translated as "Brother Minister" who, I think I can safely assume, was István Csepcsányi. The bishop complains that the Gustav Adolf women's union (*Frauenverein*) had been turned into a Hungarian organization from which Germans felt excluded. This letter was written during the German occupation, which goes to show that things were never simple in Becskerek.

Then there was the matter of the "cynical, derisive smile" that the next-door neighbor Bozović saw on the minister's face. The file includes a handwritten pencil note by my father showing that at the trial, Csepcsányi's facial expression noticed by the neighbor was qualified an "anti-people smile" by the prosecutor. This clearly defined which side of the political divide the Lutheran minister stood on, even when hiding behind the window in his vicarage.

I suppose that the wave of the hand must also have been interpreted an anti-people gesture. In momentous epochs the notion of "the people" gets extremely simplified. At that time, and not only then, there was a large number of mixed marriages and a mishmash of identities in Becskerek. I found some forty or fifty files from the years right after the war which all hinged on whether a person with a German name was to be regarded as a German or a Hungarian (because, if proved a German, his property would be confiscated). I had a classmate who himself couldn't decide if he was Slovak or Hungarian. An acquaintance of ours with a Serbian name considered himself to be Hungarian. Thus, it was often anything but obvious where you belonged. Once being called "the people," however, everything would become simple. There were no more dilemmas. Not for the first time, and very probably not for the last, the notion of the people covered only those who were enthusiastic enough. Perhaps it was their own freedom from thought and doubt which was regarded as the measure of being "mentally pure" (the concept being modelled on "racially pure") by the more radically-thinking "members of the people." It meant that anyone who had doubts or merely waved things aside could not belong to the people but was standing on the opposite side.

When confronted with neighbor Božović's evidence, Pastor Csepcsányi tried to rely on a different neighbor, a woman. He proposed that at the verbal trial to be held on November 5, 1947, as a witness, Rozi Maron should be heard. She lived at 18 Cara Dušana Street, and would prove "that I did not watch the entry of the Red Army with cynical derision." 18 Cara Dušana was the address also of the house in which the minister lived, so Rozi Maron must have been another next-door neighbor. We lived under 10 Cara Dušana Street until the section of the street to which our house belonged was demolished. To move a little closer to the people, István Csepcsányi also proposed that the farmer Đorđe Cvejić be heard, who lived on Čehoslovačka Street; this was the cross street on the corner of which there stood the Slovak Church. Neighbor Cvejić was expected to verify that Csepcsányi "took an active part in running the affairs of the Popular Front and assisted the Street Secretary's work." This was the first time ever that I heard about the Popular Front having had street secretaries too. But then there may be many more things I don't know about. This means that Csepcsányi did not (and could not) get rid of the "either pro-people or anti-people" straitjacket but tried to limp in it. Within the straitened options, he tried to get some push towards the pro-people tagging with the help of witnesses. Which was not easy.

Rozi Maron was not summoned to the court. Neither were most of the other witnesses proposed by the defense. That means Csepcsányi's efforts to move slowly ahead were in vain. He was overtaken by the prosecutor who had apparently hitched his wagon to world history itself.

To get away a little from the papers in the archives, I read some poetry last night, and I came upon poem entitled "The Idle Season Is Here," by the celebrated Hungarian writer Antal Szerb. The first lines point to a rather different direction:

Dear Master Nikita
You can take a happy break
There is no more
World history to make

But this was written in 1913, and the poet was Antal Szerb. In 1945, the Nikitas of Becskerek could just not take a break from world history. And the idle season is still far off, up to this day.

What Made the Slovak, German and Hungarian Church Communities Unite?

The problem took on a special importance during the criminal trial. There are several witness testimonies, submissions, documents and notes trying to explain it in one way or another. I will make an effort first to give, as far as I am able, an unbiassed account of what happened in order to make the arguments and categorizations set against each other in the trial easier to understand.

The territory of the state of Yugoslavia established after World War One saw several organizations and reorganizations in the Lutheran Church of Christians of the Augustan Confession. Language and ethnicity were playing a role too, and there were also solutions involving specific dioceses only. Basically, there were two main units: German and Slovak. Hungarians as well as Slovenes (the latter are called "'Wendish" in some of the documents) were attached to the German branch. On April 16, 1930, the Kingdom of Yugoslavia actually enacted a law on the Lutheran and Reformed (Calvinist) churches. The text of that law is also included in the file, thus providing more familiar and also more solid ground for me. According to Article One, followers of the Lutheran Church of Christians of the Augustan Confession have two churches, a Slovak and a German. Paragraph Three also rules that the two are allowed to establish an alliance "for the sake of their common ecclesiastic interests."

It is revealed by the documents that until 1932, German, Slovak and Hungarian believers belonged to a common organization. I don't know in which year the cooperation actually began. After that, the Slovak congregation separated from the others. Csepcsányi was appointed pastor of the German-Hungarian congregation in 1935. Then came the date critical from the point of view of the criminal proceedings. In 1941, the Slovak, German and Hungarian believers reunited in Becskerek under the authority of the of the Pancsova Diocese (*senioratus*). At this point the protagonists of the process saw a new chance carved out by history, and the dispute shifted over to whether the congregations had genuinely wanted to unite, or if unification had been forced on them by the Fascist occupiers and their collaborators.

Behind all of this there was also a long-lasting personal rivalry between Pastor Juranji and Csepcsányi who succeeded him (or replaced him). And just as in the case of Jemricsnéni and Sürlemon, the parties did not want to miss the possibility inherent in drawing fascism (and now also anti-fascism and communism) into the dispute. The accusation was made by Juranji on April 3, 1945. Next, Juranji was interrogated by the prosecutor on August 17. According to the record of the interrogation, the departure of Germans and Hungarians from the common Lutheran congregation in 1935 was Csepcsányi's doing. The rest of the documents put the date of the separation to 1932. By Juranji's testimony, on May 17, 1941 when the German invaders were already in the Banat, Csepcsanyi went to see him in the company of Kund, the German Archdeacon of Pancsova. Kund told him action was being taken against him, and he would be executed unless he resigned in favor of Csepcsányi. After that, it was Csepcsányi who convened the general assembly of the parishioners, at which they all decided (including the Slovaks) to leave their earlier diocese and join the new Slovak-German-Hungarian diocese with its center in Pancsova. In his evidence, Juranji also said: "I don't know which side he claimed to support during the occupation. All I know is that he was the darling of the German authorities." According to the closing sentence of the testimony, after the liberation, on October 30, 1944, the vicarage was taken once again by Juranji.

There are many details that I would like to investigate but all the facts relevant to these details are absent from the court sentence. Did Kund (and Csepcsányi) have so much power as to be able to decide whether Juranji should be executed? According to Juranji's evidence, Kund informed him that "a big action is being mounted against him, and therefore he will be executed," but he (Kund) will save him if he resigns and gives up leading the congregation. Juranji, however, fails to mention on what grounds the "big action" was being taken. It would have been logical, and, in August 1944, hardly dangerous, to name some heroic anti-fascist feat carrying the risk of execution back then. But nothing specific is mentioned. Then the next question to arise is how could the "big action" be stopped by Kund, perhaps along with Csepcsányi, so completely that Juranji could go on living in Becskerek without harassment. Or did Kund really say something of the sort but was only bluffing? If I were a novelist, I could not even discount the unlikely case of Juranji's home having been invaded by armed bandits shouting: "Your parish or your life!"

Csepcsányi denied having had anything to do with the separation of the Slovak, German-Hungarian congregations, especially as it took place in 1932, whereas he moved to Becskerek from Verbász only in 1935. This was supported by other data as well. According to Csepcsányi, the real cause of the separation of the community in 1932 had actually been Juranji who provoked disagreement and "called every Slovak reluctant to obey him a "leftist." To prove that Juranji had been the one who had provoked the quarrel, my father proposed that the joiner Josef Hulina should be heard. His name also appears in the handwritten list. I remember him too. I was several times in his workshop, and we called him Uncle Jóska Hulina. We spoke with him in Hungarian and Serbian. He was a Slovak, or at least had Slovak roots. But I can find no trace of him having been actually heard by the court among the documents.

In both his deposition and his submission, Csepcsányi testified that the German-Hungarian and Slovak congregations decided to reunite at a general assembly held in September 1941, and he was elected to head the parish. The majority of the believers were Slovak. In October 1944 they separated again, but no German parish was formed this time, only a Slovak and a Hungarian one. Juranji was elected leader of the Slovak community. This was emphasized by Juranji himself as well. Csepcsányi, however, adds that as soon as 1945, Juranji was dismissed again by the Slovak congregation. Csepcsányi's evidence also confirms that Kund had used threats. There is no mention of "serious action" leading to execution, though, only a Church procedure is mentioned, the documents do not reveal what it was about. Csepcsányi adds that he was indeed present in May 1941, but he did not take part in the conversation. Kund and Juranji made a deal that Juranji would continue to draw his salary till the end of the year but hand over the parish immediately. Next, an inventory was being drawn up by a committee consisting of Pavel Litavski, István Göttel and István Csepcsányi.

There were financial reasons as well. The church, which I came to know as Tóttemplom, was built in 1837. The vicarage, however, was raised by Juranji (against the will of the Slovak believers, Csepcsányi said) in 1926. The prosecutor argued that when taking over the vicarage, Csepcsányi won undeserved profit. This was, however, contradicted by Pavel Litavski's evidence given on August 20, 1945. According to the prosecutor's record of this testimony, "Litavski Paja" said substantial debts had accumulated in connection with the real properties of the church. The Slovaks found themselves unable to meet these debts on their own. That was why they wanted to unite with the German and Hungarian congregations in the first place. The position of the property in the real estate register remained unchanged. The properties were registered as owned by the Lutheran congregation both before and after Csepcsányi. Litavski also said the unification had been actually blessed by the Slovak Archdeacon Josip Lanis.

The file includes a letter by Archdeacon Janis. He wrote it in Hungarian to Archdeacon Kund of Pancsova. Kund then verified it and authenticated it with his seal. In his testimony, Litavski said the unification had been "blessed" by the Slovak archdeacon. While the word "blessing" is missing from the letter, he clearly unequivocally recognized the unification based on old ties, and also added: "I acknowledge the duty of the common congregation to repay all liabilities that have been taken over." The letter of Archdeacon Janis reads:

> The Very Reverend Archdeacon, Sir,
> I have thoughtfully studied and hereby accept your formal Notice Number 511/1941, dated November 17 of the current year, as well as the resolution on the unification of the two Lutheran Church congregations of Nagybecskerek, namely the German-Hungarian and the Slovak congregations, declared on September 28, 1941. Similarly, I also accept, on the basis of the old ties, the union of the trilingual German-Hungarian-Slovak followers of the Lutheran faith of the Augustan confession of Nagybecskerek into a single, common Lutheran congregation of the Augustan confession and its joining the Lutheran diocese of the Evangelical confession of the Banat, the current seat of which is in Pancsova. At the same time, I also acknowledge the duty of the common congregation to repay all liabilities that have been taken over.
>
> Greetings from your brother in faith:
>
> József Janis
> Archdeacon

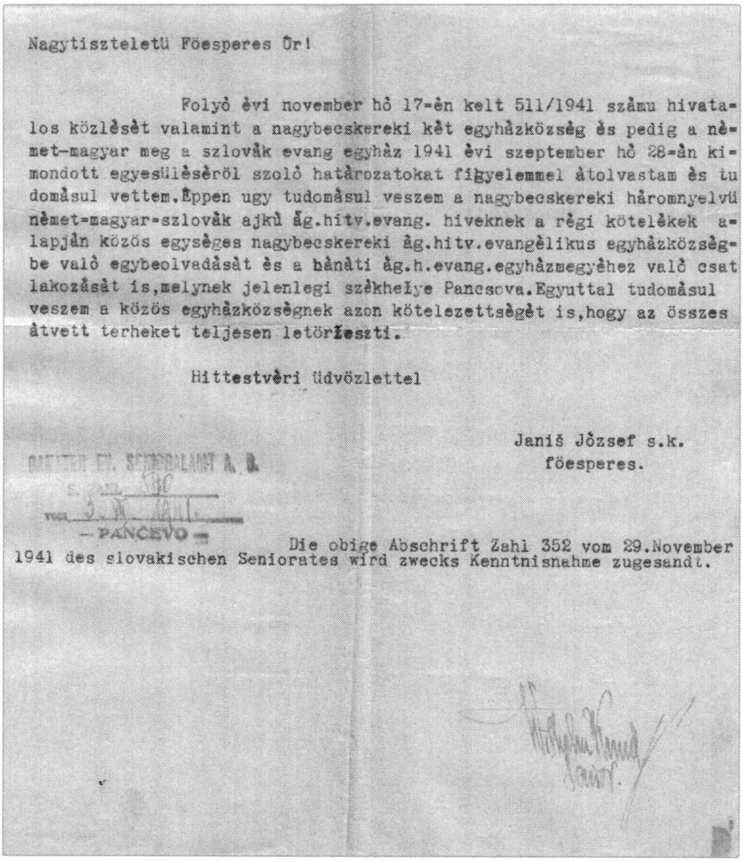

Nagytiszteletü Föesperes Ůr!

Folyò èvi november hò 17-èn kelt 511/1941 szàmu hivatalos közlèsèt valamint a nagybecskereki kèt egyhàzközsèg ès pedig a nèmet-magyar meg a szlovàk evang egyhàz 1941 èvi szeptember hò 28-àn kimondott egyesülèsèröl szolò hatàrozatokat figyelemmel àtolvastam ès tudomàsul vettem.Èppen ugy tudomàsul veszem a nagybecskereki hàromnyelvü nèmet-magyar-szlovàk ajkù àg.hitv.evang. hiveknek a règi kötelèkek alapjàn közös egysèges nagybecskereki àg.hitv.evangèlikus egyhàzközsègbe valò egybeolvadàsàt ès a bànàti àg.h.evang.egyhàzmegyèhez valò csatlakozàsàt is,melynek jelenlegi szèkhelye Pancsova.Egyuttal tudomàsul veszem a közös egyhàzközsègnek azon kötelezettsègèt is,hogy az összes àtvett terheket teljesen letörlieszti.

Hittestvèri üdvözlettel

Janiš Jòzsef s.k.
föesperes.

– PANČEVO –

Die obige Abschrift Zahl 352 vom 29.November 1941 des slovakischen Seniorates wird zwecks Kenntnisnahme zugesandt.

My first reaction upon reading this letter is a rush of Banat pride. We have every reason to rejoice over our linguistic skills. The Slovak archdeacon's letter is written in nearly faultless Hungarian. He obviously knew Serbian, and very probably German too. The only reason he wrote in Hungarian must have been that he felt on a surer footing. Nor was it a problem that he wrote to the German archdeacon Kund in Hungarian because the latter's Hungarian must have been just as good. In one of Csepcsányi's notes I read that he held services in Hungarian, German and Slovak (and I am sure he knew Serbian too).

Cross-contamination of languages was not rare either in this multilingual world of ours. Sometimes it involved no more than a bit of additional flavor, but it could also result in real misunderstandings or even quarrels. The documents include a letter written on a small piece of paper. It was written by Pal Lalis (or Pavel Lalis) to Pastor Csepcsányi. I suppose my father kept it because it was evidence that Juranji was rather disliked by his own (Slovak) flock who had more trust in Csepcsányi. Lalis wrote his letter in Hungarian, but using Slovak characters, and Slovak idioms are also discernible behind some of his odd turns of (Hungarian) language. And not all is completely clear either. The meaning of the first two lines remains somewhat mysterious even when Hungarian characters are substituted for the Slovak ones. "Reverend, Sir, would you please bury this little child?" But then it continues with the explanation that if a release (or receipt?) is written out by Csepcsányi, should Brother Poljak wish it so, then Juranji has nothing. Was the debate about who should bury a small child, Csepcsányi or Juranji? Hard to know for certain.

Another example comes to mind which produced not only a special flavor but also a serious misunderstanding. One of my classmates recalled that in his family by the mid-fifties things got so loose that sometimes even spicier stories were told by parents in front of their children, who were teenagers by this time. This one involved my friend's Aunt Juci, and the events related must have taken place in 1945. At the end of the war a partisan had been quartered in Aunt Juci's house, as they had been in ours. As the war became more distant, people began to be preoccupied by more peacetime concerns, and the partisan (whose name was Slavko) was visited by a lady a couple of times. For the time of these visits the partisan would lock the door of his room overlooking the courtyard, but the sounds overheard made it possible for Aunt Juci and her mother to follow developments in the room. On one occasion, things took such a turn that Aunt Juci made to discard her usual tactfulness, knocked on the door noisily several times, then shouted in Serbian, "Slavko, tu si otac!" (Slavko, you are a father here!) Now I don't know if Slavko took Aunt Juci for a prophetess, a seer or maybe a witch, but, as I was told, he took the warning so seriously that he rushed out of the room and appeared in the doorway in a complete alarm barefoot, wearing nothing but a pair of shorts and a tank top despite the cold December weather. As far as my classmate knew, the relationship between the partisan and his lady was of a temporary nature, so the issue of starting a family never arose. However, condoms were not available in Becskerek at the time, so Slavko's alarm was not entirely groundless. The truth of the prophecy came to light later, when tensions had relaxed a bit. The piece of information that Aunt Juci had meant to convey in Serbian was not "here you are (or became) a father," but "your father is here," as the old man had turned up unexpectedly from southern Serbia to visit Slavko.

Another event I remember well was that, also in the years after the war, a gentleman wearing a French-style beret on his head shouted over to another man walking in the opposite direction on *Tsara Dušana* Street, as he passed by: "Go fuck your mother, Herr Volkmann!" What is interesting is that not even the use of such strong language (in Hungarian) could shake the deeply ingrained German form of address. It would not do to just say "Volkmann." That would not have been the real thing. The word "Herr" just had to be added, as always, so it would be unequivocally clear whom the gentleman with the French beret on his head is encouraging to commit such an unseemly act.

I am wondering if these little twists actually disrupted the idyll of multilingual Banat, or was exactly this that made up the idyll?

The Darling of the German Occupiers?

Juranji's evidence in which he accused Csepcsányi of having been the favorite of the German occupiers furnished the ground for one of the harshest accusations of the prosecution, namely that he had "collaborated with the occupiers." The file shows that my father tried to use several lines of argument in an effort to repudiate the charge of collaboration. The documents include a letter written on November 5, 1947 by Zoltán Ambrózy, who knew the Lutheran Church from inside. This letter must have been used in a submission by my father which is unfortunately missing from the file. But the letter survived. It describes that Csepcsányi was actually arrested by the "occupiers" and kept in detention for one day (as was my father), and "friends would not be arrested."

Does this really explain it all? Not by any means. Some people were harassed, but then, or because of this, they would nevertheless join. Others did not. On the other hand, if Csepcsányi really collaborated, then there ought to be some specifics on how he did it. That is, however, absent from the file. True, Bozovic's testimony does contain the damning vision of the "cynical, derisive smile" from behind the window, and the allegation that he waited for Horthy with a bunch of flowers, but I suppose the charge of "crime against the people and the state" would have taken a little more than that. Also, the narrative of flower-purchasing, or having a bunch made by the women's union, appears anything but convincing. Moreover, there is a disagreement over Horthy. The prosecutor charges that he held a service in honor of Horthy. This is partly admitted by Csepcsányi, who, however, maintains that rather than for Nicholas Horthy, the head of the Hungarian state, the service in question was held in memory of his son István Horthy when he died. István was a fighter pilot who died at the age of 37 when his plane crashed. Csepcsányi adds that he never had any business with politics and was always keeping himself strictly to the Bible in his sermons. He never even mentioned the names of either Nicholas Horthy or King St. Stephen, Hungary's king a thousand years ago.

Csepcsányi declared that his whole parish could verify that he had nothing to do with politics in or out of church. As far as I can see, though, the court did not bother to hear any witness regarding that claim. Still, according to the sentence of the court of first instance "he conducted profascist propaganda during the occupation." There is no reference to witnesses or concrete words either. I see that earlier on, the prosecutor put witness Lalis Pavel the question as to what Csepcsányi had been preaching about. Lalis replied in his evidence given on August 20, 1945 that he did not know because he never listened to either Csepcsányi or Juranji preach. So how did they know that he gave pro-fascist (*profašističke*) sermons?

The Sentences

The law on crimes against the people and the state was enacted on September 1, 1945. István Csepcsányi was charged with offenses listed under Sections 3 and 6 of Article 3. The actions were not specified. Section 3 covers a long list of offenses including war crimes (whether by organizing or commanding it), then murder, execution, the declaration of death sentence, torture, deportation to concentration camp, the ordering of forced labor, forced separation from the people, terrorism, arson, inhumane treatment of prisoners, rape, forcing to prostitution, and coerced conversion to a different faith. Section 6 mentions political collaboration with foreign occupiers, that is, playing a role in the administrative bodies of enemy rule, deprivation from food, or other violent actions against the population of Yugoslavia.

In other words, a wide range of criminal acts are found in Sections 3 and 6 of Article 3. The sentences of both the court of the first instance and the appellate court relied on these sections of the Criminal Code without actually specifying what acts the crimes of Csepcsányi consisted of. It is interesting that enemy propaganda is directly mentioned in Article 9, and the court did rule that Csepcsányi had conducted fascist propaganda, yet Article 9 did not figure among the underpinnings of the sentence. What it relied on was Article 3 (murder, declaration of death sentence, deportation to concentration camp, terrorism, arson, rape, forcing to prostitution, and all the other things). I cannot stifle the compulsion to note that had I been the prosecutor, I would have much rather relied on Article 9. But I would not want to have been prosecutor in this case. I would have preferred the defense's side.

The penalties specified in the law were harsh. Article 4 prescribes a minimum of 3 years imprisonment and hard labor for the perpetrators. In the case of aggravating circumstances, the death sentence would ensue. If the criminal acts were committed at the time of war or danger of war, then the punishment could not be less than 5 years. According to Article 17, the procedure in all cases must be subject to summary proceedings. And that's what it was in the Csepcsányi case…

I began to read the sentence with excitement. The main focus was on the unification of the churches in 1941. To be able to arrive at a sentence, the court should to have clarified (in principle, at least) if the reorganization was motivated by personal rivalry between Juranji and Csepcsányi, or if it was a fascist conspiracy that led to the reunification of the Slovak, German and Hungarian congregations. In other words, the question was whether unification was a goal that the Slovak believers had also wished for, among other things, because in that way the debts of the Slovak community regarding the parish would turn into joint liability. I expected the fact to emerge sooner or later that the three congregations used to belong together up to 1932. Indeed, I waited for it. This unity was seen as a positive thing both by Juranji and Csepcsányi; they were only blaming each other for the disintegration. I was also interested in finding out if any other wrongdoing incriminating Csepcsányi was established, something I had missed in the documents preceding the sentence. I also thought there might be some explanation as to why the reunion of the three churches was considered to have served the interests of the fascists. As a matter of fact, one could easily argue that, quite to the contrary, the separation of the German church could have been in the interest of German nationalism.

The sentence was terribly simple. On November 25, 1947, the District Court of Nagybecskerek (Zrenjanin, by that time) ruled that István Csepcsányi was guilty because, "led by his commitment to fascism, he threatened Juranji together with Archdeacon Kund, after which, following political goals, they united the Slovak, German and Hungarian Lutheran Churches." In that way he collaborated with the occupiers. The sentence also contained that he had "conducted pro-fascist propaganda."

I have encountered this pattern of justification many times in life. The condemnation of bad behavior is always applauded, even when it cannot be proven that the person condemned really behaved badly. That is when statements serving as substitute facts come into play. "Alternative facts," one might say. I have now followed for many years the annual selection of the "Non-word of the Year" (*Unwort des Jahres*) in Germany, a serious cultural event. The jury consists of linguists from Frankfurt. In 2017 the title was won by "Alternative Fakten" (alternative facts). I had noted earlier that, for instance, in 2006 the non-word of the year was "Human Kapital" (human capital), which illustrated that not only money or real estate but also people counted as capital, the fact being made somewhat more palatable by the addition of the more philanthropic flavor of the word "human." When I moved to Budapest, I noticed the rapid and large-scale conquest of the word "human" as the big companies (and even our university) hastened to adopt the term "department of human resources" as the new name of their "cadre departments" developed during the communist era, which were a bit more direct. We are on the side of humanity, are we not?

In 1999, the "non-word of the year" was inspired by the bombing of Serbia by NATO air power. Since civilian victims had to be fit into a pro-human-rights rhetoric, the expression "collateral damage" emerged. So, the people who lost their life in the bombing of a hospital or in Belgrade Television, which was also bombed by NATO planes, were not victims of evil acts, but only "collateral damage," the unwanted by-products of otherwise noble-minded, rightful action. The expression also merited the *Unwort des Jahres* prize. In my view, by the way, one of the real collateral damages done by the NATO bombings was that Milošević became somewhat more accepted (thankfully, not really accepted even then) and Serbia's joining NATO is still not on the agenda. I suffered some collateral damage myself. I was teaching in Atlanta, when one day, spread across the front page of *The New York Times*, I saw our house in Novi Sad. NATO had bombed a bridge in Novi Sad which was about a hundred meters from our home. The bridge was completely demolished. The apartment was undamaged, but the explosion blew out every window, and the wall was also cracked in a few places. It was a small thing. There were bigger problems at that time. Miroslav Mandić was staying in our apartment just then. The same Miroslav Mandić who was imprisoned in the 1970s for a piece of writing he had published in *Új Symposion*. Luckily, this time he escaped with a mere shock.

Then, at the end of 2017, the title of pseudo-word or non-word of the year went to the term "Alternative Fakten," i.e. "alternative facts." The justification was read out by Ms. Janich, a linguist, who explained that the term (or pseudo-term) was eminently well-suited for furnishing the ground for the increasingly frequent practice of replacing genuine facts with unproven observations. Ms. Janich recalled when Kellyanne Conway, President Trump's senior adviser, defended then White House Speaker Sean Spicer's allegation that the crowds drawn by Trump's inauguration in January 2017 had been the largest ever seen at an inauguration. When challenged, Conway said this was an "alternative fact." What was the number of people who attended the Trump inauguration? How many people attended earlier inaugurations? This is now irrelevant. What we have in front of us, is the "alternative" fact that "there were more people than ever before."

I continue to follow the announcement of the *Unwort des Jahres* year after year with sympathy. All I am wondering is whether the present does not overestimate itself when it regards alternative facts as its own new discovery. In Becskerek, this kind of thing was encountered a great deal earlier, especially in momentous times. Not only Jemricsnéni, but also certain prosecutors and judges saw the chance in fascism (or anti-fascism) for substituting facts. When sentencing Csepcsányi, the judge did not waste time on insignificant details, like, for instance, explaining why on earth had the unification of the churches served the interest of the occupiers, or analyzing what was and what was not said in the sermons of Csepcsányi. The profile had been developed anyway (and, after all, here was a man who had the nerve to smile cynically and derisively in his room while the Red Army itself was marching outside in the street). Looking back today, it is clear throughout that we are seeing in action a prosecutor and then a judge who are doing their best against fascism and have an easy ride, practically sliding forward. Somewhat similar to those people in Becskerek who made us stop in out tracks and watch mesmerized as, rather than swim, they slid over the River Bega by clinging to the anchor chains of the steamboat.

Thus, the thorough work of argumentation is being replaced by the comfortable ride provided by alternative facts. All of which is made even easier when the riders of alternative facts also put their boats in a powerful stream. Maybe all that the *Unwort des Jahres* adds is making us aware that the issue is not what the communists or Nazis are like, or the party currently in power or the one in power before that. There are times when it is more obvious that we live together with alternative facts because they are pouring forth loudly from everywhere. At others they are less rough and more modest, but they are present all the same. We had better be aware that alternative facts are also a part of our life. They live with us.

And there are also the convictions. Especially the ones that succeed in developing into a full environment. At any rate, most people do not read Nietzsche, according to whom "convictions are more dangerous enemies of truth than lies."

On November 25, 1947, István Csepcsányi was sentenced by the District Court of Nagybecskerek to one-year imprisonment and hard labor. This was in fact considerably less than would have followed from the law. Crimes falling under Article 3 carried a minimum penalty of three years, and if the acts were committed in wartime, a minimum of five years. How a more lenient sentence was arrived at was not explained by the court. It was also ruled that the confiscation of properties was waived since Csepcsányi had no property anyway. Trial expenses had to be borne by the defendant, but these were deemed "unrecoverable" by the court, which meant that he did not have to cover the costs. Since Csepcsányi had been in prison since September 18, those two months were deducted as time already spent. After sentencing he was sent to Zabela prison in Požarevac, one of the toughest in Serbia at the time. The appeal was decided with extreme speed by the Supreme Court of the Vojvodina. I can't see when it was submitted by my father. Presumably the first half of December 1947. The appeal was rejected as early as December 27. The appeal argued that Csepcsányi had no part in threatening Juranji, whatever it was that he had been threatened with. The Supreme Court, however, saw everything clearly again. According to the appellate sentence, "in Juranji's home Csepcsányi was not passive, he was only silent to what Archdeacon Kund demanded from Juranji, which he accepted at once. In this situation the silence of the defendant was equal to agreement with Archdeacon Kund." The expression "silent to" — "ćutao na to" in Serbian—is not entirely clear in the Serb text either. "Silent when" could be somewhat more precise, but it is not in my power to change the original wording of the sentence. Thus, according to the court, it does not follow from the silence of the defendant that he was passive. Nor does it matter that Kund's proposal was "accepted at once" by Juranji. The judge also added that Csepcsányi had gained "success" from the resignation of Juranji. And, according to the concluding sentence of the verdict, "Such success could only be achieved by collaborators of the occupiers."

The appeal for clemency is next, written in the name of Mrs. Csepcsányi. It was submitted on March 15, 1948. The arguments include that the couple has a son in the third year of elementary school (that was Pupsi), and without her husband, Mrs. Csepcsányi could not support the family. Also, a new development is brought up concerning Juranji. Since one of the witnesses, Lalis, alleged in his evidence that earlier on "Juranji had relied on the police apparatus of the old Yugoslavia in settling accounts with his adversaries," Juranji sued him for libel, but he failed. The court dismissed the libel charge. Still, the file does not include any reply, which seems to indicate that the appeal for clemency was rejected. This is also shown by a subsequent attempt. On July 27, 1948, Mrs. Csepcsányi requests that the court release her husband on probation, which would hardly have been necessary if the appeal for clemency had been successful.

I don't know anything about the result of the new petition submitted on July 27. Decision on that must have been made sometime in August. The one-year sentence was to be completed in September 1948, which could have been the date Pastor Csepcsányi was actually released. That, or maybe a little earlier. After his release and return, he continued to live in No. 18, *Tsara Dušana* Street. If my memory serves well, the vicarage was shared with another family. From time to time he walked into the front room with windows looking on the street, but, at least every time when I was there, he seemed to avoid the windows, the "scene of the crime" where he had committed a cynical, derisive, anti-people smile. Then came the days which Pupsi and I spent guessing if the next vehicle to pass would be drawn by a single horse or two, maybe three. And I was struck by the aloofness of Pupsi's dad standing behind us.

Things have become even simpler since then. The vicarage still stands but it is uninhabited. The front windows facing the street appear shuttered for good. Today any army could march by toward the center of Becskerek without the risk of being smiled at.